DEMOCRACY AND ELECTIONS

Electoral systems and their political consequences

edited by

VERNON BOGDANOR

Fellow of Brasenose College, Oxford

and

DAVID BUTLER

Fellow of Nuffield College, Oxford

CAMBRIDGE UNIVERSITY PRESS

Cambridge

London   New York   New Rochelle
Melbourne   Sydney

CAMBRIDGE UNIVERSITY PRESS
Cambridge, New York, Melbourne, Madrid, Cape Town,
Singapore, São Paulo, Delhi, Tokyo, Mexico City

Cambridge University Press
The Edinburgh Building, Cambridge CB2 8RU, UK

Published in the United States of America by Cambridge University Press, New York

www.cambridge.org
Information on this title: www.cambridge.org/9780521272827

First published 1983
Re-issued 2011

A catalogue record for this publication is available from the British Library

Library of Congress Catalogue Card Number: 82-25300

ISBN 978-0-521-25295-9 Hardback
ISBN 978-0-521-27282-7 Paperback

Contents

Contributors

Vernon Bogdanor, *Fellow of Brasenose College, Oxford, and University Lecturer in Politics*

David Butler, *Fellow of Nuffield College, Oxford, and Special University Lecturer in Politics*

Richard Clogg, *Lecturer, Department of Modern Greek and Byzantine Studies, King's College, London*

David Goldey, *Fellow of Lincoln College, Oxford, and University Lecturer in Politics*

Dick Leonard, *Brussels Correspondent, 'The Economist'*

Paul McKee, *Deputy Chief Executive, ITN, and a member of the SSRC Electoral Studies Panel*

Peter Pulzer, *Student of Christ Church, Oxford, and University Lecturer in Politics*

Richard Rose, *Professor of Politics, University of Strathclyde, and Director, Centre for the Study of Public Policy*

Bo Särlvik, *Professor of Politics, University of Göteborg*

Christopher Seton-Watson, *Fellow of Oriel College, Oxford, and University Lecturer in Politics*

Michael Steed, *Senior Lecturer, Department of Government, Victoria University of Manchester*

J.A.A. Stockwin, *Professor of Modern Japanese Studies, University of Oxford, and Fellow of St Antony's College*

Philip Williams, *Fellow of Nuffield College, Oxford, and University Lecturer in Politics*

Preface

Our aim in *Democracy and Elections* has been to analyse electoral systems in their political context. For electoral systems are not merely technical devices whose effects can be analysed mechanically; the same systems can yield very different consequences when introduced into different societies with contrasting historical traditions.

Electoral reformers, through ignoring the historical factors that have shaped the social development of their country, often see their impatient hopes frustrated.

The political history of France in the twentieth century is sufficient to show how fallacious it can be to assume that reforms of the electoral system alone will alter long-established norms of political behaviour. Yet, for good or ill, electoral systems do exert long-run effects upon the style and character of a country's political life. There is a reciprocal interaction between social and electoral change, and it is this interaction which we have tried to explore.

Many of the chapters in *Democracy and Elections* were first delivered at a seminar which we conducted at Nuffield College, Oxford, in Hilary Term 1982, and we are grateful to those who participated in these seminars for their stimulating contributions. We are grateful to our Oxford colleges, Brasenose and Nuffield for much material support: and for providing environments so conducive to research. We could not have produced the book without the aid of Brenda Lambourn and Audrey Skeats. We are also grateful to Stephen Barr of the Cambridge University Press. Finally, we would like to thank our wives and children, for tolerating our obsessive preoccupation with the consequences of electoral systems.

9 August 1982

VERNON BOGDANOR

DAVID BUTLER

Glossary

Additional member system: this is exemplified by the proportional system used in Germany. Half the members are elected by first-past-the-post voting in single-member constituencies. The other half are allocated to party lists in such a way that the seats in the full assembly are proportionate to the votes cast in the country as a whole (subject to certain threshold rules). A variant of this system proposed by the Hansard Society in 1976 provided for the additional members to be chosen from defeated constituency candidates rather than party lists.

Alternative vote: this refers to the use of preferential voting within single-member constituencies. For the Australian Lower House, for example, every elector is required to number all the candidates in order of preference; the candidate with fewest first preferences is eliminated and the second preferences are redistributed and the process continues until one candidate has a clear majority.

Andrae system: an alternative name for the single transferable vote system.

Apparentement: a provision in a list system of voting by which separate parties can declare themselves linked for the purposes of vote counting and seat allocation (France 1951, 1956, Italy 1953).

Constituency: this is the most common term for the geographic areas into which a country is divided for electoral purposes. A constituency may send one or several members to the legislature. Other terms include district (USA), riding (Canada), *circonscription* (France), electorate (Australia and New Zealand), and division (UK).

Cube law: a formula which has been used to describe the way in which first-past-the-post systems exaggerate majorities in votes into much greater majorities in seats. If votes are divided in the ratio A:B, seats are likely to be divided in the ratio A^3:B^3.

Cumulative voting: a rarely used system of voting in a multi-member constituency in which electors can cast more than one of their votes for a single candidate.

D'Hondt system: the formula used in most list systems of proportional representation to allocate seats. It is also known as the highest-average system. Briefly, it ensures that in a constituency no reallocation of seats would reduce discrepancies in the shares of the vote received by the winners.

Droop quota: the formula used in most single transferable vote systems to allocate seats. It can be stated $[\text{votes}/(\text{seats}+1)]+1$.

First-past-the-post (FPTP) system: this, the oldest kind of voting arrangement, still predominates in English-speaking countries. It usually involves single-member districts. Each elector has one vote, and the candidate who gets most votes wins, even if he does not secure an absolute majority. This is also known as the relative majority or plurality system.

Gerrymandering: the drawing of constituency boundaries deliberately to secure party advantage.

Hagenbach-Bischoff method: a method of allocation using the Droop quota in the first stage and the D'Hondt system in later stages.

Hare quota: votes divided by the number of seats.

Largest remainder system: the formula for allocating seats in list systems that is most favourable to smaller parties. After one seat has been distributed for every full quota (the quota being derived simply by dividing votes by seats), any remaining seats are allocated in turn to the parties with the largest residues.

Limited vote: a system of voting in multi-member constituencies with a majoritarian system in which electors have fewer votes than there are seats to fill (now used only in Japan; tried in a few UK constituencies 1867–85).

Panachage: a provision in a list system of proportional representation in which the elector is given the opportunity to vary the order of candidates on his party's list.

Preferential voting: a system of voting in which the elector expresses a rank order of preference between candidates. The alternative vote and the single transferable vote are systems of preferential voting.

Proportional representation (PR): this is a generic term for all the systems of election which seek, by multi-member seats or reserve lists, to relate seats to votes more proportionately than is possible under a single-member-constituency system.

Redistribution: the British term for two processes distinguished in American usage: 'redistricting', the redrawing of constituency boundaries, and 'reapportionment', the reallocation of seats among states.

Sainte-Laguë system: a formula used to allocate seats in some Scandinavian list systems of proportional representation. The use of a divisor larger than the number of seats available ensures a more proportional result than the d'Hondt system.

Second ballot: this refers to the system used in Third and Fifth Republic France, under which, in a single-member-constituency system, there is a second vote a week after the first one if no candidate has an absolute majority. It is analogous to the run-off arrangements in some American primary elections.

Single transferable vote (STV): this refers to the use of preferential voting in multi-member constituencies. It is used in the Irish Dail and the Australian Senate. Electors are asked to number the candidates in order of preference. Any votes surplus to a Droop quota are reallocated according to second preferences. Then the bottom candidates are successively eliminated and their preferences redistributed until all the seats are filled.

Threshold: a minimum condition for securing representation. This device limits purely proportional results, for example, by distributing seats only to parties securing a minimum of 5% of the vote (as in Germany) or by having constituencies with so few members that a party needs a substantial vote to have any chance of securing a seat (as in Ireland).

1

Introduction

VERNON BOGDANOR

I

Elections lie at the heart of the democratic process; and it is through the act of voting that government by consent is secured. Yet no country has solved the riddle first posed by Oliver Cromwell who was 'as much for government by consent as any man, but if you ask me how it is to be done, I confess I do not know'. For modern democracies use a wide variety of different electoral systems, and there is no hint of agreement as to which is best, each system having its characteristic virtues and defects. In addition, there are electoral systems which exist on paper but not in reality. Indeed, the only Royal Commission ever appointed in Britain to inquire into electoral systems declared in its report, published in 1910, that there were over 300 systems then in existence.[1] There are, no doubt, many more now. Yet a classification of electoral systems does not have to be just a lengthy catalogue listing them one by one; for they can be analysed as variations upon a small number of basic types.

Electoral systems are the practical instruments through which notions such as consent and representation are translated into reality. For an electoral system is above all a method of converting votes cast by electors into seats in a legislature. The purpose of this chapter is to categorise the main types of system actually employed in democracies, as a preliminary to the chapters on individual countries which explore their political consequences in different cultures.

II

The central factor differentiating one electoral system from another is the method by which it allocates seats. There are, broadly, three ways in which this can be done. Seats can be allocated to a candidate or candidates obtaining a *plurality* of the vote, to a candidate or candidates obtaining a *majority* of the vote, or *proportionately*. There are, therefore, *plurality* systems, *majority* systems and *proportional* systems of election.

But there are a number of different methods of allocating seats proportionately. The central distinction is between a method based upon preferential

voting in multi-member constituencies – *the single transferable vote* – and a
method of allocation based upon *party lists*. List systems can in turn be
subdivided into those which allocate seats *nationally*, and those allocating
within *multi-member constituencies*, and further subdivided according to the
methods by which *candidates* are chosen. A system may require the elector to
vote soley for a party list, the particular candidates elected being determined by
their order on the list, or offer varying degrees of choice of candidate within a
party list, or even across party lists.

It is, therefore, a mistake to refer to 'proportional representation' as if it
denotes a single type of electoral system. 'Proportional representation' is in
fact a generic term denoting a number of different systems sharing only the
common aim of proportionality between seats and votes. This common aim,
however, does not prevent the various proportional systems diverging
considerably, one from another; and their political consequences, therefore,
can be quite different.

The electoral system which a country adopts depends more upon its political
tradition than upon abstract considerations of electoral justice or good
government. There is a striking geographical dividing line between those
countries using the plurality system and those employing proportional
systems. For it is only in countries which have come under British political
influence – Commonwealth countries, the United States and Britain herself –
that the plurality system is still used for the election of the legislature. It is not
used in any Continental country. Every Continental democracy except France
uses a list system, a method which has not been favoured in any Commonwealth country except Guyana and Sri Lanka. The single transferable
vote method of proportional representation, by contrast, is the 'Anglo-
Saxon' method of proportional representation. For it has been employed
only in Commonwealth or ex-Commonwealth countries: it has been used in
elections to the Irish and Tasmanian Lower Houses, the Australian
Upper House, and the Maltese legislature. It is also the only proportional
system to have been tried in Britain; it was used in Northern Ireland – for local
government elections from 1920 to 1923 and since 1972, for elections to the
Northern Ireland Parliament between 1921 and 1929, and to the Assembly in
1973, Convention in 1975, European Parliament in 1979, and Assembly in
1982 – it was also used in the United Kingdom for four university constituencies between 1918 and 1950, and in Scotland for local education
authorities between 1919 and 1930. But the single transferable vote has never
been used in any Continental country, with the exception of an experiment in
Denmark in the nineteenth century.

III

The plurality system, as it developed in Britain and in countries influenced by
Britain, was profoundly linked to the notion of territorial representation. 'The

ancient idea of representation', according to Maitland, comprised 'the representation of communities, of organised bodies of men, bodies which, whether called boroughs or counties, constantly acts as wholes, and have common rights and duties.'[2] MPs represented not segments of opinion, nor of course political parties, but constituencies. They were attorneys seeking the redress of grievances before committing their constituencies to the payment of the expenses of government. 'Representation was nowise regarded as a means of expressing individual right or forwarding individual interests. It was communities, and not individuals who were taxed in parliaments.'[3] It was this notion of representation which came to be adopted by the American colonists whose 'surroundings had recreated to a significant extent the conditions that had shaped the earlier experiences of the English people.' For:

> The colonial towns and counties, like their mediaeval counterparts, were largely autonomous, and they stood to lose more than they were likely to gain from a loose acquiescence in the action of central government . . . Having little reason to identify their interests with those of the central government, they sought to keep the voices of local interests clear and distinct.[4]

It was indeed in America in the eighteenth century in the constitutions of the colonies that the single-member constituency originated. Indeed, the single-member constituency formed the predominant basis of representation in Canada, Australia, New Zealand and the United States before it came to be accepted as the norm in Britain. From the fifteenth century, the plurality system operated in Britain mainly in two-member constituencies, and until the 1832 Reform Act, 'the *preponderant tradition* in English electoral practice was probably *the tradition of uncontested elections'*.[5] The single-member constituency was not introduced into Britain until 1707, and it did not become the predominant basis of representation until 1885, a step which 'marked a new and deliberate departure. Hitherto single-member constituencies had only existed because they were too small to be entitled to more than one member, now they became the unit on which all representation was to be calculated and all future schemes of redistribution must rest.'[6]

Paradoxically, by the time the plurality system in single-member constituencies came to be the norm in Britain, the idea of representation upon which it was based already seemed unreal; for it had been eclipsed by the growth of party; and already in the eighteenth century Burke had insisted that Parliament was

> not a *congress* of ambassadors from different and hostile interests, which interests each must maintain as an agent and advocate against other agents and advocates; but Parliament is a *deliberative* assembly of *one* nation, with *one* interest, that of the whole, where, not local purposes, not local prejudices ought to guide, but the general good, resulting from the general reason of the whole.[7]

With the growth of party and the eclipse of older ideas of territorial representation, the plurality system could no longer be defended as securing the representation of communities, and it came under attack from advocates of proportional representation who insisted that it failed to meet ideal norms of democratic representation. To such an attack, there was, it seemed, little reply, but the defence has been a pragmatic one. The plurality system is seen as a means to stable and effective government which forces the voter to decide his priorities. It is conceded that the plurality system gives disproportional representation, but this is held to secure a positive benefit, since it is likely to yield single-party government without the need for coalitions. The plurality system secures this effect by systematically exaggerating the support of large parties while under-representing small parties (unless they are territorially concentrated). Where the basic cleavage in an industrialised country is socio-economic rather than territorial, it will encourage the growth of a two-party system, and moderate government is a likely result. Where, on the other hand, the political culture is less homogeneous, but riven with territorial or ethnic cleavages, the system will work very differently, emphasising geographical concentrations of support, and stressing territorial issues at the expense of socio-economic, as in Canada, for example. It is not surprising, therefore, that the plurality system is found to be least workable in such divided societies. It presupposes consensus, but may also help to reinforce it.

The plurality system normally operates through single-member con-stituencies. But there is a variant generally known as the block vote, whereby each elector in a multi-member constituency has as many votes as there are candidates to be elected. This system is used in various local elections in Britain – in elections for the London boroughs and for some district councils. It too predates the rise of the party and was introduced to Britain in the Municipal Corporations Act of 1835, establishing elected local institutions. If the candidates are independents, then use of the block vote may secure the election of the most popular candidates, but if the candidates are organised in parties, the block vote exaggerates still further a characteristic feature of the plurality system in single-member constituencies, namely, its tendency to give a large bonus of seats to the largest party. In a single-member constituency with three candidates standing, it is perfectly possible for a candidate to win election with 34% of the vote; in a multi-member constituency, with three candidates from each of three parties standing, and the elector having three votes, it is possible, if party voting is solid, as it usually is, for three candidates to be elected from the party gaining 34% of the vote, while the other parties win no seats at all. Thus a party may obtain all the places in a constituency with no more than a bare plurality of votes.

IV

Majority systems seek to do away with the possibility of a candidate winning a constituency on a minority vote. There are two types – the second ballot, used in elections for the French National Assembly and the Presidency, and the alternative vote used in elections for the Australian House of Representatives.

Under the former system, a second ballot is held shortly after the first, if no candidate has won an absolute majority of the vote. The rules concerning who can participate in the second ballot have varied quite considerably. In Third Republic France, any candidate could participate in the second ballot, whether or not he had competed in the first. In National Assembly elections in the Fifth Republic, the only candidates who can now compete in the second ballot are those who have gained the votes of $12\frac{1}{2}\%$ of the *registered electorate* – equivalent, perhaps, to 15% of the vote – in the first ballot. For presidential elections, only the top two candidates in the first ballot can compete in the second.

The alternative vote is a preferential system of voting in single-member constituencies. The elector votes by expressing his first preference, and such subsequent preferences as he chooses. If no candidate has an absolute majority of the vote, the candidate with the fewest votes is eliminated, and his second preferences redistributed. This process continues until one candidate has an absolute majority of the vote.

Both the second ballot and the alternative vote seek to prevent any candidate from being elected on a minority vote. They therefore encourage alliances between parties, since the allies can each put up candidates without fear of splitting the vote; whereas under the plurality system, the only form of electoral alliance possible between like-minded parties is a mutual withdrawal of candidates, so that only one candidate from the alliance stands in each constituency. For this reason, the second ballot and alternative vote are likely to offer the elector a wider choice of candidate, and they allow, but do not necessarily encourage, party fragmentation. Conversely, these systems are likely to discriminate against 'anti-system parties' which cannot find allies – the German Social Democrats before 1914 and the French Communists in the years immediately after 1958.

Although both the second ballot (in most of its variants) and the alternative vote ensure that no candidate can win a seat unless he has the support of a majority of the voters in the constituency, they do not ensure that the party winning the election in the country as a whole will necessarily enjoy a majority of the votes. They do not achieve, and indeed do not purport to achieve, a proportional relationship between votes and seats. In France, for example, in 1981 the non-Communist Left secured 62% of the seats in the National Assembly for only 38% of the vote in the first ballot, and 50% of the vote in the *tour décisif* (a total of the party vote in seats won on each ballot).

	% Votes	% Seats
Liberals	38.3	53.2
National Country Party	9.7	14.5
Liberal/National Country Party coalition	48.0	67.7
Labour	40.0	28.2
Australian Democrat	9.3	0
Others	2.7	0

In the Australian House of Representatives the result in 1977 was as above. The Liberals gained an absolute majority of seats with fewer votes than Labour which secured only a quarter of the seats, and the Liberal/National Country Party alliance secured a large majority of the seats on a minority of the popular vote.

The effect of the alternative vote in Australia has been like the effect of first-past-the-post in Britain or New Zealand: it has produced vastly exaggerated majorities. In 1975, for example, a 10% lead in votes for the government parties produced a 44% lead in seats while in 1980 a 1% lead in votes produced an 18% lead in seats.

Whether majority systems do or do not secure accurate representation will depend, as with plurality systems, upon the distribution of votes. Where the party which, under a plurality system, would benefit from disproportionality wins a large number of seats as a result of a split vote for the opposing parties, use of a majority system will increase the degree of proportionality; but in other circumstances, where a party benefiting from disproportionality is *not* vulnerable, the degree of disproportionality may actually be increased.

In Britain, for example, assuming that the Liberal Party (or Liberal/SDP Alliance) draws votes evenly from the Conservative and Labour Parties, a majority system would deprive the Conservatives of more seats than Labour; for in the 1979 general election, the Liberals were second in 79 Conservative seats, but only in 2 Labour seats. Thus more Conservative than Labour seats would be vulnerable to the alternative vote or second ballot, because of the geographical distribution of Conservative and Labour seats. So a majority system would increase the degree of proportionality in Britain only in years such as 1970 and 1979 when the Conservatives won disproportionately. In years such as 1945 and 1966, when Labour benefited, a majority system would probably have *increased* the degree of disproportionality. Thus, whether a majority system produces proportionality depends upon purely contingent factors.

For majority or plurality systems share one fundamental feature: the number of seats which a party receives depends not only upon the number of votes which it gains, but upon where these votes are located. Under the plurality system, the number of seats which a party gains will depend upon the distribution as well as the size of its support. Under the alternative vote and second-ballot systems, the ability of a party to form alliances with like-minded parties will be a further factor determining its electoral success. No system of election using only single-member constituencies can ensure proportional representation, since votes for those supporting losing candidates are 'wasted'. There is, therefore, a very profound conflict between the idea of *territorial* representation and the ideal of *proportional* representation: or between the representation of *territories* and the representation of *opinion* or *party*.

V

If the elector has one less vote in a multi-member constituency than the number of candidates to be elected, rather than as many votes as there are candidates to be elected, as with the block vote, then the system of election is known as the limited vote. It was used for parliamentary elections in some constituencies in Britain between 1867 and 1885, when electors were given two votes in thirteen three-member constituencies, and three votes in one four-member constituency. The purpose of this system was to secure minority representation, and, provided that the minority party in a constituency did not put up more candidates than the elector had votes, so that support for its candidates was not too thinly spread, it could gain representation in a three-member constituency with two-fifths of the vote. The single non-transferable vote, as used in Japan, is a special case of the limited vote giving the elector only one vote in a multi-member constituency. In this case, the minority party will gain representation if it puts up one candidate and secures just over a third of the vote in a two-member constituency, or just over a quarter of the vote in a three-member constituency. In general, a minority will gain representation under the limited vote and single non-transferable vote systems, assuming that it does not put up more candidates than the elector has votes, if its support is just over $\frac{L}{N+L}$ of the votes, where each elector has L votes and there are N places to be filled.[8]

Both the limited vote and the single non-transferable vote attempt to remedy a weakness in the plurality system – the inability of the minority in a constituency to secure representation. Yet these systems are not generally regarded with much favour by electoral reformers. For, although they facilitate the representation of minorities, they do not ensure a proportional relationship between votes and seats, as the following example from the 1969 House of Representatives election in Japan shows.[9]

	% Votes	% Seats
Liberal Democratic Party	47.6	59.2
Socialists	21.4	18.5
Democratic Socialist Party	7.7	6.4
Kōmeitō	10.9	9.7
Communists	6.8	2.9
Other small parties	0.1	0
Independents	5.5	3.3

Indeed, the relationship between seats and votes will depend upon how many candidates each party puts up – if too few, a party may sacrifice winnable seats, if too many and its vote is evenly spread, it will also fail to maximise the number of seats won from a given vote. Further, a party must be able to locate its supporters and instruct them which candidate to vote for when it puts up more than one; otherwise one candidate may accumulate a large surplus vote which is wasted, but which could have helped elect another candidate from the same party. Like the cumulative vote – used for the election of local school boards in England and Wales, 1870–1902 – the limited vote and the single non-transferable vote have the effect of placing a good deal of power in the hands of the party caucus, while providing only rough accuracy of representation. These systems can, perhaps, be best regarded as crude approximations to proportional systems; and indeed, in her book, *How Democracies Vote*, Enid Lakeman describes them as semi-proportional systems.[10]

VI

The single transferable vote – the Anglo-Saxon version of proportional representation – was developed by the English lawyer Thomas Hare (1806–91) and endorsed by John Stuart Mill. It was a product of Victorian individualism, and its starting-point was a radically different conception of representation from that embodied in the plurality system. Whereas representation under the plurality system was conceived of as *territorial* in nature – as representation of communities – advocates of the single transferable vote saw representation as fundamentally *personal*; indeed in its early years, the system was often described by the term 'personal representation'. The elector was not properly represented simply because he voted for an MP who reflected the interests of the community; true representation required that he had an MP who reflected his own point of view. That is why adherents of the single transferable vote regard electors who disagree with the policies of their MP as unrepresented, and their votes wasted. The aim of the system is to ensure that the number of wasted votes is minimised and that as many of the electorate as possible are able to elect an MP of their choice.

The nineteenth-century advocates of the single transferable vote were well aware that the territorial principle, supposedly embodied in the plurality system, was rapidly being overcome by the growth and development of organised political parties. The plurality system, in their view, fundamentally altered its nature when representation became that of party rather than that of territory. MPs of independent outlook would be squeezed out by the twin forces of the tyranny of the majority and the party machine. Hare's scheme, which in its original form involved one nationwide constituency enabling a candidate to be elected on a vote equal to one divided by the total number of MPs, would provide a role for the independent-minded and the Victorian clerisy. For this reason, investigation of the Hare system convinced John Stuart Mill that it was, after all, possible to reconcile democracy with respect for the claims of intellect; and this realisation struck Mill with the force of revelation: 'You appear to me', he wrote to Hare, 'to have exactly, and for the first time, solved the difficulty of popular representation; and by doing so, to have raised up the cloud of gloom and uncertainty which hung over the futurity of representative government and therefore, of civilisation.'[11]

The single transferable vote is a method of election providing for preferential voting in multi-member constituencies. Its two central features are the attempt to secure proportional representation of political opinion, and the provision for choice of candidate within, as well as between, parties. Proportionality would be secured since few votes are wasted; instead they are transferred, so that a fair representation of opinion would be secured within each multi-member constituency. Votes which could not be used to help elect a candidate – either because they were surplus to what he needed to secure election, or because the candidate had too few votes to be elected – were transferred to second and third choice candidates. The only votes which did not help to elect a candidate would be those cast for the runner-up, and those votes which could not be used because they were non-transferable, i.e., because the voter had refused to indicate a full list of preferences. Thus, each elector would be represented by a candidate of the party of his choice, and the vast majority of electors would be represented by individual candidates of their choice. Only in this way could personal representation – which was real representation – become a reality.

The single transferable vote gives the elector the power to choose between candidates of the same party. This differentiates it sharply from list systems of proportional representation, most of which offer only minimal choice or no choice at all. To the individualists who sponsored the single transferable vote, the representation of opinion was as important as the representation of party, and the voter ought to be allowed not only to decide which party was to govern the state, but also to influence the policies it should follow. A central characteristic, therefore, of the single transferable vote is that it contains a built-in primary election, and one which allows every elector, whether or not a registered member of a political party, to play a part. In conception, therefore, the single transferable vote may be seen as an attempt to translate into practical terms, the principle of 'the free development of individuality' which Mill wrote *On Liberty* to defend as 'one of the leading essentials of well-being'.[12]

As so often happens, the hopes of the enthusiasts were to be disappointed, and the single transferable vote has worked out very differently in practice. Admittedly, the areas in which it has operated – the Irish Republic, Northern Ireland, Malta and Tasmania – can hardly be regarded as a representative sample of the world's democracies. The single transferable vote has, with the exception of Australia, only been used in small, rural societies where political affiliations have been organised on 'tribal' lines rather than being based upon socio-economic cleavages. The characteristic features of the transferable vote have fitted well into such societies. But it is, in consequence, difficult for the political scientist to distinguish between the effects of the electoral system itself and those which flow from the nature of the society in which it operates. From the political scientist's point of view, it is perhaps a pity that no large industrialised society has ever thought to experiment with this electoral system!

As we have seen, a central concern of early advocates of the single transferable vote was to weaken the role of the party machine. Some – Ostrogorski, for example – even hoped that it might lead to the abolition of parties altogether and their replacement by single-issue groups. And yet, in those areas where the system operates, parties and party government are not noticeably weaker than in other countries. In Ireland and in Tasmania, the parties have often circumvented the purpose of the system – to provide a choice of candidate – by dividing multi-member constituencies geographically into bailiwicks, each candidate confining himself to one bailiwick and each bailiwick functioning as a single-member constituency. In addition, Ireland and Malta have seen the growth of personal political machines, organisations whose loyalty is owed to a particular candidate rather than to the party as a whole.

The hopes of Hare and Mill that the single transferable vote would lead to legislatures of high intellectual quality have also been confounded. Indeed, there have been frequent complaints of the calibre both of members of the Irish Dail and of the Tasmanian House of Representatives. Legislators are said to be narrow and parochial, more interested in servicing their constituents and filling the pork-barrel than in holding the executive to account on policy issues. Yet these may be criticisms more of the roles and expectations of rural societies than of the electoral system itself.

The single transferable vote has been found to yield a high degree of proportionality, not as great as list systems, but far higher than plurality or majority systems. Yet, there have often been anomalies. In the elections in Malta in 1981, with only two parties competing, the system yielded, for the first time in sixty years in that country, an anomalous result, the Labour Party securing 49.1% of the first preference votes and 34 seats, while the Nationalists with 50.9% of first preference votes gained only 31 seats.

In Ireland, also, there has been some disproportionality. Consider, for example, the results of the general elections in 1965, 1969 and 1973.

	% First preference votes	% Seats
1965		
Fianna Fail	47.7	50.3
Fine Gael	34.1	32.9
Labour	15.4	14.7
Clann na Poblachta	0.7	0.7
Independents	2.1	1.4
1969		
Fianna Fail	45.7	51.7
Fine Gael	34.1	35.0
Labour	17.0	12.6
Independent	3.2	0.7
1973		
Fianna Fail	46.2	47.6
Fine Gael	35.1	37.8
Labour	13.7	13.3
Sinn Fein	1.1	0
Aontacht Eireann	0.9	0
Independents	3.0	1.4

In both 1965 and 1969, Fianna Fail won an absolute majority of the seats on less than 50% of the vote, and on a smaller vote than the two main opposition parties – Fine Gael and Labour – combined. In 1969, the Fianna Fail vote fell to 45.7% and the two main opposition parties gained 51.1% of the vote; yet Fianna Fail remained in government and even increased its share of seats. In 1973, by contrast, the Fianna Fail vote was higher than in 1969, and the vote of the two main opposition parties – 48.8% – lower than in 1969. Yet the Fianna Fail share of seats fell to 47.6%, and it lost power to the Fine Gael/Labour coalition. In the first two elections, therefore, – in 1965 and 1969 – the electoral system yielded a Fianna Fail majority on a minority of the popular vote; while in the third, in 1973, it resulted in a Fine Gael/Labour government on a minority vote.

There are four main reasons why the single transferable vote yields deviations from full proportionality. The first is that in each constituency some votes for candidates who do not reach the quota, i.e., a sixth of the votes in a five-member constituency, and a fifth of the votes in a four-member constituency – in general $\frac{L}{N+L}$ votes in a n-member constituency – will not have helped to elect anyone. If these votes are unevenly spread amongst the parties, there will be disproportionality. Small parties which are unable to reach the quota, or able to reach it only in a small number of constituencies will, of course, be under-represented.

Secondly, votes cast for candidates who are runners-up will not have helped to elect anyone. If the number of runners-up is distributed unevenly amongst the parties, then, again, there will be disproportionality. A combination of the first and second causes seems responsible for the anomalous result in Malta in 1981.

Thirdly, it may be that there are a large number of non-transferable votes, so that the last candidate in some constituencies is elected without reaching the quota. In Ireland, for example, Fianna Fail voters frequently fail to use their later preferences for Labour or Fine Gael candidates. If candidates elected without reaching the quota are drawn disproportionately from one party, fewer votes will be needed to elect them than are needed to elect candidates from other parties. It is for this reason that in Ireland Fianna Fail has gained more seats than it was entitled to under a strict rule of proportionality in every general election it has fought.

Finally, the number of votes needed to elect candidates may vary as a result of differences in constituency size. A three-member constituency yields more benefit to the stronger party than a four-member constituency, for in a three-member constituency, the stronger party will be likely to win two seats, whereas in a four-member constituency in Ireland it may need over 60% of the vote to win more than two seats. The weaker party can gain two seats on as little as 37.5% of the vote, and can always secure two seats on 42% of the vote. Thus, a party strong in the areas where there are three-member constituencies, but weak in areas where there are four-member constituencies, will gain a disproportionate advantage from the system.

Supporters of the single transferable vote profess themselves relatively untroubled by these anomalies. The purpose of the system, in their view, is not to secure proportional representation of parties, but proportional representation of opinion, and, in particular, of opinion which cuts across party lines. But since they do not give a clear operational definition enabling one to measure 'proportionality of opinion', it becomes difficult to offer any evaluation of their claim. Even so, defenders of the system can plausibly assert that it provides the voter with a greater degree of effective choice than other electoral systems. But critics would argue that this value is not worth pursuing if it means the introduction of large multi-member constituencies and intra-party factionalism which, in their view, will militate against strong and effective government.

VII

List systems, as used by every Continental country except for France, constitute the other main type of proportional representation. Until recently, they were regarded as unsuitable by advocates of proportional representation in Anglo-Saxon countries. In 1976, however, the Hansard Society's Commission on Electoral Reform, under the chairmanship of Lord Blake, recommended that Britain adopt a variant of the West German electoral system, while in 1977 the Labour government proposed a version of the Finnish electoral system for Britain's first elections to the European Parliament. But this proposal was turned down by the Commons.

List systems are of many different types with varying political consequences, and it is a mistake to speak of 'the list system' as if there was only one type. They can be classified according to four criteria: (a) whether the list is national or sub-national, i.e., regional or local; (b) whether the proportional allocation of seats is at national level or in multi-member constituencies; (c) whether the system allows voters to choose between different candidates of their preferred party – or even across parties – or whether it confines them to voting for a party list, with the order of candidates being determined by the party; and (d) the nature and size of the threshold.

(a) National list systems are used only by Israel and the Netherlands. Israel has no constituencies at all. In the Netherlands constituencies do not determine how many seats each party wins. But they may determine which candidates fill the party seats. Other countries using list systems employ regional or local lists with multi-member constituencies, except for West Germany which combines regional lists with single-member constituencies.

(b) Countries using national list systems allocate seats proportionately at national level. Other countries can choose to allocate seats either regionally or nationally. Countries using regional or local constituencies but allocating seats proportionately at the national level include Germany, Denmark and Italy. National proportionality is secured through the allocation of supplementary seats from a national pool. Allocation at national level will result in greater proportionality than allocation at regional or local level. In addition, small parties which cannot gain representation under a system requiring regional allocation – because they do not have sufficient strength in any one region – might secure representation under a system requiring national allocation, by acquiring support in a number of regions.

(c) List systems may or may not allow the elector to choose between candidates of the same party. Israel is an example of a country where there is no choice at all: the elector simply votes for the party symbol, and the candidates elected to the legislature are decided by the parties. Such a system is an example of the *closed list*. The West German system also allows the elector no choice between candidates of the same party; while the variant of it

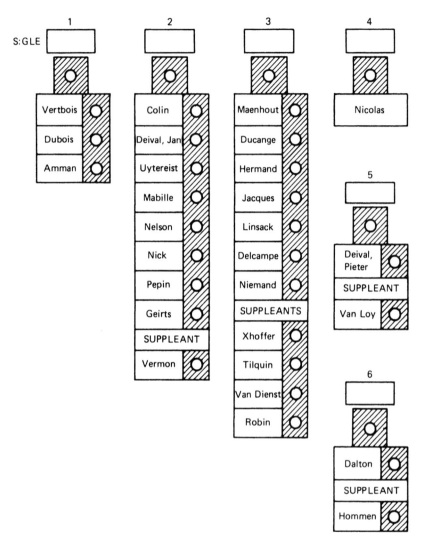

Figure 1 Sample voting paper (French language version)
Arrondissement.....................................
Election de...........................représentants
Election de............................sénateurs

recommended by the Hansard Society Commission in 1976, whereby proportionality is secured through the election of the 'best losers' in single-member constituencies, may be seen as a 'hidden list' system, in that the names of the candidates on the list do not have to be presented to the electorate, as candidates on an actual list must be. Most countries allow some choice of candidate, but this is often very limited. A typical ballot paper of a system allowing some limited choice – which we may call the *flexible list* – is the Belgian shown in Figure 1. On this ballot paper, the elector can either vote for the list in the order decided by the party, in which case he marks the top of the ballot paper – the so-called *case de tête* – or he may vote instead for a particular candidate by ticking a name on the list.

The possibility of a greater degree of electoral choice can be illustrated by the example of the *open list* system in Finland, where there is no *case de tête*, and the elector is not presented with an ordered list at all, but instead with a series of names in alphabetical order. He votes by marking a space beside the candidate of his choice.

Finally, there is the case of the so-called *free list* in Switzerland and Luxembourg where, again, the candidates are not placed in any order of preference by the parties, but, by contrast to Finland, the elector has not one vote, but as many votes as there are candidates to be elected. He may cast his votes for candidates of different parties and cumulate two votes on any one candidate if he wishes. Rae offers the intriguing suggestion that such wide scope for preference voting can be afforded only by 'relatively homogeneous, high consensus societies, in which the divisive forces on which opposition parties thrive are quite weak'.[13]

Both the open list and the free list systems give the voter control of the party list, so that the list is no longer an *ordered* one. But they are still party list systems in that they share this central feature, 'that every vote (whether or not given in the first instance to an individual candidate) is, automatically and without further reference to the voter's wishes, added to the total of the list on which that candidate appears'.[14] Thus a vote for one candidate on a party list can help elect another candidate on the list of the same party, whom the voter might not support, and might not approve of. Such a result can never happen under the single transferable vote; on the other hand, party list systems are likely to provide, especially when allocation is at national level, a greater degree of proportionality than the single transferable vote.

(d) However, not even the purest national list systems, such as Israel and the Netherlands, offer complete proportionality. In every system there is a threshold, either implicit or explicit, limiting small parties. The Netherlands has a national threshold established by the number of members elected to the Lower House of the legislature – 150. This means that any party which cannot attract the support of 1/150 of the voters, i.e., 0.67%, will not secure representation. In Israel, there is a statutory threshold of 1% – the lowest explicit threshold in any democracy; the highest is West Germany's where it is 5%.

For countries operating a regional or local constituency system, there is an implicit threshold set by the size of the constituency, except where the threshold is overcome by national allocation of seats. Parties which might have sufficient national support to gain seats where there is allocation at national level, may, if their support is very evenly spread, fail to secure sufficient votes in any one constituency to secure representation where allocation is at sub-national level. Under the single transferable vote system, of course, the threshold is set by the size of the quota, and any party unable to secure enough votes to reach the quota anywhere will be unrepresented. A further factor which may limit small parties is the *formula* used for the allocation of seats, the d'Hondt formula being less favourable to smaller parties than Sainte-Laguë.

Broadly, the larger the size of the unit of allocation of seats, the greater the degree of proportionality, the most proportional systems being the national list or national allocation systems in the Netherlands, Israel and West Germany (except for the threshold) with the other limiting case being the plurality system in the single-member constituency where, in theory, a party with 49% of the vote in every constituency in a two-party system could fail to win a single seat.

VIII

It is now possible to schematise the various electoral systems as shown in Figure 2. This diagram differs in important respects from that presented in Vernon Bogdanor, *The People and the Party System*, p. 215, since that book was concerned with the question of the most appropriate electoral system for Britain, whereas the diagram here is intended to be more comprehensive. It illustrates the main types of electoral systems. Proportional systems are clearly the most complex. For proportionality is determined by a number of different factors – the size of constituency or unit of allocation of seats, the precise formula used for allocation and whether or not there is a threshold. In addition, proportional systems may or may not allow for choice of candidate. Yet these variables are, to some extent at least, *independent* of each other in that they may be combined and recombined in different ways. So, although the main electoral systems are probably already known, there are undoubtedly many ingenious ways of breeding new combinations. But – as many of the chapters of *Democracy and Elections* will show – electoral engineering is a highly inexact science and one liable to rebound upon those who try to practise it.

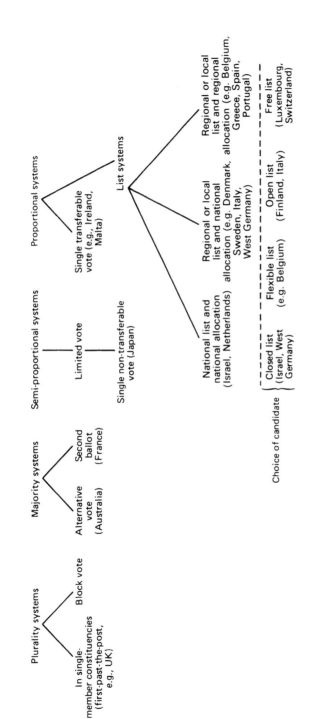

Figure 2 A classification of electoral systems

NOTES

1 Report of Royal Commission Appointed to Enquire into Electoral Systems, Cd. 5163, 1910, para. 45.
2 F. W. Maitland, *The Constitutional History of England* (Cambridge, 1909), p. 363.
3 A. F. Pollard, *The Evolution of Parliament* (London, 1920), p. 155.
4 Bernard Bailyn, *The Ideological Origins of the American Revolution* (Cambridge, Mass., 1967), p. 164.
5 Sir Goronwy Edwards, 'The Emergence of Majority Rule in English Parliamentary Elections' *Transactions of the Royal Historical Society* (1964), p. 185 (italics in original).
6 Report of Royal Commission, para. 5.
7 Speech to the electors of Bristol.
8 Robert A. Newland, *Comparative Electoral Systems* (London, 1982), p. 33.
9 Enid Lakeman: *How Democracies Vote: A Study of Electoral Systems*, 4th edn (London, 1974), p. 86.
10 Ibid, chap. 4.
11 J. S. Mill, *Collected Works*, vol. 15 (Toronto, 1977), pp. 598–9.
12 J. S. Mill, *On Liberty*, chap. 3.
13 Douglas Rae, *The Political Consequences of Electoral Laws*, revised edn (New Haven, 1971), pp. 128–9.
14 Lakeman, *How Democracies Vote*, p. 110.

SUGGESTIONS FOR FURTHER READING

(a) Historical

Thomas Hare, *The Election of Representatives, Parliamentary and Municipal: A Treatise* 1st edn (London, 1857)
John Stuart Mill, *Considerations on Representative Government* (1861), chap. 7
Victor d'Hondt, *La Représentation Proportionelle des Partis* (Ghent, 1878)
   Représentation Proportionelle (Brussels, 1882)
Poul Andrae, *Andrae and His Invention: The Proportional Representation Method* (Philadelphia, 1926)
Andrew McLaren Carstairs, *A Short History of Electoral Systems in Western Europe* (London, 1980)

(b) Contemporary

W. J. M. Mackenzie, *Free Elections* (London, 1958)
Douglas Rae, *The Political Consequences of Electoral Laws*, revised edn (New Haven, 1971)
Enid Lakeman, *How Democracies Vote: A Study of Electoral Systems*, 4th edn (London, 1974)
Geoffrey Hand, Jacques Georgel and Christoph Sasse, eds, *European Electoral Systems Handbook* (London, 1979)
Robert A. Newland, *Comparative Electoral Systems* (London, 1982)

Shorter accounts can be found in:

Stein Rokkan, *Electoral Systems*, in *International Encyclopaedia of the Social Sciences* (New York, 1968), vol. 5, pp. 6–21, and in revised form as chap. 4 of *Citizens, Elections, Parties* (Oslo, 1970)

David Butler, in David Butler, Howard R. Penniman and Austin Ranney, eds., *Democracy at the Polls*, American Enterprise Institute (Washington, DC, 1981)

Vernon Bogdanor, *The People and the Party System* (Cambridge, 1981), pp. 209–16

2

Elections and electoral systems: choices and alternatives

RICHARD ROSE

Elections offer a multiplicity of choices, and the most important choices are made by politicians. The authors of a country's constitution and laws decide how elections will be held, what offices will be filled by popular election and how votes will be translated into seats in Parliament. In countries where the rules of the electoral system were established a generation or more ago, these rules are usually taken for granted. But where competitive elections are new, only recently restored or under fresh challenge as in Britain, major choices arise about implementing the principle of free elections. Western nations holding free elections today may be grouped into three broad categories;

i) *Electoral systems established by evolution.* English-speaking and Scandinavian countries have had long histories of free elections; their electoral systems are a century or more old.

ii) *Electoral systems established following a constitutional disruption a generation ago.* France, Germany, Italy and Austria today have well-established electoral systems. But in each country the present constitution was only established after the Second World War, and the change of regime was normally accompanied by a change in electoral system. What is taken for granted in the 1980s was uncertain a generation ago. Moreover, the electoral system can display different properties in its rapid evolution. For example, in Germany the Social Democrats and Christian Democrats together secured 87% of the vote and 89% of the seats in the 1980 German election, but in 1949 won only 60% of the vote and 67% of the parliamentary representation.

iii) *Electoral systems newly established following a constitutional disruption.* Spain, Portugal and Greece today have competitive elections – but the electoral system of a country freshly enjoying free electoral choice after a period of authoritarian rule cannot yet be fully institutionalised.

The object of this chapter is to identify what decisions must necessarily be made about the procedures of competitive elections, and to show to what extent European nations make the same or different choices from a repertoire of alternatives. The chapter also discusses the political consequences of different choices in electoral systems, for the selection of a particular system is much influenced by what it is instrumentally expected to produce. Choices about electoral systems are a significant set of decisions that politicians can and must make to secure representative government. The first section considers constitutional decisions about the scope and nature of elected offices, and the second, decisions about eligibility to vote. Laws regulating the conduct of the ballot are covered in the third section. The conversion of votes to seats by simple plurality or proportional representation methods is given detailed consideration in the following two sections. The conclusion reviews problems of assessing electoral systems.

This chapter concentrates attention upon the electoral systems of the nine nations of the European Community with well-established electoral systems: Belgium, Denmark, France, Germany, Ireland, Italy, Luxembourg, the Netherlands and the United Kingdom.[1] These nations collectively display a variety of choices. Where different choices are employed in other Western nations outside the European Community, reference will be made as appropriate.[2] All the nations examined here have maintained competitive electoral systems successfully since the Second World War.

I CONSTITUTIONAL CHOICES

Elections may decide who governs, but constitutions decide what the government is. A constitution not only establishes a set of rules for conducting elections; even more important, it identifies the institutions and offices of government for which the electorate can vote.

The election of a representative assembly is a *sine qua non* of democratic government. If the chief executive is the only elected office-holder, as in the Bonapartist tradition, then an election can easily degenerate into a plebiscite meant to endorse the authority of an individual. The norm in the European Community is to have a bicameral Parliament, with the Lower Chamber popularly elected and the Upper Chamber filled by other means. Hence, it is customary in English to use the term Parliament to refer to the popularly elected Lower Chamber of a bicameral legislature (e.g., the British House of Commons, the French Assemblée Nationale, the German Bundestag, the Italian Camera dei Deputati, etc.), as well as using the term to describe both chambers together. A consequence of having only one chamber directly elected is that this chamber can uniquely claim to represent the whole electorate.

The permutations in forms of Parliaments are numerous. At one extreme, a Parliament can be unicameral: this is found in only six of twenty-one Western nations – Denmark, Finland, Israel, Luxembourg, New Zealand and Sweden – all with comparatively small populations. At the other extreme, the Upper House as well as the Lower House can be popularly elected, as in Australia, Japan, Switzerland and the United States, and virtually so in Italy. The norm for Western nations is a two-chamber Parliament, with the Lower House directly elected by popular vote, and the Upper House filled by indirect election by provincial bodies, holders of particular positions and/or appointment (Table 1).

Federalism is neither a necessary nor a sufficient condition for having a predominantly elected Upper House. Among the six federal systems in our universe of review, three have appointed or indirectly elected second chambers (Austria, Canada and Germany) and three (Australia, Switzerland and the United States), popularly elected second chambers with the constituent states of the federal union as electoral districts. Allocating seats to states creates extremes in the number of voters represented by a given representative. In the United States, one vote for a Senator in Alaska can be worth more than fifty times the vote for a Senator in California.

The whole of a country's territory may be treated uniformly for electoral purposes, or exceptional arrangements can be made for a limited area. Ironically, federalism tends to uniformity, inasmuch as a federal constitution usually stipulates the same status for all signatories to the federal compact. For example, in the United States the constitution gives each state, whatever its size, two Senators, and in West Germany the constitution stipulates the number of representatives that each *land* can send to the Upper House, the Bundesrat, with only a limited allowance for population differences.

The majority of members of the European Community make some territorial exceptions in their electoral laws. Belgium adopted an exceptional procedure for Brussels in the election of the European Parliament in 1979: French- and Flemish-speaking electors there could cast their ballot for the linguistic constituency of their choice. Germany includes in the Bundestag non-voting representatives from Berlin, the old Imperial capital; they are chosen by West Berlin's House of Representatives and not directly by voters. For designated minority parties Germany is also prepared to waive its 5% threshold for votes to qualify for a seat. To date, only the South Schleswig Voters League, representing a Danish-speaking minority, has benefited, winning one seat in 1949. Italy has one single-member constituency, the French-speaking Val d'Aosta, where proportional representation cannot apply. Denmark gives two seats in the Folketing to the Faroe Islands and two to Greenland; each territory also has a substantial amount of internal self-government. In the United Kingdom since 1950 all MPs have been elected for single-member constituencies, but a variety of electoral franchise experiments have occurred since 1973 in Northern Ireland, and a special border referendum for Northern Ireland and devolution referendums for Scotland and Wales have also departed from the rule of territorial uniformity.

Territorial uniformity in electoral laws is the rule to a very high degree. Exceptions can be made, but these usually appear to be justified de minimis. By definition, national parties compete nationwide for votes, and do so under the same electoral rules everywhere. Regional or nationalist (that is, indepen-

Table 1. *The scope for voting in national elections*

	Lower House		Upper House			Other
	N seats	Votes per MP	N elected	N total	Referendums since 1945	national elections
Belgium	212	28,500	106	182	1	None
Denmark	175	18,250		Unicameral	11	None
France	474	52,250	0	283	8	President
Germany	496	76,500	0	45	0	None
Ireland	166	10,250	0	60	6	President
Italy	630	60,500	315	323	5	None
Luxembourg	59	3,000		Unicameral	0	None
Netherlands	150	58,000	0	75	0	None
United Kingdom	635	49,250	0	1,075[a]	1	None

[a] House of Lords membership fluctuates around this figure.
Sources: Mackie and Rose, *International Almanac*; Inter-Parliamentary Union, 1976, table 2; Butler and Ranney, *Referendums*, appendix A.

dence or autonomist) parties can secure representation, according to their electoral strength, where they choose to contest seats. It is *lack of popular support* rather than electoral laws that limits representation by autonomist parties.[3]

The size of a Parliament is only very roughly related to population. The ratio of votes cast to representatives elected in the four large countries of the European Community ranges from 76,500 in Germany to 49,250 in the United Kingdom. Among smaller countries, the Netherlands is distinctive in having only one representative in its Lower House for every 58,000 votes, a higher ratio of votes to seats than Britain. Among the other Community countries there is a substantial range from one representative for 28,500 votes in Belgium to one representative for 10,250 votes in Ireland and 3,000 votes in Luxembourg.

The election of a Parliament is not the only nationwide ballot held. A majority of members of the European Community have held at least one referendum since the Second World War. But a referendum is neither necessary nor frequently used by representative governments.[4] Three of the nine Community countries – Germany, Luxembourg and the Netherlands – have not held a single referendum since 1945, and the number of issues voted on have been few in the six other countries, averaging only one referendum per decade. Voters can expect to choose their representatives, but not to vote upon individual laws. The concept of representative government distinguishes clearly between decisions taken by electors and decisions taken by elected representatives.

The election of a President is as important as the election of a representative assembly in France and in the United States, but these two Western nations are unusual in vesting substantial powers in a President. Moreover, each system also vests significant political powers in its assembly, albeit less in France than in the United States. It is not necessary to choose a President in the monarchies of Belgium, Denmark, Luxembourg, the Netherlands and the United Kingdom. In Germany and Italy the President is indirectly elected. Ireland is the only member nation of the European Community with provision for a directly elected figurehead President, and Ireland's President is sometimes returned unopposed.

National elections are not the only elections that concern citizens. Every Western nation makes provision for the election of local as well as national government officials, and European Community nations for the election of Members of the European Parliament as well. The United States is extreme in the number of elected officeholders. In addition to federal elections there are three tiers of election for executive (and some judicial) legislative posts at state, county and town level. The frequency of elections and the quantity of elected officials is no guide to their significance. By definition, sub-national elections affect only a portion of a country. In the United States, the existence of more than 50,000 separate electoral jurisdictions means that the average elected official will be concerned with a small population and limited functions. By definition, nationwide elections are the ballots of greatest importance for national government.

In broad terms Western constitutional provisions for elections in nations can be divided into two basic categories. 1) An *all-in-one* ballot as the sole expression of popular preference for national government within the life of the Parliament elected. Britain and the Netherlands are examples of constitutional systems that have a single nationwide election. 2) *Concurring elections* in which a multiplicity of nationwide votes must occur. Examples include the separate popular election of a President and an Assembly in France and the United States; of a second chamber, as in Australia and Italy; or the frequent use of the referendum as in Switzerland. Popular election of lower-tier authorities in a federal system is another institutional check upon central government's exclusive claim to speak for the electorate. The criteria for choosing between these alternative types of elections are political, not technical; elections are simply a means to the end of constitutional government.

II ELIGIBILITY TO VOTE

The achievement of universal suffrage was neither easy nor quick in most European nations. The establishment of parliamentary institutions antedated the adoption of universal suffrage by decades, generations or, in the extreme case of England, by six centuries.[5] Whereas the creation of a Parliament strong enough to wrest control of government from a monarch is typically a nineteenth-century European innovation, the grant of universal suffrage to men (and, even more, to women) is typically a twentieth-century pheno-menon.[6] The achievement of universal suffrage reflected ideas and influences common to all Western nations. Hence, laws determining who votes tend to be common throughout the European Community and, for that matter, among all Western nations (Table 2).

Citizenship is the basic requirement for voting in a country's election. Even this requirement may be waived. In the 1979 election to the European Parliament, Ireland and the Netherlands allowed citizens of other European Community countries resident there to vote. The United Kingdom allows Irish citizens to vote in British general elections if resident in Great Britain, because of historical anomalies arising from Ireland's secession from the United Kingdom in 1921.

The basic requirement of citizenship is qualified on more or less common and uncontroversial grounds in every country (Table 2). *Age* is the chief ground for limiting the right of citizens to vote. Today, an individual must be eighteen years old to vote. The age qualification is usually consistent with statutes determining when an individual legally comes of age. No Western nation allows the vote to persons younger than eighteen, and until the 1960s or 1970s twenty-one was the normal age for qualifying to vote. Conviction on a criminal charge, bankruptcy or being declared mentally incompetent by a court is the second limitation upon the franchise. Ireland is unique in the European Community in imposing no disqualification of this type upon adult citizens. The number affected by legal disqualifications is trivial.

Every government in Europe takes positive measures to facilitate voting. The most common measure is to assume responsibility for compiling the *electoral register*. Meeting the formal legal criteria for voting is not sufficient for a person to cast a vote; an individual must also have his or her name upon the register of electors of a given constituency. An electoral register must be compiled in advance of polling day, showing who is eligible to cast a ballot in a given constituency. Compiling the register is an administrative task, and one that is greatly simplified in countries that have identity cards or registration of residence. The United States is unique in the Western world in still following the nineteenth-century practice of placing the burden for registering to vote upon citizens, thus disqualifying tens of millions of otherwise eligible electors.

Voting can be made easier for an individual if an election is held on a *public rest day*, such as Sunday, or if polling day is made a legal holiday. This greatly increases the number of hours when the ordinary voter is able to cast a ballot. If polling is on a normal working day, then a working person who spends up to ten hours away from home will have very little time in which to vote at a polling station based on residence. Five of the nine countries in the European Community with well-established electoral systems hold elections on a rest day. Italy is exceptional in letting the ballot extend into the following Monday as well. Inevitably, a portion of the electorate will not be near home on election day,

Table 2 *Determination and facilitation of right to vote*

Country	Government compiles register	Qualifying Age	Disquali- fications for cause	Vote Rest day	Compul- sory	Absentee ballot	Turnout %
Belgium	Yes	18	Yes	Yes	Yes	Yes	86
Denmark	Yes	18	Yes	No	No	Yes	83
France	Yes	18	Yes	Yes	No	Yes	70
Germany	Yes	18	Yes	Yes	No	Yes	88
Ireland	Yes	18	No	No	No	Yes	77
Italy	Yes	18	Yes	Yes	Yes	Yes	87
Luxembourg	Yes	18	Yes	Yes	Yes	No	83
Netherlands	Yes	18	Yes	No	Formerly	Yes	87
United Kingdom	Yes	18	Yes	No	No	Yes	76

Sources: See Inter-Parliamentary Union, 1976, tables 3–4; Mackie and Rose, *International Almanac.*

and some may be ill or otherwise incapacitated from going to the poll. Every European Community nation except Luxembourg makes some provision for *absentee voting,* whether by postal vote, proxy vote or both. The proportion of postal votes can be substantial; in the October 1974 election in Britain 2.9% of all votes cast (850,000) were postal votes, and in a close general election the postal vote can be sufficient to influence the overall outcome, inasmuch as the absentee ballot tends to favour parties supported by more educated voters. In a country with a large number of emigrants, granting a postal vote to emigrant workers is also significant. Some countries with substantial numbers of emigrants, such as Australia and New Zealand, allow emigrants to vote at their embassies abroad.

In the belief that voting is a duty, and not just an optional right of citizens, voting is made compulsory in a limited number of Western nations, including Belgium, Italy, Luxembourg and, formerly, the Netherlands. While the penalties for not voting are slight and rarely enforced, compulsory voting does generate a higher turnout of voters. A multivariate statistical analysis by Powell found that compulsory voting and government responsibility for voter registration are strongly correlated with higher voter turnout.[7] By contrast measures of economic wellbeing such as GNP per capita are not so strong an influence upon voter turnout in Western nations.

A well administered registration system and polling on a rest day can honestly record the votes of upwards of 90% of the populace. This is true even if a substantial portion is poor or has only basic literacy. In postwar Italian elections, where voting is compulsory but the social and economic conditions thought to encourage political participation are unfavourable, the mean level of voting in elections since 1945 has been 92%.

Overall, the pattern is clear: European governments want every eligible elector to be able to vote, and do much to facilitate voting. Governments differ only in their readiness to facilitate voting; none intentionally places obstacles in the path of adult citizens exercising their legal right to vote. There is variation in the extent to which individuals actually do turn out to vote, ranging from 88% in Germany to 70% in France at the latest general elections. But differential voter response to an election does not detract from the common characteristics of laws governing eligibility to vote in European nations today.

III REGULATING THE BALLOT

While an election campaign is pre-eminently an occasion for politicians to display their strategic skills, rules laid down by government do affect the conduct of the campaign in important respects: the timing of an election; the nomination of candidates; the exposure of candidates to the electorate; and the adjudication of disputes arising from contested election results.

Every European Community country sets a maximum length to the life of a Parliament, four or five years, and, in Sweden and New Zealand, three years. Every EEC country makes provision for an election to be held before a Parliament's statutory life is complete, because the governing party or coalition lacks the confidence of Parliament, or because the government judges that the time is suited for testing its electoral support (Table 3).

In a Western parliamentary system it is unusual for a Parliament to run its full term; Germany is the only government in the European Community that has gone the full term in seven out of eight postwar ballots. Norway, Switzerland and the United States have fixed-date elections and in Luxembourg, New Zealand and Sweden elections are almost invariably held on a consistent schedule. In practice, the median Parliament lasts for 75% of its statutory length, that is, about three years. Given that the shadow of a forthcoming election campaign is cast well in advance of polling day, this means that a government will have less than three full years without being subject to the pressures of an election campaign. Nor is a French President normally elected for a seven-year term of office; of the first three Presidents to hold office since direct election in 1962, only one, Giscard d'Estaing, has served a full term; de Gaulle resigned and Pompidou died in office.

The governing party usually cannot time a general election to its electoral advantage,[8] because most governments in the European Community are coalitions. Only Britain normally has single-party government. When a coalition forms a government, then the withdrawal of one partner can be sufficient to precipitate a ballot. Nor can a coalition government normally time a general election to its electoral advantage. An analysis of postwar general elections in Western nations found that in two-thirds of elections parties in government lose votes.[9]

Table 3 *The frequency of general elections 1945–1982*

	Maximum life of Parliament	Average life	Average life as % maximum
Belgium	4	3 yrs	75
Denmark	4	2 yrs 5 mo.	60
France	5	3 yrs 9 mo.	74[a]
Germany	4	3 yrs 11 mo.	98
Ireland	5	3 yrs 5 mo.	68
Italy	5	4 yrs 1 mo.	82
Luxembourg	5[b]	5 yrs	100
Netherlands	4	3 yrs 6 mo.	87
United Kingdom	5	3 yrs 5 mo.	68

[a] Fifth Republic only.
[b] Luxembourg changed to a five-year Parliament in 1956; exceptional arrangements prevailed, 1968–74.
Source: Mackie and Rose, *International Almanac*. The average life of a Parliament is calculated from the first Parliament elected after the Second World War to the most recent election as of June 1982.

To have a chance to win votes, candidates must be named on the ballot. European countries have an 'open-entry' attitude toward the nomination of candidates and the entry of new parties to the ballot.[10] To be named on the ballot, a minimum number of signatures is required, ranging from as few as ten in Britain to twenty-five per district in the Netherlands or 1,000 in Italy. France and Ireland do not require any nominating signatures. Only four Community countries require a candidate to make a cash deposit, to be returned upon securing a stipulated share of the vote. The vote required to save a deposit is not high, and the deposit is low, e.g., £150 in Britain. The minimum age for candidates is slightly higher than that set for voting; it is lowest in Denmark, twenty, and highest, twenty-five, in Belgium, France, Italy and the Netherlands. The formal requirements for a party or candidate securing a place on the ballot are few, encouraging would-be parliamentarians to test their popular support.

Anti-system parties – that is, parties challenging the democratic basis of the constitution or its territorial scope – present a distinctive question of eligibility. The problem was seen as particularly important in the founding of the Federal Republic of Germany, given the history of Weimar and the Third Reich. Article 21 of the basic law declared ineligible for election parties seeking to impair or destroy the democratic basic order or endanger the existence of the Federal Republic of Germany. The Federal Constitutional Court decides questions of constitutionality. On that basis, the neo-Nazi Socialist Reich Party was outlawed in 1953, and the Communist Party in 1956. Other countries such as Australia, Finland and the United States have at times outlawed the

Communist Party. One practical weakness of such a move is that the leaders of a banned party may proceed to set up a 'front' organisation under another name to gain ballot recognition and votes.

The dilemma facing democratic regimes confronting an anti-system party is more apparent than real. If an anti-system party has very little popular support, then allowing it to contest free elections will actually reveal its weakness. If an anti-system party has a large amount of support, then trying to ban it is futile, given its mass base of support. In European countries, allowing anti-system parties to contest elections reveals their weakness (Table 4). Three types of anti-system vote can be identified in European Community countries. Historically, the Communist Party has claimed that it is anti-system. Yet where its vote has been highest – Italy and France – it has been supporting a regime (the *compromesso storico* in Italy), or even taking seats in government in Mitterrand's administration in France.

Aggressively 'hard Left' anti-system parties are found, but they have polled derisory votes. Armed terrorism, rather than electoral competition, is the mark of the extreme Left (or extreme Right) today. On the extreme Right, most European countries have no party courting votes on an anti-democratic platform. Only in Italy can a right-wing group claim more than a derisory vote. Nationalist parties are more widespread, but their share of the total nationwide vote is usually very small. Belgium is unusual in that all of its major parties are now linguistic parties but fragmentation has had the incidental effect of isolating secessionist political groups. Ireland (and Northern Ireland) is the place where nationalist groups make the biggest impact, but they do so by force of arms; candidates linked with the IRA (Irish Republican Army) usually poll badly, except when tension is very high.

In contemporary European elections, there is little opportunity for fraud or dispute about election results. But as long as the possibility exists, it is necessary to establish rules to deal with disputed elections. The majority of European Community countries leave the task of resolving election disputes to the courts, which do not have the partisan interest of MPs. Once an individual is seated in Parliament, the seat cannot be forfeit in Belgium, Ireland and Italy, for there is no mechanism for expulsion or disqualification. In other European Community countries, the only ground for expulsion is if an MP loses eligibility for election, say, by taking an office incompatible with being an elected representative, or being convicted of a crime that deprives the felon of civil rights.[11]

European countries seek to hold elections under rules that are fair to all parties, and fair to all candidates. The requirements for securing a place on a ballot are few, and disqualifications of anti-system parties or adult citizens virtually non-existent.[12] While all parties cannot enjoy equal popular support, Western elections are held under laws that are fair and open to competition. Constitutions put trust in the voters to choose between the wide array of candidates who campaign for support.

Table 4 *The weakness of anti-system parties*

	Extreme Left	Extreme Right	Nationalists
		(% votes, latest election)	
Belgium	2.3[a]	0	11.9 (Flemish)
Denmark	1.1[a]	0	0
France	1.3	0	0
Germany	0.2	0.2	0
Ireland	0	0	4.2
Italy	1.4	5.3	0.9
Luxembourg	5.8[a]	0	0
Netherlands	2.1[a]	0	0
United Kingdom	0.1	0.6	2.6

[a] Extra-system Communist Party vote.
Source: Compiled from Mackie and Rose, *International Almanac.*

IV CONVERTING VOTES TO SEATS: PLURALITY ELECTION SYSTEMS

Whereas voters choose what party they support, the electoral system determines what effect votes have in allocating seats in a national Parliament. There is nothing automatic about the translation of votes into seats; how this is done depends upon the choice between different electoral systems. Broadly speaking, there are two types of electoral system. The oldest type is the plurality or first-past-the-post system that awards a seat to the candidate who gets a plurality of votes in a given constituency, whether a relative plurality (the largest number) or an absolute majority (at least one more than half). Proportional representation systems, intended to allocate seats in proportion to votes, are the most common in Western nations today.

The chief justification for plurality elections is that they concentrate attention upon the choice of government. The plurality system is meant to be a means of manufacturing a parliamentary majority. The mathematical representation of preferences, the principal feature of proportional representation, is seen as less important than creating a choice in which one party is clearly responsible for government, as in Schumpeter's definition of democracy as competition between two parties, the In party and the Out party.[13] The electorate knows which party has been governing the country, and can vote accordingly for or against the government. In a parliamentary system, the plurality ballot enhances the likelihood that one party will win a majority.

A plurality electoral system is a mechanism of *disproportional* representation; the candidate wins who is first-past-the-post (that is, has the largest share of the vote in a constituency), whatever his share of the vote, just as the winner in a horse race is the horse that runs faster than every other horse in that particular race. Of the seven Western countries using one or another form of the plurality systems, five are derived directly from the British system.

In a *simple plurality* election system each constituency normally returns only a single member. This is justified in Britain as encouraging close ties between a representative and his electorate. But this goal is unattainable when the electorate is above a certain size. By the standards of New Zealand, with one MP for every 19,500 votes, British single-member constituencies are unreasonably large; this is even more true of single-member districts in the United States Congress, with hundreds of thousands of electors.

A second distinctive feature of a simple plurality electoral system is that the share of the vote needed to win a given seat cannot be known in advance: it is a function of the number of candidates and the distribution of votes between candidates in a given constituency. The winning candidate will only be sure of taking more than half the vote if there are only two candidates in the constituency. But this is not normal in the United Kingdom. The average number of candidates per constituency has been three at postwar British elections, and in 1979 it was four. In a contest between three or more candidates, there is no necessary requirement that the winner gain half the vote. The likelihood of one candidate winning at least half the vote depends upon a constituency's socio-economic characteristics as well as the number of candidates. For example, a heavily working-class constituency is likely to produce a disproportionately large Labour vote. But the fit between social characteristics and vote is not so strong that it guarantees a majority for one candidate in every seat. Many constituencies are socially mixed, or predisposed to divide votes among three or more candidates. In the February 1974 British general election, 64% of seats were won by candidates with less than half the vote in their constituency and in 1979, 32% of seats.

A consequence of awarding seats in Parliament to candidates winning less than half the vote is that a governing party with an absolute majority in Parliament may not have an absolute (or even a relative) majority in popular votes. In Britain, the Conservatives won a majority of seats after finishing second to Labour in popular votes in 1951, and in February 1974 Labour won control of government with 37.2% of the vote, 2.7% less than the Conservative share. In the 1981 New Zealand election, the Labour Party won the largest share of the vote, 39.0%, against 38.8% for the National Party. But the National Party took 51% of the seats in the House of Representatives, as against 46.7% for Labour, and 2.2% for Social Credit, which won 20.7% of the popular vote. No governing party in Britain has won as much as half the popular vote since 1935, and the Labour Party has never won an absolute majority of the popular vote. Similarly, the Liberal Party has dominated the politics of Canada for more than half a century, even though it last won an absolute majority of the popular vote in 1908.

The *alternative vote* – used only in Australia – is an attempt to overcome one principal objection to the simple plurality system. In the alternative vote system, the winning candidate in a constituency must secure an absolute majority, that is, at least one vote more than 50% of the total. An absolute majority may be obtained on the first count of votes, but with three or more candidates this is by no means certain. Hence, each voter is required to rank alternative candidates in order of preference 1, 2, 3, etc. If no majority is secured on the first count, the candidate with the fewest votes is eliminated, and his second preferences redistributed among the remaining candidates. If this does not produce an absolute majority, then the next lowest candidate is eliminated, and his second preferences redistributed, until one candidate wins an absolute majority.

The alternative vote is a method for ensuring majority representation in each constituency; for that reason, it remains a system of disproportional representation. The minority candidate's party gets nil representation in a constituency. In Australia, a party with as much as 9% of the national vote – the Australian Democrats in 1977 – can win no seats because it lacks a majority in any one constituency.

The alternative vote system prevents a party from manufacturing a majority if it cannot secure second preference votes from supporters of other parties. In Australia, the Labor Party has won the largest share of the popular vote at every Australian general election bar one since 1937. Yet it has won a majority of seats in the Australian House of Representatives in only four of the eighteen elections held in the past forty-five years. This is because of a second feature of the alternative vote system: it allows two parties to run in a competitive alliance. In the first count, the two parties can compete against each other (or against third-party candidates). The whole electorate can vote their first preference, knowing that splitting the vote among several anti-Labor parties will not allow the party they like least to win the seat on a minority vote. The subsequent distribution of preferences for the lesser parties allows anti-Socialist votes to combine in an absolute majority. The logic of the alternative vote system is not ipso facto anti-Socialist. It will work against any party that appeals to a substantial group – but repels a majority of the electorate.

The *two-ballot* plurality system used in the Fifth French Republic is a variant on the alternative vote. Instead of voters marking their preferences in order at a single point in time, the French system calls for two ballots. The results of the first election determine which candidates in a constituency may contest the second ballot. In the strictest formula, only the two highest-ranking candidates contest the second or 'runoff' election, in order to ensure that one candidate has an absolute majority. This is the system used in the second ballot in the French Presidential contest, and in many gubernatorial elections in the American South. In elections to the French Assembly, withdrawal is mandatory only for candidates with less than 12.5% of the electorate. In actuality, the second ballot is often a straight fight between two candidates, one of the Left (Socialist or Communist) and the other of the Centre-Right. The difference between the Australian and French forms of alternative vote is limited, but of practical political importance. Both systems seek the election of representatives by an absolute majority of the vote, and are therefore disproportional. Both candidates heavily penalise parties which have a large vote, but more enemies than supporters. Both ask voters to state more than one preference. But the Australian system leaves it to the voter to decide his preference, ordering candidates all at once in a single ballot. By contrast, the French system also gives an initiative to the candidates and parties after the results of the first ballot are in. In search of a constituency victory, a candidate can engage in *combinazione* or *transformismo*, trying to put together a majority coalition, with each participant seeking a maximum price for promises of second-ballot support.

The *limited vote* is a distinctively different form of plurality voting; it is only used in Japan (and the Upper House of the Spanish Cortes) today. A limited vote system has multi-member constituencies, with each elector having fewer votes than there are MPs to be elected by the constituency. In Japan each elector has one vote, and a constituency returns up to five MPs (see chapter 11).

A single vote in a multi-member constituency has two consequences. The first is that each party's candidates are to some extent running against each other. There is considerable uncertainty about the outcome in many constituencies because it is not known what share of the total vote is needed to win or which of a party's candidates will be returned. Secondly, the limited vote plurality system is less disproportional than a plurality vote in a single-member constituency. It forces even the strongest party to concede some seats to its opponents by nominating fewer candidates than there are seats to be allocated.[14]

A simple plurality electoral system usually does *not* produce a two-party Parliament. In the six Western parliamentary governments using variants of the simple plurality system, there are anything from three to nine parties in Parliament (Table 5). The United Kingdom, long considered the exemplar of two-party politics, today has MPs from a Scottish, a Welsh and four Ulster parties, concentrating their appeal territorially in order to turn votes into seats, as well as the historic 'third' party, the Liberals, who fail to win many seats because their vote is evenly spread around hundreds of constituencies. Among the six systems, only the smallest, New Zealand, has normally had a two-party Parliament in the postwar era.

The first-past-the-post electoral system is usually successful in manufacturing a parliamentary majority for one party, notwithstanding its failure to win half the vote (Table 5). In all six of the most recent elections examined, a majority of seats was won by a single party. Shares of vote ranged from 48% for the Liberal Democratic Party in Japan, which thereby won 56% of seats, to 38%

Table 5 *The tendency of plurality systems toward majority party government*

| Country | Number of parties winning[a] | | Largest party's % share[a] | | Largest party wins | |
	1% plus vote	Any seats in Parliament	Vote	Seats	Half vote	Half seats
					(% postwar elections)	
Australia	4	3	46[b]	59[b]	7	100[b]
Britain	4	9	44	53	0	91
Canada	5	3	44	52	8	54
France (Fifth Republic)	7	6	38	56	0	28
Japan	6	6	48	56	20	53
New Zealand	3	3	39[c]	51[c]	23	100

[a] At latest election.
[b] Liberal–Country coalition here treated as a single party.
[c] Figures for National Party, first in seats but second in votes.
Source: Calculated from Mackie and Rose, *International Almanac.*

for the French Socialists, which also won 56% of seats. In five of the six countries, one party usually wins a majority of seats, and in Australia and New Zealand, this has happened at every general election since the war. In no country is it normal for one party to win as much as half the vote. Moreover, the tendency of plurality systems to manufacture a single-party majority government is really strong only in the cricket playing parts of the Commonwealth. It does not apply regularly in Canada, in Japan or France. In the Fifth French Republic, with at least four parties likely to take a sixth or more of the vote, no overall majority has been usual, an outcome that could become familiar in Britain too, if the Liberal and Social Democratic Party Alliance establishes itself as a significant third force.[15]

V CONVERTING VOTES TO SEATS: PROPORTIONAL REPRESENTATION
SYSTEMS

In proportional representation electoral systems, a general election is principally a means of representing popular preferences. An election is meant to produce as close as possible a match between a party's share of the vote and its share of representation in the national Parliament. The election is an end in itself, and not, as in plurality systems, a means to the end of forming a single-party government.

Because the electorate rarely gives any party half its vote under any system, an invariable consequence of proportional representation is the maintenance of a multi-party (that is more than two-party) system. In the seven PR systems

Table 6 *The distribution of seats by party in proportional representation elections*

| | Parties winning seats | % Seats won by | | | |
		Largest party	Two largest	Three largest	Four largest
Belgium	13	20	37	50	62
Denmark	9	34	49	61	72
Germany	3	45	89	100	—
Ireland	6	47	86	95	96
Italy	12	41	73	83	88
Luxembourg	6	41	66	90	93
Netherlands	10	32	61	79	90

Source: Mackie and Rose, *International Almanac*.

of the European Community, an average of eight parties win at least one seat in Parliament (Table 6). By contrast, in the six plurality systems, the norm is representation by five parties, with two much larger than the rest (Table 5).

Proportional representation is likely to create a multiplicity of winners and losers in a general election, for with half a dozen to a dozen parties competing for seats, several are likely to have their total vote rise and several have their vote fall. Nor can a single winner take control of government when no party wins a majority and, especially, when the largest single party wins less than a third of the vote, as happens, say, in Belgium or the Netherlands. The extent to which parties dominate representation is very variable between proportional representation systems (Table 6). The largest party can win anything from 20% to 47% of the seats; together the two largest parties can take anything from 37% to 89% of the seats. PR by itself does not determine the number of parties in a national Parliament. It simply encourages more parties than do plurality systems, and tends to be biased against (but does not necessarily preclude) the emergence of one or two large parties.

Proportional representation systems require the election of MPs from multi-member constituencies.[16] Only if two or more representatives are returned can the minority as well as the majority be sure of a parliamentary voice. But the division of a country into constituencies varies greatly within the European Community (Table 7). At one extreme, the Netherlands treats the whole nation of 9.9 million electors as a single constituency electing all members of the 150-seat Tweede Kamer. But every other Western country using proportional representation except Israel divides the country into a multiplicity of constituencies. The resulting constituencies can be very large, containing more than a million voters.

The basic rule is: *the more MPs returned from a constituency, the greater the*

Table 7 *Constituencies in proportional representation systems*

	Total seats	N constituencies	Seats per constituency		Average electors per constituency
			Average	Range	
Belgium	212	30	7	5–48	229,000
Denmark	175	18	10	2–40	209,000
Germany					
a) Direct	248	248	1	0	174,000
b) PR	248	1	248	0	43,000,000
Ireland	166	41	4	3–5	55,000
Italy	630	31	20	1–35	1,360,000
Luxembourg	59	4	15	6–24	53,000
Netherlands	150	1	150	0	9,960,000

Sources: Mackie and Rose, *International Almanac*; Inter-Parliamentary Union, 1976, table 9.

degree of proportionality. If the quota for election is the total number of votes cast divided by the number of seats in a constituency plus one, then in a constituency with two members, a third of the vote is needed to win a seat; with three members a quarter of the vote; with four members, a fifth of the vote, and so on. In a constituency with ten members, a party can win a seat with less than a tenth of the vote. The number of members elected by a constituency sets the threshold of votes a party must obtain to be sure of a seat in a PR system. In European Community nations, the tendency is to have relatively large constituencies (Table 7). The median country is Luxembourg, where the average constituency elects fifteen MPs.

The size of a constituency is determined primarily by the distribution of population within a country. No country with proportional representation divides the country into constituencies of equal size. Sparsely populated areas receive fewer representatives. Historic boundaries of provinces, regions or cities are usually respected, and as population varies between these (e.g., in Germany by a factor of 1:24 between Bremen and North Rhine-Westphalia) the number of representatives for a given multi-member constituency will also vary. Two consequences follow. There is no best or right number of representatives in a multi-member PR district. Furthermore, there is no maximum size for the number of electors in a constituency. Differences in size between constituencies within a given nation are likely to be greater than differences in the average size of constituency between nations. In Denmark, the number of MPs per constituency ranges from two to forty, in Belgium from five to forty-eight, and in Italy from one to thirty-five.

In allocating seats within a constituency, the first requirement is to establish a *quota*, that is, the minimum number of votes a party requires to be sure of winning a seat. The quota can be calculated by the Hare, Droop, Hagenbach-Bischoff or Imperiali method. After determining the electoral quota for a multi-member constituency, the next step is to allocate seats according to parties, by the largest remainder, the highest average d'Hondt or the Sainte-Laguë formula (see Glossary).

The system for allocating seats according to votes affects the minimum number of votes a party needs to secure representation, and the maximum number of 'wasted votes'.[17] Proportional representation systems vary according to their formula for allocating seats to parties, and also according to the distribution of votes among parties in a given constituency.[18] The possible differences can be explored mathematically, and examples produced of anomalies under extreme assumptions about the number of parties competing, the number of seats to be allocated in a constituency and the particular distribution of votes. Yet the nuances differentiating the largest remainder, d'Hondt, and Sainte-Laguë systems should not obscure their basic common feature: the tendency to approach proportionality in the distribution of seats.

Nearly every proportional electoral system sets a *threshold*, the minimum number of votes (and the constituency concentration of that vote) a party must have to be sure of gaining a seat. In a constituency with only a few seats, this threshold will be high. In a three-seat constituency, for example, a party must win at least a third of the vote to be sure of achieving a Hare quota, and more than a quarter of the vote to be sure of achieving a Droop quota. In a large constituency, say with twenty seats, the threshold is low; a party must win only 4% to be sure of a seat with a Hare quota, and with a Droop quota it can win a seat with slightly less than 4%. The problem of large remainders or 'wasted votes' in a constituency (that is, votes insufficient to win a seat) is common to every proportional representation system.

A great variety of methods can be found to deal with the risk of 'wasted' votes. At one extreme is the Irish system, which has small constituencies and no provision for wasted votes. A party failing to win a seat in a constituency cannot transfer its votes for use elsewhere in allocating seats. With a maximum of five seats per constituency and some three-seat constituencies, this tends to make the Irish system more disproportional; a party that polls about 10% of the vote could theoretically find itself with no representation, according to the dispersion of the vote among constituencies. At the other extreme, the Dutch system has only one very large national constituency and requires no provision for wasted votes. The minimum vote needed to win a seat in the 150-member Tweede Kamer is very low, 0.67%. In an electoral system such as the Dutch, the threshold could only be lowered further by increasing the size of the national assembly. In Luxembourg, seats are also allocated only within constituencies, but as an average of 15 seats are to be won in a constituency, the threshold a party must clear to be sure of winning a seat by the Hagenbach-Bischoff quota is usually not high. The majority of proportional representation systems in the European Community make some positive provision for topping up representation by creating a national-level constituency to pool 'wasted' votes, that is, votes that did not win a seat in a given constituency allocation. Arrangements vary from country to country. The norm is to have relatively large electoral districts, and to have a second-stage pool to top up representation for the smaller parties, thus reducing wasted votes and increasing the overall proportionality of the system.

In Italy there is a bias toward exact proportionality arising from the very large constituencies and the Imperiali quota. Parties having wasted votes there have their votes pooled nationally, provided that they have already won at least one seat and 300,000 votes nationwide. The seats not distributed by constituency quotas are then distributed from the national pool, thus reducing the proportion of wasted votes. In Denmark, 40 of the 175 seats in the Folketing are distributed by a similar national topping up system for all parties meeting low minimum standards of popular support. In Belgium, there is provision for transferring votes wasted at the constituency stage to a provincial pool, where seats can be allocated to individual parties or combinations (*apparentement*) formed by groups of parties to avoid wasting individual remainders.

Germany has a unique system of topping up representation, for half the Bundestag is elected by proportional representation and half by single-member districts. To qualify for the distribution of proportional representation seats, a party must win at least 5% of the total national vote or victory in at least three *Wahlkreis* (constituencies). The barrier was set at this height to prevent representation of extremist parties, and to prevent the proliferation of small parties, both considered problems fostered by the Weimar electoral system. The distribution of seats at the *Wahlkreis* level is usually disproportional, because it is done by simple plurality. For example, in 1972 the Social Democratic Party (SPD) won 46% of the vote and 61% of the constituency seats, whereas in 1976, when its vote dropped by 3%, its share of constituency seats dropped almost 15%.[19] The award of half the seats by PR compensates effectively for the disproportionality of the plurality distribution. In 1972, for example, the SPD received only 31% of the seats in the PR distribution, because it had done disproportionately well in the constituency contests. In 1976 its share of seats in the PR distribution rose by 9%, because its success at the constituency level had fallen. The Free Democratic Party does disproportion-ally well in the PR distribution, taking 15.9% of seats. Since 1961 it has won from 5.8 to 12.8% of the vote but has not won a single constituency seat in six elections.

The final stage in a proportional representation system is the allocation of seats to particular candidates, who then become the Members of Parliament. Logically, there are two alternatives: an elector may be asked to vote for a party, which lists the order in which its candidates should be elected, or an elector may vote for a candidate, with votes cast for all the candidates of a party totalled to establish its number of seats, and seats allocated to their candidates who secure the most votes as individuals. The use of pure alternatives is relatively rare. Germany is the only member of the European Community that uses the strict party list, but a voter can also express a preference for individual candidates at the *Wahlkreis* level. Israel and Spain also use the strict party list. At the other extreme, in Ireland (see below) an elector can only vote for individual candidates. In Italy, the parties give no indication of the rank order in which candidates should be elected; this is determined by those who vote for the party's list. The candidates elected reflect the preference votes that individual candidates of the party secure votes additional to the vote for the party list.

Most proportional representation systems make some allowance for an elector to express a preference between candidates of a given party, as well as allowing each party to indicate the order in which it wishes its candidates elected. The ranking of candidates has an important effect upon a party's representation (and upon the influence of those doing the ranking upon their representatives), for the top person on a list is normally certain of election, and the bottom person normally certain of defeat. The usual procedure is to ask a voter to indicate a party preference, and also to allow the voter to vary the party's rank ordering of candidates, if the voter so wishes.

The Irish electoral system is best discussed on its own (see chapter 9). Its most distinctive feature is that it makes voters express a choice for individual candidates rather than party lists. In practice, there is a strong tendency for voters to confine preferences within their first choice party, and to put the top candidate of their second party below the bottom candidate of their first party. But the relationship is not exact, and control of government has turned on the extent to which transfers have been regular, especially when Fine Gael and Labour have run in coalition. The practical political effect of STV PR is to weaken party discipline, because the winning candidates are not beholden to the party for a high position on the party list. To win a seat a successful candidate normally must defeat another member of his own party. For example, in a constituency in which a party hopes to win two seats it will nominate three candidates, who then compete against each other. The Irish ballot thus combines elements of an American-style primary election with a general election.

The empirical significance of different choices between electoral systems is easily exaggerated by looking only at their theoretical differences. Particular elements of a system tending to increase or reduce proportionality may be cancelled out by devices having the opposite effect. Moreover, plurality systems distort but do not negate the preferences of electors. There remains a correlation between a party's share of the vote and its share of the seats.

The difference in proportionality between the median election under proportional representation and plurality systems is very limited: 7% (Table 8). The median Western countries with proportional representation are Finland and Italy, where the distribution of seats is 95% proportional to votes. The median plurality system country is Australia, where the distribution of seats is 87% proportional to votes.

Notwithstanding the common intent of proportional representation systems, there is a considerable difference in the degree of proportionality actually achieved currently. The most proportional system is Austria, which matches seats and votes to within 1%. The least proportional is Spain, which deviates by 17% from pure proportionality, and Greece, which deviates by 12%. A major reason for this is that the two countries tend to return a small number of MPs per constituency, five on average in Greece and six in Spain, the smallest among the seventeen countries reviewed here except for Ireland. Moreover Spain has an unusually fragmented party system because of regionalist political pressures, and in Greece high thresholds for winning seats significantly reduce the actual proportionality at several stages. The range of proportionality is also substantial among plurality systems. Elections to the 1980 United States Congress have been within 6% of proportionality, whereas in France the election of the 1981 National Assembly deviated by 21% from pure proportionality.

While ideal-type systems can be delineated for purposes of exposition, it is not meaningful to select any one country as typical of a proportional representation or a plurality system. The specifics of a nation's history, social structure and political culture will also affect how an electoral system is used by parties and by the electorate, and thus what it produces.

The effective difference between representation in proportional representation and plurality systems is *a matter of degree, not kind.* On average, the seventeen PR systems examined are 8% more proportional than the seven plurality systems. The most proportional PR system, Austria, is 20% more proportional than the French plurality system but only 5% more proportional than the most proportional plurality system, the United States Congress. The departure of every electoral system from pure proportionality is not surprising. It is a condition of allowing free access to the ballot that many parties will lose an election, and some will fail to gain any representation at all. What is most noteworthy is the general tendency of *all* electoral systems to allocate representation in Parliament in keeping with the broad distribution of the popular vote.

VI ASSESSING ELECTORAL SYSTEMS

Electoral rules cannot be assessed independently of political criteria and values. This is most obviously the case in deciding about an acceptable level of

Table 8 *Comparing the proportionality of*
PR and plurality systems

	Index of proportionality
PR systems	
Austria	99
Germany	98
Sweden	98
Denmark	97
Iceland	96
Ireland	96
Netherlands	96
Switzerland	96
Finland	95
Italy	95
Israel	94
Portugal	93
Belgium	91
Norway	91
Luxembourg	90
Greece	88
Spain	83
Plurality systems	
United States (House, 1980)	94
Japan	91
Canada	88
Australia	87
Britain	85
New Zealand	80
France	79

Note: The index of proportionality is calculated as
the sum of the differences between each party's
share of seats and its share of votes, divided by two
and subtracted from 100.
Source: Mackie and Rose, *International Almanac*,
table A. 5.

proportionality in an electoral system. No one would defend a system
that consistently gave the most seats in Parliament to parties with the least
votes. On the other hand, even a Parliament elected by nationwide proportional representation leaves some parties without any representation. In the
case of the Netherlands in 1981, three parties with 2.0% of the vote,
notionally worth three seats, won nothing. Whether the proportionality of a
PR or a plurality system is enough depends upon the degree of perfectionism
demanded, or imperfection deemed acceptable.

Insofar as elections are viewed as a means to the end of constituting government, which is prima facie an object as important as representation, then judgements about electoral systems become subordinate to judgements about the most desirable way of constituting government. A simple plurality system is most likely to manufacture a majority for one party. But most European societies cannot have their political cleavages reduced to a single bipolar choice. Parties divide along a multiplicity of lines: religion, territorial identity and language – as well as (or instead of) class.[20] Fixing responsibility upon a single governing party only creates competitive politics if the pendulum swings, that is, if the governing party is ejected from office from time to time. But this is *not* normally the case. Britain is atypical because its two parties usually alternate in office. In Western nations since 1945, single-party hegemony is the norm.[21]

Insofar as a choice of proportional representation or plurality electoral systems influences the likelihood of single-party or coalition government, an assessment of electoral systems can turn upon the consequences of different types of government. A coalition government is more subject to internal constraint, because the concurrence of its member parties is needed to maintain a coalition majority. But a very large party, with nearly half a nation's vote, is likely to be a coalition too. The Democratic and Republican Parties in the United States are extreme examples of large 'catch-all' parties. The evidence of disagreements within the Conservative and Labour Parties is a reminder that each is a coalition of groups with a variety of outlooks. Moreover, a party in government must deal with a coalition of disparate interests. There is 'something stronger than parties' that makes a governing party recognise the need to bargain with pressure groups of many kinds including supporters of their electoral opponents.[22]

The problem of looking after minorities in a democracy based on majority rule cannot be resolved by electoral systems. By definition, in any reasonably fair electoral systems *minorities must always lose*. Only in a chronically fragmented society, such as the United States, can a minority hope to exercise persisting leverage as a potential partner in governing coalitions. Permanent minorities anxious to protect their rights must look to non-electoral constitutional guarantees, such as a federal structure, to accommodate diverse territorial groups or nations; concurring or 'more than majority' constitutional provisions for national decision-making; and justiciable rights resolved in a court that is *not* governed by an elected majority.[23]

For the majority of politicians and the majority of voters, the decisions taken about electoral laws are important. They are constituent judgements, because they concern the very rules by which government is constituted, prior to decisions about particular issues of public policy. Immediate party or policy concerns can influence the rules chosen. But however transitory the reason, once chosen, electoral rules tend to persist by their own inertia. These rules apply in future circumstances that cannot be known at the moment of choice. Hence, the golden rule for politicians confronted with choices about electoral systems is to ask: *how would I like it if the rules were applied in circumstances unfavourable to me and my party as well as in favourable circumstances?* This principle of equity[24] is of fundamental importance, for in any system of free elections politicians who immediately benefit will still be asked to endorse the system, when the rules that once made them winners turn them into losers.

NOTES

An earlier draft of this chapter was presented at a Workshop on Electoral Law organised by the Centro de Estudios Constitucionales, Madrid, 25–26 February 1982. I am indebted to Thomas T. Mackie for many comments on the draft.

1 The tenth member of the European Community, Greece, is omitted, because it has not yet demonstrated continuity in elections.
2 The term 'Western nations' is used to refer to the twenty-one countries with well-established competitive electoral systems with full data reported in Thomas T. Mackie and Richard Rose, *The International Almanac of Electoral History*, 2nd edn (London, 1982): Australia, Austria, Belgium, Canada, Denmark, Finland, France, Germany, Iceland, Ireland, Israel, Italy, Japan, Luxembourg, Netherlands, New Zealand, Norway, Sweden, Switzerland, the United Kingdom and the United States. When reference is made to an illustrative election result for a nation, it is the latest result as of 1 January 1982, unless otherwise stated.
3 Richard Rose and D. W. Urwin, *Regional Differentiation and Political Unity in Western Nations*, Sage Professional Papers in Contemporary Political Sociology 06–007 (London and Beverly Hills, 1975).
4 D. E. Butler and Austin Ranney, eds., *Referendums*, American Enterprise Institute (Washington, DC, 1978).
5 Stein Rokkan, *Citizens, Elections, Parties* (Oslo, 1970).
6 Dieter Nohlen, *Wahlsysteme der Welt* (Munich and Zurich, 1978), pp. 36f.
7 G. Bingham Powell, 'Voting Turnout in Thirty Democracies: Partisan, Legal and Socio-Economic Influences', in R. Rose, ed., *Electoral Participation* (London and Beverly Hills, 1980), pp. 24–6.
8 In proportional representation systems, a government usually need not fear losing a seat at a by-election. When a seat falls vacant during the life of a Parliament, it is awarded to the next candidate in line on the list of the party that has just lost a member. Exceptionally, Ireland holds by-elections, with a single member elected by the alternative vote.
9 Richard Rose and Thomas T. Mackie, *Incumbency in Government: Liability or Asset?*, University of Strathclyde Studies in Public Policy, No. 54 (Glasgow, 1980), p. 10.
10 Inter-Parliamentary Union, *Parliaments of the World*, compiled by Valentine Herman with Françoise Mendel (London, 1976), Tables 5 and 6.
11 Inter-Parliamentary Union, *Parliaments of the World*, Tables 13–14, 17–18.
12 Furthermore, parties contesting an election usually receive significant subsidies in kind from broadcasting authorities, see Anthony Smith, 'Mass Communications', in D. E. Butler, H. R. Penniman and Austin Ranney, eds., *Democracy at the Polls*,

American Enterprise Institute (Washington, DC, 1981), and often cash subsidies as well, see K. Z. Paltiel, 'Campaign Finance: Contrasting Practices and Reforms', in Butler, Penniman and Ranney, *Democracy at the Polls*, pp. 138–72.

13 Joseph Schumpeter, *Capitalism, Socialism and Democracy*, 4th edn (London, 1952).

14 Cf. Enid Lakeman, *How Democracies Vote: A Study of Electoral Systems* (London, 1970), pp. 80–5.

15 D. E. Butler, 'Mark Your Card for the Next Election', *The Sunday Times* (8 November 1981).

16 West Germany is a partial exception, employing single-member districts for half the members of the Bundestag – but only because the whole of the nation then becomes a proportional representation constituency to offset the imbalance introduced by the allocation of single-member seats.

17 See e.g. A. Lijphart and R. W. Gibberd, 'Thresholds and Payoffs in List Systems of Proportional Representation', *European Journal of Political Research*, 5, 3 (September 1977), pp. 219–44.

18 See Rein Taagepera and Markku Laakso, 'Proportionality Profiles of West European Electoral Systems', *European Journal of Political Research*, 8, 4 (December 1980), pp. 423–46.

19 Nohlen, *Wahlsysteme der Welt*, p. 305.

20 Richard Rose, *Electoral Behavior: A Comparative Handbook* (New York, 1974).

21 R. M. Punnett, *Alternating Governments*, University of Strathclyde Studies in Public Policy, No. 93 (Glasgow, 1981).

22 Richard Rose, *Do Parties Make a Difference?* (London, 1980), chap. 8.

23 Richard Rose, 'On the Priorities of Citizenship in the Deep South and Northern Ireland', *Journal of Politics*, 38, 2 (1976), pp. 247–91.

24 John Rawls, *A Theory of Justice* (Oxford, 1972).

SUGGESTIONS FOR FURTHER READING

Butler, D. E., 'Mark Your Card for the Next Election', *The Sunday Times* (8 November 1981)
    and Ranney, Austin, eds., *Referendums* (Washington, DC, 1978)
    Penniman, H. R. and Ranney, Austin, eds., *Democracy at the Polls* (Washington, DC, 1981)
*Inter-Parliamentary Union, *Parliaments of the World*, compiled by Valentine Herman with Françoise Mendel (London, 1976)
*Lakeman, Enid, *How Democracies Vote: A Study of Electoral Systems* (London, 1970)
Lijphart, A. and Gibberd, R. W., 'Thresholds and Payoffs in List Systems of Proportional Representation', *European Journal of Political Research*, 5, 3 (September 1977) pp. 219–44
*Mackie, Thomas T. and Rose, Richard, *The International Almanac of Electoral History*, 2nd edn (London, 1982)
Nohlen, Dieter, *Wahlsysteme der Welt* (Munich and Zurich, 1978)
Paltiel, K. Z., 'Campaign Finance: Contrasting Practices and Reforms', in Butler, Penniman and Ranney, eds., *Democracy at the Polls*, pp. 138–72

Powell, C. Bingham, 'Voting Turnout in Thirty Democracies: Partisan, Legal and Socio-Economic Influences', in R. Rose, ed., *Electoral Participation* (London and Beverly Hills, 1980), pp. 5–34

Punnett, R. M., *Alternating Governments*, University of Strathclyde Studies in Public Policy, No. 93 (Glasgow, 1981)

Rawls, John, *A Theory of Justice* (Oxford, 1972)

*Rokkan, Stein, *Citizens, Elections, Parties* (Oslo, 1970)

*Rose, Richard, *Electoral Behavior: A Comparative Handbook* (New York, 1974)

'On the Priorities of Citizenship in the Deep South and Northern Ireland', *Journal of Politics*, 38, 2 (1976), pp. 247–91

Do Parties Make a Difference? (London, 1980)

and Mackie, Thomas T., *Incumbency in Government: Liability or Asset?*, University of Strathclyde Studies in Public Policy, No. 54 (Glasgow, 1980)

and Urwin, D. W., *Regional Differentiation and Political Unity in Western Nations*, Sage Professional Papers in Contemporary Political Sociology 06–007 (London and Beverly Hills, 1975)

Schumpeter, Joseph, *Capitalism, Socialism and Democracy*, 4th edn (London, 1952)

Smith, Anthony, 'Mass Communications', in Butler, Penniman and Ranney, eds., *Democracy at the Polls*, pp. 173–95

Taagepera, Rein and Laakso, Markku, 'Proportionality Profiles of West European Electoral Systems', *European Journal of Political Research*, 8, 4 (December 1980), pp. 423–46

*Particularly recommended for a comparative overview of electoral systems.

3

Variants of the Westminster model

DAVID BUTLER

The British electoral system is very old and very widely disseminated. It has been much admired. Yet no major democracy that has not been under British rule actually uses it today. British electoral arrangements are supposed to foster two-party systems and majority governments. Yet most countries that have adopted them have in practice had multi-party systems and frequent minority situations.

The consequences of first-past-the-post voting are full of paradox. They are sometimes predictable, sometimes unpredictable, sometimes stabilising, sometimes destabilising. They are certainly not uniform. First-past-the-post voting was the instrument that ended Mrs Gandhi's emergency in 1977, and two years later it was the instrument that restored her to full power. It was the instrument that brought in apartheid in South Africa in 1948 on a mere 40% of the white vote and it was the instrument that, in the postwar period in Britain, gave full power to government after government without one of them receiving 50% of the ballots cast. Yet a general verdict would be that, for good or ill, the electoral system is one that has provided 'strong government' and 'stable government' in these – and other – countries.

This chapter seeks, in most summary form, to consider the impact of majoritarian voting in seven countries. Electoral systems lie at the heart of the democratic process and their consequences can be infinitely ramifying, shaping the nature of parties, the operation of pressure groups, the style of the legislature, the authority and stability of government and the unity and cohesion of the nation. The experience of Britain and the major countries that have followed its basic pattern, in terms of voting systems, have been in many ways different. Here we look out from the original model to the four countries that made up the self-governing Dominions of pre-war days, together with India (the largest member of the New Commonwealth and one of its few surviving democracies) and the United States, the most important exponent of first-past-the-post voting.

I BRITAIN

Until the 1832 Reform Act, the mediaeval arrangements for sending a Burgesses and Knights to Westminster had not the least pretence of proportionality.

46

Communities large and small – and, indeed, non-existent – returned members on a non-secret ballot and often as a result of crude bribery or intimidation. But the last century has brought in the notions of equality – equality of franchise (one man, one vote – later, one man or woman, one vote) and equality of constituency size (at least in broad principle). It has seen the elimination of money and intimidation as significant influences in elections. But it has also seen the rise of organised parties, fighting nationwide and winning votes that can be aggregated and percentaged, and then compared with the number of seats won. The concepts of equality brought into the electoral system, step by step, over the last century inevitably brought in their train a questioning about proportionality. Elections yielded disproportional representation – and an awareness that representation was disproportional. The defenders of the system, indeed, have made a virtue of its necessary disproportionality: how else, when no party commands 50% of the vote, could there be single-party majority governments, taking full responsibility for the nation's affairs?

Britain has had since 1950 a pure system of single-member seats, roughly equal in size. Northern Ireland has been systematically under-represented, while Wales and even more Scotland have been consistently over-represented.[1] The continuance of these anomalies emphasises the political rather than the principled underpinnings of the system. Parliamentary boundaries have been redrawn infrequently (and by a very cumbersome procedure). This has produced a regular cycle in the direction and the degree of bias that the system has shown as between the major parties. That bias is not great, since a 2% lead in votes has always guaranteed the larger of the two parties a lead in seats. However, it did allow the Conservatives to win a clear majority in 1951 although 1% behind Labour, and it did allow Labour to win most seats in 1929 and in February 1974 although 1% behind the Conservatives. For a long while Labour seemed to suffer more from the system, because it wasted votes piling up huge majorities in rock solid seats in mining areas and city centres. But population movements have recurrently hurt the Conservatives; as boundaries get more out of date, Labour has become over-represented in the depopulated cities and the Conservatives under-represented in the developing suburbs.

On a more fundamental level, the properties of the system seem to have changed over time. The way in which it crushes minorities (unless, like the Welsh and Scottish Nationalists and the various Ulster groupings, they are regionally concentrated) has seemed more brutal as the minorities have grown bigger. In February 1974 the Liberals with almost 20% of the vote won only 2% of the seats. But the regularity of the system's working has also come under challenge. In 1981–2, as the rise of the SDP/Liberal Alliance raised the spectre of three parties with almost equal mass support, simulations showed that 33% of the vote would be likely to give Labour 290 seats, the Conservatives 260 seats, and the Alliance only 79.[2]

Even in a two-party situation the properties of the system are changing. The relation between seats and votes, crudely expressed in the 'cube law',[3] which had, more or less, held good between 1931 and 1964, ceased to apply so accurately. By 1979 it seemed that the system was almost following a 'square law' (i.e., votes in the ratio A:B means seats A^2:B^2; this would involve only 11 seats out of 600 changing for a 1% swing). The reasons for this development lie partly in the growing polarisation of the electoral map, with Labour unrepresented in rural seats and Conservatives almost driven out of city centres, and with Labour declining in the South and the Conservatives in the North and in Scotland. These developments have significantly reduced the number of marginal seats.

These changes in the working of the system offer a warning against universal a priori conclusions about the consequences of particular electoral arrangements.[4] If the passage of a few years can so alter their impact in a single country, how much less reason is there to suppose that they should have standard consequences in different polities.

Yet some broad points can be made about the extent to which British political practice has been shaped by the British electoral system. It has almost always produced decisive electoral results with a single party being given full power to carry out its programme without any scapegoating excuses against coalition partners. Parties on the whole had to be broad-based and tolerant, mindful of middle-of-the-road swinging voters as they planned how to secure a majority at the next election. When minor parties produce good, vote-winning ideas, these have tended to be taken over by one or both of the two main contenders. Each of the two had its turn in office and the alternation has lent freshness to the political system with new faces and new approaches. The fact that a 1% switch in votes could produce a 3% switch in seats has given life to elections even when the movements of public opinion have been at their most sluggish. The relation between seats and votes, as far as the two main parties are concerned, has not been too unfair.

Yet the costs of the system are great. The oscillation between rival philosophies and policies in government has been unsettling and expensive. The unfairness to minor parties can be extreme and generate cynicism about the democratic process. An arrangement that worked well in the 1950s when 94% of the United Kingdom votes were divided between Labour and Conservatives became less acceptable in the 1970s when only 77% were so allocated.

One other snag latent in the system but not apparent since 1945 has been the tendency to overdo things. In all but one of the elections in the first half of the century, over 100 seats changed hands. Overwhelming landslides occurred in 1906, 1918, 1924, 1931, 1935 and 1945; it is widely agreed that the 1931 election, when seats were divided 556 to 59 between government and opposition, provided one of the most unsatisfactory parliaments in British

Table 1 *UK election results 1922–1979*

	% Voting	% of votes					% of seats					Government majority in seats
		Con.	Lib.	Lab.	Nat.[a]	Other	Con.	Lib.	Lab.	Nat.[a]	Other	
1922	71	38	29	30		3	56	19	23	–	2	Con.	75
1923	71	38	30	30		2	42	25	31	–	1	Lab.	−233
1924	77	48	18	33		1	68	7	25	–	1	Con.	233
1929	76	38	23	37		2	42	10	47	–	1	Lab.	−35
1931	76	67		31		2	85	6	8	–	1	Con.	493
1935	71	54	6	38		2	70	3	25	–	1	Con.	249
1945	73	40	9	48		3	33	2	61	–	3	Lab.	146
1950	84	44	9	46		1	47	1	50	–	–	Lab.	5
1951	83	48	2	49		1	51	1	47	–	–	Con.	17
1955	77	50	3	46		1	55	1	44	–	–	Con.	58
1959	79	49	6	44		1	58	1	41	–	–	Con.	100
1964	77	43	11	44		2	48	1	50	–	–	Lab.	4
1966	76	42	9	48		1	40	2	58	–	–	Lab.	96
1970	72	46	8	43	2	1	52	1	46	–	1	Con.	30
F 1974	79	38	19	37	3	3	47	2	47	1	2	Lab.	−34
O 1974	73	36	18	38	4	4	44	2	50	2	2	Lab.	3
1979	76	44	14	37	2	3	53	2	42	1	2	Con.	43

[a] Scotland and Wales.

Source: Adapted from D. E. Butler and A. Sloman, *British Political Facts, 1900–1979* (London, 1980).

history. The increased volatility of the voter so evident in the opinion polls of the 1960s and 1970s and still more in the opinion polls of 1981–2 makes it likely that, sooner or later, an election will once again be called at a particularly low point in the fortunes of one or other party and will result in a Parliament more lopsided than has been known for a generation.

II NEW ZEALAND

New Zealand is the smallest country to be considered here. In the second half of the last century it imported the Westminster model very comprehensively and, despite shedding its second chamber, its practices are still nearer to Westminster than those of any other country. Its population and interests have been sufficiently homogeneous for a two-party system to have flourished for most of its history. Every election since 1928 has produced a clear majority and indeed from 1946 to 1966 no general election produced any MPs who were not attached to one of the two main parties. And the cube law worked according to form, exaggerating switches in votes into much bigger switches in seats. But in recent years Social Credit has emerged as a third force. The result of the election in November 1981 certainly offered evidence for electoral reformers to exploit, as Table 2 shows. The party with fewer votes won, and a party that got 21% of the votes secured only 2% of the seats. On entirely plausible assumptions about swings in party support the next New Zealand elections could yield an utterly anomalous outcome.

But even before the rise of Social Credit there was anxiety about the system. Rural seats were virtually monopolised by the National Party while Labour was mainly urban. This situation is familiar enough in Britain – but in Britain agriculture matters much less. The fact that, when New Zealand Labour was in power, there were few farmers on its benches was certainly a source of weakness; if, through a different electoral system, Labour had been given a strong motive to echo rural interests (and indeed if the National Party had had more cause to look for votes from organised urban workers), the whole New Zealand economy might have benefited. But one must not exaggerate the polarisation of New Zealand politics. It has seen the adversarial system work with the due restraint essential to its success. The electorate has alternated between confirming governments in power and throwing them out. Elections have produced clear results and stable three-year Parliaments. And there has been no serious pressure for a change in the electoral system.

III INDIA

India, as democracy was doled out to her, naturally used the British system. And for a people with a large illiterate element the simplicity of first-past-the-post voting had obvious attractions. When independence came there was no serious move to experiment with proportional representation. The Congress Party, with its pre-eminent position, was happy with a system that favoured strong parties – and for thirty years Congress romped to overwhelming majorities in the Lok Sabha, defeating a divided opposition of many parties that consistently split the anti-Congress vote. In fact the Congress vote had declined to a mere 44% by 1971 but it won 68% of the seats. When the opposition formed a common front against Mrs Gandhi's emergency in 1977, it was not surprising that Congress was trounced. The Congress share of the vote only fell from 44% to 34% but its share of seats fell from 68% to 28%. Little more than two years later, the old divisions reasserted themselves and the Indira Congress Party with 43% of the vote won 67% of the seats.

Indian democracy is a far cry from Britain's. It has a low level of literacy and its constituencies each contain over a million people. Yet it continues to have a competitive party system. Relatively free voting and a genuine choice of government exist in few developing countries. The survival of Indian democracy, spectacularly demonstrated in the alternations of 1977 and 1980, may be a tribute to the electoral system. The sub-continent is not easy to rule

Table 2 *New Zealand election results 1946–1981*

	% of votes				% of seats				Government majority in seats	
	Nat.	Lab.	Soc. C	Other	Nat.	Lab.	Soc. C	Other		
1946	49	51	–	–	47	53	–	–	Lab.	4
1949	52	47	–	1	58	42	–	–	Nat.	12
1951	54	46	–	–	63	37	–	–	Nat.	20
1954	44	44	11	1	56	44	–	–	Nat.	10
1957	44	48	7	–	49	51	–	–	Lab.	2
1960	48	43	9	–	58	42	–	–	Nat.	12
1963	47	44	8	1	56	44	–	–	Nat.	10
1966	44	42	14	–	55	44	1	–	Nat.	8
1969	45	44	9	2	54	46	–	–	Nat.	6
1972	42	48	7	3	37	63	–	–	Lab.	23
1975	48	40	7	5	63	37	–	–	Nat.	23
1978	40 –	40 +	16	2	55	44	1	–	Nat.	8
1981	39 –	39 +	21	1	51	47	2	–	Nat.	4

Source: S. Levine, *The New Zealand Political System* (Sydney, 1979), pp. 193–5.

and, without the clear majorities that first-past-the-post voting so consistently produced, it is possible that the political chaos would have been on a scale to provoke even the Indian Army into attempting a takeover of a sort so frequently seen elsewhere.

IV SOUTH AFRICA

In South Africa the survival, over the last thirty years, of democratic procedures (for whites only, of course) is perhaps as surprising as the survival of democracy in India. But the same voting system has worked in a very different way. For the last twenty years the Nationalist Party has won over 50% of the votes and over 75% of the seats. The electoral system survives because it reinforces the dominance of the ruling party; it has prevented its not insignificant right-wing dissidents in the Herstigte Nasionale Party from getting a toehold in Parliament; oddly enough, it also allowed the more radical Progressives to oust the former United Party as the principal opposition.

Moreover the Nationalists have also to thank the quirks of the British electoral system for their original rise to power. In the election of 1948 the Nationalist/Afrikaner Alliance, with 42% of the vote, won 79 seats and beat the United Party/Labour government which, with 52% of the vote, got 71 seats. Geography and the drawing of boundaries have favoured the National-ists. The National Party represents smaller rural constituencies and it wastes fewer votes in safe seats. Since 1948 its support has increased steadily, partly

Table 3 *Indian election results 1952–1980*

	% of votes					% of seats					Government majority in seats
	Congress	Janata	Various Socialist	Various Communist	Other	Congress	Janata	Various Socialist	Various Communist	Other	
1952	45	3	11	3	39	75	1	2	3	19	C 239
1957	48	6	10	9	27	75	1	4	5	15	C 248
1962	45	6+8	9	10	20	75	1	4	6	11	C 223
1967	40	9+9	3	5+4	20	54	15	8	4+4	15	C 46
1971	44	28	–	5+5	18	68	10	–	4+5	15	C 186
1977	34	43	–	3+4	16	28	55	–	1+4	11	J 54
1980	43+5	19+9	–	3+6	15	67+2	6+8	–	2+7	8	C 220

Sources: 1951–71: N. D. Palmer, *Elections and Political Development* (London, 1975), p. 35; 1971–7: M. Weiner, *India at the Polls* (Washington, DC, 1978); 1980: *Keesing's Contemporary Archives*.

Table 4 *South African elections 1948–1981*

	% of votes				% of seats				Government majority in seats
	Nat. P	United P	Lab.	Other	Nat. P	United P	Lab.	Other	
		Afr.							
1948	38 4	49	3	6	47 + 6	43	3	–	Nat./Afr. 8
1953	50	47	3	–	60	36	–	–	Nat. 32
1958	55	43	–	2	66	34	–	–	Nat. 50
			Prog.				Prog.		
1961	46	35	9	10	67	32	1	–	Nat. 54
1966	58	37	3	2	76	24	1	–	Nat. 86
		HNP							
1970	54 4	37	4	1	71	28	1	–	Nat. 48
1974	57 4	33	5	1	72	24	4	–	Nat. 75
		N. Rep.							
1977	66 3	12	17	2	82	6	10	2	Nat. 105
1981	57 14	8	19	2	79	5	16	–	Nat. 97

Note: Unopposed returns which have varied from 11 (1970) to 70 (1961) greatly distort the voting figures. In 1958 when there were 24 unopposed returns it has been calculated that if every seat had been fought by the Nationalist Party and the United Party the vote would have been almost exactly 49–49 not 55–43 (R. R. Farquharson in D. E. Butler, ed. *Elections Abroad* (London, 1959).
Source: T. T. Mackie and R. Rose, *The International Almanac of Electoral History* 1st edn (London, 1974).

through birthrate trends and partly through the pressures to stay united in the White laager. But the bias in the system has increased even more. By 1958 when the Nationalist government got virtually the same percentage as the United Party opposition the Nationalists won by 103 seats to 53: Robin Farquharson calculated that the United Party would have needed to win by 60% – 40% in votes to get a majority in seats.[5] And this bias, it should be noted, was far more due to the geographic distribution of support than to any gerrymandering. The solid anti-Nationalist areas returned opposition candidates with large majorities: the Nationalists had fewer vote-wasting concentrations of overwhelming support. It is natural to be chary of using South Africa as an illustration in arguments over democratic procedures. But it is plain that for reasons inherent in the electoral system, and not because of explicit rigging, it provides the extreme example of the first-past-the-post system working, not just in a disproportionate way exaggerating majorities, but also in a heavily loaded way, favouring one side far more than the other. However, for over thirty years, it has given the white electorate a stable single-party government.

V UNITED STATES

In the United States political practice is so far removed from the British model
that it may seem hardly suitable to deal with it here. Yet because it is a
majoritarian system, with origins that go back to Britain, it is worth stressing
the similarities and the differences between US Lower House contests and those
that take place in the Commonwealth. The relation between seats and votes is
very different: Congressmen serve as ambassadors for their districts; unlike
MPs the prime function is not to choose and then support a government; the
primaries weaken party ties and foster individualism; there are much greater
incumbent advantages than in parliamentary systems and much wider local
variations from the national swing. Yet party majorities do go up and down on
national tides and the movement in seats can exaggerate the movement in
votes. Over the last thirty-four years votes have fluctuated from 49% to 59%
Democratic, but seats have fluctuated from 49% to 68%. In 1978, 53% of the
major party vote won the Democrats 64% of seats; in 1980, 49% won them 56%
of seats. That means that, for a 4% switch in votes, the Republicans only got a
8% switch in seats, little more than half what the cube law would have
predicted.

The cube law has in fact never worked in the USA. There was a time when
the unresponsiveness of the system could be blamed on the South with low
turnouts, unopposed returns and a solid phalanx of Democrats. But now that
every state has real contests and some Republican representation it is plain
that the cause lies elsewhere. It is to be found primarily in the advantages of
incumbency.

Congressmen learn by observation of what has happened to others, in
primaries and in the final elections; they can see that it is each for oneself. A
Congressman's fate depends only marginally on his party's fortunes. He will
survive if he gathers favours for his constituents and sympathetic publicity for
himself; to be seen as a staunch party loyalist does not help him much in
getting re-elected. As so often in life, the bad boy may extort more favours from
the powers that be than the good boy can. The political system and the
electoral system of the US demand very special reflexes from the Congressman,
quite different from those needed by British MPs or Australian MHRs.

Indeed the US variant of first-past-the-post is so special in its workings that it
is probably of little value to consider it in the Westminster context (except as a
warning against mechanistic assumptions about the operation of electoral
systems). Yet one cannot leave electoral arrangements of the US without
drawing attention to the Electoral College. American presidential contests do
demonstrate the extreme forms of majoritarian exaggeration. The fifty states
which each cast their votes *en bloc* in the Electoral College are involved in a
variant of first-past-the-post voting.

Table 5 *Popular votes and Electoral College votes*

| | Victorious Party's percentages of | | |
	2-party vote	States	Electoral College
1960	50	46	56
1964	61	88	90
1968	50	64	56
1972	62	98	97
1976	51	46	55
1980	55	88	91

Table 6 *US Congressional elections 1946–1980*

| | % of votes | | % of seats | | Government majority in seats | |
	Dem.	Rep.	Dem.	Rep.		
1946	44	54	43	57	Rep.	58
1948	52	45	60	40	Dem.	92
1950	49	49	54	46	Dem.	35
1952	49	49	49	51	Rep.	8
1954	52	47	53	47	Dem.	29
1956	51	49	54	46	Dem.	33
1958	56	44	65	35	Dem.	129
1960	54	45	60	40	Dem.	89
1962	52	47	59	41	Dem.	83
1964	59	42	68	32	Dem.	155
1966	51	48	57	43	Dem.	61
1968	50	48	56	44	Dem.	51
1970	53	45	59	41	Dem.	75
1972	52	46	56	44	Dem.	51
1974	57	41	67	33	Dem.	147
1976	56	42	67	33	Dem.	149
1978	53	45	64	36	Dem.	119
1980	49	49	56	44	Dem.	61

Source: J. F. Bibby, et al., *Vital Statistics on Congress 1980* (Washington, 1981).

In three of the last six contests a majority of 6 to 4 in popular votes has produced a majority of more than 9 to 1 in the Electoral College. In the other three a hair's breadth margin in popular votes has still provided a comfortable margin in the Electoral College.

VI AUSTRALIA

Australia is different electorally from the rest of the Old Commonwealth in three main respects. First, it has compulsory voting; second, it has the alternative vote for the Lower House; and third, it has proportional representation with the single transferable vote for the Upper House. Yet in practice its electoral system operates more like Britain's than any other country except New Zealand. Despite what happened in 1975 the Senate and Senate elections do not loom very large in Australia's politics, and compulsory voting, while simplifying the task of electioneering, does not seem greatly to affect party support. The alternative vote instituted in 1919 has not led to a proliferation of parties. Since 1949, a party rebel has only once been elected to the Federal Lower House; every other seat has gone to a member of the Liberal/Country Party coalition or to a Labor candidate. The alternative vote has enabled the coalition partners, the Liberal and Country Parties, to fight a few public battles over who owns a seat without letting Labor in on a split vote. The alternative vote also permitted the breakaway Democratic Labor Party to flourish for several elections even though it never got near to winning a seat; the 5%–10% of anti-Evatt Catholics could cast a loyal vote for the DLP and then give their second preference to a Liberal candidate, to do down the hated Evatt-, Calwell-, Whitlam-led Labor Party. And in 1977 and 1980 the new Centrist Australian Democrat Party could get 9% and 6% of the protest vote; its supporters ran no risk of wasting their votes; they were deliberately given no guidance on their second preferences and in fact they divided them remarkably equally between the other parties. But these have not been important factors in the broad logic of postwar Australian elections. There has been a two-sided battle. In almost every constituency government and opposition have provided the top two at the poll; after the distribution of preferences (actual or notional), seats have been divided much as the cube law would suggest. There is a slight anti-Labor bias in the system. Labor has needed almost 51% of the preferred vote[6] to get a majority of seats. This is due to the slightly smaller rural electorates and not to gerrymandering or to any aspect of the alternative vote.

Australia shows, at least in one context, that the alternative vote is closer to the first-past-the-post system than to any kind of proportional representation.[7] In a country that is very evenly divided between two major groupings, government have consistently won clear majorities.

VII CANADA

Canada offers a contrasting story. It has stuck to the British system of voting (though the province of Alberta had a rather disastrous experiment with the alternative vote where on one occasion 58% of the vote got the victor 100% of the seats), but the nature of the country has meant that, in terms of

Table 7 *Australian election results 1946–1980 (House of Representatives)*

	% of 1st preference votes					% of seats				Government majority in seats
	Lib.	CP	DLP	ALP	Other	Lib.	CP	ALP	Other	
1946	33	11		50	7	24	15	58	3	ALP 10
1949	39	11		46	4	45	16	39	–	Lib./CP 27
1951	41	10		48	2	43	14	43	–	Lib./CP 17
1954	39	9	–	50	3	39	14	47	–	Lib./CP 7
1955	40	8	5	45	3	47	15	39	–	Lib./CP 28
1958	37	9	9	43	1	48	16	37	–	Lib./CP 32
1961	34	9	9	48	1	37	14	49	–	Lib./CP 2
1963	37	9	7	46	1	43	16	41	–	Lib./CP 22
1966	40	10	7	40	3	50	16	33	1	Lib./CP 39
1969	35	9	6	47	4	37	16	47	–	Lib./CP 7
1972	32	9	5	50	4	30	16	54	–	Lab. 9
1974	35	10	1	49	4	32	16	51	–	Lab. 3
1975	42	11	1	43	3	54	18	28	–	Lib./CP 55
			A. Dem							
1977	38	10	9	40	3	54	15	31	–	Lib./CP 48
1980	37	9	7	45	2	43	16	41	–	Lib./CP 23

Sources: D. E. Butler, *The Canberra Model* (Melbourne, 1973); Howard R. Penniman, ed. *Australia at the Polls* (Washington, DC, 1977); Howard R. Penniman, ed. *The Australian National Elections of 1977* (Washington, DC, 1979).

proportionality and of regional representation, the picture has been very different. Canada is effectively 7,000 miles long by 100 miles deep and its ten provinces each have their separate politics. It is noteworthy that in 1980 when the Liberals won a comfortable Federal victory, they did not control a single provincial legislature. Federally two parties have long been dominant, alternating in power since 1867. But in Francophone Quebec the Conservatives have had no place. Minor parties have flourished there, as well as in the Western provinces. And, despite the electoral system, the Canadian version of Labour (the CCF, now the NDP), has kept a toehold in Ottawa for the last forty years. But though the electoral system has fostered two-party dominance it has not of late yielded firm majorities. From 1867 to 1953 there was a decisive result in every election but one (1925). But since 1957 six out of ten elections have failed to produce a clear lead for any party. The consequence has not, however, been coalition government but minority government. The largest party has, without ever making an explicit deal, run affairs for up to three years without being defeated on an issue involving confidence.

And minority governments have not been weak governments. In three cases a general election has turned a minority into a majority for the incumbents. Only one minority government has actually been defeated at the

DAVID BUTLER

Table 8 *Canadian Election Results 1945–1980*

	% of votes					% of seats					Government
			CCP/					CCP/			majority
	Con.	Lib.	NDP	Soc. C	Other	Con.	Lib.	NDP	Soc. C	Other	in seats
1945	27	41	16	4	12	27	51	12	5	5	Lib.	5
1949	30	49	13	4	4	15	74	5	4	2	Lib.	69
1953	31	49	11	5	4	19	65	9	5	2	Lib.	77
1957	39	41	11	7	2	42	40	9	7	2	Con.	−55
1958	54	34	9	2	1	79	18	3	–	–	Con.	151
1962	37	37	14	12	–	44	28	7	11	–	Lib.	−65
1963	33	42	13	12	–	36	49	6	9	–	Lib.	−7
1965	32	40	18	9	1	37	49	8	5	1	Lib.	−4
1968	31	41	17	4	1	27	59	9	5	–	Lib.	46
1972	35	38	18	8	1	41	41	12	6	1	Lib.	−46
1974	36	43	15	5	1	36	54	6	4	–	Lib.	18
1979	36	40	18	6	1	48	41	9	2	–	Con.	−10
1980	33	44	20	1	2	37	52	11	–	–	Lib.	12

Source: Adapted from H. G. Thorburn, ed., *Party Politics in Canada* (Toronto, 1963).

polls following an appeal to the country. Canada is a living refutation of the thesis that only majority governments are strong governments just as it is a refutation of the thesis that first-past-the-post elections must produce clear majorities.

The first-past-the-post system is currently under challenge in Canada. In Quebec the governing party Quebecois continues to talk about PR, which it espoused when it was in under-represented opposition. It has now won full power twice on less than half the votes but, with a fine consistency, some at least of its members are keeping alive the discussion of PR.

At the federal level a modest form of PR is being advocated as a cure for the regional imbalance which threatens Canada's shaky federal structure. In 1980 the ruling Liberal government won no seats west of Winnipeg – and over half its federal MPs came from Quebec. The Conservative opposition, with only 12% of the vote in Quebec, won only one of the Province's 75 seats. The NDP has no seats in Quebec or the Maritimes.

It has now been seriously suggested that 50 seats should be allocated to parties proportionately to the aggregate vote in each of four regions. This would not much alter the overall proportionality of the House of Commons but it would ensure that each party had an interest in gathering votes everywhere in the country and that its caucus contained spokesmen for every region.[8]

Canada has not been ill-governed under the Westminster electoral system. But it has not worked in the Westminster way, even though the relation between seats and votes for the two dominant parties has been remarkably regular.

VIII   CONCLUSION

If this diverse chronicle of seven countries has a moral, it is that one should be sceptical about attributing fixed qualities to electoral systems. Seven polities have had very different experiences of the way in which first-past-the-post elections translate votes into seats. Moreover, in some of the polities the system has worked erratically, conforming to different formulae at different periods of time. Although electoral systems are among the most quantifiable of political phenomena, they do not conform to mechanistic rules.

Yet, with that reservation, some tentative generalisations about the British voting system can in most circumstances be sustained.

1. Unless they have great concentrations of local strength, minor parties are alway penalised, in the sense that their proportion of seats is much less than their proportion of votes.
2. First-past-the-post voting does foster either a two-party system or the establishment of one dominant party.
3. Where there are two main parties, it usually, but not always, treats them fairly equally, producing parallel disproportion in the results, yielding landslide victories to whichever party has a clear lead in votes.
4. Where there are three or more major parties, it is likely to produce very capricious results.
5. It sometimes follows the logic of Anthony Downs and fosters moderate parties, as the rivals seek to maximise their support among middle-of-the-road floating voters. Since extreme parties have little chance, the main parties are in no danger of being outflanked and fight each other on the central ground, choosing leaders and policies with a wide appeal.

But each of these propositions, except perhaps the first, has at least one exception among the countries considered here. The lesson of this chapter must above all be that one should be humble in generalising about the consequences of any particular electoral system.

NOTES

1 In 1979 these were the actual and the proportionate division of seats between the components of the UK:

	Actual	Proportionate
England	516	528
Wales	36	32
Scotland	71	59
Northern Ireland	12	16

2 *Sunday Times*, 8 Nov. 1981
3 The cube law states: 'If votes are divided in the ratio A:B seats will be divided $A^3:B^3$'.
  According to the cube law in a 600-member Parliament, eighteen seats will change
  hands for each 1% swing nationwide between two relatively equal parties.
4 The changes in the working of the system are explored thoroughly in a pioneering
  article by J. Curtice and M. Steed, 'Electoral Choice and the Production of
  Government: The Changing Operation of the Electoral System in the United Kingdom
  since 1955', *British Journal of Political Science*, 12 (1982), pp. 249–98.
5 See R. Farquharson in D. E. Butler, ed., *Elections Abroad* (London, 1959), pp. 269–71.
6 I.e., the major party vote after the actual or notional redistribution of preferences.
7 At the Senate level, where there is proportional representation, the behaviour of the
  voters upsets a lot of the generalisations about the single transferable vote which
  observers of its working in Ireland are tempted to purvey. It has done little to foster
  the free choice of candidates. In thirty-two years, there have never been enough
  individualist voters to disturb the order of candidates as set out in the official party
  'How to vote' cards (although it has allowed in a few independent and minor party
  representatives).
8 Incidentally the NDP is suspicious of the proposal just for that reason. Having totally
  replaced the Liberals as the alternative party in the four Western states, they dislike
  the idea of Liberal MPs getting in through a back door and laying claim to the local
  patronage that is at the disposal of the Federal Liberal government.

SUGGESTIONS FOR FURTHER READING

Britain

David Butler, *The British Electoral System since 1918*, 2nd edn (Oxford, 1963)
John Curtice and Michael Steed, 'Electoral Choice and the Production of Government:
    The Changing Operation of the Electoral System in the United Kingdom since 1955',
    British Journal of Political Science, 12 (1982)
Electoral Reform: First Report of the Joint Liberal/SDP Commission on Constitutional Reform
    (London, 1982)
G. Gudgin and P. J. Taylor, *Seats, Votes and the Spatial Organisation of Elections* (London,
    1979)
Angus Maude and John Szemerey, *Why Electoral Reform?* (Conservative Political
    Centre, 1982)
Report of the Hansard Society Commission on Electoral Reform, Chairman, Lord Blake
    (London, 1976)

New Zealand

S. Levine, *The New Zealand Political System* (Sydney, 1979)
Howard R. Penniman, *New Zealand at the Polls: The General Election of 1978*
    (Washington, DC, 1978)

India

N. D. Palmer, *Elections and Political Development: The South Asian Experience* (Durham, North Carolina, 1975)

Myron Weiner *India at the Polls: The Parliamentary Elections of 1977* (Washington, DC, 1978)

South Africa

Kenneth A. Heard, *General Elections in South Africa 1943–1970* (Oxford, 1974)

United States

Kleppner, P., et al., *The Evolution of American Electoral Systems* (Westport, Conn., 1981)

Australia

Don Aitkin and Brian Jinks, *Australian Political Institutions*, 2nd edn (Pitman, Australia, 1982)

David Butler, *The Canberra Model* (Melbourne, 1973)

Dean Jaensch, 'Australian Electoral Systems, in Richard Lucy, ed., *The Pieces of Politics* (South Melbourne, 1975)

Howard R. Penniman, ed., *Australia at the Polls: The National Elections of 1975* (Washington, DC, 1977)

ed., *The Australian National Elections of 1977* (Washington, DC, 1979)

J. F. H. Wright, *Mirror of the Nation's Mind: Australia's Electoral Experiments* (Sydney, 1980)

Canada

Robert Burns, *One Citizen, One Vote: Green Paper on the Reform of the Electoral System* (Quebec, 1979)

William P. Irvine, *Does Canada Need a New Electoral System?* (Queen's University, Kingston, Ontario, 1979)

W. E. Lyons, *One Man – One Vote* (Toronto, 1970)

Howard R. Penniman, ed., *Canada at the Polls: The General Election of 1974* (Washington, DC, 1975)

ed., *Canada at the Polls, 1979 and 1980: A Study of the General Elections* (Washington, DC, 1981)

T. H. Qualter, *The Election Process in Canada* (Toronto, 1970)

Duff Spafford, 'The Electoral System of Canada', *American Political Science Review* (1970)

4

France

DAVID GOLDEY AND PHILIP WILLIAMS

Comparative studies tend to neglect or ignore the simple truth that working politicians cannot favour electoral systems simply for their arithmetical attractions or their moralising effects. For them, electoral systems are less important as means by which the voter controls his representatives, than as devices to constrain and restrict their occasional master, the electorate.

In France, the instability of governments and regimes has reinforced the natural obsession of competing politicians for survival, and the characteristic concern of competing social groups and parties to try to fit the electoral system to their changing needs. The issue of electoral reform has thus been more often on than off the boil. Much of the public discussion has been normative, in terms of fairness, good government, representativeness and political stability – often disguising more mundane ends of political advantage. Nonetheless, the quest for a fair and neutral system has not been without effect, particularly when fed by public revulsion against the electoral engineering of previous authoritarian or unstable regimes. Alas, the remedies adopted, while characteristically justified in the name of great principles, have more often been influenced by the narrow, immediate self-interest of governing groups. The consequence has been that French electoral systems have been seen not as a set of relatively fair, permanent and neutral ground rules, but as devices to be manipulated regularly for partisan advantage, often justified as protecting the regime (necessarily by helping to re-elect those who support and profit from it). This tendency to tinker with voting arrangements has hardly contributed to the acceptance of the results by those who could too easily attribute defeat to the system rather than the voter, and has thus helped sap the legitimacy of parliaments, governments and regimes.

The longevity of the much criticised single-member two-ballot majority system is a tribute to the capacity of French voters to prefer single-member districts with the access it gives them to *their* deputy, while believing that only proportional systems are really fair; and to the capacity of most French politicians to turn the system to their advantage, corresponding with their own need to root national political careers in a firm, controllable, local base. Electoral reform has, then, usually been accepted only when the previous system seemed more likely to cost more deputies their seats than to assure their re-election. It has often been a compromise between different groups, concerned with different outcomes; results have often betrayed expectations. Reformers without direct political power have attributed too much to electoral arrangements; politicians have been too exclusively concerned with immediate personal and partisan advantage. The French experience confirms the general rule that electoral systems are but one of the factors that conditions a country's politics, and not usually the most important or durable one.

Universal manhood suffrage was introduced to France in 1848 – and then seduced by Louis Napoleon. In the Second Empire constituency boundaries were rigged; the register was arbitrarily compiled; the administration intervened in campaigns, and regularly rewarded faithful supporters with spoils. The press was censored, the Church mobilised, the opposition harassed, voters intimidated and ballot boxes stuffed. When the Empire fell, twenty years' experience of the manipulation of universal suffrage had left its own heritage. The first lesson was to do to your opponents what they had done, or would do to you, if they got the chance. As the Republic established itself, it became more difficult to justify administrative interference in elections; prefects themselves became more cautious and conciliatory, since all governments were unstable coalitions, and most serious politicians had impregnable local bases anyway. The Council of State increasingly protected electors (and officials) from arbitrary pressures. The secret ballot was made effective only in 1914; in that year the Socialists first returned over 100 members.

Governments were still not trusted to filter candidatures or draw constituency boundaries: any citizen might stand at either ballot, and constituencies were defined as the permanent territorial units of the departments or their internal divisions, the *arrondissements*. That solved the problem of gerrymandering at the price of over-representing rural areas, magnified by the indirect electoral system for the Senate – a permanent characteristic of all subsequent French systems. The rural areas appreciated most the single-member constituency, with the representative more subject to local interest and individual concerns. MPs were not elected to support governments, but rather to constrain their arbitrary exercise of administrative authority, if necessary by bringing them down. That was perhaps the most lasting – and least beneficial – heritage of the Second Empire. Republicans converted its electoral system to make sovereign a representative assembly and subordinate the executive to it.

In the hundred years since the Third Republic was established in 1875, France has frequently changed her electoral system. Three times, single-member districts have been abolished and replaced by large constituencies; three times they have been restored. In these single-member constituencies the winner must have a clear majority of votes cast to be returned, otherwise there is a second ballot, a week or two later, when the candidate with most votes wins. Clearly the French favourite, this system has prevailed over 76 of those

107 years, and for twenty of the twenty-eight elections held during that time. But it has had different political consequences at different periods, and demonstrated how, in a new social and political context, the same mechanism can operate in quite a different way, first reinforcing and then polarising the Centre.

All the alternative systems have used large constituencies (generally the department) contested mainly by rival party lists. The Republicans at first thought this would help them against local grandees hostile to the new regime. In 1885 there were two ballots, with an absolute majority needed on the first; but in every twentieth-century list election there has been only one ballot, and some provision for proportional representation (PR) – effective (within limits) on four occasions, highly ineffective on the other three.

Under the single-member system in the Third Republic, *arrondissements* formed the districts, the largest of them being divided; in the Fifth, new districts were created, not quite so glaringly unequal as the old ones. As before, first-ballot winners needed to poll a clear majority of votes cast and at least a quarter of the registered electorate. But second-ballot candidatures were severely restricted. Up to 1940 complete newcomers could enter without having stood at all before (in 1936, 503 candidates did so). In 1958, only those who had polled 5% of the votes at the first round were allowed to go forward to the second; in 1967 that threshold was raised substantially, to 10% of the *electorate* (very roughly equivalent to the level at which a deposit is saved in Britain); and in 1975 it was put up still higher, to $12\frac{1}{2}\%$ of the electorate. The new rules, the party political factors working in the same direction – probably with even greater effect – and direct election of the President, with only the top two candidates qualifying for the run-off, together drastically limited the competition at the final ballot.

Between the Third and Fifth Republics, France had her first experiment with effective PR. At the first three elections after the Liberation, PR operated within each department or constituency in a form which gave a marginal advantage to large parties. As most districts had only four or five members, only large minorities secured representation, and the Communists, much stronger since the war, had well over a quarter of the seats. There were new pressures towards discipline among the old amorphous groups of the Right and Centre, both from the need to form large enough blocs to count, and from the fear that division elsewhere would swell the representation of the well-disciplined Communists. The practical impossibility of standing without party backing initially allowed the party organisation to determine which candidate should head the list and so have the best – usually the only – chance of election. The smaller groups competed for marginal votes to win the last seat, or to stop a strong party from picking up a second. The main contests were fought out between ideological neighbours – between Communists and Socialists for the left-wing vote, between varieties of Catholic (Gaullists, MRP or traditional conservatives) on the Right. Parties like the Socialists and MRP, which had to compromise if a government was to be formed at all, were constantly outbid by opposition groups – from opposite sides – taking an intransigent stand on issues calculated to appeal to their respective clienteles. In 1951 the system was modified to give an advantage to Centrist parties capable of forming alliances; it led to many anomalous results at its first trial, but at the second, in different political circumstances in 1956, it had no effect and the outcome was the same as the unmodified PR system would have produced (see Table 3).

By 1951 many members had held their seats for five or six years, and for voters of similar outlook they symbolised the party locally; it could no longer afford to replace them with another candidate. Indeed a deputy could occasionally change his party label – and carry his voters with him. The Communist threat no longer appeared imminent, and the party discipline which had once been so rigid – and so irksome to those politicians who had never known it before – eroded fairly completely on the Right and Centre and even to some degree on the Left, where it had traditionally been more acceptable. When the Fourth Republic collapsed in 1958, it had reverted a long way towards the rampant political individualism and indiscipline which, under a very different electoral system, had been so widely blamed for the paralysis of its predecessor before 1940.

Opinions about the political consequences of that system, called *scrutin d'arrondissement* – single-member constituencies with two ballots – reflected its operation between the two world wars, when it increased the size, but reduced the discipline, of the parties of the Centre. Majorities in the Chamber of Deputies were insecure, governments were weak and frequently reshuffled, and their survival depended on elaborate manoeuvres and unstable combinations among several loose and shifting (or even shifty) parliamentary groups, rather than on any clear choice by the electorate. This was the parliamentary reflection of a society divided after the First World War by two principal cleavages, respectively pitting clericals against anti-clericals and socialists against anti-socialists. The primary beneficiaries of the electoral system were those politicians who were 'anti-both', particularly the ill-disciplined Radical party and the protean little groups which often associated with it (see Table 2). For in right-wing regions like the West, only a Radical could hope to defeat the clerical candidate and he could therefore count on support from the entire Left, while in left-wing regions like the South only a Radical could beat the Socialist – and clericals therefore often found him the lesser evil. Not many deputies – fewer than 50 out of 600 in 1928 – were elected without adding second-ballot support from one or the other wing to their Centrist base. Thus the Radical and Centrist ranks were swollen but their cohesion was destroyed, since half of them feared to forfeit essential second-ballot support by leaning too far to the Right, the other half by leaning to the Left.

At election times, most Radicals preferred the latter, traditional alliance, but on three occasions between the wars such left-wing coalitions won the general election only to split, usually over finance, midway through the four-year Parliament. With few seats settled at the first round, individualism flourished. Local mayors could build a popular reputation and then, with a secure constituency base, seek whatever parliamentary association seemed most profitable, combining with others in little Centre groups without ideological commitment, assembled to maximise their bargaining power in the frequent cabinet changes which punctuated the regular rightward drift; such small groups with a marginal position could raise 'a record crop of ministerial jobs to the acre'. Sometimes on the Right, and frequently in the Centre, there was only a tenuous connection between the uninformative label under which the deputy had fought the election and the vague allegiance he professed in the Chamber itself.

In this period, politics operated quite differently at the two ballots. On the first round, a whole series of candidates could stand with little fear of splitting the vote for their side and letting the enemy in. No party contested every, or even nearly every, seat, except for the Communists. As before the First World War, the Centre groups, crucial for majorities in the Chamber, stood in only a minority of districts; left-wing parties bunched in left-leaning areas and conservative candidates in right-wing, often clerical, departments. For partisan strength was then much more heavily concentrated geographically than it is today, and politics much more localised.

The concentration of support allowed competition in safe Right or Left seats between political neighbours who would be likely allies in the Chamber. In general, however, on the second ballot, the contest would be clear cut, usually between Left and Right, as it had been between republicans and monarchists before the turn of the century. But in some districts the Left was represented by a Socialist, in others by the least conservative non-Socialist, who in other constituencies stood as the Right's standard bearer. The second ballot simplified the choice in most constituencies without clarifying the national outcome. In 1928, fewer than 23% of seats had more than two serious candidates, and only a handful had more than three. Party politicians were expected to observe coalition discipline – at least in marginal seats – withdrawing in favour of the strongest candidate of their side, whether Right or Left. Those who failed to do so were very likely to find their supporters withdrawing their votes. The first round allowed an indication of preference, the second a repudiation of the enemy – when, in most places, turnout rose: 'Choose on the first round, eliminate on the second.'

This became the justification of the system – and its attraction for those loosely disciplined parties that profited from it on the second ballot, above all the Radicals. The functional virtue of the two-ballot system was one often advanced for PR: that in profoundly divided polities unable either to produce genuine majorities or accept the rule of those artificially created by the electoral system, modification of the single-ballot majority rule is not only desirable but necessary. The French two-ballot election encouraged wide competition on the first round, without the risk of returning minority members; on the second it allowed a bipolar contest between Left and Right, represented by different parties in different constituencies. That was the best to be hoped for in a political landscape riven by multiple cleavages, where voters preferred local worthies committed to constituency interests rather than disciplined party hacks. These circumstances explain the multiplication of candidatures to which the two-ballot system contributed. But when the system was adopted, these consequences were not foreseen.

In early Third Republic elections, the overwhelming majority of seats (never less than four-fifths) were decided on the first round, a comfortable majority right down to the First World War. That was because the line was drawn – as in the early Fifth Republic – between proponents and opponents of the new regime. Party was at an early stage of development and national parties non-existent; most groups fought only a limited number of seats while numerous seats were effectively uncontested (22% in 1881). In that profoundly rural and still hierarchical society, with support intensely concentrated by region, marginal seats were fewer and most candidates were local notables, elected for their status rather than gaining prestige through election. Until the last decade of the nineteenth century and again after the Dreyfus Affair the one political division that really mattered was that separating assorted clericals, monarchists and reactionaries from their republican antagonists. When a monarchist President dissolved a republican Chamber in 1877, the ensuing election was fought between the two united and disciplined coalitions, and only 15 seats (out of 526) went to a second ballot. The republicans ran only one candidate per constituency, won the election, invalidated seventy-seven of their successful opponents (only ten were returned again in the consequent by-elections), and drove the President to resign. For eighty years a dissolution became politically unthinkable – and divided, undisciplined Chambers that much harder for governments to manage.

With the decline of the anti-regime Right, republicans could more safely squabble amongst themselves. In the intensely polarised elections of the early Third Republic, as also in 1902 and 1936, the Centre was squeezed; in calmer times it prospered. Moreover, parties organised and presented candidates, generalising contests within as well as between coalitions, particularly on the first ballot. In the seven elections during the last quarter century before 1914, the older simple clash was complicated by the division of anti-clericals into moderate republicans, Radicals and Socialists; and of the clericals between last-ditch defenders of former regimes, and the *Ralliés*, Catholics rallied to the Republic. There was therefore some increase in the number of candidates contesting the first ballot, and the number of seats in which a run-off was

Table 1 *Extent of political competition*

General elections	Seats (metropolitan France)	% Abstain first ballot	% Seats filled at first ballot	Average candidates per seat first ballot
1876	526	26	80	
1877	526	19	98	2
1881	541	31	86	22% of seats
1889	560	23	75	uncontested
1893	565	29	63	
1898	570	24	69	$3\frac{1}{2}$
1902	575	21	71	2 +
1906	575	20	73	
1910	580	22.5	61	3
1914	586	23	57	
1928	593	16	31	6
1932	596	16.5	42	6
1936	598	15.5	29	8
1958	465	23	8	6
1962	465	31	21	5
1967	470	19	15	5
1968	470	20	33	5
1973	473	19	10	6
1978	474	17	13	9
1981	474	29	33	6

Sources: For 1876–1936, adapted from Peter Campbell, *French Electoral Systems and Elections since 1789*, 2nd edn (London, 1965); G. Lachapelle, *Les Régimes Électoraux* (Paris, 1934); M. Dogan, 'Changement de Régime et Changement de Personnel', in François Goguel, et al., *Le Référendum de Septembre et les Élections de Novembre 1958* (Paris, 1960); Alain Lancelot, *L'Abstentionnism Électoral en France* (Paris, 1968); for 1958–81, adapted from *Le Monde* and J. R. Frears and Jean-Luc Parodi, *War Will Not Take Place* (London, 1979).

necessary rose above a quarter of the total, occasionally approaching two-fifths and at last, in 1914, reaching 43% (see Table 1). France was urbanising and industrialising, rural areas were being drawn into the market by improved communications; the battle between the clericals and their opponents and then the separation of Church and State had mobilised energies, encouraged party organisation and redistributed some important political cards. It had left deep resentments, but partly cleared the decks for greater concentration on economic and social questions. Already the parties nearest the Centre were the main beneficiaries of the system, but in a few seats (sometimes tacitly) an 'unnatural' alliance would be struck at the second ballot, Socialists or conservatives (including Catholics) – all advocates of PR – transferring their votes to the rival extreme against the Radical, to elect an advocate of electoral reform or to bring pressure on the presumptive Centrist partner who was refusing concessions, or both. Sometimes the Centre parties were simply victims of bloody-mindedness from their potential allies, the '*politique du pire*'; but the second ballot choice remained basically bipolar. In 1893 there were more than two serious candidates in the run-off in 12% of seats, in 1902 in 10%, and in 1906 in only 6% – a quarter of the 1928 figure.

The rise of the *Ralliés* on the Right and of the Socialists on the Left, made a government of conservative republicans and moderate Catholics a possible parliamentary formula; but the clerical issue remained the divide between Left and Right in the constituencies. So moderate men on both sides of that cleavage looked to PR as one solution, and so did the Socialists. The conservatives wanted to stem the Socialist tide and rescue the *Ralliés* from the reactionaries; the Socialists to liberate their party from the Radical incubus, in order to keep it *pur, dur* and disciplined. But the Radicals remained wedded to the system which awarded them power, and were joined by Centrists who preferred the system they knew. There was no majority for real PR and no longer one for the *scrutin d'arrondissement*, blamed for the scandals and sectarianism of Third Republic politics. But deputies (and senators) were loath to move too far from the majority system they understood.

The law was changed in 1919 and the 1919 and 1924 elections were fought with the department as the usual constituency on a bastard PR list system, whose proportionality was fatally undermined by the proviso that any candidate with a majority won a seat, followed by any list candidates whose vote exceeded the constituency quotient (valid votes divided by number of seats). These rules simply transferred the problem of second-round alliances to the first ballot. In 1919 the Socialists were divided from the Radicals and the Right won; in 1924 the Right split, and Socialists and Radicals were allied and victorious.

The creation of the Communist Party faced the parliamentary republic with a growing enemy on the Left. Both in 1928 and 1932, the Communists chose isolation and maintained their candidates on the second ballot; that cost the Left seats, particularly in 1928, but it cost the Communists control of their electorate, especially in 1932. Their sectarianism lost them substantial support on the first round; and on the second nearly half their voters deserted to support the best-placed 'republican' candidate. In 1936, the Communists changed tack, joined the Popular Front and reaped much benefit from the alliance.

By this time the splintering effects of the system were at work, powerfully abetted by the same sorts of problems and pressures that destroyed parliamentary democracy in the Weimar Republic. Constituencies were contested on average by half a dozen or more candidates, and a large majority of seats needed a second ballot (see Table 1). Swings between Left and Right were relatively minor: support remained regionally concentrated, politics rooted in the parochial concerns of the crucial local base, and success dependent,

Table 2 *Political bias between the wars: first-ballot % of the vote and seats won*

	Rad. and RS	Soc.	CP	Right[a]	Rad/Soc. minus Right
Seats won					
1928	167	100	14	307	
1932	194	129	12	259	
1936	165	149	72	222	
Entitled under PR					
1928	131	108	68	272	
1932	148	122	50	280	
1936	135	121	93	259	
Bias of system					
1928	+36	−8	−54	+35[a]	−7
1932	+46	+7	−38	−21	+74
1936	+30	+28	−21	−37	+95

[a] Moderate groups accounted for the entire 'bonus' of 35 seats in 1928; in 1932 they won 9 more seats than the extreme Right, though 'entitled' to 4 fewer. Here, too, Centrists gained most.

Source: Adapted from Peter Campbell, *French Electoral Systems and Elections since 1789*, 2nd edn (London, 1965); G. Lachapelle, *Les Régimes Électoraux* (Paris, 1934) and *Élections Législatives 1936* (Paris, 1936).

especially for the Right, the Centre and the Radicals, on diligent and persistent constituency service.

The Radicals and their minor Centrist allies profited from the system, which gave them and the Socialists an advantage over the Right, in a parliamentary division, of from 50 to nearly 120 seats in a house of 600 (see Table 2). This meant a big bonus for the moderate Left if they stayed united, but they rarely did so for long. The Socialists were pulled away by fear of Communist competition, and the Radicals were pulled apart by their deputies' differing interests in retaining the various votes which returned them at the second ballot. Small groups in the Centre could hope to profit from cabinet changes to advance their members' careers. A crucial role was played by the Senate, indirectly elected for long terms by local authority delegates, in which the countryside was vastly over-represented. A stronghold of conservative anti-clericals, essential to pass budgets and legislation, it stood guard against woman suffrage, PR and social reform, and was always ready to strike a blow at a faltering government of the Left and to encourage the familiar rightward drift of the Radical and Centre deputies which would change the majority in the Chamber.

Defeat in the Second World War left this system thoroughly discredited; only the hopelessly shrunken Radical party wanted to return to either the old electoral or the old parliamentary system. The Socialists survived intact, but were outstripped by the Communists, who regularly polled over a quarter of the votes in the Fourth Republic and became the largest party, and at first by MRP, Christian Democrats of a moderately reforming kind who attracted a huge disoriented right-wing vote which exerted a growing pressure on them. Socialists and Christian Democrats had long been committed to PR (MRP in particular seeing any return to the second ballot as lethal): for reasons of principle; because it spared them difficult or compromising second-ballot alliances which weakened the internal party discipline reinforced by party control of lists; and because they had strong regional concentrations of supporters but also national support spread unevenly across the country as powerless minorities. The third governing party, the Communists, preferred PR for all the above reasons, and because they regarded elections as the pre-1914 Socialists once had: as much exercises in mobilisation and propaganda as a source of legitimacy. With PR they could collect incompatible protest votes from electors constrained neither by considerations of wasted votes, nor of whether they really wanted a Communist majority (since with PR none was possible). That system, however, ensured that the Communists received at least a quarter of the seats and, after 1947 when they went into intransigent opposition over both domestic and foreign issues, made it impossible to assemble a stable majority from among the remaining three-quarters of the Assembly, covering as they did what in Britain would be the whole political spectrum (see Table 3). In particular this strategic situation, which allowed marginal right-wing groups to extract a high price for their votes, made it impossible to take any decisive action to avert or limit the collapse of French power overseas, in Indo-China and then in Algeria.

In 1958 the army took power in Algeria, protesting at the paralysis in Paris, and sought to install General de Gaulle. As the liberator who had handed over power to the politicians in 1946, he was acceptable to Parliament which elected him Prime Minister to avert a military coup. His new constitution was approved overwhelmingly by referendum in September, and a general election followed two months later. The right-wing diehards – who had called on de Gaulle in order to keep Algeria French – expected to win a plurality of votes, by exploiting his popularity for their purposes, maximising their number of seats through a majority system of party lists combining Gaullists and Conservatives in large constituencies. The Socialists had split over de Gaulle, but both wings favoured a return to the pre-war system, believing that single-member districts would help the established local politicians and limit the impact of the coming right-wing sweep, and that the second ballot would benefit them as the new party of the Centre. Shared by all politicians on both sides and by every detached observer, these expectations led de Gaulle, to the general surprise, to choose the system advocated by some of his leading opponents over the one

Table 3 % *Seats and votes in the Fourth Republic (metropolitan France)*

| | 1945 | | June 1946 | | Nov. 1946 | | 1951 | | 1956 | |
	Votes	Seats	Votes	Seats	Votes	Seats	Votes	Seats	Votes	Seats
Poujadists									12.3	9.6
Conservatives	13.3	11.9	12.8	11.9	12.8	12.9	14.0	16.0	14.6	17.3
Gaullist					3.0	0.0	21.7	19.6	5.9	3.5
MRP	24.9	27.0	28.1	30.6	26.3	29.0	12.5	15.1	11.1	13.0
Radicals, etc.	11.1	6.7	11.5	7.5	11.1	11.0	10.0	14.2	15.2	13.7
Socialists	23.8	25.7	21.1	22.0	17.9	16.6	14.5	17.3	15.0	16.2
Communists, etc.	26.1	28.4	26.2	28.0	28.6	30.5	26.9	17.8	25.9	26.7
Others	0.8	0.3	0.3	0.0	0.3	0.0	0.4	0.0		

Note: The PR system used in 1945–6 was changed in 1951 to give an advantage to parties which could form alliances against those which could not. It produced this effect at the first trial in 1951, but not at the second, in 1956. For further details see: P. M. Williams, *Crisis and Compromise* (London, 1964) and Peter Campbell, *French Electoral Systems and Elections since 1789* (London, 1965), from which this Table is adapted.

proposed by his vociferous supporters. For he had no wish to encumber himself with a Parliament full of rigid diehards over the Algerian question, and hoped to balance them with Socialists and others, who would be critics on some issues but might respond to his appeals over the most crucial problem of all, thus giving him more freedom of manoeuvre.

The unexpected decision had even more unexpected consequences: to everyone's astonishment it was the new Gaullist party, the UNR, and not the Socialists who profited from the system. Proclaiming loyalty to de Gaulle, it was seen both as a force for stable government – the first appearance of that motive in a French election – and as the true Centre party, able to attract second-ballot support from both sides against the Communists (or the Right). The Gaullist gains could not be explained by gerrymandering, for boundaries were not rigged against the Socialists; the Communists did suffer somewhat (some large towns were split up) but far less than they did from the voters' stern determination to switch at the second round to the candidate best able to keep them out. Candidates were again numerous – about six per seat on average – and fewer deputies than ever were returned with a clear majority: a mere thirty-nine. Even on the second ballot, straight fights – which usually predominated – occurred in only a fifth of the seats. For the last time, *scrutin d'arrondissement* had worked, however surprisingly, to reinforce the presumed Centre party (as Tables 1 and 4 show).

Since 1962 the French have used their system to return moderate majoritarian parties able to support governments through the life of a Parliament. At first Gaullists and allies had a monopoly of these virtues and so

Table 4 *Political bias in the Fifth Republic: first ballot % of the vote and seats won (metropolitan France)*

	Gaull.	Soc.	CP	Cons.
Seats won				
1958	187	65	10	203
1962	256	105	41	61
1967	231	115	72	48
1968	348	57	33	32
1973	257	102	73	40
1978	144	112	86	132
1981	83	285	43	66
Entitled under PR				
1958	96	114	90	155
1962	166	94	103	89
1967	180	88	106	81
1968	218	81	93	56
1973	171	97	99	79
1978	108	123	97	119
1981	99	183	76	103
Bias of system				
1958	+91	−49	−80	+48
1962	+90	+11	−62	−29
1967	+51	+27	−34	−33
1968	+130	−24	−60	−24
1973	+86	+5	−26	−39
1978	+36	−11	−11	+13
1981	−16	+102	−33	−37

Note: Party coalitions are loosely defined: many Conservatives count as Gaulists 1962–73; some Radicals as Gaullists, Conservatives or Socialists at different dates; Conservative includes opposition Centre 1962–73, Giscardians and Centre allies 1978–81.
Sources: Adapted from P. M. Williams, *French Politicians and Elections 1951–1969* (Cambridge, 1970) and *Le Monde*.

benefited most. Their success squeezed the old independent Centre to the profit of the reviving Socialist party and, even more, to the benefit of non-Gaullist elements of the ruling conservative majority, until Giscard d'Estaing took the Presidency in 1974. The presidential contest, where only the two leading candidates were allowed to stand on the second round, favoured the less sectarian partner in both the Left coalition (the Socialists) and the Right (the Giscardians and their Centrist friends). Since their men were more attractive to the floating Centre voters who decided elections – in parliamentary as well as in presidential contests – there was also an incentive for more partisan electors to vote usefully from the first ballot, choosing on the first round whichever candidate of their coalition was most likely to succeed on the second. Incumbency indicated that choice on the Right, and to some extent on the Left too; otherwise, the Communists were placed at a distinct disadvantage. The old rule has thus been partly amended: 'Eliminate on the first round, choose on the second.'

So the same electoral system has produced strikingly different results in two Republics. It took the fall of two regimes; the prolonged trauma of the Algerian war and the threat of civil war; the massive presence of General de Gaulle; and the delayed industrialisation, urbanisation and secularisation of France, to achieve through the old single-member two-ballot majority system what French electoral reformers had once argued could be accomplished only through PR: stable, effective, majoritarian government, acceptable to the nation.

In 1958, the UNR profited from its loyalty to the General, who was judged the only effective alternative to civil war: the Centre alternative *par excellence*. The sequel showed that, in seeing the UNR in that unexpected perspective, the voters had judged more shrewdly than most people supposed. Faced over the next four years with the unwelcome choice between following de Gaulle (now President) or clinging to French rule in Algeria, most of its deputies took the former course. In April 1962 a referendum ratified Algerian independence and marked the disappearance of the parliamentary (though the beginning of the terrorist) threat to the regime from the extreme Right. However, as de Gaulle was well aware, the Algerian settlement also completed the service which the old politicians had counted on him to render; but he remained an obstacle to the renewal of their old parliamentary games, to be removed as soon as possible. Anticipating their offensive, he proposed that the President be directly elected by the voters – a popular move which the parties were almost bound to oppose – carried it against them in an (unconstitutional) referendum, and swamped them in the subsequent general election which they fought in utter disarray. Again seen as a middle party, the Gaullists did even better than before, but now thanks to a much higher vote on the first ballot rather than to transfers from all sides on the second. For on the Left the unthinkable happened: Socialists and Communists, for fifteen years perhaps the bitterest enemies in all French politics, began a timid rapprochement on the second ballot. It was to develop much further in later years, but 1962 was the point of transition when the old electoral system began to operate in a new way.

Long-term developments in French society were simplifying the political scene by reducing the number of cleavages. Clericalism was steadily declining as a cause of bitter conflict as the Church became less powerful and much less uniformly reactionary. The two parties which had most clearly defined themselves in relation to it had been badly discredited and had never recovered: the Radicals, anti-clerical but socially conservative, in the Third Republic; and MRP, Catholics seeking a progressive clientele and finding only a conservative one, in the Fourth. More important, the Communist threat, which for so long had deterred many alarmed voters from plumping for the Left, receded after 1958 when the party lost a third of its supporters, some permanently. Preaching partnership with other parties of the Left (though not practising it from 1977 to 1981), it could not liberalise or distance itself from Moscow sufficiently to convince enough voters of its democratic *bona fides*. Instead, Mitterrand was able to revive the Socialist party and make it, for the first time since 1936, the dominant party of the Left. With the political threats from both Left and Right less serious, and the security of the new regime apparently assured in 1969 by a peaceful succession to de Gaulle without diminution of the presidential office, the cleavage over economic and social policy at last became the critical dividing line both for politicians and voters.

The reaction of the major parties to the nationalisation of support and issues and the new discipline of the electorate has taken two forms. On the first ballot they must present candidates in almost every seat or share out seats with partners under a national portmanteau label. For the second they need a national agreement, perhaps supported by a common programme, to stand down for the best-placed candidate of their putative coalition (desistment), even if both partners have contested virtually every seat on the first round. The Gaullists were the first to understand the necessity for nationwide candidatures; only since 1973 has any substantial number of seats been contested by several conservative coalition contestants, in 'primaries', with the usual promise to withdraw on the run-off for the partner with the best vote. The Communists have regularly contested every seat; only in 1967 did the non-Communist Left first manage to present a single candidate in most seats, and negotiate a national second-ballot withdrawal agreement with the Communists.

These developments have meant that small Centre groups generally could no longer win through to the second ballot and so to Parliament as they had in the Third Republic; even when they did, they had no leverage there against stable governing majorities. First their electorates, then their leaders, have been progressively absorbed, mostly by the Right, because of their instinctive anti-Communist reflex. But the revival of the Socialists and the erosion of the old clerical issue meant that once Centre leaders formally joined Giscard's majority they could no longer hold their more liberal supporters. Elections in the Fifth Republic continue to be won in the Centre: no longer by Centre parties but by the Centrist partner of the Right or Left coalition who can most plausibly appeal to these floating voters. That bipolarising tendency has been partly masked by the variation in the number of first-round candidates; it is exemplified by the regularly increasing number of duels between Left and Right on the run-off (as Table 5 makes clear).

Table 5 *Second-ballot contests 1958–1981 (metropolitan France)*

	% Seats won first round	Second-ballot seats	Uncon-tested[a]	Four-cornered and more	Three-cornered	% Duel –	– of which % Rt/Lt[b]
1958	8	426	–	30%	50%	20	71[c]
1962	21	396	1	3%	35%	62	77
1967	15	398	–	1 contest	16%	84	75
1968	33	316	1	–	15%	85	88
1973	10	424	1	1 contest	16%	84	89
1978	13	418	8	–	1 contest	99	99
1981	33	320	10	–	1 contest	99	100

[a] Where no candidate has got a majority of votes (and a quarter of the register) on the first round, but where opponents are eliminated (by the 5%, 10% or $12\frac{1}{2}$% rule) and partners withdraw as agreed, leaving only one candidate on the run-off, usually in safe Left or Right seats.
[b] Gaullists/Giscardians and allies v. Communists/Socialists and allies (remainder involve at least one Centrist).
[c] UNR/Conservatives v. Communists/Socialists; in 50.0% of duels the Right's candidate was UNR.
Sources: Adapted from J.-L. Parodi 'L'Échec des Gauches', *Revue Politique et Parlementaire*, 873 (March–April, 1978) and *Le Monde*.

The inflation of candidatures in the 1970s (see Table 1) was due to the multiplication of hopeless contestants seeking free campaign television time. All were eliminated by the $12\frac{1}{2}$% rule. Serious candidatures increased marginally, because of primaries on the Right and more Socialists standing. Politicians now had to run under the label of one of the four major national parties, with nominees throughout the country, and standard national desistment agreements with their coalition partners: the guarantees that they would be numerous and disciplined enough to support a stable government. Here was the great contrast with the Third Republic, not in the average number of candidates per seat: more numerous since 1958 than before 1914, less so than between the wars. Nor is the number of seats decided on the first round simply a function of the number of candidates standing (see Table 1).

The proportion of candidates elected on the first round varied from less than a tenth in 1958, when there were fewer candidates per seat than before the war, to the pre-war average of a third in 1968 and 1981, years of first a Gaullist and then a Socialist landslide. The average number of seats won in the initial contest since 1958 is under a fifth; 15.5% if the two landslides are discounted. First-ballot victors have declined because of the nationalisation of support for the parties and the spread of national candidatures, both the results of profound social changes; the nationalisation of issues and the media; and the impact of presidential elections.

Minor candidates, then, are now political kamikaze pilots: with no hope themselves they may destroy the chances of others by taking the marginal percentage necessary to come ahead within their own camp and thus proceed to the run-off. Their direct clout has been reduced by the instinct of electors to vote usefully from the first ballot, and to transfer their votes to the second in predictable, disciplined, national patterns, usually in accord with the public positions of their parties, much more so than between the wars. It is the national pattern of desistments amongst the big battalions and the disciplined reflex of their voters that create majorities in the Fifth Republic and distinguish it from the Third. The run-off gives a better measure of polarisation than first-round candidacies or victories (as Table 5 shows).

In 1958 Socialists and Communists, then still bitter enemies, fought each other in almost half the seats on the second round on which Gaullists and Conservatives also opposed each other. The UNR garnered everyone's votes, Right and Left on the run-off, to punish the Communists and reward de Gaulle. There were few offers of Communist desistment for Socialists and fewer accepted. By 1962, common hostility to the Algerian war and to the new regime provided a fragile bridge between the two main parties of the Left, whose continued competition threatened to scuttle them both. Second-ballot agreements were hastily patched up, and the Communists brought themselves back into the *pays légal* by demonstrating the utility for others of their disciplined electorate. Socialist voters remained reluctant to transfer to a Communist, but the pattern of Fifth Republic politics was now established: only the Gaullist coalition and the Socialist–Communist alliance remained as serious contenders for power (see Table 5). Only they could present candidates everywhere and survive to the second round where exclusive desistment arrangements now applied. The Centre, once the beneficiary of the second-ballot system in the Third Republic, was thus ground between Left and Right in the Fifth. Centre voters could still help decide the outcome between Left and Right on the run-off: although the Socialists benefited marginally from their favour, only in 1967 and 1981 did Centre voters substantially desert the conservative coalition.

By 1978 relations between the parties of the Left and within the governing coalition had soured, but not the bipolarisation of the electorate nor thus the logic of the system. On the Right Chirac feared Giscard's designs on the RPR; on the Left, the Communists risked becoming the cockboat to the Socialist man of war. Under these circumstances, the inclination to vote usefully from the first ballot, and national desistment agreements for the second, might destroy one partner for the benefit of the other, turning a bipolar into a bipartisan party system. But neither Left nor Right voters would tolerate denunciation of the desistment agreements, so handing the election to their opponents. No party could defy that constraint without putting at risk seats that depended on alliances formed over fifteen years. Chirac's solution to that dilemma was to pose as the only effective leader of the conservative coalition, against its

President. The Communists' was to attack the Socialists before the first round, alienating a quarter of their own support in 1981 and falling to 15% of the poll, their 1936 score. Communist strategy thus produced the result it was designed to avoid: the marginalisation of the party. For its voters wanted a Left government regardless who led it; others found that prospect acceptable so long as the Communists could not.

The same electoral system has thus not only helped to produce different results in different Republics, but differential advantages for various contenders at different periods in them. Since 1962, the Right has remained fundamentally more united and homogeneous than the Left; at elections it has more often than not shared out candidatures amongst its different components than systematically fought out its internecine quarrels on the first ballot. That has not been possible on the Left, with a well-entrenched Communist party dominating a fifth of the electorate until 1981. There primaries have necessarily been the rule, and the sharing of the potential spoils of office has been more a divisive than unifying factor; for the Communists remain the most isolated and suspect of major French parties, and a victory of the Left over the Right was likely to be achieved by the Socialists at the expense of Communists and conservatives alike.

Unlike the Centre, the Communists have regularly stood in every seat, and maintained a national withdrawal pact for the run-off with another national party, the Socialists. Because they suffered at the second round from the reluctance or unwillingness of others to vote for their candidates, their capacity to return members, like the Centre's, has been diminished. In the end, that has affected the ability of both to mobilise support on the first ballot; both were left with a few rock solid constituencies and the prospect of marginalisation elsewhere. That drove the Centre into the conservative coalition in 1973, and the Communists to try and destroy the Socialists from 1977 to 1981. The problem for both Centre and Communists may best be appreciated by comparing the share of the vote on the *tour décisif** with Assembly seats won (see Table 6). Taking the two ballots together also illustrates the functional argument for two ballots in a multi-party system with three or four relatively equal contenders: partisan preferences expressed at the first ballot can be generalised and simplified at the second through party alliances and the transfer of votes to the most – or away from the least – acceptable alternative. In other words, the second ballot functions in some ways like the alternative or single transferable vote: it allows electors not simply a crude first preference, but to express distance from or proximity to other parties. Coalition partners are thus designated by the voter at the polls rather than by party cabal in Parliament (the usual consequence of proportional list systems), where a single ballot risks producing not only unacceptable but also wholly unpredictable and arbitrary results.

* The *tour décisif* cumulates the party vote in seats won on the first ballot with their vote in the more numerous districts won on the second.

Table 6 Comparison of results (% of the vote) first ballot and tour décisif 1958–1981 with % seats in Assembly (metropolitan France only)

% Vote

	1958		1962		1967		1968		1973		1978		1981	
	First ballot	Tour décisif	First ballot	Tour décisif	First ballot	Tour décisif	First ballot	Tour décisif	First ballot	Tour décisif	First ballot	Tour décisif	First ballot	Tour décisif
Communists	19	20	22	20	22.5	21	20	19	21	21	20.5	18	16	5
Non-Communist Left	20	22	20	20	19	22	17	19	21	23.5	26	30	38	50
Gaullists and allies[a]	20.5	26	36	43	38.5	44	46	51	37	46	23	26	21	23
Conservatives, Centrists, Giscardians[b]	38	32	19	15	17	12	12	10	17	9	25	25	22	22

Note: Columns do not total 100% because minor parties, none of which returned members, are excluded.

% Seats

	1958		1962		1967		1968		1973		1978		1981	
Communists		2		9		15		7		15		18		9
Non-Communist Left		14		23		26		12		22		24		62
Gaullists and allies[a]		40		55		49		74		54		30		15
Conservatives, Centrists, Giscardians[b]		44		13		10		7		8.5		28		14
Total (metropolitan) Assembly seats		465		465		470		470		473		474		474

[a] Includes Giscardians until 1973.
[b] Opposition Conservatives and Centre until 1973; then Giscardians and allies.

Since no party can (normally) hope for a majority by itself, strong allies are essential. The problem of course is that effective allies with votes to deliver on the second round are more dangerous competitors on the first for a place in the run-off. A party must choose between isolation and being swamped by a more powerful partner: the first danger drove the Communists to the Socialists in 1962, after the desperate consequences of isolation and rejection had been made clear to it in 1958; the second into effective opposition to its nominal partner from 1977 to 1981. The Centre too has suffered from both difficulties. In 1958 Conservatives and Centrists supported the return of General de Gaulle; in 1962, when most of them turned against him, they were deserted by most of their electorate on the first ballot, but refused to join any alliance for the second in which the Communists also participated. With insufficient candidates and support on the first round they were also without prospects on the second for want of allies. Regularly squeezed on the *tour décisif* they quickly lost credibility as an alternative, until they joined with Giscard on the 1974 presidential first ballot.

But if the second-ballot pact is to be sustainable over time, neither party must feel its partner is likely to benefit disproportionately and at its own expense. When Communists and Socialists first stood down for each other in 1962 and for the next decade, their electorates were largely complementary: the Socialists were older, more rural, more middle class, concentrated south of the Loire; the Communists younger, more urban, more working class. Relations were worst where they traditionally competed for the same vote. As the Socialists gathered steam they became the first party of the Left in an increasing number of districts; increased their share of the working-class vote by two-thirds to 27% in 1973; overtook the Communists as the first party of the Left on the first ballot in 1978; and took two and a half times the Communist vote and almost double its share of working-class votes in 1981. For desistment to be of mutual advantage, the two parties had to share the first-ballot lead in about as many seats. Otherwise, it risked subordinating one partner to another, and even perhaps eventually removing it from serious contention for power – a prospect no party, certainly no Communist party, could entertain with equanimity.

On the Right, the Gaullists initially triumphed by snaffling the bulk of the Conservative–Centrist electorate from its former leaders and adding to it a specifically Gaullist component: less Catholic, more progressive, urban and working class, concentrated north of the Loire. With the departure of de Gaulle and the progressive rallying of former opposition Centrists, support for the governmental coalition became increasingly homogeneous and conservative: rural, Catholic, feminine, middle class. Competing for the same voters, the coalition found it could no longer share out seats, and primaries became the rule in 1978. At the second ballot both Left and Right regrouped for bipolar confrontation, where conservative discipline was regularly better than on the Left (see Tables 5 and 6).

In the Fifth Republic, then, the majority system has worked as it ought, minor shifts in the vote at both rounds producing important variations in parliamentary seats. The system worked that way in the early Third Republic when a single clear issue was dominant: the nature of the regime. Between the wars, when issues were blurred and cleavages cross-cutting and contradictory, small shifts in first-round vote mattered less than alliance patterns for the second ballot. But the Centre parties, who profited most from that system by changing allies between elections according to circumstance and advantage, could not control their deputies or their voters. In the Fifth Republic, the same pattern of second-ballot alliances has held since 1962 (in fact, if not at first formally) on the Centre and Right. MPs who have objected to that pattern have had to give in, or get out – either of their party of origin or of serious politics altogether. No well-entrenched moderate, Radical or Independent Socialist would have been inclined or constrained to take such a principled – or defeatist – view of his prospects between the wars. There are still a very few local *bonzes* (on the Right and Centre) who can afford to stand without a national ticket; other local notables are ignored by their parties at both their perils; but most members now depend on party endorsement on the first ballot, and the assurance of desistment on the second, for their success. The discipline thus guaranteed is more readily and easily accepted in some parties than in others, but it is imposed on all of them by an electorate that wants coherent parties supporting stable governments. That reflex might survive a change in the electoral system, or it might succumb to it, depending on circumstances.

How important then has the revision of electoral arrangements been for the political system of the Fifth Republic? Alongside changes in party structure and aims, and the alteration in voting behaviour that has accompanied them, its effect is marginal. So are other factors: the way constituencies are drawn and party support is concentrated in them; or even party organisation. On the run-off in 1978, the Communists won a fifth of their seats with margins of under 1% while other parties averaged only 10% of their deputies returned by so narrow a margin.

Nonetheless, departmental majority list systems or PR with *apparentement* would have made it more difficult for Gaullists to resist the siren embrace of the *Algérie française* Right in joint lists; increasing the strength of the Algerian ultras in France, Algeria, and within the army, with incalculable and very likely catastrophic political consequences. A real proportional system would surely have deprived the UNR of its dominant position in the Assembly, and given the Communists closer to 80 seats than the 10 they actually won; for the clear discrimination in favour of the former and against the latter was much magnified on the second round.

In 1962, no proportional list system would have given the Gaullists their majority, or forced together Communists and Socialists; the Centre would certainly have suffered, but not as desperately as it did, particularly if *apparentement* were allowed. That result would have seriously inflected the political development of the Fifth Republic, by reducing bipolarising pressures – at least until the 1965 presidential election. But then, a Socialist–Centrist opponent for de Gaulle might have been more plausible than he could ever be after the actual 1962 result. Since 1962, the single-member two-ballot majority system has given an advantage in seats to the dominant coalition, and to the dominant partner within it. That advantage has influenced presidential prospects just as having a plausible pretender to that office has benefited the parliamentary prospects of parties so blessed. It cannot then be argued that the electoral system has been indifferent to the political evolution of the Fifth Republic, any more than it has been responsible for it. It has probably been a necessary condition; it has certainly not been a sufficient one.

Fear of isolation; a sufficient community of outlook, interests and ambitions; social and geographical complementarity of support; and the tendency for the electorate to accept the consistent and continuing second-ballot pacts negotiated by party leaders – and then to impose their continuation on them – are necessary for the second-ballot system to work as it has so far done under the Fifth Republic. Support for republican parties was more complementary at the beginning of the Third Republic – perhaps because it was so much more personalised and regionalised – than it later became, when Socialists poached on Radicals, Communists battened on Socialists, and second-ballot success for one party implied first-ballot failure for another. But the importance of the regime in the early years of the Republic also served to unite voters whose social and economic concerns were dissimilar. As these issues became more prominent, first-ballot competition became more widespread, second-ballot desistments and discipline more problematical – and the demand for electoral reform more insistent.

The incentive for first-ballot competition within coalitions partly springs from the nationalisation and homogenisation of coalition support, intensified by the bipolarising effects of second ballots fought with desistment agreements. Parties and candidates are necessarily preoccupied with their own showing (even at their partner's expense) on the first round. Increasingly, voters have become more concerned with coalition outcomes on the second. Their initial vote is thus affected by notions of which coalition candidate seems most likely to win on the run-off – just as in the presidential contest. The bipolarising effect of the second ballot is thus transmitted to the first, and in the process perhaps transmutes a bipolar into a bipartisan contest – just as the British and American single-ballot systems reputedly do. In other words, the effects of the system are contingent, complicated and perhaps contradictory.

Proportional representation was advocated before 1939 as the best – and only – means of restoring principled politics, disciplined parties, stable government and the legitimacy of the regime. The experience of the Fourth Republic hardly justified these exaggerated expectations. Instead, the last three (at least) have been achieved in the Fifth with the very electoral system that supposedly precluded them before the war. Since 1958, it has allowed a multi-party system to be structured in a bipolar way, producing acceptable majorities from the second ballot and stable government. Whether France is fundamentally a multi-party country in bipolar disguise, or is moving from a multi-party base through a bipolar phase to a bipartisan system cannot be predicted; cannot even be sensibly discussed in the abstract; and certainly does not entirely depend on the electoral system adopted.

SUGGESTIONS FOR FURTHER READING

In English

*Peter Campbell, *French Electoral Systems and Elections since 1789*, 2nd edn (London, 1965)

*D. B. Goldey and R. W. Johnson, 'The French General Election of March 1978: The Redistribution of Support Within and Between Right and Left', *Parliamentary Affairs*, 31, 3 (Summer 1978)

*and A. F. Knapp, 'Time for a Change: The French Elections of 1981. II. The National Assembly Elections', *Electoral Studies*, 1, 2, (August 1982)

*A. J. Milnor, *Elections and Political Stability* (Boston, 1969)

Roy Pierce, 'French Legislative Elections: The Historical Background', in Howard R. Penniman, ed., *The French National Assembly Elections of 1978* (Washington, DC, 1980)

*P. M. Williams, *Crisis and Compromise: Politics in the Fourth Republic* (London, 1964)
French Politicians and Elections 1951–1969 (Cambridge, 1970)

In French

*Frédéric Bon, *Les Elections en France: Histoire et Sociologie* (Paris, 1978)

*Jean Charlot, 'Rapport sur les Modes de Scrutins en France depuis 1945', unpublished paper, delivered at Journées Internationales d'Études Comparatives, Jan. 1977

J-M. Cotteret and C. Emeri, *Les Systèmes Électoraux* (Paris, 1973)

C. Emeri and P. Lalumière, *Lois Électorales et inégalités de représentation en France (1936–1960)* (Paris, 1960)

*M. Dogan, 'Changement de Régime et Changement de Personnel', in Jean Touchard, et al., *L'Etablissement de la Cinquième République: Le Référendum de Septembre et les Élections de Novembre 1958* (Paris, 1960)

*Francois Goguel, *La Politique des Partis sous la IIIe République* (Paris, 1946)

*G. Lachapelle, *La Représentation Proportionnelle en France et en Belgique* (Paris, 1911)
Les Régimes Électoraux (Paris, 1934)

*Alain Lancelot, *L'Abstentionisme Électoral en France* (Paris, 1968)

*M-T. and A. Lancelot, *Atlas des Circonscriptions Électorales en France depuis 1875* (Paris, 1970)

J-P. Charnay, *Les Scrutins Politiques en France de 1815 à 1962* (Paris, 1964).

*Indicates a work used in preparing this chapter.

5

Germany

PETER PULZER

The political debates on the electoral system in Britain and Germany start from entirely contrary presuppositions. In Britain parliamentary institutions are a source of national pride. How different in Germany, where the very legitimacy of parliamentary institutions and the desirability of partisan conflict have been in question for much of the nineteenth and twentieth centuries. Germany has suffered what one historian has called the 'trauma of parliamentary helplessness'[1] beginning at Frankfurt in 1848–9 and reaching its climax in the Weimar Republic. The folk memory of the multi-party chaos of Weimar has affected postwar political debate much as the memory of the inflation has dominated economic thinking. In Britain the usual reaction of politicians and citizens to proposals for political reform is: 'If it works, don't fix it.' In Germany the dominant question in the minds of political mechanics has been: 'How can we stop an imminent break-down?'

Shutting the Weimar stable door has been the principal theme of the debate on electoral systems since 1945. To understand the debate we have to try to understand what went wrong in Weimar and why; and that in turn means bearing in mind the experience of parties and elections before 1918.

For much of the nineteenth century the question of how to turn votes into seats was a subordinate part of the franchise debate. Its main components were, naturally enough, for or against universal suffrage, direct or indirect election, open voting or secret ballot. The first German democratic electoral law, that was passed by the Frankfurt Assembly in March 1849 but never implemented, called for universal male suffrage and direct, secret voting. Election was to be by single-member constituencies and absolute majority at the first or second ballots, and a simple majority at the third and final ballot.[2] There was some debate at Frankfurt on a theme that has never since been absent from German political concerns: how to prevent a fragmentation of votes,[3] and some rather more abstract debate on the merits of absolute and relative majorities.[4] In fact, the 1849 law was merely following Continental practice. The three-ballot system was borrowed from France, where it was used for the elections to the Third Estate in 1789 and for parliamentary elections after the Restoration (but not, paradoxically, for those of April 1848, which the Frankfurt delegates would have had most in mind). Absolute majorities had also been required in the electoral colleges of the German states, where indirect elections were usual before 1848.

When Bismarck resuscitated the electoral law of Frankfurt to serve the Reichstag of the North German Confederation in 1867 and of the new Reich in 1871 it was amended in only one respect. Absolute majorities were to be achieved, where necessary, in two ballots, the second restricted to the two leading candidates of the first ballot. As in 1848–9, the mechanism of this system seemed of minor importance in the framework of the general constitutional debate, but political developments in the lifetime of the Empire made the electoral system increasingly controversial.

The first of these developments was the increase in the number of candidates and therefore of the complexity of the contests. Economic transformation brought the rise of a mass Social Democratic Party, and of minor special-interest parties, chiefly agrarian; religious disputes led to the rise of a Catholic defence party in the form of the Zentrum; and the general growth of political awareness and organisation meant the extension of party activity from original regional strongholds to a wider area. As a result, the proportion of deputies elected at the first ballot dropped from 88.2% at the first Reichstag election in 1871 to 51.9% in 1912, the last pre-revolutionary election.[5] The second development was the 'passive gerrymander', whereby constituency boundaries were not redrawn to keep pace with the movement of population. Initially of approximately equal size, the electorates in 1912 ranged from 13,407* to 338,798. 7,941 votes sufficed to elect a Conservative in East Prussia, but 64,833 votes failed to elect a Social Democrat in Bochum in the Ruhr.

This imbalance was one reason why electoral reform appeared on the agenda in the years before the First World War; the other was the pressure for the reform of the franchise in the individual states, which had been left untouched by Bismarck's law. The only party that was specifically committed to proportional representation in Imperial Germany was the Social Democratic Party,[6] not only for the obvious reason that it was most disadvantaged by the existing system, but even more on theoretical grounds. The SPD was not primarily interested in taking power in the existing constitutional system. It saw parliamentary elections as a propagandistic and agitational exercise of which the counting of heads was the most important component, and since it interpreted the political process in class terms, proportionality would best express class interests. But an older element of radical-democratic ideology also pointed the SPD in the direction of PR. This saw universal suffrage as an expression of political equality and popular sovereignty, and combined it with direct democracy: the 1891 Erfurt programme that enshrined the demand for PR also called for the referendum and the initiative.

---

* The smallest constituency of all, Schaumburg–Lippe, 10,707 electors, was protected by the constitutional provision that entitled all states to at least one deputy.

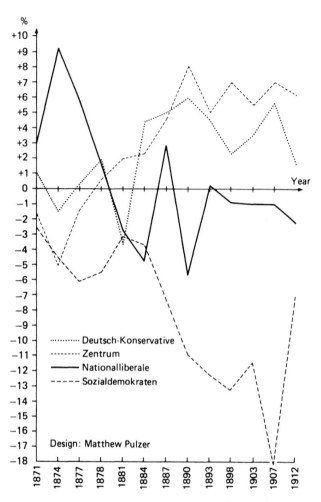

Table 1 Shares of seats of four parties in relation to shares of votes in Reichstag elections 1871–1912

The only dissent from PR orthodoxy within the SPD came from revisionists, notably Eduard Bernstein. Concerned with establishing parliamentary democracy and with transcending Marxian class analysis he saw parties as more than the mere expression of class interest.[7] For him a two-party system was 'of the essence of parliamentarism';[8] a fragmented Reichstag, the probable consequence of PR, would mean 'sacrificing democratic practice to a presumed democratic principle'.[9] Bernstein was strongly influenced by British Labour thinking, and by Ramsay MacDonald in particular, and contributed a preface to the German edition of *Socialism and Government*. Notwithstanding this, electoral systems were not of major interest to him, and he did not devote systematic attention to them.

Table 2 *First- and second-ballot results in Reichstag elections*

Parties	Elections of 1907			Elections of 1912		
	(a)	(b)	(c)	(a)	(b)	(c)
Conservatives	67	60	−7	53	43	−10
Moderate Conservatives (Reichspartei)	24	24	0	13	14	+1
National Liberals	47	54	+7	25	45	+20
Progressives	30	42	+12	14	42	+28
Anti-Semites	12	16	+4	2	3	+1
Zentrum	101	105	+4	98	91	−7
SPD	73	43	−30	144	110	−34
National minorities	29	29	0	34	33	−1
Others	14	24	+10	14	16	+2

(a) N of first-ballot leads.
(b) N of seats won.
(c) (b)−(a).

The pre-1918 electoral system favoured those parties that were geographically concentrated, had strong rural support and were eligible for second-ballot support from other parties. The Conservatives and the Catholic Zentrum scored on the first two criteria but not the third: as Table 1 shows they benefited on balance. The Social Democrats were also second-ballot lepers and their base was urban: therefore, the system, as the Table shows, discriminated against them. But geographical concentration became a growing asset and by 1912 they were approaching the threshold where the system could turn in their favour. In some parts of Germany this had already happened: in the kingdom of Saxony the SPD won 19 out of 23 Reichstag seats in 1912 with 55% of the vote. Indeed, under first-past-the-post the SPD would already have broken through this threshold: in 1912 they led the field in 144 seats, or 36%, on a national vote share of 34.4%.

The SPD, as indicated, favoured PR on doctrinal more than pragmatic grounds; the other parties were, in varying degrees, suspicious of a reform that would strengthen the Left and undermine their privileges in the states and municipalities.

The most ambiguous situation was that of the Liberal groupings. Their ability to capture seats at the first ballot declined sharply; on the other hand, like the Radicals of the Third French Republic, they benefited disproportionately from the second ballot, as is shown in Table 2. Even so, they were on balance under-represented. While self-interest pointed one way, doctrine pointed another. After the 1890 Reichstag elections, in which the National Liberals did particularly badly, moves towards PR found some favour. But most National Liberals preferred a political culture dominated by local notables and one in which national unity was at a higher premium than partisanship or individual rights. Their theorists went to great lengths to reject the premises of English advocates of PR. Rudolf von Gneist could think of 'no more thorough way of breaking the ligaments of constitutions' than Thomas Hare's scheme[10] and Heinrich Bernhard Oppenheim despised J. S. Mill's 'atomistic form of representation'.[11] The Left Liberals or Progressives, on the other hand, inclined more strongly towards PR, especially as they became more heavily dependent in the final years of the Empire on second-ballot support from the SPD. An SPD motion in favour of PR failed by one vote in the Reichstag in 1913, with the Progressives voting in support, the National Liberals against.

The only German experience of PR before 1918 was in state elections. It was adopted only in Württemberg in 1906, with the creation of a Lower House based on universal male suffrage: the existing one-member constituencies were supplemented by a six-member seat for the capital, Stuttgart, and two multi-member constituencies totalling 17 seats for the rest of the state, all using straight list systems. A revised plural voting system in Hamburg also incorporated PR.

A final experiment in PR came in 1918 when the government attempted a partial redistribution of Reichstag seats, on much the same lines as proposed by the contemporaneous Constitutional Conference in the UK: the thirty-four largest constituencies were turned into multi-member constituencies, returning seventy-eight members by the d'Hondt method. But this scheme was overtaken by the end of the war, the abdication of the Kaiser and the outbreak of the revolution, and by the establishment of that parliamentary republic that became a by-word for all that parliamentary republics ought not to be.

In the beginning was PR, with a national assembly at Weimar, elected by the d'Hondt method, that drew up a constitution which prescribed the principle of PR for all Reichstag and state elections.[12] As at the beginning of the Empire, other problems overshadowed that of the choice of an electoral system; but the choice, once made, created powerful vested interests and these stood in the way of any moves towards change.

PR was adopted virtually without debate by the provisional government of the two Social Democratic parties, MSPD and USPD,* as the self-evident concomitant of democracy in accordance with the party programme. It was accepted by the non-Socialist parties as a defence against the expected Red landslide. There were also practical arguments in favour of PR at this stage. An equitable redistribution of constituencies would have been impossible in the time available; moreover, the first elections, both nationally and in the states, were for constituent assemblies in which, it could be argued, 'mirror representation' was a virtue.

The chief reason for the adoption of PR was, however, doctrinal. Indeed the electoral law of 1920 expressed the doctrine at its purest. It replaced the

---

* The SPD had split in 1917 on the question of support for the government's war aims.

Table 3 *Successful and unsuccessful parties 1919–1932*

Year	No. of parties contesting	elected	% of votes for unrepresented parties	No. of candidates
1919	19	10	0.1	2,360
1920	24	10	1.1	3,604
May 1924	27	12	2.8	4,947
Dec. 1924	24	11	2.0	4,716
1928	35	15	2.8	6,209
1930	27	15	1.7	7,115
July 1932	42	14	0.4	
Nov. 1932	36	13	0.7	

Sources: Vogel, et al., *Wahlen in Deutschland,* p. 300; G. Kaisenberg, 'Wahlreform', *Zeitschrift für die gesamte Staatswissenschaft* (1931), p. 458.

d'Hondt system with the even more proportional 'automatic system': there was to be one Reichstag deputy for every 60,000 votes cast, the votes to be distributed at three levels – one of the thirty-five multi-member constituencies, a multi-constituency grouping and the entire country. Any party list (which might comprise more than one party) would qualify, provided it had presented candidates in the whole of the area concerned.[13]

Few voices were raised initially against the equation of PR with democracy. The Liberal Friedrich Naumann was alone in the Weimar constituent assembly in claiming that 'parliamentary government and PR are mutually exclusive . . . If we want to govern ourselves according to the English party system, we have to accept the English electoral system.'[14] But Naumann, whether or not he gave the right answer, had at least thought of the right question: does a change in the system of government require a change in the behaviour of parties?

What followed the adoption of PR was not so much a limitless fragmentation of Parliament as the perpetuation of a fragmentation inherited from the Empire. True, as Table 3 shows, the number of parties contesting elections escalated, reaching forty-two in July 1932. But most of these parties failed to clear even the minimal hurdles set by the 1920 law, so that a sizeable proportion of votes were wasted. The number of successful parties was not much greater than in the Empire: if one excludes the national minority parties, whose geographical base was removed by the Versailles treaty, the 1912 Reichstag had contained eleven parties. What had happened was a change not in the party system but in the constitution. The parties that had grown up in the Empire reflected the role of the Reichstag: they were required to represent, not to govern. Under Weimar, they found themselves burdened overnight with the obligations of responsible government.

Their failure to operate a parliamentary system led to the search for institutional solutions, among them electoral reform. Proponents and opponents of reform agreed that the principal problems to be addressed were those reducing the gap between the elector and the government, and of political recruitment. The strongest impetus for a move away from pure PR came from politicians and academics close to the Catholic Zentrum. This was not because the party saw itself as potentially majoritarian: it was, indeed, the archetypal pivotal party, essential to all coalitions and providing the Chancellor in nine of Weimar Republic's twenty cabinets. But its leaders' commitment was less to popular sovereignty than to the maintenance of legitimate authority and to the rooting of representation in community, in accordance with Catholic social teaching. They therefore viewed electoral systems functionally: Chancellor Brüning, presenting the last of many abortive bills in 1930, saw its aim as 'enabling parliament to provide the state with leadership'.[15] The straightforward view that behaviour could be changed by a change in rules and that nothing but first-past-the-post would do is expressed by F. A. Hermens, who was close to the Zentrum:

The integrating effect of the electoral system will give battle to whatever disintegrating forces there are in the country and it seems that in this fight the distribution of forces is such that democracy is bound to come off victoriously. In other words, the majority system of voting, instead of presupposing basic homogeneity in a country, will tend to create it.[16]

If one believed that, one could also believe that 'if PR had not been in operation . . . the National Socialists would long since have disappeared from the scene . . . and Hitler would have found it more profitable to go back to the painting of houses'.[17]

It should, in fairness, be said that these 'Cleopatra's nose' theses date from the retrospective debate (Hermens' *Democracy or Anarchy?* came out in 1941 and it is evident from his pre-1933 writings that he regarded coalition government as inevitable, and absolute majority voting as preferable to first-past-the-post[18]); in the lifetime of the Weimar Republic itself more modest expectations were voiced. The aim of most reform schemes was to produce not two parties but fewer and bigger ones, to reduce the power of party machines through more numerous and smaller constituencies and, by both these devices, to discourage anti-system parties. The two principal legislative proposals, those of 1924 and 1930, shared these aims.[19]

They were all modified proportional systems, if only because any more radical measure would have required constitutional amendment. None got off the ground and might well, if they had, been struck down by the Supreme Court which had declared as unconstitutional a number of much more limited modifications by individual states, e.g., a deposit requirement, a higher signature requirement for new parties or a minimum percentage hurdle for representation.[20]

Among Liberals and Social Democrats there was an equal concern with political integration, governmental stability and leadership selection, but their conclusions tended more often in the direction of PR. This was particularly true of those scholars of historicist inspiration who constituted the house intelligentsia of the fledgling republic. If one agreed, not with Hermens, that Germans were waiting to be guided into voting for moderation, but with Ernst Troeltsch, that they were like the Nibelungs, 'destroying each other in hatred and obstinacy',[21] then a two-party system would simply mean a polarisation between pro- and anti-democratic forces: it would accelerate, not retard, the rise of fascism.[22] But there was, in addition, the argument from social reality. Max Weber asserted that multi-partism was an inescapable consequence of modern social structures – even the British two-party system would not survive the rise of Labour[23] – and in the German context even major parties like the Zentrum and the SPD were doomed to minority status.[24]

On the Left support for PR as the institutionalisation of social cleavage was even stronger. Academic advocates of it, like Otto Kirchheimer, conceded that 'German elections have certain similarities to those carried on under the Bolshevik and fascist electoral laws in so far as they do not decisively affect the stream of political events.'[25] The virtue of Weimar PR is that it enables 'class boundaries to be mirrored with mathematical exactness'.[26] Attempts to restore nineteenth-century parliamentarism would simply disguise the infra-structural truth: 'it is more honest to let each voter know which class interests his deputy represents than if the various local notables whom an election reform might possibly bring into parliament were to be "captured" by various organized interests without the knowledge of their voters.'[27]

That the list system of Weimar PR was failing to recruit notables or promote leaders was widely acknowledged. Centralised nomination favoured party hacks and pressure-group nominees, resulting – in Max Weber's often-cited complaint – in a *Banausenparlament*, a Parliament of nonentities and philistines. His own solution, which was indeed adopted, was a directly elected President[28]; Troeltsch was prepared to shrug the whole problem off as teething troubles.[29] Some Socialists, including Kautsky, positively welcomed the anonymity of lists: it ensured the subordination of deputies to the party organisation.[30] But a group of younger party revisionists, grouped in the 'Hofgeismar circle', which included Willy Brandt's mentor, Julius Leber, wanted the SPD to take a more positive attitude to the Weimar state and to involve parliamentarism in leadership selection. Hugo Sinzheimer com-plained, 'We lack the brains and the capacity to really be able to govern, and the party does everything it can to keep its distance from such qualities. It therefore does not create a bridge to the intellectual figures of our time.'[31] Carlo Mierendorff put it more bluntly. Thanks to the list system 'the deputy cannot be dismissed. His seat is absolutely guaranteed against the will of the people once he has acquired a safe place in the list. In consequence, the election ceases to be an election.'[32]

There was a generational element in these grievances that reflected the

Table 4 *Weimar Republic: simulated results of single-member constituencies*

Year		KPD %	SPD %	Zentrum %	Lib. parties %	DNVP (Cons.) %	NSDAP %	Others %
Dec. 1924[a]	Votes	12.6	20.5	16.6	14.9	19.5	6.6	7.5
	Seats	1.0	44.8	31.0	0.5	19.5	–	3.2
1928[a]	Votes	10.6	29.8	15.2	13.6	14.2	2.6	13.9
	Seats	3.0	56.3	28.5	0.5	9.3	–	2.4
1930[b]	Votes	13.1	24.5	14.8	8.3	7.0	18.3	14.0
	Seats	10.2	46.5	27.5	–	2.0	12.0	1.8
July 1932[c]	Votes	14.6	21.6	15.7	2.2	5.9	37.4	2.6
	Seats	5.0	10.0	25.0	–	–	60.0	–

Sources: [a] Johannes Schauff, *Neues Wahlrecht: Vorschläge zur Wahlreform* (Berlin, 1928); [b] Hermens, *Democracy or Anarchy?*, p. 258: [c] S. S. Nilson, *Zeitschrift für die gesamte Staatswissenschaft* (1954), pp. 283–4.

composition of the SPD's Reichstag delegation. In 1930, out of 143 deputies fifty-six were party or trade union officials and sixteen others civil servants. Only twenty were under forty years old, compared with fifty-five out of seventy-seven in the SPD's principal rival, the KPD.[33]

How many of the Weimar Republic's problems could have been solved by electoral tinkering must remain speculative. For the early years there is little doubt that Troeltsch was right: survival entailed consensus and that, in turn, meant a coalition of the pro-system parties. What now seems a gratuitously self-inflicted injury was the 1920 move from d'Hondt to pure proportionality: the retention of d'Hondt would have given the most loyal Republican parties, the SPD and the Zentrum a bonus of about ten seats each. A change to a majority system at a later stage, when tempers were calmer, would have run other risks. Table 4 shows the simulated results of four Weimar elections if they had been fought in single-member constituencies. The estimate for 1932 supports the claim of that eminent psephologist Hermann Goering at the Nuremberg trial that his party would have done better, not worse, under first-past-the-post. But that is to caricature the argument of the Hermens school: their claim is that a different electoral system would have inhibited party fragmentation and cabinet instability, saved the credit of the Republic and neutralised the appeal of extremism. The estimates for the earlier Weimar elections do indeed show working majorities for parties loyal to the Republic, but only at the cost of great violence to electoral opinion. One sector of opinion virtually unrepresented was the Protestant middle class, numbering about 40%. How this socially and economically powerful stratum, whose allegiance to Weimar was in any case dubious, would have reacted to this disfranchisement is doubtful.

What such a reform might have done is to oblige the Liberal and Centre-Right parties to amalgamate, at least for electoral purposes: there is, of course, no guarantee that they would have done this. They might have been more willing to do so on the basis of Brüning's 1930 reform. Even the raising of the electoral quota from 60,000 to 70,000 votes, one of the bill's proposals, would, on the figures of the 1930 election, have raised the SPD share of seats from 24.8% to 29.4%, that of the Zentrum from 15.0% to 17.2%; it would have eliminated at least one minor list and would presumably have encouraged some amalgamation.[34] Both Communists and Nazis were by then too strong to be edged out by tinkering.

Hitler's Enabling Law put an end to such speculations in Germany, though they were, of course, the stuff of exile politics. Hermens was close to ex-Chancellor Brüning, now in the USA, and to Zentrum exiles. This group provided important continuity between the Catholic social theorising of the 1920s and the electoral thinking of the CDU after 1945. More significant was the move away from PR on the part of the SPD, already begun, as we have noted, before 1933. Especially under the impact of their Anglo-Saxon environment, SPD exiles sought to learn from the mistakes of Weimar. In London Erich Ollenhauer declared in 1941: 'We German Social Democrats must put into practice the experiences of British democracy . . . by adopting smaller constituencies and abolishing electoral lists.'[35]

However, when the war ended, electoral systems were not to be in the gift of German politicians. As politics gradually revived in 1946 and 1947 both occupiers and occupied saw the limitation of the number of parties as desirable. The Allies used the licensing mechanism, for ease of control as much as for any other reason; the Germans moved fairly quickly towards party amalgamations, the chief products of which were the CDU and FDP, as yet under a variety of different labels. But in the matter of electoral systems the occupying powers were less adventurous: as in 1867 and 1918 crucial decisions, entailing long-term consequences, were taken by default.

The Soviets were in no doubt that they favoured PR for the five *Länder* in their zone, both to protect the minority status of the KPD and to ensure centralised control over nominations. Indeed at the 1947 foreign ministers' conference in Moscow, Molotov insisted on PR as a pre-condition for all-German elections, not only nationally, but for *Land* and local elections.[36]

Rather more surprisingly, a variety of PR systems were also quickly adopted in the French and American zones. In the French zone there was little consultation between occupiers and occupied.[37] Two of the three *Länder* of the French zone, Rhineland–Palatinate and Baden, incorporated the principle of PR in their constitutions; the third, Württemberg–Hohenzollern, did not. A year later, in 1948, Rhineland–Palatinate introduced into its electoral law a hurdle requiring a minimum 5% of the vote for representation in the *Landtag*. In the US zone, in contrast with the French, much more initiative was left to

German politicians and officials, most of whom favoured the principle of PR.[38] So, too, did a number of the military administration's advisers, including James K. Pollock, Richard M. Scammon and Karl Loewenstein. What emerged were mixed systems with multi-member constituencies and *Land* lists. The US *Länder* also pioneered the minimum percentage hurdle, 5% in Hesse and Württemberg–Baden, 10% in any one of the five provinces of Bavaria. Their constitutions (except that of Bremen)* also enshrined PR and minimum percentage hurdles.

Given the bad odour of Weimar-style PR these decisions might seem surprising. On the other hand it could be argued that the municipal and *Land* authorities to which elections were being organised were consultative rather than executive – indeed those of the US zone were specifically constituent assemblies – and that PR was therefore quite appropriate. The Americans in particular were anxious to govern by consensus, i.e., coalition, and wished to avoid the emergence of 'oppositions' which might easily turn into oppositions to occupation policies. At this stage the Western allies lacked any view on the ultimate German constitutional structure; there were therefore no criteria for the functionality of an electoral system. Nor had the prospects of a unified German state disappeared in 1947 and there was much to be said for sticking to institutions that would be acceptable to all four powers. When, by 1948 and 1949, these prospects had receded and the US moved towards setting up a Western-orientated Federal Republic, it also moved towards the majority electoral system favoured by the CDU, and it was primarily American opposition that ensured that PR would not be enshrined in the Basic Law. But by then a party constellation had emerged that would make anything other than PR very difficult to enact.

The only occupying power determined to reform German electoral habits were the British. The local elections of 1946 were fought on a system that combined simple majorities with some proportionality.[39] Especially in the Protestant areas, where the anti-Socialist vote was fairly evenly split, this led to serious distortions as Table 5 shows for Hamburg. In the *Land* elections that followed in 1947, Lower Saxony and North Rhine–Westphalia adopted single-member constituencies with compensatory list seats, subject to a 5% hurdle – in fact, a system very close to that finally chosen for the Federal Republic – while Schleswig–Holstein stayed closer to the model adopted for Hamburg and Bremen.* None of the British zone *Land* constitutions, which were all adopted after the Federal Republic had come into being, specifies the electoral system.

Hamburg, as Table 5 shows, was something of a laboratory for the effect of electoral systems on party systems. In 1949 the CDU and FDP formed an alliance to counter the SPD's advantage, but since there was now a further

---

* Bremen was originally in the British zone and transferred to the US zone only after the first elections.

Table 5 *Votes and seats for Hamburg Diet 1946–1957*

Year		SPD %	CDU %	FDP %	DP %	KPD %	Others %
1946	Votes	43.1	26.7	18.2	–	10.4	1.6
	Seats	75.5	14.5	6.4	–	3.6	–
1949	Votes	42.8	34.5		13.3	7.4	2.0
	Seats	54.2	33.3		7.5	4.2	0.8
1953	Votes	45.2	50.0			3.2	1.6
	Seats	48.3	51.7			–	–
1957	Votes	53.9	32.2	8.6	4.1	–	1.2
	Seats	57.5	34.2	8.3	–	–	–

right-wing party, the German Party, splitting the anti-Socialist vote their success was limited. In 1953 the German Party joined the alliance and the SPD was defeated; but the electoral allies remained separate parties and used their majority to institute PR. In spite of this the SPD displaced them in 1957, this time by topping 50% of the vote. But it was still over-represented, because the votes for the German Party, now below 5%, were wasted.

Hamburg was the last *Land* to drop a predominantly British electoral system. By the time the *Land* electoral systems had been homogenised in the early 1950s the Federal Republic had come into existence. Although the Basic Law of the Federal Republic did not, on the insistence of the Allies, contain any provision concerning the electoral system, the Parliamentary Council that drew up the Basic Law had to decide on an electoral law for the first Bundestag: its decision in this respect reflected its party composition, which in turn reflected the composition of the Landtage, which in turn derived from the decisions made by the Allies about electoral systems in 1946–7. (CDU and SPD had 27 seats each in the Council, FDP 5, others 6.)

Though it had been the Allies who primarily determined local government and *Land* electoral systems, that for the Bundestag was predominantly the product of German politicians. The major new factor in German politics was the CDU, made up of the bulk of the old Zentrum and a wide range of former Protestant liberal and conservative forces. Both these components helped to turn the new party away from the German PR tradition. The organisation of the CDU went ahead fastest in the North Rhine–Westphalia, the old Zentrum heartland, and here the Catholic influence was strongest. The founders of the party emphasised both the need to repudiate the anonymity of the list system and the call for creating workable majorities. In the predominantly Protestant areas a different imperative – that of aggregating an electorate of diverse former allegiances – pointed in a similar direction.

Initially there was no unanimity on this point. In particular, the Christian Democrats of the Soviet zone, led by Jakob Kaiser and Ernst Lemmer, urged that nationwide parties would need strong central organisations. It was less obvious to them that the CDU would profit from first-past-the-post in all-German elections and they were anxious not to press for a system unacceptable to the Soviet authorities. But as the prospect of all-German elections receded after 1947, so did the attractiveness of PR. In May 1948 the CDU/CSU's constitutional executive unanimously recommended a system of 'personal election': 'Only such an electoral system appears, in the eyes of the executive committee, to guarantee that the creation of clear majorities are possible inside parliament and, further, that the immediate relationship between electors and elected is restored.'[40]

Within the SPD the trend was in the opposite direction. When the party emerged from illegality in 1945 it organised itself much as it had existed before 1933, often with the same local officials. Whereas the CDU was aiming at creating ad hoc coalitions of diverse groups of voters and therefore wanted an electoral system with a low premium on partisanship, the SPD hoped to attract its voters on the basis of a strongly delineated identity. It was anxious to demarcate itself not merely against the Right but against the Left, and to resist Soviet-inspired moves towards 'working-class unity'. Those SPD exiles and academics sympathetic to the SPD who wanted to move away from PR therefore found themselves in a minority. Nevertheless, the pressures not to resume where Weimar had left off were sufficient to elicit a compromise formula from the party executive in 1948 which stated that the question of an electoral system was not one of party principle and did not need incorporating in a constitution. It favoured a mixed system of constituencies and lists, with no party entitled to more list seats than constituency seats, and a 5% hurdle[41] – in other words proportionality biased in favour of the bigger parties.

When the debate in the Parliamentary Council began, therefore, both major parties had fairly well-defined positions and fairly reliable evidence of their respective electoral strengths. The debate itself, though no doubt dominated by tactical manoeuvrings, revealed many of the anxieties of the Federal Republic's founding fathers.

Those who advocated a purely majority system, like the CDU spokesman Adolf Süsterhenn, did so for two reasons, both related to the Weimar trauma.

The re-introduction of a parliamentary system of government in Germany can be justified only if an electoral system is formed, following the Anglo-Saxon example, without slavish imitation, which pushes back the party apparatus, brings political personality into the foreground and makes the creation of clear majorities possible.[42]

This is an illuminating misunderstanding of the Anglo-Saxon example, since the British branch of Anglo-Saxonia maintains clear majorities by favouring party discipline at the expense of the personality, while the American branch does the opposite.

The minor parties were the strongest opponents of majority voting. Helene Wessel of the revived Zentrum feared that this would lead to a polarisation between clerical and anti-clerical forces and also that it would disadvantage women.[43] But it was Carlo Schmid of the SPD who expressed the burnt child's crucial lack of confidence in his fellow citizens' ability to operate a system based on mutual trust. He acknowledged all the advantages of a two-party system, but also felt: 'We need an electoral system that will not lead to the brutal outbreak of latent crises . . . we need an electoral system that loads the burden onto broader and more numerous shoulders . . . when we have got a bit further, we can talk about this again.'[44]

In the end the choice was between a CDU proposal for 300 simple-majority constituencies supplemented by 100 list members and an SPD proposal for six-member constituences, with lists subject to panachage and votes distributed by d'Hondt, and a further 25% of members drawn from national or regional lists. The final compromise, produced by the SPD, was, as indicated, a system much like that of Lower Saxony. 60% of members were to be elected by simple majority, the other 40% by compensatory lists, subject to a minimum of one directly elected member or 5% of the vote in any one *Land*. The proportional element was to be determined by the d'Hondt method. It was accepted with the votes of the minor parties against those of the CDU. It has, in its essentials, remained in operation ever since. The principal changes have been a raising of the hurdle, first to a national 5% minimum, then to three directly elected members; an increase in the proportion of list seats to 50%; and, from 1953 onwards, the separation of the constituency from the list vote, enabling the voter to split his ticket. One anomaly of this system is that parties that gain more constituency seats in any one *Land* than the total to which their share of the vote would entitle them to, retain these as a bonus (see last column of Table 6). The combined effect of these hurdles and of the d'Hondt method has been, as Table 8 shows, to bestow consistent over-representation on the CDU/CSU and SPD, approximate proportionality on the FDP and under-representation on all other parties.

But though the electoral law has remained virtually unchanged, the party landscape has been transformed. This was by no means predictable. Despite some party fusion, the 1949 federal election in many respects resumed where party politics had left off, if not in 1932 then in 1928. Ten parties were elected to the first Bundestag and after the Allies gave up their licensing prerogative there was a rash of new formations. But the trend was sharply reversed in 1953 by what might be justifiably called 'the German electoral miracle'.[45] 1953 was not a re-aligning election: the ideological frontier continued to run where it had settled a couple of generations earlier. But it was, in V. O. Key's sense, critical: it set the terms for electoral contests for the next generation. What happened in 1953 was that for the first time in German electoral history an incumbent head of government, Konrad Adenauer, campaigned for re-election. That he was successful no doubt helped to institutionalise the habit, and though the SPD did not formally respond by running a shadow chancellor until 1961, earlier contests were in effect plebiscitary competitions for executive leadership. Moreover, the pattern quickly spread to a number of *Länder* including SPD-governed ones, like Hamburg in 1953 and Hesse in 1956. The SPD had, in fact, slipped into adversary politics without intending to. Their postwar preference was for great coalitions. It was the CDU that tried to exclude them from policy-making, initially in the Economic Council of the Anglo-American bi-zone and then in the first federal cabinet. The SPD leader, Kurt Schumacher, obliged, not because he believed in a two-party system – he did not – but because he believed that sharing power on unfavourable terms had been the SPD's undoing under Weimar. A concomitant of the electoral miracle was that five of the parties elected in 1949 failed to clear the hurdle in 1953, two more in 1957 (including the Refugee Party, first elected in 1953) and another in 1961, leaving the current three parties in the Bundestag. Moreover, two parties, the Zentrum in 1953 and the German Party in 1957, survived only by accepting piggy-back constituency seats from the CDU, thus surrendering their independence.

The debate on electoral reform did not entirely disappear during the 1950s either among the parties or in public debate. The principal intellectual lobby for majority voting was the Deutsche Wählergesellschaft, founded in 1947 by Dolf Sternberger, with cross-party, though predominantly right-of-centre, support. Sternberger did not see entirely eye-to-eye with the CDU's advocacy, which was based on the need for strong government, whereas he was more concerned with the emancipation of the individual elector: 'In a political election deputies, that is to say persons, are elected to a parliament, that is to say a corporate body. That is done by us, the voters. A simple description of the process tells us all the essentials.'[46] Even when, as in 1957, the CDU gained an absolute majority of the votes, he regarded this as less of a victory for efficient government than for the electorate 'over the privilege of parties, and especially of party executives, in the formation of governments' and 'over the electoral law'.[47]

What the Deutsche Wählergesellschaft did establish in a survey was the strong support majority voting had in the first Bundestag: 145 of the 402 members favoured it, including twenty-nine of the SPD and nine of the FDP. Adenauer himself had always favoured it, but although the CDU held absolute Bundestag majorities from 1953 to 1961, he formed maximum anti-SPD coalitions in order to get the Western integration treaties through the Upper House. But electoral reform did feature as a weapon in coalition politics. In 1956 the FDP switched coalition partners from the CDU to the SPD in North Rhine–Westphalia in order to block a CDU reform project. This resulted in the departure of the FDP from the Bonn coalition and a split in its Bundestag delegation. When the CDU lost its absolute majority in 1961 and again required the FDP as a partner it twice used the threat of a great coalition and its concomitant, electoral reform: in 1961, when the FDP tried, without success, to insist on the retirement of Adenauer as a price of joining the government, and in 1962 when the FDP, successfully this time, insisted on the dismissal of Strauss after the *Spiegel* affair.

When, therefore, the FDP pulled the plug on the Erhard government in 1966, the CDU was determined to eradicate this source of instability. The Great Coalition of CDU + SPD, formed at the end of 1966, proclaimed its commitment to a 'majority-creating electoral system', if necessary with an interim measure for the 1969 election. However, cup and lip have not met, despite several tremulous rapprochements. Academic opinion on the whole favoured a move towards Anglo-Saxon practice. When in 1968 the government set up a commission with the remit to recommend 'which electoral system offered the best prospects of ensuring the proper functioning of democracy through clear-cut majorities',[48] this commission unsurprisingly reported in favour of first-past-the-post; but its members included several favourable to the SPD, e.g., Wilhelm Hennis, Erwin Scheuch and Thomas Ellwein. Within the parties, however, there was no unanimity.

CDU leaders in SPD strongholds feared that their regions would now be unrepresented and that if the reform were extended to *Land* elections they would be all but eliminated in Hamburg, Bremen and Hesse. Discord was greater within the SPD. The advocates of majority voting were, in the main, the national leaders of the party's reformist wing – Herbert Wehner, Helmut Schmidt, Fritz Erler, Carlo Schmid. For them, the Great Coalition and a two-party system were a logical culmination of the party reform of Bad Godesberg. These views were not strongly shared by back-benchers, *Land* leaders and the Left. The Left feared a loss of identity: competition between two catch-all parties, they argued, would mean competition on the basis of the status quo. They became more attracted by the FDP as a coalition partner, especially as the FDP began moving to the Left after 1967.

Above all, there were uncertainties about the electoral effects of first-past-the-post. An analysis of the 1961 and 1965 elections showed that there was a bias in the system against the CDU, due to its massive majorities in Catholic rural seats. This bias amounted to 2 to $2\frac{1}{2}$%: it would be reduced, but by no means eliminated, were the parties to draw level. First-past-the-post ought therefore to favour the SPD. The SPD's polling organisation, *Infas*, conducted an elaborate simulation exercise, based not only on juggling with figures but on social-structural and political identification data: it concluded that the SPD was in a 'structural minority', that its chances under a two-party system were therefore poor and that the risks of a 2/3 CDU majority in the Bundestag were high. Table 6 shows that in 1961 and 1965, when less than 10% separated the main parties, the SPD's share of constituency seats was only just above the one third level of eighty-three.

Table 6 *Constituency and list seats in Bundestag elections 1949–1980*

	CDU/CSU			SPD			FDP			Others			Surplus seats
	(a)	(b)	Total	(a)	(b)	Total	(a)	(b)	Total	(a)	(b)	Total	
1949	115	24	139	96	35	131	12	40	52	19	42	61	1 CDU, 1 SPD
1953	172	71	243	45	106	151	14	34	48	11	23	34	2 CDU, 1 DP
1957	194	76	270	46	123	169	1	40	41	6	5	11	3 CDU
1961	158	86	244	91	99	190		67	67				5 CDU
1965	154	91	245	94	108	202		49	49				
1969	121	121	242	127	97	224		30	30				
1972	96	129	225	152	78	230		41	41				
1976	134	109	243	114	100	214		39	39				
1980	121	105	226	127	91	218		53	53				1 SPD

(a) Constituency seats
(b) List seats

Though the parties' rival academic teams diverged in their conclusion they were agreed on the issues. SPD pessimists and CDU optimists agreed that if the FDP vote collapsed it would split in favour of the CDU. *Infas* concluded that the SPD was at a structural disadvantage, its opponents that social change was working to produce an equality of opportunity. Above all, the risks of a highly distorted result led all participants to devise a series of mixed systems.

Hermens, in a minority report of the government's commission, proposed a system combining simple majority voting with a small number of list seats (25% of the total) to compensate the seat-winning parties for any bias. This is in effect PR with the FDP not allowed to play. A proposal favoured by the CDU was PR by the d'Hondt method in four-member constituencies. This would avoid violent swings in seat distribution, but also favoured parties with very safe seats, since 66.7% of the two-party vote would be needed to achieve a 3:1 division of seats. This is in effect PR with a 17% hurdle. A proposal favoured by the SPD was PR by the d'Hondt system in three-member seats. This would ensure minority representation in most seats, make 2/3 parliamentary majorities difficult to achieve and maximise the number of marginal seats in which the critical contest would take place. It is in effect PR with a 20% hurdle. Neither the three-member nor the four-member constituencies would necess-arily have eliminated the FDP: it had sufficient regional strongholds in the 1960s to retain some seats even against a 20% threshold, but it would have been badly under-represented.

Perhaps of greatest interest to students of British psephology was another proposal by Hermens: to give statutory effect to the cube law. Seats would simply be distributed in the ratios that were the cube of their ratios of the popular vote. This would apply to all contesting parties, not just the two leading ones. Minor parties would be under-represented, but not eliminated. The relationship of votes to seats would be as below.[49]

	Case A		Case B		Case C	
	% Votes	% Seats	% Votes	% Seats	% Votes	% Seats
Party X	50	57.8	48	59.5	45	64.2
Party Y	45	42.14	42	39.9	35	30.1
Party Z	5	0.06	10	0.6	20	5.7

There were many reasons why nothing came of all this relentless ingenuity. Political calculation was the most important. The SPD got cold feet, firstly because of the *Infas* exercise, secondly because of severe losses in *Landtag* elections, thirdly because it wished increasingly to put an end to the Great Coalition and was increasingly drawn to the FDP to this end. SPD–FDP *Land* coalitions, especially in crucial North Rhine–Westphalia, and SPD–FDP co-operation in electing Gustav Heinemann Federal President in 1969 all implied repudiation of electoral reform by the SPD.

Public opinion, one suspects, also played a part. There was no one clear-cut proposal for reform. The multiplicity of elaborate schemes merely caused confusion and suspicion. Nor was there a self-evident need for change. Bonn was not Weimar. If it works, don't fix it. Dolf Sternberger, the veteran advocate of majority voting, conceded in 1963 that 'the development of the party system in the Federal Republic has drastically contradicted some of our fearful forecasts'.[50] The more the reform looked as a mere device for killing off the FDP, the less people liked it. There is among the German public what Rudolf Wildenmann has called a 'horror majoritatis'.[51] Opinion polls have consistently shown distrust of single-party government and a preference for a three-party Bundestag.

What finally removed reform from the agenda was the 1969 election result, which made an SPD–FDP coalition possible. If the neo-Nazi NDP had won 230,000 more votes it would have gained Bundestag representation, and a continued Great Coalition would have been politically as well as mathematically necessary. There is little doubt that under those circumstances some form of electoral reform would have emerged, if only to kill off the NPD.

The 'social–liberal' coalition that governed West Germany from 1969 to 1982 lasted longer and was more fully integrated than any previous one. Electoral campaigning and voter behaviour has responded accordingly. Under Adenauer and Erhard *chancellors* sought re-election and so, to some extent, did *parties*, but not *governments*. Participants in incumbent coalitions gave no pledges about post-electoral behaviour. In 1972, 1976 and 1980 *coalitions* sought re-election as *coalitions*. One consequence of that has been a growth of ticket splitting. This was first noticeable in 1969 when, contrary to all the forecasts, the SPD won a majority of constituency seats. In part this was due to the bias since, as Table 8 shows, the SPD was 2.6% behind even on constituency votes. But it was 3.4% behind on list votes and the difference was made up by FDP list voters casting tactical constituency votes. Table 7 shows the development of this tendency. Two factors, it seems, favour ticket splitting: (1) a highly polarised election and (2) a clear government coalition. Where neither is present, as in 1957, ticket splitting is low: list and constituency votes for the three main parties were within 0.2% of each other in that year. Where one factor is present, it is higher. In 1961 and 1969 there was polarisation, but no alliance; in 1965 and 1976 an alliance, but no polarisation. In 1972 and 1980, where both were present, splitting is at its highest.

We cannot assume that this bipolar electoral contest, with its consequences for the particular forms of voter rationality that we have observed, will continue into the eighties. The FDP may enter future elections without a coalition commitment; new parties may take votes unevenly from existing ones and even enter the Bundestag: the 'Green' Party of environmentalists quite possibly, a left-splinter SPD rather less conceivably. The FDP itself is never wholly safe. All these are circumstances under which coalition

Table 7 *Constituency vote of FDP list voters 1961–1980 (%)*

Constituency Vote to	1961	1965	1969	1972	1976	1980
CDU/CSU	7.9	20.9	10.6	7.9	8.0	13.3
SPD	3.1	6.7	24.8	52.9	29.9	35.5
FDP	86.5	70.3	62.0	38.2	60.7	48.5

Source: Statistisches Bundesamt, *Wahl zum 9. Deutschen Bundestag am 5. Oktober 1980*, Heft 8, pp. 24–5.

Table 8 *Share of votes and share of seats (%)*

	CDU/CSU		FDP		SPD		Others	
	Votes	Seats	Votes	Seats	Votes	Seats	Votes	Seats
1949	31.0	34.6	11.9	12.9	29.2	32.6	27.9	19.7
1953	45.2	49.9	9.5	9.9	28.8	31.0	16.5	9.2
1957	50.2	54.3	7.7	8.2	31.8	34.0	10.3	3.4
1961	45.3	48.5	12.8	13.4	36.2	38.1	3.7	–
1965	47.6	49.4	9.5	9.9	39.3	40.7	3.6	–
1969	46.1	48.8	5.8	6.0	42.7	45.2	5.4	–
1972	44.9	45.4	8.4	8.3	45.8	46.4	1.8	–
1976	48.6	49.0	7.9	7.9	42.6	43.1	1.7	–
1980	44.5	45.5	10.6	10.6	42.9	43.9	2.0	–

formation would once more become difficult, causing electoral reform to reappear on the agenda.

Within the *Länder* there have been some adjustments of the electoral system, without a departure from the principle of PR. Baden–Württemberg, for instance, now operates the 'additional member' system which was favoured by the Hansard Society's Commission on Electoral Reform in 1976 and which is one of the principal candidates for consideration in Britain.

What are the morals to be drawn from these tales? Firstly, that the world is pregnant with unintended consequences and that Robert Burns had a point about well-laid plans. Secondly, that constitutional controversies can persist for a very long time, conducted in scarcely changing terms even though the world around is transformed beyond recognition. The PR debate surfaced in the *belle époque* – the first Reichstag vote on it was in 1913 – and is still with us, only temporarily submerged by Armageddon.

The broad strands of the argument show considerable continuity. True, the traditional conservative cure for multi-partism, that of strengthening the executive – whether monarchical or republican – against an incompetent legislature, lost salience. So has the nineteenth-century liberal vision of independent voters electing independent parliamentarians, which entails small, preferably single-member, constituencies. Its last notable advocates were Dolf Sternberger and his Deutsche Wählergesellschaft.

But the intellectual traditions of Catholic social theory, with an essentially functional view of the electoral system, designed to sustain on the one hand the authority of government and on the other the autonomy of social organis-ation, has survived through the CDU and the intellectuals grouped round it. So has the tradition of regarding parties as the representatives of well-defined and legitimate interests. This, expressed largely by the SPD and its theorists, regards multi-partism and the list system as the expression of this essential infrastructural truth, and any attempt to fiddle with the system as an attempt to disguise this truth. Even the technicalities of the present electoral system have an ancient lineage. Mixed constituency and list systems were first proposed before 1914.[52] In 1926 Walter Jallinek, an influential figure in the US zone after 1945, proposed alternative schemes: a predominantly majority system with list supplementation, and a system closely resembling the additional member.[53] The nearest presentiment to the present-day system was proposed by C. H. Bornemann in 1931, complete with a 2% minimum-vote hurdle.[54]

Under the two-ballot system of the Empire moderate multi-partism flourish-ed, a multi-partism that reflected the religious and ideological cleavages ante-dating the formation of the Empire, and the industrial cleavage that followed its foundation. Since there was no responsible parliamentary government under the Empire the question of effective government-formation through parties did not arise. But since the Reichstag did have considerable legislative and budgetary powers its partisan composition mattered. Towards the end of the Imperial period ideologically contiguous parties were more and more inclined to come to first-ballot arrangements to avoid mutual elimination, and to make national – albeit informal and not easily enforced – alliances for the second ballot. A change to PR would presumably have halted any further developments in this direction. One reason for the defeat of PR before 1914 was the fear of the right-wing parties that it would lead to the introduction of equal suffrage in state and municipal elections. In other words, the issue of PR was subordinate to the general debate on constitutional reform.

In the Weimar Republic, on the other hand, PR was a central issue. Its very existence was tied up with the ideology of the republic and frequently defended as one of the achievements of the revolution.[55] It did not, of course, inhibit the survival of the multi-partism inherited from the Empire; it was indeed initially designed to ensure its survival. Some modification of it would probably have counter-acted the fragmentation of the Centre-Right in the late twenties, and lengthened the average life of cabinets. Whether that would have sufficed to neutralise the structural difficulties of the German economy, the dubious loyalty of the army, of the public service and of large sections of the academic intelligentsia, and the despair induced by the burden of reparations and the Great Depression is less certain. Czechoslovakia's inter-war democracy survived much better with an electoral system identical to that of Weimar, which raises important questions about cause and effect.

What has enabled parliamentary government to flourish in the Federal Republic, apart from an undoubted desire to learn from the past, was a more favourable economic climate and a more manageable diplomatic environment. All political controversies, including that concerning electoral systems, have been conducted in a milder tone. Whether the Federal Republic would have fared better or worse under another electoral system is nevertheless worth discussing.

One development that seems to be independent of the electoral system is the ability of parties to recruit political leaders. All post-1949 Chancellors and Presidents, and the great majority of cabinet ministers, have been partisan figures, many of high calibre. This suggests that the lack of political leadership in the Weimar Republic, and the frequent resort to non-partisan 'expert' or 'caretaker' figures, reflected the immaturity of German parliamentary practice rather than – as its critics frequently asserted – specific defects of the list system.

The 5% hurdle has certainly kept splinter and extremist parties out of the Bundestag and, together with the d'Hondt system which is biased in favour of big parties, has helped party concentration. However, the hurdle only just excluded the NPD in 1969 and may not exclude the 'Greens' in 1983. But since both groups got into various Landtage without disastrous consequences, the system is likely to survive this challenge, too.

The biggest contrast in the political atmospheres of Weimar and the Federal Republic is in the growth of consensus. Experience no doubt played a part. The Third Reich and Soviet occupation practice did not do much for the prestige of the anti-parliamentary Right and Left. But did the re-adoption of PR help or hinder the process? Had the CDU prevailed in 1949, majority voting could well have driven the SPD into a minority ghetto – a position it had after all occupied before – and delayed the integration of the left-wing working-class sub-culture into civil society. A change to majority voting in the 1960s would no doubt have achieved the short-term aim of eliminating the FDP – but beyond that? It could hardly have prevented the SPD from gaining power in 1969, but it could conceivably have led to a CDU victory in 1976.

Whether the prevalence of coalition government has materially helped consensus-building is more doubtful. Widely based coalitions are more usual on a municipal and, to a lesser extent, *Land* basis. Bonn politics have, since 1949, been adversary; on occasion intensely so. Except in the years 1966 and 1969, one of the major parties has been out of power. But perhaps the adversary electoral contests are only part of the story. Institutional causes of

consensus can be found most readily in the Bundestag, where party co-
operation in the committees is the rule, and in federalism. *Land* politics has
enabled the Bonn opposition to retain a base for influence and patronage and
to form coalitions that may be in contradiction to that in power federally. In
addition, one should not ignore the effect of industrial co-determination,
arguably the expression of a political culture inclined towards *Proporzdemokratie*
– the harmonisation of interests by coalition.

Politics, it would appear, is a multi-faceted game and the electoral rules are
only one set among many. Sometimes they are decisive. More often they are
not.

NOTES

1 Gerhard A. Ritter, *Gesellschaft, Parlament und Regierung: zur Geschichte des
  Parlamentarismus in Deutschland* (Düsseldorf, 1974), p. 18.
2 *Reichsgesetz über die Wahlen der Abgeordneten zum Volkshause vom 2. März 1849*, Arts.
  III & V. See Gerhard Schilfert, *Sieg und Niederlage des demokratischen Wahlrechts in der
  deutschen Revolution 1848/9* (E. Berlin, 1952), pp. 355–60.
3 *Stenographische Berichte über die Verhandlungen der deutschen constituierenden
  Nationalversammlung zu Frankfurt-am-Main*, Herausgegeben . . . von Prof. Franz
  Wiegand (Frankfurt, 1849), vol. 7. See the speeches of Prof. Georg Waitz, rapporteur
  of the electoral law committee (p. 5228), Peter Reichensperger (p. 5510) and Prof.
  Bruno Hildebrand (p. 5212).
4 E.g., Waitz, ibid., vol. 7, p. 5228.
5 Ritter, *Gesellschaft*, p. 213.
6 For a general survey of the SPD's views on electoral systems see Axel Misch, *Das
  Wahlsystem zwischen Theorie und Taktik, Zur Frage der Mehrheitswahl und Verhältniswahl in der Programmatik der Sozialdemokratie bis 1933* (Berlin, 1974), pp. 65–173.
7 Eduard Bernstein, 'Parteien und Klassen', *Sozialistische Monatshefte* (1902) pt 2, p.
  853.
8 Eduard Bernstein, 'Ein Ausblick auf die bevorstehenden Reichstagwahlen', *Sozialistische Monatshefte* (1903), pt 1, p. 186.
9 [Eduard Bernstein], 'Das demokratische Prinzip und seine Anwendung', *Neue Zeit*
  (1896/7), pt 1, p. 23.
10 Rudolf von Gneist, *Die national Rechtsidee von den Ständen und das preussische
   Dreiklassenwahlsystem: Eine sozialhistorische Studie* (Berlin, 1894), p. 9.
11 Quoted in Walter Gagel, *Die Wahlrechtsfrage in der Geschichte der deutschen liberalen
   Parteien, 1848–1918* (Düsseldorf, 1958), p. 129.
12 *Die Verfassung des Deutschen Reiches vom 11 August 1919*, Arts. 17, 22.
13 *Reichswahlgesetz vom 27 April 1920*, sects. 30–3.
14 *Verhandlungen der Verfassunggebenden deutschen Nationalversammlung, 8. Ausschuss*
   (4 April 1919), vol. 336, p. 242.
15 Friedrich Schäfer, 'Zur Frage des Wahlrechts in der Weimarer Republik', in
   Ferdinand A. Hermens and Theodor Schieder, eds., *Staat, Wirtschaft und Politik:
   Festschrift für Heinrich Brüning* (Berlin, 1967), pp. 133–4.

16 Ferdinand A. Hermens, *Democracy or Anarchy? A Study of Proportional Representation* (Notre Dame, 1941), pp. 24–5.

17 Ibid., pp. 257, 228.

18 E.g., 'Wahlrecht und Verfassungskrise', *Hochland* (May, 1932), pp. 98, 110. Quoted in Erhard H. M. Lange, *Wahlrecht und Innenpolitik: Entstehungsgeschichte und Analyse der Wahlgesetzgebung und Wahlrechtsdiskussion im westlichen Nachkriegsdeutschland, 1945–1956* (Meisenheim, 1975), p. 172.

19 For details see Karl Braunias, *Das parlamentarische Wahlrecht: Ein Handbuch über die gesetzgebenden Körperschaften Europas* (Berlin, Leipzig, 1932), vol. 1, pp. 91–2.

20 Ibid., vol. 1. pp. 114–15.

21 Ernst Troeltsch, *Spektator-Briefe: Aufsätze über die deutsche Revolution und die Weltpolitik, 1918–1922* (Tübingen, 1922), p. 56.

22 Ibid., pp. 208–9

23 Max Weber, 'Parlament und Regierung im neugeordneten Deutschland', in *Gesammelte Politische Schriften*, 2nd edn (Tübingen, 1959), pp. 371–2. English translation: Max Weber, *Economy and Society: An Outline of Interpretive Sociology* (New York, 1968), p. 1443.

24 Weber, 'Politik als Beruf', ibid., p. 530. English translation: H. H. Gerth and C. Wright Mills, eds., *From Max Weber: Essays in Sociology* (Glencoe, Ill., 1948), p. 111.

25 Otto Kirchheimer, 'Weimar – and Then What', in *Politics, Law and Social Change, Selected Essays* ed. by Frederic S. Burin and Kurt L. Shell (London, 1969), p. 46.

26 Ibid., p. 46.

27 Ibid., p. 47.

28 Weber, 'Der Reichspräsident', in *Gesammelte Politische Schriften*, p. 488.

29 Troeltsch, *Spektator-Briefe*, p. 110.

30 Karl Kautsky, *Die proletarische Revolution und ihr Programm* (Stuttgart, Berlin, 1922), p. 126. Quoted by Misch, *Das Wahlsystem*, p. 185, n. 88.

31 Letter to Wilhelm Sollmann, 7 May 1924. Quoted in Richard Breitmann, *German Socialism and Weimar Democracy* (Chapel Hill, 1981), p. 2.

32 Carlo Mierendorff, 'Wahlreform, die Losung der jüngeren Generation', *Neue Blätter für den Sozialismus* (1930), p. 342–9, quoted in Lange, *Wahlrecht*, p. 232. See also Julius Leber, 'Konservatives Wahlrecht', *Ein Mann geht seinen Weg: Schriften, Reden und Briefe* (Berlin, Frankfurt, 1952), pp. 104–5.

33 Richard N. Hunt, *German Social Democracy 1918–1933* (New Haven, 1964), pp. 89, 93.

34 Georg Kaisenberg, 'Wahlreform', *Zeitschrift für die gesamte Staatswissenschaft* (1931), p. 471.

35 Anthony P. Glees, *Exile Politics during the Second World War: The German Social Democrats in Britain* (Oxford, 1982), p. 97.

36 'On the State Structure of Germany', *Documents on International Affairs 1947–1948* (Oxford, 1952), p. 453. I owe this gem to my colleague Dr Jonathan Wright.

37 Roger H. Wells, 'State Governments', in Edward H. Litchfield, ed., *Governing Postwar Germany* (Ithaca, NY, 1953), p. 100.

38 Richard M. Scammon, 'Postwar Elections and Electoral Processes', ibid., p. 525.

39 For details and a good survey of British thinking, see Raymond Ebsworth, *Restoring Democracy in Germany: The British Contribution* (London, 1960), pp. 50–77.

40 Lange, *Wahlrecht*, pp. 222–3.

41 Friedrich Schäfer, 'Sozialdemokratie und Wahlrecht: Der Beitrag der Sozialdemokratie zur Gestaltung des Wahlrechts in Deutschland', *Verfassung und Verfassungswirklichkeit* (1967), p. 186.

42 *Stenographische Berichte über die Sitzungen des Parlamentarischen Rates über das Grundgesetz* (Bonn, 1948–9), 8 Sept. 1948, p. 22.

43 Ibid., 21 Oct. 1948, p. 122; 24 Feb. 1949, p. 144.
44 Ibid., 24 Feb. 1949, p. 131.
45 The phrase was coined by Dolf Sternberger in *Die Gegenwart*, 12 Sept. 1953.
46 Dolf Sternberger, 'Über das Wählen, die Wahl und das Wahlverfahren' (1946), *Die grosse Wahlreform* (Cologne, 1964), p. 15.
47 'Der Wähler hat gesiegt' (1957), ibid., p. 168.
48 Thomas von der Vring, *Reform oder Manipulation? Zur Diskussion eines neuen Wahlrechts* (Frankfurt, 1968), p. 123, n. 190.
49 Ferdinand A. Hermens and Hermann Unkelbach, 'Die Wissenschaft und das Wahlrecht', *Politische Vierteljahresschrift* (1967), p. 19.
50 Sternberger, 'Kontinuität und Elastizität in der Regierung' (1963), *Die grosse Wahlreform*, p. 246.
51 Rudolf Wildenmann, *Macht und Konsens als Problem der Innen- und Aussenpolitik* (Frankfurt, 1963), p. 6.
52 Gustav von Hartmann, *Ein neues Wahlverfahren*, (Berlin, 1966); H. U. Kantorowicz, 'Demokratie und Proportionalwahl-system', *Zeitschrift für Politik* (1910), pp. 552ff.
53 Walter Jellinek, 'Verhältniswahl und Führerauslese', *Archiv des öffentlichen Rechts* (1926), pp. 90–3, 96–8.
54 C. H. Bornemann, 'Einzelwahlkreis und Proporz: Ein Vorschlag zur Reichswahlreform', *Zeitschrift für Politik* (1931), pp. 43–9.
55 E.g., Wilhelm Keil, *Verhandlungen der Verfassunggebenden deutschen Nationalversammlung*, Verfassungsausschuss, vol. 336, p. 243.

SUGGESTIONS FOR FURTHER READING

Burkett, Tony, *Parties and Elections in West Germany: The Search for Stability* (London, 1975)
Büsch, Otto, Wölk, Monika and Wölk, Wolfgang, eds., *Wählerbewegung in der deutschen Geschichte Analysen und Berichte zu den Reichstagswahlen 1871–1933* (Berlin, 1979)
Conradt, David P., 'Electoral Law Politics in West Germany', *Political Studies*, 18 (Sept. 1970)
Ebsworth, Raymond, *Restoring Democracy in Germany: The British Contribution* (London, 1960)
Fenske, Hans, *Wahlrecht und Parteiensystem: Ein Beitrag zur deutschen Parteiengeschichte* (Frankfurt, 1972)
Jellinek, Walter, *Die deutschen Wahlgesetze* (Berlin, 1926)
Kitzinger, Uwe W., *German Electoral Politics: A Study of the 1957 Campaign* (Oxford, 1960)
Loewenberg, Gerhard, 'The Remaking of the German Party System', *Polity*, 1 (1968)
Merkl, Peter H., *The Origins of the West German Republic* (New York, 1963)
Milatz, Alfred, *Wähler und Wahlen in der Weimarer Republik* (Bonn, 1965)
Nipperdey, Thomas, *Die Organisation der deutschen Parteien vor 1918* (Düsseldorf, 1961)
Pollock, James K., 'The West German Electoral Law of 1953', *American Political Science Review*, 49 (1955)
Preece, Rodney J. C., *Land Elections in the German Federal Republic* (London, 1968)

Ritter, Gerhard A. and Niehuss, M., *Wahlgeschichtliches Arbeitsbuch: Materiallen zur Statistik des Kaiserreichs 1871–1918* (Munich, 1980)

Roberts, G. K., 'The Federal Republic of Germany' in Finer, S. E., ed., *Adversary Politics and Electoral Reform* (London, 1975)

Vogel, Bernhard, Nohlen, Dieter, Schulze, Rainer-Olaf, *Wahlen in Deutschland: Theorie-Geschichte-Dokumente* (Berlin, 1971)

Von der Vring, Thomas, *Reform oder Manipulation? Diskussion eines neuen Wahlrechts* (Frankfurt, 1968)

Ziegler, D. J., *Prelude to Democracy: A Study of Proportional Representation and the Heritage of Germany 1871–1920* University of Nebraska Studies, new series 20 (1958)

6

Italy

CHRISTOPHER SETON-WATSON

Italy has one of the most proportional and complex of electoral systems. It reflects all too faithfully the fragmentation and immobility of the Italian electorate. While it cannot be held responsible for creating the acute political difficulties from which Italy suffers, it can certainly be criticised for failing to contribute to their alleviation.

When the Kingdom of Italy came into existence in 1861, it took over from the Kingdom of Piedmont, together with much else, its electoral system. This was a single-member constituency, plurality system. It worked much as the French electoral system worked at that time: there were no organised parties, and elections were fought mainly by competing notables or loose ad hoc associations, most of them calling themselves 'liberal' or 'democratic'. Under 2% of the population had the vote in 1861, but successive extensions of the suffrage had increased the percentage to 23 by 1913, still exclusively male. Women did not receive the vote until 1946. It was in 1919 that mass Catholic and Socialist parties appeared for the first time, forced the adoption of proportional representation and transformed the political system, ending the hegemony of the old liberal elites. After only two elections the fascist party came to power and changed the electoral system to its own advantage. A few years later free elections ceased altogether.

When democracy was restored after 1945, PR was restored with it (though not in exactly the same form as in 1919–21). It was a natural decision. It was clear that Italian politics would be dominated by the same two mass parties, plus the Communists, who had hailed the introduction of PR in 1919 as a decisive step towards the democratisation of liberal Italy. The liberals wished to revert to the pre-1919 system, but they were now hopelessly outnumbered. In the chosen form of PR the principle of proportionality was given high priority. The system was also designed to ensure a major role in the electoral process for party organisation. It was used for the election of the Constituent Assembly in June 1946, the first free election for twenty-five years, and for the Chamber of Deputies; it has remained unchanged, save for a few very minor details, down to the present day.

Italy has a bicameral legislature. The Chamber of Deputies and the Senate are equal in power and prestige. The Senate's electorate is smaller than the

Chamber's, the minimum voting age being twenty-five not eighteen, and it is almost exactly half the size: 315 elected, and at present seven nominated or *ex officio* life members, compared with 630 in the Chamber of Deputies. The constituencies for the Senate are single-member, a concession to conservative opinion in the Constituent Assembly, and a candidate is elected if he wins 65% of the votes. This is a very rare occurrence (only two cases in 1976), so that normally the seats are allocated proportionately on a regional basis by the 'd'Hondt highest average' method. The difference in composition of the two chambers is therefore small.

The 630 members of the Lower House are elected in thirty-two constituencies. Except in one, the French-speaking Valle d'Aosta, whose size entitles it to only one seat, the 'Imperiali highest remainder' method of PR is used. Seats are allotted to the constituencies proportionally to their population (roughly one deputy per 80,000 inhabitants). They vary in size from 4 seats to 53 (the national average at the last election being 20.3).[1] In each constituency each competing party presents a list of candidates, one per seat. In 1979 nine national and three regional lists secured representation. There is no residence rule, though a local power base is often a determining factor in success. Candidates may stand in up to three constituencies, and concurrently for both Houses. If elected in more than one, they have free choice as to which to represent. When a deputy or senator dies or retires, his place is automatically filled by the next highest unelected candidate on the party list. There are therefore no by-elections. Voting is compulsory, but the only penalty incurred by an offender is to have his name posted outside the town hall in his commune of residence, and to have his 'certificate of good conduct', now largely fallen into disuse, stamped 'Did not vote' for five years. Turnout is extremely high: 89.1% in 1946, between 92.2% and 93.8% from 1948 to 1976. In 1979 it fell back to 89.1% – an index, it would seem, of voters' disgust with the recent malfunctioning of the political system.[2]

In addition each voter has a limited number of preference votes at his disposal: up to three in a constituency of fifteen members or less, and up to four in one of sixteen or more. He can thus indicate his order of preference for the candidates in the party list which he has chosen. The names or numbers of the candidates have to be written in, as only the party emblems appear on the ballot form.

The mechanics of the electoral process for the Chamber of Deputies are complex. After the votes are counted in each constituency, the total number cast is divided by the number of seats plus 2, to give the constituency quotient. To take the Como-Sondrio-Varese constituency in 1976 as an example (see Table 3), the quotient was 54,073. The Christian Democratic (DC) vote was 516,128, which gave it 9 seats ($9 \times 54,073 = 486,657$) and 29,471 remainders. After the same calculation had been made for all lists, 16 of the 19 seats had been allotted: 9 to DC, 5 to the Communists (PCI) and 2 to the Socialists (PSI): leaving 3 seats to be allotted from the national pool (*collegio unico nazionale*).

The total number of seats in the national pool in 1976 was 60 (out of 630).

The purpose of the 'corrected quotient' (i.e., dividing the total number of votes by the number of seats plus 2) is to lower the quotient and the 'cost' of the first seat, and so favour the smaller parties. It also has the effect of reducing the gap between the percentage of votes and the percentage of seats, and reducing the number of seats needing transfer to the national pool.

In order to obtain a share of the national pool, a party list must obtain at least one seat on a constituency quotient, and win a total of at least 300,000 votes nationally. In 1976 three parties failed to fulfil this condition, and three qualified for a share in the pool only by the bare minimum of one constituency seat (the Radical Party by only 351 votes). The national pool is administered by a central office under the Court of Cassation. It is made up of the sum of all remainders from all constituencies of all eligible parties. This sum is divided by the total number of unallocated seats, to give the national quotient. Each party's sum of remainders is then divided by the national quotient, and the seats are allocated first to each party nationally, by the same method as for the constituencies. Each party then allocates its share of seats to the constituencies in which the ratios of its remainders to the constituency quotient are largest. There is thus no national list. Finally, each party's allocation to individual candidates within each constituency is determined by the preferences expressed by the voters.

What are the political consequences of this system? Four stand out: (A) perpetuation of a multi-party system; (B) perpetual and unstable coalition government; (C) predominance of parties over government and parliament (what the Italians call *partitocrazia*); and (D) aggravation of internal party factionalism.

(A) PERPETUATION OF A MULTI-PARTY SYSTEM

In the 1979 Parliament twelve parties were represented in the Chamber of Deputies, ten in the Senate. Despite the priority given to proportionality, the match between votes and seats is not perfect. The two large parties, DC and PCI, have consistently obtained a slightly larger percentage of seats than of votes, while for all the other parties the percentage has (except for the PSI in 1972 and 1979) consistently been slightly smaller.[3] In 1976 it took just about twice as many votes to elect a Radical or Liberal deputy as a Communist or Christian Democrat. One of the causes of this distortion is the variation in the size of constituencies. Nevertheless, the system does produce a better match than most others, and certainly allows smaller parties to survive.

(B) PERPETUAL AND UNSTABLE COALITION GOVERNMENT

Table 1 shows that since the formation of the Centre–Left coalition in 1963, there have been twenty-one governments. The number since 1946 is thirty-nine, with an average life of 10.5 months. Two observations, however, must be made. First, that the image of instability is exaggerated unless it is realised that many of the changes in government shown in Table 1 would be called 'reshuffles' in Great Britain, and many ministries have been occupied by the same minister throughout several governments. Hence, though there have been thirty-six governments (by the Italian definition) since 1948, there have been only fifteen Prime Ministers, with an average tenure of 26.6 months, and the average tenure of the Ministry of Interior has been 29.3.

Second, though clearly a multi-party system, it is marked by the presence of two dominant parties, DC and PCI (see Table 2). In 1976 they together polled 73.1% of the votes and won 77.8% of the seats in the Chamber of Deputies, the most highly polarised result yet achieved. In 1979 the trend was reversed: the two dominant parties' combined vote dropped to 68.8% and the share of the three small Centre parties recovered from 7.8% to 8.8%.

Of the two dominant parties, one (DC) has been permanently in government, either by itself or in coalition, since 1944, and provided every Prime Minister from December 1945 down to June 1981. The other (PCI) has been permanently in opposition since 1947, except for the years 1976–9 when it first abstained and then entered the governmental majority, but not the government. In 1948 the DC won a majority of seats in the Chamber of Deputies, but its leader, De Gasperi, chose to continue his coalition with three small parties, the Liberal PLI, the Republican PRI and the Social Democrat PSDI. Since 1953 the DC has had no option: often it has formed single-party (*monocolore*) governments, but these have been dependent for survival upon the support, or at least abstention, of the small parties until 1962, and since 1962 of the PSI. The return of the PSI from the ghetto of opposition in 1962–3, to form the Centre–Left coalition, did not affect the DC's hegemony: the PSI, it is true, was larger than the PLI, PRI or PSDI, but it always remained subordinate.

This permanence of the DC in power, the most striking aspect of the Italian political system, is not the result of the electoral system, but of the nature of the other dominant party, the PCI. A majority of Italians still regard the PCI as an anti-system party which cannot be trusted to govern. There has therefore been no alternation of parties or coalitions in power. Such political change as *has* occurred has been within a very narrow range, and the result either of a shift in the balance of factions within the DC, or of a change of coalition partners (as in 1962–3), or sometimes of a coincidence of both.

In 1975–9 it seemed for the first time since 1947 that change was possible. The voting figures over thirty-one years (see Table 2) show a gradual decline of the DC and a gradual rise of the PCI. In the regional elections of 1975 the PCI vote was only 1.9% behind the DC's, and the parliamentary election which took place a year later took on some of the characteristics of a British general election: everyone was asking, would the PCI overtake (*sorpassare*) the DC, would the PCI or the DC be 'first-past-the-post'? Communist expectations were disappointed: the gap widened to 4.2%. In the next election, in June 1979, it widened further, to 7.7%, and the PCI vote dropped 4%, the first reverse since 1953. The electoral deadlock, the state of *immobilismo*, seemed more insoluble than ever. Despite the PCI's recent polemics with the CPSU over Poland, which seem to have brought the two parties very near to total rupture, there will still no doubt be many millions of Italians who doubt the reality of the change and continue to refuse to take the risk of voting the PCI into power. The possibility of a 'Left alternative', the formation of a left-wing coalition capable of replacing the DC and its partners, still seems remote. But should it occur, there will be no reason to change the electoral system.

One of the consequences of the multi-party system has been that the President of the Republic has often been obliged to play an active role in coalition-building. The present incumbent, Sandro Pertini, a Socialist elected in 1978 at the age of seventy-eight, has exercised the constitutional powers of his office to the limits, some would say even beyond. Not only has he conspicuously avoided calling upon those DC leaders whose reputations had been tarnished by scandal, but on two occasions he has endeavoured to obtain a non-DC Prime Minister. On the first occasion he failed, but on the second, in July 1981, his choice of the leader of the PRI, Giovanni Spadolini, was successful.

(c) PARTITOCRAZIA

The parties draw up the lists which are presented to the electors. As Duverger stated many years ago, in a multi-party system 'the internal oligarchy reigns supreme'.[4] The procedure for composing the lists varies between the parties. Both dominant parties have 'safe seats' at the top of their lists, and can therefore ensure that no leader, nor candidate particularly favoured by the leadership, are defeated. In this way the PCI, and to a lesser extent the DC, recruit sympathetic 'independents', without inflicting upon them the ordeal of the hustings. The DC is the more democratic in its procedure, leaving the major part of selection to its constituency branches. In the PCI the practice of democratic centralism is followed, and the national secretariat has the major say. The 'parachuting' of a candidate into a constituency by the secretariat is not uncommon. In such a system, given the size of the constituencies, the relationship between elector and deputy is bound to be remote.

The *partitocrazia* is also very potent at the later stage of the electoral process – that of coalition-building. In Italian parliamentary elections voters do not decide who shall lead the next government: rather, they register the success or failure of the current coalition, and can sometimes express, indirectly, a preference as to the composition of its successor. Sartori calls this process 'peripheral rotation'. It has been particularly evident in the last ten years. In the last three elections, 1972, 1976 and 1979, Parliament was dissolved before the end of its five-year term. On all these occasions the hopes of breaking the electoral deadlock proved vain. Nevertheless, the electorate has to a certain extent influenced the parties' internal balance of power and their alliance strategies.

To take one recent example: in 1975, after its dramatic defeat in the regional elections, the DC dismissed its intransigently anti-Communist National Secretary, Fanfani, and replaced him by Zaccagnini, a close ally of Moro and an advocate of a policy of accommodation (*confronto*) with the PCI. The swing to the Left in the 1976 parliamentary election strengthened the hands of Moro and Zaccagnini, and in 1977 the PCI entered the governmental majority in support of a five-party programme of 'national solidarity'. In 1978 Moro was assassinated by the Red Brigades and Zaccagnini announced his intention to resign. The 1979 election showed a swing back to the Right, and the DC followed suit at its congress in March 1980. Next month 'national solidarity' was decisively abandoned when the PSI entered the government in a reincarnation of the Centre-Left, and the PCI resumed its more familiar role of opposition. It can therefore be argued that in these last five years the influence of the electorate has not been wholly insignificant, but it has been very indirect.

(D) AGGRAVATION OF FACTIONALISM

The fragmentation of parties into *frazioni* or *correnti*, particularly marked in the DC, has been intensified by the preference vote system. About 30% of the voters make use of it. It is most used (sometimes by over 50%) in the South, where personalised clientelistic politics still widely prevail, and least in the northern cities, where its use sometimes falls below 15%. The DC makes more use of it than any other party.[5] Electors tend to concentrate their votes on leaders of national stature or on representatives of sectional interests (e.g., trade union, agricultural, confessional). A few thousand preference votes can separate a successful from an unsuccessful candidate, and 50% of those who receive preference votes are in fact elected.

All parties issue instructions to their supporters for the use of their preference votes. In the PCI these instructions are loyally carried out. In the DC the number of preference votes won is taken as an index of power, both for the person and for his *corrente*, and plays a vital role in internal party elections. It is also becoming more common for a politician, who has built up a regional or provincial base of power, to appeal directly to his electorate for preference votes in order to establish his claim to national recognition. A striking example was that of a young right-wing Christian Democrat, Massimo De Carolis, who was almost unknown in Rome until elected by a huge preference vote at Milan in 1976.

Preference votes can also be used negatively. In the 1976 election Zaccagnini, in an attempt to refurbish the DC's corrupt image, urged his supporters not to vote for those leaders whose reputations had been tarnished. As a result the ex-Prime Minister Rumor, who was under suspicion of involvement in the Lockheed scandal, was subjected to the humiliation of being displaced from the top of his party's list in his own fief of Venetia. The system of preference votes also has the effect of reinforcing the diffusion of power within the DC. Since De Gasperi it has had no single acknowledged leader. Instead power is spread both between the chiefs of the competing *correnti*, and between the party's President and Secretary, the Prime Minister and ministers, and the leaders of the party in the Chamber of Deputies and the Senate. Thus elections do not, as in the UK, strengthen or weaken the authority of the Prime Minister or leader of the opposition, but rather intensify the multi-leader character of the DC by indicating those members who must be found leading ministerial posts and receive appropriate patronage for their *correnti*.

The manifest malfunctions of the electoral system have in recent years encouraged some Italians to advocate reform. So far none of their proposals have got beyond the talking stage, and there the sceptics expect them to remain. Since 1946 only one substantial attempt has been made, in 1953. De Gasperi's coalition had won a decisive majority in the 1948 election, and in the tense atmosphere of the Cold War it wished to preserve that majority in the interests of stable democracy by manipulating the electoral system. According to the new law, passed after some of the stormiest battles in Italian parliamentary history, any combination (*apparentamento*) of parties which obtained 50% plus one of the votes would obtain a 'majority premium' of 65% of the seats in the Chamber of Deputies. The law was modelled on the French electoral law of 1951, but because of its unfortunate resemblance to the Acerbo law of 1923, which had given the fascists an artificial parliamentary majority,[6] it was convincingly denounced by the opposition as a *legge truffa* (swindle law), a label that has stuck till this day. At the subsequent election on 7 June 1953, De Gasperi's coalition failed to reach the 50% plus 1 by 0.85%. This discredited the whole idea of electoral reform for about twenty years. In July 1954 Parliament decided to swing to the opposite extreme and revert to proportional representation in a decisively proportional form.

Today the favourite model, advocated by both the recently elected Secretary of the DC, Ciriaco De Mita, and Bettino Craxi, the leader of the PSI, is that of West Germany. This, if adopted, would, according to an article in the weekly *Panorama* in October 1979, not much alter the electoral performance of the two dominant parties, nor of the two medium-size parties (PSI and the neo-fascist MSI): their gain or loss in votes would be between 1% and 2%. But the 5% rule would eliminate the small parties, including the PLI, PSDI, PRI, Radicals and Extreme Left, while the Südtiroler Volkspartei, with a strong ethnic base in the single region of Trentino-Alto Adige, would survive. Both DC and PSI would obviously be competitors for the votes of the eliminated parties. The DC could hope to attract former PLI and PSDI voters, and so strengthen its hegemonic position. The PSI could hope to attract former PRI and Radical voters, and possibly some anti-clerical liberals as well. Craxi's ambition to build up a centre bloc between the DC and the PCI, which would play a commanding role like that of the FDP in West Germany, is well known.

The French Fifth Republic's double-ballot system also has its supporters. The veteran Socialist, Francesco De Martino, former party Secretary, argues that by forcing the small parties to coalesce, it would open the way for alternation of right- and left-wing coalitions in power. A leading political scientist, Domenico Fisichella, argues the same case in his chapter in *Adversary Politics and Electoral Reform*, and asserts that a double-ballot system would diminish the parliamentary strength of the PCI, just as it diminished that of the PCF in France.[7]

Nobody seems to want to adopt the Westminster model. The *Panorama* article, referred to above, calculated that, given present voting patterns, the British electoral system would in June 1979 have given 72.2% of the seats in the Chamber of Deputies to the DC, 27.4% to the PCI and 0.6% to the List for Trieste, a party confined to the single region of Friuli-Venezia Giulia. The inevitable consequence, given the present constraints on the PCI's appeal, would be the consolidation of the DC's permanence in power. By eliminating the smaller parties and removing the need for coalition-making, that element of flexibility in the Italian party system, which provides the only opportunity for change, would disappear.[8] It was this spectre that worried many Italians in 1976, when the increased polarisation seemed to indicate movement towards a battle between the two ideologically opposed giants, *muro contro muro* (brick wall against brick wall) which pessimists foretold might lead even to civil war.

In conclusion it must be emphasised that adversary politics are deeply alien to the Italian political culture. There have of course been periods when Italy was split by one single cleavage: the pro-war parties versus the anti-war parties in 1914–19; fascism versus anti-fascism between 1943 and 1945; and pro-communism versus anti-communism between 1947 and 1956. But the dominant tradition is one of accommodation and compromise. The process of convergence towards the Centre, and of absorption of anti-system forces, has been called by many different names during the last 130 years: Cavour's *connubio* in 1852, Depretis' *trasformismo* in the 1880s, *giolittismo* between 1903 and 1914;[9] and since 1945 the Centre-Left of 1962–3, Berlinguer's 'historic compromise' of 1973 and Moro's *confronto* of 1976 with the PCI. Its essence was the blurring of the difference between government and opposition and indulgence in the intricate game of coalition-building, in a search for a consensus which will soothe rather than exacerbate the social and ideological divisions from which Italy still suffers. This is the case for retaining the Italian electoral system.

Table 1 *Italian governments 1963–1981*

	Prime Minister	Participants	Support in Parliament	Abstention in Parliament
Dec. 1963	Moro I	DC, PSI, PSDI, PRI		
Jul. 1964	Moro II	DC, PSI, PSDI, PRI		
Feb. 1966	Moro III	DC, PSI, PSDI, PRI		
Jun. 1968	Leone II	DC	PSU, PRI	
Dec. 1968	Rumor I	DC, PSU, PRI		
Aug. 1969	Rumor II	DC	PSI, PSDI	PRI
Mar. 1970	Rumor III	DC, PSI, PSDI, PRI		
Aug. 1970	Colombo	DC, PSI, PSDI, PRI		
Feb. 1972	Andreotti I	DC	PLI, PSDI, PRI	
Jun. 1972	Andreotti II	DC, PSDI, PLI	PRI	
Jul. 1973	Rumor IV	DC, PSI, PSDI, PRI		
Mar. 1974	Rumor V	DC, PSI, PSDI	PRI	
Nov. 1974	Moro IV	DC, PRI	PSI, PSDI	PLI
Feb. 1976	Moro V	DC	PSDI	PSI, PRI, PLI
Jul. 1976	Andreotti III	DC		PCI, PSI, PSDI, PRI, PLI
Mar. 1978	Andreotti IV	DC	PCI, PSI, PSDI, PRI	PLI
Mar. 1979	Andreotti V	DC, PSDI, PRI	PSI	PCI, PLI
Aug. 1979	Cossiga I	DC, PSDI, PLI	PSI, PRI	
Apr. 1980	Cossiga II	DC, PSI, PRI		PSDI, PLI
Oct. 1980	Forlani	DC, PSI, PSDI, PRI		PLI
Jun. 1981	Spadolini	PRI, DC, PSI, PSDI, PLI		

DC: Democrazia cristiana
PCI: Partito comunista italiano
PLI: Partito liberale italiano
PRI: Partito republicano italiano
PSDI: Partito socialista democratico italiano
PSI: Partito socialista italiano
PSU: Partiti socialisti unificati (union of PSI and PSDI, 1966–9)

Table 2 *Elections to Chamber of Deputies 1946–1979*

| | % Votes | | | | | | | | | % of seats |
	1946[a]	1948	1953	1958	1963	1968	1972	1976	1979	1979
PCI	19.0	31.0	22.6	22.7	25.3	26.9	27.2	34.4	30.4	32.0
PSI	20.7		12.7	14.2	13.8	14.5[b]	9.6	9.6	9.8	9.9
PR	–	–	–	–	–	–	–	1.1	3.5	2.9
PSDI	–	7.1	4.5	4.5	6.1	[b]	5.1	3.4	3.8	3.3
PRI	4.4	2.5	1.6	1.4	1.4	2.0	2.9	3.1	3.0	2.4
DC	35.2	48.5	40.1	42.4	38.3	39.1	38.7	38.7	38.4	41.5
PLI	6.8	3.8	3.0	3.5	7.0	5.8	3.9	1.3	2.0	1.4
Extreme right	5.3	4.8	12.7	9.6	6.8	5.7	8.7	6.1	5.3	4.9

| | % Share of votes and share of seats | | | | | | | | |
| | Christian Democrats | | | Communists | | | Socialists | | |
	Votes	Seats		Votes	Seats		Votes	Seats	
1946[a]	35.2	37.3	+2.1	19.0	18.7	−0.3	20.7	20.7	–
1948	48.5	53.1	+4.6	31.0[c]	31.9[c]	+0.9[c]	c	c	c
1953	40.1	44.6	+4.5	22.6	24.2	+1.6	12.7	12.7	–
1958	42.4	45.8	+3.4	22.7	23.5	+0.8	14.2	14.1	−0.1
1963	38.3	41.3	+3.0	25.3	26.3	+1.0	13.8	13.8	–
1968	39.1	42.2	+3.1	26.9	28.1	+1.2	14.5	14.4	−0.1
1972	38.7	42.0	+3.3	27.2	28.4	+1.2	9.6	9.7	+0.1
1976	38.7	41.6	+2.9	34.4	36.2	+1.8	9.6	9.1	−0.5
1979	38.4	41.5	+3.1	30.4	32.0	+1.6	9.8	9.9	+0.1

Note: Minor parties were in almost all cases slightly underrepresented but the difference between votes and seats never exceeded 1.0% except for the PSDI on two occasions (1948 – votes 7.1%, seats 5.8%; 1953 – votes 4.5%, seats 3.2%).
[a] Constituent Assembly.
[b] The Socialists and PSDI fought the 1968 election as a single united party (PSU).
[c] The Socialists and Communists fought the 1948 election in alliance.
Source: based on tables in Alberto Spreafico, 'Notes de Scrutin et de Referendum en Italie'.

Table 3 *Operation of the Imperiali largest remainder formula: 1976 Chamber election, Como-Sondrio-Varese district*

Party	Popular vote	Seats at district level[a]	Remainders to national pool	National pool seats in district[b]	Total seats
Christian Democrats	516,128	9	29,471	0	9
Communists	308,661	5	38,296	0	5
Socialists	134,574	2	26,428	0	2
Social Democrats	42,563	0	42,563	0	0
Republicans	37,860	0	37,860	1	1
Liberals	20,040	0	20,040	0	0
Italian Social Movement	41,237	0	41,237	1	1
Proletarian Democracy	23,138	0	23,138	1	1
Radicals	11,398	0	11,398	0	0

[a] To determine the initial seats and remainders:

$$(1)\ \text{quota} = \frac{\text{total votes cast in district}}{\text{seats plus two}}$$

$$\text{quota} = \frac{1,135,539}{19+2}$$

$$\text{quota} = 54,073$$

$$(2)\ \frac{\text{Seats}}{+} \atop \text{remainder} = \frac{\text{votes for party}}{\text{quota}}$$

For the DC,

$$\frac{\text{seats}}{+} \atop \text{remainder} = \frac{516,128}{54,073}$$

$$\frac{\text{seats}}{+} \atop \text{remainder} = \frac{9}{+} \atop 29,471$$

[b] This was the sixth of seven national pool seats for the Republicans, the fourth of eight for the Italian Social Movement and the fifth of five for the Proletarian Democracy, based on the ratio of the remainder to the district quota.

Source: Howard R. Penniman, ed., *Italy at the Polls: The Parliamentary Elections of 1976* (Washington, DC, 1977), p. 46.

NOTES

1 The boundaries of the constituencies were determined by a governmental decree of March 1946 on no apparent general principle. They do not always coincide with provincial and regional boundaries. No move has been made since 1946 to revise them.
2 The highest turnout in liberal pre-fascist Italy was 65% in 1909.
3 Since 1958 the maximum percentage discrepancy has been +3.4 for DC, +1.8 for PCI, −1.9 for Extreme Right, and −1.0 for all the others. For the percentages of votes and seats, see Table 2.
4 Maurice Duverger: *Political Parties*, 2nd edn (London, 1959), pp. 151–2.
5 In 1972 the national average percentage of DC preference votes cast was 39.1, the highest (66.8) in the southern constituency of Benevento-Avellino-Salerno, the lowest (13.1) in Trieste. 'The struggle for the preference vote is the nub of Neapolitan politics', writes P. A. Allum in *Politics and Society in Post-War Naples* (Cambridge, 1973), p. 154.
6 An important difference was that in 1923 the percentage of votes required to obtain the 'majority premium' was only twenty-five.
7 Domenico Fisichella, 'The Italian Experience', in S. E. Finer, ed., *Adversary Politics and Electoral Reform* (London, 1975), pp. 261–4.
8 It should be noted that the smaller parties have contributed far more than their share of competent, distinguished and respected political leaders, including the former Prime Minister, Senator Spadolini, whose party (PRI) won only 3.4% of the votes and six of the 315 seats in the senatorial election of 1979. President Pertini has recently described the smaller parties as 'the salt' of the Italian political system.
9 The *connubio* was a coalition between Cavour's Right Centre and Rattazzi's Left Centre: *trasformismo* was originally a coalition between Depretis' moderate Left and Minghetti's moderate Right; *giolittismo* was the method of government whereby Giolitti attempted, with considerable success, to draw into the political system the hitherto anti-system forces of catholicism and socialism.

SUGGESTIONS FOR FURTHER READING

J. C. Adams and P. Barile, *The Government of Republican Italy*, 3rd edn (Boston, Mass., 1972)
P. A. Allum, *Italy – Republic without Government?* (London, 1973)
  Politics and Society in Post-War Naples (Cambridge, 1973)
Domenico Fisichella, 'The Italian Experience', in S. E. Finer, ed., *Adversary Politics and Electoral Reform* (London, 1975)
Dante Germino and Stefano Passigli, *The Government and Politics of Contemporary Italy* (New York, 1968)
Howard R. Penniman, ed., *Italy at the Polls: The Parliamentary Elections of 1976* (Washington, DC, 1977), especially chap. 2: D. Wertman, 'The Italian Electoral Process'
  ed., *Italy at the Polls: A Study of the Parliamentary Elections of 1979* (Washington, DC, 1981)
Giovanni Schepis, 'Storia dei sistemi elettorali in Italia', in *Enciclopedia del Diritto*, vol 14
R. Zariski, *Italy: The Politics of Uneven Development* (New York, 1971)

7

Scandinavia

BO SÄRLVIK

There are not many of the existing methods of translating votes of a national electorate into seats in a Parliament that have not been tried at one time or another in at least one of the Nordic countries.* Denmark is of course the historical origin of the single transferable vote (in Andrae's version), although it was then practised in a severely restricted suffrage in elections for a Second Chamber.

During the period immediately before the transition to proportional representation, Denmark and Sweden elected their Lower Chambers in single-member constituencies with the first-past-the-post system, whereas the Norwegian Storting was elected in two-round elections (with an absolute majority required for election of a candidate in the first round) in single-member constituencies. Finland went directly from the old Four Estate Diet, in 1906, to a unicameral Parliament, and at the same time followed Belgium's example by introducing proportional representation in multi-member con-stituencies. In Sweden, the first elections of the Lower Chamber of the Riksdag under a proportional system were held in 1911. Denmark adopted a fully proportional system for election of the Lower Chamber of its Parliament in 1920, and Norway changed at about the same time with the first proportional elections being held in 1921. Like Finland, all these three countries employed the d'Hondt method for allocation of seats to parties in the multi-member constituencies. But Denmark also used the Sainte-Laguë formula for the allocation of 'additional seats'.

In the early fifties, Sweden replaced the d'Hondt proportional method with a modified version of the Sainte-Laguë method, and soon after the same formula was adopted in both Denmark and Norway, although the three election systems still differed in other respects. At about the same time Denmark abolished the Second Chamber of its Parliament. It is only to be expected, perhaps, that

---

* This chapter is concerned only with Denmark, Finland, Norway and Sweden, but the Nordic countries as a political and cultural region do, of course, also include Iceland. Moreover, although the Faroes and Greenland are represented in the Danish Parliament, they have an autonomous status and representative assemblies of their own; likewise, the island of Åland has a degree of autonomy although it is part of Finland.

constitutional forms and election procedures tried out in one country are later adopted, albeit often in a modified form, by one or more of the others, given the similarity and the close contacts among the political systems in the Nordic regions. Denmark's electoral system included since 1918 a national pool of parliamentary seats which in each election were allocated so as to even out deviations from proportionality. When Sweden abandoned the two-chamber system, it was its turn to follow Denmark's example by introducing a similar national pool of additional seats; the new system came into effect at the first election of the unicameral Riksdag in 1970.

Both the introduction of proportional representation and the subsequent changes in the electoral order of each of these Nordic countries have undoubtedly had significant consequences for their party systems. But, equally, the developments in these countries can be taken to illustrate how the electoral order was adapted to the requirements of multi-party systems that pre-dated the change to proportional representation. Finland is, perhaps, a partial exception, inasmuch as a national party system was only emerging at the time of the 1906 reform. But it was already obvious that more than two significant forces were in existence, and none of these political groupings were inclined to take the risk of being squeezed out by the effects of the first-past-the-post system. In Denmark, Norway and Sweden the extension of the suffrage meant that a rapidly growing Social Democrat Party was added to the old dualism between a conservative Right and a liberal Left; in Denmark the transition to a parliamentary system of government was fraught with controversies that resulted in the splitting of the old Left. It is true, however, that the proportional system almost immediately after its introduction enabled Communist parties to win parliamentary seats and created conditions under which the agrarian parties in Norway and Sweden could be established as significant political forces. Likewise, through the following decades each of these four countries has seen the emergence of parties, and party splits, to which proportional representation has (at the least) been conducive.

When one looks back at the ways in which the electoral systems have developed in the four countries, it becomes apparent that changes in the electoral order have always come about as a result of a change in the balance of forces or in the structure of the party systems. Electoral systems are devised by political parties in response to political circumstances; in no case has a single party commanded a parliamentary strength of its own that could have allowed it to impose an electoral order against the opposition of all other parties. Changes in the electoral system have been the outcome of protracted negotiations, alliances and deals that finally led to a decision supported by more than one party. Thus, in Sweden the introduction of proportional representation was a concession that the Conservatives demanded in exchange for general suffrage. In Norway the change was delayed to 1919 when the disproportionality in the representation of the country's six parties caused widespread dismay, and when it had ceased to sustain a parliamentary majority for the Left – the dominant party in the preceding period; until then the two-round elections had consistently ensured that the Labour Party was under-represented in the Storting. The change to proportional representation in Denmark was part of a protracted process of democratisation of the constitution and was actually finalised in the midst of a heated political crisis. In all instances, the change was made for a well-understood purpose: the election system was adapted to the existing party system. The concrete political contexts in which this happened were not identical, but they had two common features. The party (or parties) that stood to lose because of the change was in a position that made it necessary to make concessions, and the parties that wished a change could not achieve this without also granting proportional representation (or nearly so) for all significant parties. By settling for proportional representation, the major parties ensured that none of them was likely to be squeezed out by under-representation. It became, of course, more difficult for any party to win an overall majority, but at the time this did not in any case seem a very likely prospect (with the exception, possibly, of the Social Democrat parties). There was, however, a cost to the major parties: the door was opened to at least some further fractionalisation of the party system. The 1920s became a period of minority governments and coalition government. In Denmark, Norway and Sweden, the era of Social Democratic dominance from the 1930s to the 1960s (Norway) or 1970s (Sweden) was a period of greater governmental stability (although it was often based on coalitions or alliances between the large Social Democrat Party and another party). When that era came to an end, the performance of the parliamentary system of government again took on some of the features that are normally associated with a multi-party system under proportional representation: unstable coalition governments, minority governments and a further proliferation of parties.

Yet, the party systems in Denmark, Norway and Sweden still retain much of their common historical pattern: a large Social Democrat Party, flanked on the Left by a Left-Socialist or Communist Party of at least some significance, at the opposite pole a traditional Conservative Party (since the 1970s competing with right-wing populist parties in Denmark and Norway), and a political centre which includes more than one party and where the differences between the parties partly reflect old rural–urban and cultural cleavages. The structure of the Finnish party system does not entirely lack these common features, but the rupture during the civil war, the impact of the wars with the Soviet Union during the Second World War and the much larger agricultural sector have all made for significant differences. The Communists (or more precisely the People's Democratic League in which the Communists are the dominant component) is one of the larger parties, and the Social Democrats are correspondingly weaker; the Centre (formerly Agrarian) Party has been a natural member of the coalition governments that have been in office throughout the postwar period; the Conservative Party is placed in a somewhat isolated position for foreign policy reasons; and there is, finally, a small but politically significant Centre Party that represents the Swedish-speaking minority.

Historically, the major parties in Scandinavia are rooted in political movements which already enjoyed a considerable degree of organisational articulation and substantial memberships at the time of the extension of the suffrage, and the establishing of a parliamentary system of government, first in Norway, then in Denmark, Finland and Sweden. The ties between parties and other organisations with mass memberships were often strong: the trade unions, farmers' organisations and, especially in the early stages, the temperance movements and the free churches all had links or at least bonds of ideological affinity with political movements. The resulting pattern could not easily be subsumed under one political dualism in the party system; and there was anyhow enough of geographical variation to prevent any one dualism from becoming the predominant one in the entire national electorate. Already in its early stages, the emergence of the party system coincided with battles over national political issues that had continued for decades and now found their expression in the parties: Members of Parliament came early to be seen as representatives of national parties and as legislators rather than as representatives for (even less as delegates for) localities. If political representation is at all tied to localities, this is in the form of a correspondence between constituencies and administrative and local government units (counties), whose boundaries are often embedded in historical tradition; these have provided a natural framework for multi-member constituencies, with representation according to population size. All these traits in the political culture contributed to make the transition to proportional representation an almost natural part of the democratisation process that occurred in the four countries during the decades before the First World War and was completed throughout the region in the years immediately after the war. And they still make the proportional translation of votes for parties into parliamentary seats a rarely challenged assumption about how the democratic system should work.

British observers often find it hard to understand how members in large multi-member constituencies can carry out the constituency work that is presumed to be so significant a part of a British MP's duties. The answer is probably that the role of Members of Parliament in these Nordic countries is more different from that of their British counterparts than is commonly appreciated. The constitutions are different and the system of public law is different. The administrative process is essentially a legal process in which redress of grievances is achieved through legally regulated appeal procedures. Sweden has gone farther than the other countries in separating administrative decision-making from direct intervention by the central government or ministers, but the overall pattern in all of these countries is distinctly different from that of the British civil service. Moreover, local self-government has a high degree of autonomy and its own appeal procedures. There is simply not much room for a Member of Parliament to act as a 'middle man' who assists his constituents in their private dealings with authorities. The function of protecting citizens against arbitrary administrative decisions is fulfilled by other means. To put it bluntly, a substantial portion of the tasks a British MP carries out on behalf of individual constituents could in the Swedish context well be seen as attempts to exercise improper political influence on the due process of administrative law. The important linkages between the Members and their constituencies are of a different nature: a large portion of them began their career in local government, many continue to hold elected office in local government. They will certainly also be sensitive to their constituencies' needs in matters like industrial development, employment or road-building, and they will maintain contacts with local interest organisations to that end; but for the representation of such demands a constituency that comprises a region may well be more functional than a smaller locality.

We have already stressed that changes in the electoral law come about as responses to changes in the political context: public opinion plays a role when such changes occur, but there is little doubt that political parties are the decisive actors when a new electoral order is established. In the next section, we will examine how these decisions are made using Sweden as a case study. We will then go on to examine in some further detail the mechanics of the electoral systems in all the four countries. In the concluding sections we shall look at the working and political consequences of these election systems in contemporary politics. Just how proportional are they? Are the thresholds sufficiently high to prevent a proliferation of small parties? What are the consequences for the working of the parliamentary system of government?

THE POLITICS OF ELECTORAL LAW-MAKING: THE CASE OF SWEDEN

Adapting the election system to a government coalition

Why did Sweden change its electoral system just in time for the parliamentary elections of 1952? Ever since proportional representation was introduced, the d'Hondt formula for the allocation of seats had been in use. Since the 1920s elections were conducted in comparatively large constituencies with an average of around 8 seats per constituency. This did in itself serve to give smaller parties a better chance to win seats than they would have when the d'Hondt method is applied in small constituencies. Moreover, *apparentement* had been incorporated in a form that allowed a party to put forward its own party list whilst at the same time forming an 'electoral cartel' of parties. The seats won by a cartel were then divided among the participating parties through the continued use of the d'Hondt formula. (On the ballot paper, there would then appear both the name of the party and, above it, the label of the cartel.) In general, the non-socialist parties formed a cartel, whilst the Social Democrats and the Communists did not. Given that the 'bourgeois' cartel's voting support was of the same magnitude as that of the Social Democratic party, the cartel allowed the non-socialist parties to overcome the under-representation of small parties that is built into the d'Hondt method. Only the Communists were systematically under-represented, whilst the Social Democrats, as the largest party, could benefit from the election system by winning a moderate over-representation at the Communists' expense.

In 1950, the Social Democratic government yielded to the pressures from the non-socialist parties and agreed to set up a committee of inquiry to review the election system, although it was hard to discern any enthusiasm for a change to perfect proportionality among the Social Democrats. But in 1951 it all changed. The Social Democrats formed a coalition government with the Agrarian Party and parliamentary elections were due in the following year. Could a party in a coalition government go to the country in an electoral alliance with the opposition parties? The Social Democrats and the Agrarian Party had, of course, formed a coalition government previously, in the 1930s, but in no previous parliamentary election had the Agrarian Party actually been in a coalition with the Social Democrats before an election (except in the National coalition government during the war). Moreover, this time it would be a lot harder to re-establish a non-socialist cartel, even if the Agrarian Party had wished to do so. To make matters worse, the Agrarian Party leaders also feared that they would suffer a heavy loss of support if they ventured to form a cartel with the Social Democrats. The farmers that formed the large majority in the Agrarian Party's electoral base might accept the government coalition as a marriage of convenience; but it was entirely a different matter actually to ask them to cast their votes for a cartel that included the Social Democrats. The dividing line between socialist and non-socialist parties was a political and psychological reality that could not be disregarded.

What was needed – from the coalition parties' point of view – was an election system that could guarantee the Agrarian Party a proportional share of the seats without entering any electoral cartel and at the same time did not rob the Social Democrats of their moderate degree of over-representation under the d'Hondt system. To put it another way: the parties in the coalition wanted a system that preserved the under-representation of the Communist Party whilst eliminating the need for an electoral alliance between the non-socialist parties.

Luckily the committee of inquiry had considered – among other alternatives – a system that appeared to achieve precisely that result. This would be effected by a change from the use of the d'Hondt formula for the allocation of seats within constituencies to a modified version of the Sainte-Laguë formula. Both

Table 1 *The distribution of seats yielded by the d'Hondt method (with non-socialist cartel) and the Sainte-Lagüe method (without cartel) when applied to the results of the election in 1948*

	d'Hondt	Modified Sainte-Lagüe[a]	Original Sainte-Lagüe[b]	Exactly proportional
Conservatives	23	21	29	28
Liberals	57	56	53	53
Agrarian Party	30	30	30	28
Social Democrats	112	113	106	107
Communists	8	10	12	14
TOTAL	230	230	230	230

[a] Sainte-Lagüe's formula with 1.5 as first divisor.
[b] Sainte-Lagüe's formula with 1 as first divisor.
Source: Det proportionella valsättet vid val till riksdagens andra kammare: 1950 års volkomröstnings- och valsättsutrednings betänkande, I, Statens offentliga utredningar (1951), p. 114.

formulae involve the calculation of a series of quotas; a party's number of votes is successively divided by a divisor that increases for each seat that it has been allocated. Sainte-Lagüe's formula is in general more favourable than the d'Hondt formula for small- and medium-sized parties in competition with a big party. The proposed modification of the Sainte-Lagüe formula meant that the number 1.5 rather than 1.0 would be used as the first divisor. The modified version is less favourable than the original formula for a party whose share of the vote in a constituency is on the borderline between winning one seat or no seat; the raising of the first divisor increases the threshold that such a party has to pass in order to win a seat. In effect, the modified formula was designed so as to result in near-proportionality for medium-sized parties, a modest bonus to a big party and under-representation of very small parties (although slightly less so than the d'Hondt formula).

The committee report presented applications of a range of different PR formulae to a series of previous elections, thus enabling the politicians to compare them on a reasonably realistic basis. How the proposed modification of the Saint-Lagüe formula related to the result of the d'Hondt method (with a non-socialist cartel) in the 1948 election is shown in Table 1. It appeared evident that the proposed system would have yielded almost exactly the same distribution of seats as the old method – but with the difference that no electoral cartel was required.

There was one obstacle, however. The Conservatives and the Liberals argued with some vehemence that the proposed system was too favourable to the Social Democrats and wanted to further steps towards full proportionality – at least with regard to the division of seats among the Social Democrats and the non-socialist parties. The Social Democrats, on their side, wanted the election system to be sufficiently favourable to the largest party to ensure that most of the under-representation of the Communists would accrue to the Social Democrats. Some measure of accommodation was deemed necessary by the coalition parties, however. The outcome was that the Sainte-Laguë formula was adopted but with the first divisor set to 1.4 rather than 1.5; the effect was to reduce the expected over-representation for the Social Democrats slightly, but largely retain the under-representation of the Communists.

The first divisor of 1.4 emerged as the result of a great deal of political controversy. It has no specific mathematical meaning in terms of defining any uniform threshold of representation or maximising proportionality with respect to any particular criterion. But it served the purpose it was intended to serve: to do away with the need for a bourgeois cartel without otherwise changing much in the distribution of seats that the earlier election system would have produced.

Adapting the electoral system to a unicameral Riksdag

Before the 1970 elections to the first unicameral Riksdag, the election system was changed again. Of the 350 members (later changed to 349) of the Riksdag, 310 were to be elected with the same method as before in twenty-eight constituencies. But 40 (later changed to 39) seats were to be distributed among the parties so as to eliminate the deviations from overall proportionality that could result from the allocation of seats within the constituencies. (The procedure is described more fully in a following section.) At the same time, however, a new threshold was set up against very small parties. In general, no party that has received less than 4% of the vote in the country as a whole is entitled to any representation in the Riksdag. An exception is made only for parties that achieve at least 12% of the vote in a constituency but fail to achieve 4% of the national vote. Such parties keep the seats they may have won in the constituency (or constituencies) where they have got 12% of the vote but do not get any of the additional seats. This provision was tailor-made to allow the Communists to win at least some seats in their historically strongest constituency, even if they were to fail the national threshold. The new method obviously yields a virtually exactly proportional distribution of seats among the parties that have passed the 4% threshold.

The new electoral order was part of an important constitutional reform which ultimately gave the country an entirely new constitution, but its adoption with Social Democratic support also signalled that the political context had changed since the early 1950s. The Social Democrats had obviously shifted their ground on the election system. For decades they had argued for an election system that would guarantee the largest party at least a measure of over-representation in the Riksdag; indeed, only a few years before the change they had rejected a proposed election system in a committee of inquiry for that reason. Why did they now accept a system that was likely to result in virtually exactly proportional representation? One reason was certainly a desire to achieve something close to a consensus: the new system could be adopted with the support of all parties except the Communists. And anyhow the Social Democrats did not command a parliamentary majority of their own in the Riksdag when the decision was made (1968).

Yet, it must have been obvious for everyone that it would be harder than before for the Social Democrats to achieve a reasonably stable basis for a one-party government in the new Riksdag. The Upper Chamber, where an over-representation of the Social Democrats had served as a buffer in the past, was no longer there. The era when the Social Democrats could hope to stay in office with the support of the Agrarian Party had also vanished – the Agrarians had become the Centre Party with a much widened base in the centre of the party system; in the future it would be much more likely to align itself with the other bourgeois parties. And without over-representation at the expense of the Communists, the Social Democrats would not only find it difficult to win a majority of their own in the Riksdag (they had won a majority of the votes in only two second chamber elections: 1940 and 1968), but even to gain a larger number of seats than the three bourgeois parties together.

One important factor was certainly that none of the bourgeois parties was any more willing to agree to anything less than full proportionality in comparison with the Social Democrats; if there were to be spoils at the expense of small parties, they wanted them fairly divided. Another factor was that the Social Democrats and the Communists tend to some extent to win and lose votes at each others' expense. When the decision about the election system was taken, the Social Democrats were still smarting under a damaging setback in the 1966 local elections (where the Communist vote had marginally increased) and they could hardly foresee that they were to win a convincing electoral victory in 1968. In that light, the new system had certain potential advantages: if the Communists were to suffer a decline and fail the 4% threshold – then the Social Democrats would stand a good chance of winning a larger electoral support than the three bourgeois parties taken together. In that case, a strictly proportional division of the seats among the parties above the threshold would create a parliamentary majority for the Social Democrats. On the other hand, if the Communists were gaining support in an election when the Social Democrats lost votes, an under-representation of the Communists might well result in a bourgeois majority in the Riksdag even if there was a socialist majority in the electorate. Hence, when the Communist vote was too large to be insignificant for the balance in the Riksdag, it was essential that they should have proportional representation. All this required, of course, that the Communists could be counted upon to sustain Social Democratic governments when the two parties together held a majority in the Parliament; but that could be considered a fairly safe assumption.

If this makes sense, why would the bourgeois parties wish to have proportional representation with a threshold? Firstly, these parties, like the Social Democrats, certainly had a genuine wish to find a PR system that would be seen to be fair and at the same time erected a barrier against the proliferation of small parties. In addition there was a political consideration: the new Christian Democratic Party was still only a fledgling but it could conceivably drain away a crucial portion of the bourgeois parties' voting support; a threshold that discouraged small parties must have appeared a prudent safeguard.

THE MECHANICS OF PROPORTIONAL REPRESENTATION IN THE NORDIC COUNTRIES

As we have seen, elections in all the four countries are conducted in multi-member constituencies. Electors always cast their votes for a party by voting for party candidates. Only one vote is cast – in Norway and Sweden this is a vote for a list of candidates, in Denmark it is a vote for a party together with, if the elector wishes, a simultaneous preference vote for one of its candidates; in Finland the vote is cast for a candidate of the party that the voter wishes to support. No by-elections are held.[1] If a seat becomes vacant because of resignation or death, the place is always filled by the candidate 'next in turn' on the list of the party concerned. There are variations, however, in the mechanics of proportional representation which we will now look at: the use of a national pool of additional seats, thresholds for representation and preference voting for candidates.

Additional seats

It is well known that the mere division of a country into multi-member constituencies may result in deviations from a proportional distribution of the seats among the Parliament at the national level. As mentioned above, the Danish and Swedish election systems include a pool of seats that are allocated so as to even out such effects. In both countries, these additional seats can be described as geographically 'floating seats', since their allocation across parties and constituencies can only be determined after the election. Each party will receive its additional seats in those constituencies where it is found to be 'most entitled to' additional representation. The candidate elected to an additional seat in a constituency will always be the one who is 'next in turn' in the rank-ordering of the party's constituency candidates (as determined by his place on the party list or by preference votes). Thus, no separate candidate lists

Table 2 *Constituencies and seats*

	Number of constituencies	Constituency seats	Additional seats	Total	Average number of seats per constituency
Denmark: Folketing[a]	17	135	40	175 +4	8[b]
Finland: Eduskunta/					
Riksdag	15	200	–	200	14[c]
Norway: Storting	19	155	–	155	8
Sweden: Riksdag	28	310	39	349	11[b]

[a] In addition to the 175 members elected in Denmark proper, the Folketing includes 2 members each for Greenland and the Faroe Islands.
[b] Excluding additional seats.
[c] Excluding the one-member constituency of Åland.

are required for the additional seats. The numbers of constituencies, constituency seats and additional seats in the Nordic countries are shown in Table 2. As is also seen from the table, the number of seats per constituency is quite large, which in itself makes for a high degree of proportionality.

In both Denmark and Sweden, the total number of seats in the Parliament is allocated to the parties that have surpassed the threshold requirement for representation on the basis of the number of votes cast for each of these parties in the country as a whole; in Sweden the modified Sainte-Laguë formula is used for the purpose, whilst the Hare (quotient and largest remainder) formula is used at this stage in Denmark. For each of the parties, the number of seats it has already won in the constituencies is subtracted from the total number of seats it is entitled to; the difference is the number of additional seats. In Sweden, each party's additional seats are allocated to its constituency lists by the use of the original Sainte-Laguë formula (taking into account the number of constituency seats each list of candidates has already won). In Denmark, each party's additional seats are allocated, first, to larger regions and, secondly, to constituencies; this somewhat complex procedure involves the use of the original Sainte-Laguë formula as well as a divisor formula with even more steeply increasing divisors. The effect is to favour, somewhat, the less densely populated areas of the country and increase the geographical spread of a party's elected members. However, this does not affect the proportional distribution of seats among the parties – only the dispersion across constituencies of the elected members of each party.

Threshold for parliamentary representation

There is always some threshold of representation – some minimum share of the vote required to win at least one seat – built into any proportional formula.[2] The height of that threshold is to some extent dependent on the number of seats to be allocated; indeed, if an entire country is treated as one constituency in the election of a Parliament, all the commonly used formulas will yield results that are very close to perfect proportionality. Moreover, when elections are conducted in constituencies with a smaller number of seats the actual height of the threshold in each constituency will also depend on the number of parties as well as their relative size. Everything else being equal, the threshold against very small parties is, however, higher with the d'Hondt formula than with the modified Sainte-Laguë formula – and the latter sets a somewhat higher threshold than the original Sainte-Laguë formula. In addition to the mathematical effect of the PR formula, electoral systems can comprise *legal threshold rules* which entirely deny representation or exclude from proportional representation such parties whose electoral support do not fulfil certain criteria; the criteria can be defined in terms of, e.g., the party's share of the vote (either nationally or locally) or the constituency seats it has captured. The threshold rules applied in Sweden have already been described; the Swedish threshold rules exclude from proportional representation parties that obtain less than 4% of the national vote; in fact, such a party will gain no seats at all unless it surpasses an even higher constituency threshold (12%). In Denmark, the threshold is significantly lower. A party is entitled to proportional representation if it meets at least one of three criteria: that it has obtained at least 2% of the national vote, or won at least one constituency seat, or has achieved as many votes as the average number of votes cast per constituency seats within at least two of the three larger regions.[3] In Finland and Norway there are no threshold rules of this kind.

Voting for parties and candidates

The proportional election system determines how many seats a party will win in a constituency. But a system that requires voters to vote for parties, must also require that the voting results in a rank-ordering determining which candidates will be elected to the seats the party has captured. That rank-ordering can be decided by the party organisation as part of the election procedure. Or the election system can leave it open to the voter to exercise some influence on the ordering of the candidates.

Before we look at the differences between the four countries' election systems in this respect, it should be noted that the nomination of candidates is, in general, the responsibility of the parties, and usually under the firm control of the constituency party organisations. Only to a very limited extent are candidate nominations regulated by law. Norway is an exception, though, inasmuch as it has a nomination law which lays down a standard procedure for the nominations by constituency party organisations; but the law is not binding although its provisions are commonly followed.[4] Otherwise, legal regulations are largely limited to allowing parties to register party labels and the names of their adopted candidates.

A party's control over the rank-ordering of candidates is obviously at its strongest when each party nominates one list of candidates, the ordering of which cannot be changed or modified by the voter. This is the method employed in parliamentary elections in Norway. In Sweden, the voter will also have to cast his vote for a party list of candidates – but with the important difference that there can be more than one candidate list with the same party label.[5] Votes for all candidate lists with a common party label will be added together as the total vote for a party. The necessary rank-ordering of the candidates is determined by the number of votes cast for the various list types. It is possible for a dissatisfied group of party supporters to put forward their own candidate list in this way, provided only that the first name is one of the party's officially registered candidates. Far more common, however, is for the parties themselves officially to put forward more than one candidate list: the list types are then composed so as to appeal either to different geographical parts of the constituency (e.g., town and country) or to specific categories of voters (e.g., a 'youth' list or a 'Christian' list). Often, the same candidates appear on more than one list, though sometimes at different places in the rank-ordering. The use of competing party lists is largely an instrument for the parties' campaign strategies rather than for effective candidate-preference, especially since the distribution of the votes among the list types often is fairly predictable. Yet, sometimes competition between lists can be used to settle a dispute within a party about which candidates should be given an 'electable place' on the ballot. List competition is hardly a prominent feature of a Swedish constituency campaign; it rarely amounts to much more than the publishing of some campaign advertisements in the local press and, perhaps, a leaflet.

The Danish electoral law offers the voter a choice between voting for a party or for an individual party candidate. In both cases, the vote will count towards the party's total number of votes. Preference voting for candidates does affect the final rank-ordering among them, but how effective the voting for candidates will be is dependent to some extent on which one of the various ballot formats the party has chosen. In general the Social Democrats have used a ballot format that allows the party considerable control by treating the non-candidate votes as votes in support of the party's own ordering of the candidates, whilst the non-socialist parties have favoured ballot formats that give more weight to preference voting.[6] The trend in the 1970s seems to have been for preference voting to increase and for an increasing use of a ballot format that makes for more effective preference voting between candidates.

Finland offers the voters the strongest influence – indeed, a decisive influence – on the ordering of party candidates. When the Finnish voter enters the polling station, he finds there a poster displaying the names of the candidates, grouped according to party. Each candidate has a number, and the voter casts his vote by writing the number of the candidate he wants to support on the ballot paper. The vote is at the same time a vote for the candidate's party, and a party's total vote is the sum of the number of votes for its candidates. The rank-ordering of the candidates for a party is determined by the number of votes the candidates have received. This means that there is a fair element of within-party competition among candidates in Finnish election campaigns. Naturally, there is also a tendency for the most well-known candidates to attract large portions of the party vote; incumbency is among the factors that help, and this can be enhanced by having a prominent position in national politics; but experience shows that candidates can also benefit from fame gained on less political grounds, for example if he or she is a sports star or a media personality. More effectively than the Danish system, and in sharp contrast to the Norwegian and Swedish systems, the Finnish system limits the role of political parties to that of nominating candidates. Beyond that, it is the candidate's standing in the eyes of a party's supporters that decides who is to represent the party in Parliament.

HOW PROPORTIONAL?

How proportional are these election systems when it comes to reflecting the strength of the parties in the country as a whole? The answer to that question will vary somewhat from election to election, and it will depend on such factors as the portion of the total vote cast for parties that do not surpass the threshold (in Denmark and Sweden), the precise distribution of the vote among smaller and larger parties as well as the effect of electoral alliances (*apparentement*) in Finland and Norway. Table 3 illuminates how the system worked in the general elections held during the years 1979–81. (The distribution of votes and seats in all postwar elections is shown in the Appendix.)

In Denmark and Sweden the distribution of seats in the Parliament is virtually exactly proportional to the parties' voting strength – provided only the parties which have passed the threshold of representation are taken into account. If the relation of seats to numbers of votes for all parties is taken as the measure – as is the case in Table 3 – the degree of proportionality will depend on how large a proportion of the national vote is cast for minor, unrepresented parties. In the case of Denmark, the threshold is, of course, very low, but it is noteworthy that two small parties which have long been present on the Danish political scene failed to gain representation in 1981: the Communists and the Justice (Single-Tax) Party. Yet, of the nine parties that did gain seats, two would not have exceeded the Swedish threshold of 4%. In Sweden's election of 1979 – as in the previous elections in the 1970s – the degree of proportionality was very high, but this was due to the fact that the Communists gained more than 4% while the vote for the smaller parties was insignificant. Proportionality could become much less perfect in some future election if, say, the Communists were just to fail the threshold, and support for the Christian Democrats were to come to but not reach the 4% level. Though

Table 3   *Seats, votes and deviations from proportionality in elections*

	Seats	% Seats	% Votes	% Seats minus % votes
Denmark 1981[a]				
Communists	–	–	1.1	−1.1
Small socialist parties	–	–	0.2	−0.2
Left Socialists	5	2.9	2.6	+0.3
Socialist People's Party	21	12.0	11.3	+0.7
Social Democrats	59	33.7	32.9	+0.8
Centre Democrats	15	8.6	8.3	+0.3
Radical Liberals	9	5.1	5.1	–
Justice (Single-Tax) Party	–	–	1.4	−1.4
Christian People's Party	4	2.3	2.3	–
(Agrarian) Liberals	20	11.4	11.3	+0.1
Conservatives	26	14.9	14.4	+0.5
Progress Party	16	9.1	8.9	+0.2
TOTAL	175	100%	100%	
Finland 1979				
People's Democratic League[b]	35	17.5	17.9	−0.4
Socialist Workers Party	–	–	0.1	−0.1
Social Democrats	52	26.0	23.9	+2.1
Finnish Rural Party	7	3.5	4.6	−1.1
National Unity Party	–	–	0.3	−0.3
Centre (Agrarian) Party	36	18.0	17.3	+0.7
Liberal People's Party	4	2.0	3.7	−1.7
Swedish People's Party	10	5.0	4.5	+0.5
Christian League	9	4.5	4.8	−0.3
National Coalition Party (Conservatives)	47	23.5	21.7	+1.8
Constitutional Party	–	–	1.2	−1.2
TOTAL	200	100%	100%	
Norway 1981[c]				
Red Alliance	–	–	0.7	−0.7
Communists	–	–	0.3	−0.3
Socialist Left Party	4	2.6	5.0	−2.4
Labour Party	65	41.9	37.1	+4.8
Liberals	2	1.3	3.9	−2.6
Liberal People's Party	–	–	0.6	−0.6
Christian People's Party	15	9.7	9.4	+0.3
Centre Party	11	7.1	6.6	+0.5
Conservatives	54	34.8	31.8	+3.0
Progress Party	4	2.6	4.5	−1.9
Others	–	–	0.1	−0.1
TOTAL	155	100%	100%	

Table 3 (*cont.*)

	Seats	% Seats	% Votes	% Seats minus % votes
Sweden 1979				
Small Communist parties	–	–	0.4	−0.4
Communists	20	5.7	5.6	+0.1
Social Democrats	154	44.1	43.2	+0.9
Centre Party	64	18.3	18.1	+0.2
People's Party (Liberals)	38	10.9	10.6	+0.3
Christian Democratic Party	–	–	1.4	−1.4
Moderates (Conservatives)	73	20.9	20.3	+0.6
Others	–	–	0.4	−0.4
TOTAL	349	100%	100%	

[a] Excluding four Members for Greenland and the Faroe Islands.
[b] The Communist Party is a constituent and dominant component of the People's Democratic League.
[c] Votes for joint party lists (a small proportion of the total) have been apportioned to the participating parties in accordance to their strength in previous elections. Because of technical errors in the procedure, re-elections had to be held in two constituencies. The table pertains to the results reported for the general election; as a result of the re-elections, Labour gained one seat from the Conservatives.

other factors than the threshold are certainly important, it is worth noting that Sweden alone among the four countries has not experienced any increase in the number of small parties represented in its Parliament.

The adjustment of the Sainte-Laguë formula, it is also interesting to note, bears virtually no practical significance in either Denmark or Sweden: very small parties will in any case be eliminated by the threshold, and those who do achieve representation will receive their proportional share through the additional seats.

In Norway, where there are no additional seats and the adjustment of the Sainte-Laguë formula therefore has a small but real effect, there is (as is shown by the table) some over-representation of the larger parties. Thus, in the 1981 election the Labour Party got approximately 5 and the Conservatives approximately 3 seats (out of 155) more than they would have obtained under exact proportionality. The outcome for medium-sized and small parties in the Storting varies between nearly exact proportionality and an under-representation by up to 3–4 seats. In some constituencies, some of the non-socialist parties actually put forward joint candidate lists which occasionally results in the net gain of a seat and reduces the likelihood of overall under-representation. In general, it appears that smaller parties receiving between approximately 6% and 2% will win some seats, but achieve less than proportional representation. Although there is no formal threshold rule, parties with less than 2% of the national vote are unlikely to win a seat.

In Finland, the tendency for the d'Hondt formula to over-represent larger parties is not too markedly reflected in the actual election result. Three reasons seem to account for this: one is that Finland does not have any party which is very much larger than its competitors and could therefore benefit to any considerable extent from the d'Hondt method.[7] Secondly, the non-socialist parties form electoral alliances in many constituencies, which have proved to be an effective way of ensuring almost proportional results for smaller parties. Finally, the number of seats in the constituencies is large enough (see Table 2) to allow even small parties to capture a seat even under the d'Hondt formula. A change to the Sainte-Laguë formula would probably increase the degree of proportionality somewhat (at the expense of the larger parties); and that might well result in some increase in the number of parties in the Parliament, given that split-off parties crop up already under the present system.[8]

A summary of how the parties achieving representation in the Parliament were affected by deviations from exact proportionality is provided in Table 4. The table shows the total amount of over-representation as well as under-representation for the parties in each country's Parliament. Since some parties are too small to get any seats at all, at least some of the parties in the Parliament are bound to be over represented. In Denmark and Sweden – thanks to the additional seats – none of the parties in the Parliament is under-represented in this sense, and the sum total of over-representation is very small. Deviations from exact proportionality are clearly more significant in Finland and Norway. It is interesting to note that Norway – with the modified Sainte-Laguë method – shows larger deviations than Finland in terms of both over-representation and under-representation. Other things being equal, one would have expected that the use of the d'Hondt method in Finland should have had the opposite effect. But, of course, other things are not really equal.

A ROAD TO POLITICAL INSTABILITY?

If the main purpose of an electoral order is to ensure that all political parties of any significant size are represented in the Parliament at least nearly in proportion to their support in the electorate, then all the four Nordic countries fulfil that requirement. None of their election systems does much to over-represent large parties, and all allow even quite small parties effective parliamentary representation.

The late 1960s and the 1970s have been a time of unusual political instability, first in Norway and Denmark, and from the mid-1970s also in Sweden. The life-expectancy of cabinets has become shorter; unstable coalition government and minority governments have become the norm

Table 4 *Deviations from perfect proportionality in the Nordic Parliaments after elections in 1979–1981*

| | Over-representation | | Under-representation | |
	% Units	Seats	% Units	Seats
Denmark (1981)	2.9	5	0	0
Finland (1979)	5.1	10	3.5	7
Norway (1981)	8.6	13	6.8	11
Sweden (1979)	2.1	7	0	0

rather than the exception. In the summer of 1981 all three countries were governed by minority governments. Finland has been governed by often short-lived coalition governments throughout the postwar period. Is this the undesirable face of electoral justice gone too far? Would the parliamentary system of government have fared better with electoral systems less favourable to small parties? Would a little less proportionality have made much difference?

When considering these questions, it must first of all be noted that increasing instability of governments in Denmark, Norway and Sweden in recent years is not in itself the sudden effect of a proportional system that has existed for much longer. Stability of governments was primarily a concomitant of Social Democratic dominance. That era came to an end, both because the electoral support of the Social Democratic parties began to subside and because these parties found it increasingly difficult to form durable pacts with parties in the Centre. When this happened, the onus of providing a parliamentary basis for a government has from time to time shifted to the non-socialist side of the party system which has always been split, even before proportional represen-tation was introduced. And so far, the bourgeois parties have been unable to form an alternative alignment with anything like the cohesiveness that the Social Democrats achieved during the preceding era. One – but not the only – reason has been the emergence of issue cleavages that cut across the traditional socialist–bourgeois dividing line: the EEC issue in Denmark and Norway and the nuclear power issue in Sweden. Another has been the economic crisis of the 1970s. It has made it harder for all governments to govern, and it is not surprising that the strain has been hardest for coalition governments. Moreover, there have been genuine policy differences between Conservative parties and parties in the Centre – or Conservative parties have been more prepared than parties in the Centre to give up some of the welfare state's ambitions in order to cut public expenditure.

All of these developments have, in turn, contributed to the emergence of new parties, increasing support for minor parties and party splits – given that the election system already provided the preconditions. With declining popular confidence in the Social Democrats, parties to the left of them have increased in strength, especially in Denmark and Norway. In Denmark, the Social Democrats also saw the formation of a break-away party on its Right flank (the Centre Democrats). When the established bourgeois parties failed to offer a viable alternative to the Social Democrats, populist right-wing parties emerged in Denmark and Norway (the 'Progressives'). A Christian People's Party has existed for some considerable time in Norway; the new 'moral' issues (especially abortion) may help to explain why Christian Democratic parties have now been formed also in Denmark, Finland and Sweden – but it has certainly also something to do with the established parties' declining ability to attract trust and loyalty.

Proportional representation is so deeply entrenched in the Nordic countries that it is not really worth speculating about what shape their politics would have assumed under an entirely different system. But it might be worthwhile to consider how a less proportional system would have worked, say one that ensured a modest but substantial over-representation for larger parties. In fact, however, it is only in Norway and Sweden that any party – Labour and the Social Democrats – could hope to achieve an overall majority with the aid of a modest over-representation, but that was a remote possibility in the 1970s. A modest bonus for larger parties would hardly have prevented the bourgeois parties from coming to office in Sweden but neither would it have changed the structure of the bourgeois bloc. Hence it would not have been any remedy for subsequent governmental instability: the failure of the non-socialist parties to form stable coalitions and the fact that the parties have proved unwilling to join coalitions that over-ride the boundaries between the two blocs has been the major cause.

In Finland, the fine balance between socialist and non-socialist parties has not really been significant, and neither side of the party system provides a base for stable majority formation. Coalitions have tended to be over-sized and comprise parties on both sides of the socialist–bourgeois dividing-line. No modest degree of over-representation could have been the cure for a governmental instability that ultimately has its ground in the difficulty of accommodating the Communists and the Conservatives in coalition govern-ments; the need to build broad coalitions around the centre of the party system has, moreover, often forced the Social Democrats and the Centre Party into an uneasy partnership.

If modest over-representation would have done little to improve govern-mental stability, could it nevertheless be the case that the threshold of representation for really small parties has been set at too low a level? Although the election systems are different in Denmark and Norway, they have both allowed a number of small parties to gain a few seats each. This is not only the result of split-offs and the formation of new parties. A PR system with a low effective threshold of representation also allows old parties to survive even though they have declined to a minor party status. In both countries, the collection of minor parties comprises a mix of old and new parties. When it is unlikely that any party can win a parliamentary majority and when small parties can retain considerable bargaining power, there are hardly any inducements for a small party with an 'historic tradition' and a sense of ideological identity to join a broader political grouping. The number of small parties thus tends to increase both because of a high birth-rate and a low death-rate.

The fragmentation of the political Centre in Denmark and Norway has undoubtedly made it more difficult to form parliamentary majorities. This is not only because the participation of an increased number of parties is needed, it is also because the existence of minor parties is likely to increase the number of issues on which between-party compromises must be found. The failure to form a bourgeois majority government in Norway in 1981 because of the Christian People's Party's stand on the abortion issue is an illustrating case. As a consequence, the larger parties will also be engaged in electoral competition on a larger number of issue fronts.[9] However, in the case of Denmark, it is not only the small parties in the Centre that have made the formation of stable majority coalitions more difficult; at least as important is the emergence of a populist protest party of significant size to the Right of the Conservatives. No threshold at any politically acceptable level could have kept the Progressives out of the Folketing.

Apparently a lowering – rather than any heightening – of the effective threshold of representation (by means of a reduction of the first divisor in the modified Sainte-Laguë formula to, say, 1.2) is now a matter for serious discussion in Norway. One might well wonder why any of the larger parties would at all be willing to consider such a proposal. But two-bloc politics has its own logic. All the minor parties have their home in one or the other of the two blocs. In a short-term perspective, it may well appear preferable for a larger party to concede more proportional representation to very small parties, if the other bloc would otherwise stand a better chance of winning a parliamentary majority. What complicates the matter in the Norwegian case is only that it is so uncertain which of the blocs would stand to gain or lose.[10]

The d'Hondt method is supposed to discourage small parties and has probably done so, to some extent, in Finland. It is from this point of view noteworthy that the declining Liberal Party settled for a merger with the Centre Party after the presidential election of 1982. But the Finnish election system has not prevented the splitting-off of small parties from the Social Democrats, the Centre Party and the Conservative Party. Nor has it prevented the emergence of the Christian League. Some of the minor parties are likely to be short-lived, but some – like the Rural Party and the Christians – have shown remarkable resilience.

The Swedish case, finally, might be taken as a test of the effects of a significantly higher threshold of representation. Certainly the number of parties in the Riksdag has not increased; with five parties, the Swedish Parliament is now significantly less fractionalised than the others. But the fact that the bourgeois bloc consists of only three parties has not really made stable coalition governments any easier; since the Social Democrats lost office in 1976, Sweden has had a three-party coalition, followed by minority government by the small Liberal Party, followed by a new three-party government which, in turn, was succeeded by a Liberal–Centre two-party minority government. It is not altogether certain, either, that the high threshold will always come to appear quite as beneficial as at present. If one or more parties were to have a 'normal voting support' very near the threshold level, even small fluctuations could be quite disruptive for the orderly working of parliamentary politics, especially when the election period is as short as three years. It might mean that one or more parties with around 20 seats and non-negligible bargaining power could appear and disappear on the parliamentary scene at short intervals. It remains to be seen what the political response to such a situation would be. It is by no means implausible that it would result in strong pressures to lower the threshold of representation. Proportional representation, once established, creates a dynamic of its own – fairness always seems to demand that it should be taken one step further.*

---

* This chapter was written before the election of 1982, which returned the Social Democrats to office, albeit without an overall majority. The Social Democrats gained 166 seats whilst the non-socialist parties have 163 seats between them. With 20 seats the Communists hold the balance, but it is politically significant that the Social democrats will have a majority over the non-socialist parties, if the Communists abstain.

APPENDIX

Denmark: votes and seats in elections 1945–1981 (Folketing, Lower Chamber 1945–1953; unicameral 1953–)[a]

Parties	1945 V(%)	1945 S	1947 V(%)	1947 S	1950 V(%)	1950 S	1953 (Apr.) V(%)	1953 (Apr.) S	1953 (Sep.) V(%)	1953 (Sep.) S	1957 V(%)	1957 S	1960 V(%)	1960 S	1964 V(%)	1964 S
Communists	12.5	18	6.8	9	4.6	7	4.8	7	4.3	8	3.1	6	1.1	0	1.2	0
Left Socialists	—	—	—	—	—	—	—	—	—	—	—	—	—	—	—	—
Small Socialist parties	—	—	—	—	—	—	—	—	—	—	—	—	—	—	—	—
Socialist People's Party	—	—	—	—	—	—	—	—	—	—	—	—	—	—	—	—
Social Democrats	32.8	48	40.0	57	39.6	59	40.4	61	41.3	74	39.4	70	42.1	76	41.9	76
Centre Democrats	—	—	—	—	—	—	—	—	—	—	—	—	—	—	—	—
Radical Liberals	8.2	11	6.9	10	8.2	12	8.6	13	7.8	14	7.8	14	5.8	11	5.3	10
Justice (Single-Tax) Party	1.9	3	4.5	6	8.2	12	5.6	9	3.5	6	5.3	9	2.2	0	1.3	0
Christian People's Party	—	—	—	—	—	—	—	—	—	—	—	—	—	—	—	—
Liberal Centre	—	—	—	—	—	—	—	—	—	—	—	—	—	—	—	—
(Agrarian) Liberals	23.4	38	27.6	49	21.3	32	22.1	33	23.1	42	25.1	45	21.1	38	20.8	38
Conservatives	18.2	26	12.4	17	17.8	27	17.3	26	16.8	30	16.6	30	17.9	32	20.1	36
Independents Party	—	—	—	—	—	—	—	—	2.7	0	2.3	0	3.3	6	2.5	5
Progress Party	—	—	—	—	—	—	—	—	—	—	—	—	—	—	—	—
Others	3.1	4	1.8	0	0.3	0	1.2	0	0.4	1	0.4	1	0.4	1	1.1	0
TOTAL	100%	148	100%	148	100%	149	100%	149	100%	175	100%	175	100%	175	100%	175

Parties	1966 V(%)	1966 S	1968 V(%)	1968 S	1971 V(%)	1971 S	1973 V(%)	1973 S	1975 V(%)	1975 S	1977 V(%)	1977 S	1979 V(%)	1979 S	1981 V(%)	1981 S
Communists	0.8	0	1.0	0	1.4	0	3.6	6	4.2	7	3.7	7	1.9	0	1.1	0
Left Socialists	—	—	2.0	4	1.6	0	1.5	0	2.1	4	2.7	5	3.7	6	2.6	5
Small Socialist parties	—	—	—	—	—	—	—	—	—	—	—	—	0.4	0	0.2	0
Socialist People's Party	10.9	20	6.1	11	9.1	17	6.0	11	5.0	9	3.9	7	5.9	11	11.3	21
Social Democrats	38.3	69	34.2	62	37.3	70	25.6	46	29.9	53	37.0	65	38.3	68	32.9	59
Centre Democrats	—	—	—	—	—	—	7.8	14	2.2	4	6.4	11	3.2	6	8.3	15
Radical Liberals	7.3	13	15.0	27	14.4	27	11.2	20	7.1	13	3.6	6	5.4	10	5.1	9
Justice (Single-Tax) Party	0.7	0	0.7	0	1.7	0	2.9	5	1.8	0	3.3	6	2.6	5	1.4	0
Christian People's Party	—	—	—	—	2.0	0	4.0	7	5.3	9	3.4	6	2.6	5	2.3	4
Liberal Centre	2.5	4	1.3	0	—	—	—	—	—	—	—	—	—	—	—	—
(Agrarian) Liberals	19.3	35	18.6	34	15.6	30	12.3	22	23.3	42	12.0	21	12.5	22	11.3	20
Conservatives	18.7	34	20.4	37	16.7	31	9.2	16	5.5	10	8.5	15	12.5	22	14.4	26
Independents Party	1.6	0	0.5	0	—	—	—	—	—	—	—	—	—	—	—	—
Progress Party	—	—	—	—	—	—	15.9	28	13.6	24	14.6	26	11.0	20	8.9	16
Others	—	—	0.2	0	0.2	0	—	—	—	—	0.9	—	—	—	—	—
TOTAL	100%	175	100%	175	100%	175	100%	175	100%	175	100%	175	100%	175	100%	175

Note: Due to decimal rounding, the percent columns in this and the following tables do not always add up to 100.0.
a The table does not include Greenland and the Faroe Islands which elect a total of four Members of the Folketing.

Finnish: *Finland: Votes and seats in elections 1945–1979 (Eduskunta/Riksdag)*

Parties	1945 V %	1945 S	1948 V %	1948 S	1951 V %	1951 S	1954 V %	1954 S	1958 V %	1958 S	1962 V %	1962 S	1966 V %	1966 S	1970 V %	1970 S	1972 V %	1972 S	1975 V %	1975 S	1979 V %	1979 S
People's Democratic League (Communists)	23.5	49	20.0	38	21.6	43	21.6	43	23.2	50	22.0	47	21.2	41	16.6	36	17.0	37	18.9	40	17.9	35
Social Democratic League/Socialist Workers Party	–	–	–	–	–	–	–	–	1.7	3	4.4	2	2.6	7	1.4	0	1.0	0	–	–	0.1	0
Social Democrats	25.1	50	26.3	54	26.5	53	26.2	54	23.2	48	19.5	38	27.2	55	23.4	52	25.8	55	24.9	54	23.9	52
Centre (Agrarian) Party	21.3	49	24.2	56	23.2	51	24.1	53	23.1	48	23.0	53	21.2	49	17.1	36	16.4	35	17.6	39	17.3	36
Smallholders Party (1945–51) Finnish Rural Party (1962–)	1.2	0	0.3	0	0.3	0	–	–	–	–	2.2	0	1.0	1	10.5	18	9.2	18	3.6	2	4.6	7
National Unity Party	–	–	–	–	–	–	–	–	–	–	–	–	–	–	–	–	–	–	1.7	1	0.3	0
Liberal League	–	–	–	–	0.3	0	0.3	0	0.3	0	0.5	1	–	–	–	–	–	–	–	–	–	–
National Progressive Party/Liberal People's Party	5.2	9	3.9	5	5.7	10	7.9	13	5.9	8	6.3	13	6.5	9	5.9	8	5.1	7	4.3	9	3.7	4
Swedish People's Party[a]	7.9	14	7.7	14	7.6	15	7.0	13	6.7	14	6.4	14	6.0	12	5.7	12	5.4	10	4.6	10	4.5	10
Christian League of Finland	–	–	–	–	–	–	–	–	–	–	–	–	0.4	0	1.1	1	2.5	4	3.3	9	4.8	9
National Coalition Party (Conservatives)	15.0	28	17.1	33	14.6	28	12.8	24	15.3	29	15.0	32	13.8	26	18.0	37	17.6	34	18.4	35	21.7	47
Constitutional Party	–	–	–	–	–	–	–	–	–	–	–	–	–	–	–	–	–	–	1.6	1	1.2	0
Others	0.8	1	0.5	0	0.2	0	0.1	0	0.6	0	0.7	0	0.0	0	0.2	0	0.0	0	1.1	0	–	0
TOTAL	100%	200	100%	200	100%	200	100%	200	100%	200	100%	200	100%	200	100%	200	100%	200	100%	200	100%	200

a Includes votes for and one seat won by the Swedish candidate in the Åland constituency.

Norway: Elections 1945–1981 (Storting)

Parties[a]	1945 V %	1945 S	1949 V %	1949 S	1953 V %	1953 S	1957 V %	1957 S	1961 V %	1961 S	1965 V %	1965 S	1969 V %	1969 S	1973 V %	1973 S	1977 V %	1977 S	1981[b] V %	1981[b] S
Red Alliance/Other Extreme Left	–	–	–	–	–	–	–	–	–	–	–	–	–	–	0.4	0	0.6	0	0.7	0
Communists	11.9	11	5.8	0	5.1	3	3.4	1	2.9	0	1.4	0	1.0	0	–	–	0.4	0	0.3	0
Socialist People's Party/ Socialist Left	–	–	–	–	–	–	–	–	2.4	2	6.0	2	3.5	0	11.2	16	4.2	2	5.0	4
Labour Party	41.0	76	45.7	85	46.7	77	48.3	78	46.8	74	43.1	68	46.5	74	35.3	62	42.3	76	37.1	65
Liberals (Venstre)	13.8	20	13.4	21	10.0	15	9.7	15	8.9	14	10.4	18	9.4	13	3.5	2	3.2	2	3.9	2
Liberal People's Party	–	–	–	–	–	–	–	–	–	–	–	–	–	–	3.4	1	1.4	0	0.6	0
Christian People's Party	7.9	8	8.4	9	10.5	14	10.2	12	9.6	15	8.1	13	9.4	14	12.3	20	12.4	22	9.4	15
Centre Party	8.0	10	8.2	12	9.0	14	9.3	15	9.3	16	9.9	18	10.5	20	11.0	21	8.6	12	6.6	11
Conservatives	17.0	25	17.7	23	18.8	27	18.9	29	20.0	29	21.1	31	19.6	29	17.4	29	24.8	41	31.8	54
Progress Party	–	–	–	–	–	–	–	–	–	–	–	–	–	–	5.0	4	1.9	0	4.5	4
Others	0.4	0	0.7	0	0.0	0	0.2	0	0.2	0	0.0	0	0.1	0	0.5	0	0.2	0	0.1	0
TOTAL	100%	150	100%	150	100%	150	100%	150	100%	150	100%	150	100%	150	100%	155	100%	155	100%	155

[a] Votes for joint party lists have been apportioned to participating parties in accordance to their strength at previous elections.

[b] Re-elections were held in two constituencies (because of errors in the procedure at the general election). The table shows the results reported for the general election: as a result of the re-elections, Labour gained one seat from the Conservatives.

Sweden: Elections 1948–82 (Riksdag, Lower Chamber 1948–68; unicameral 1970–)

Parties	1948 V %	1948 S	1952 V %	1952 S	1956 V %	1956 S	1958 V %	1958 S	1960 V %	1960 S	1964 V %	1964 S	1968 V %	1968 S	1970 V %	1970 S	1973 V %	1973 S	1976 V %	1976 S	1979 V %	1979 S
Small Communist parties	–		–		–		–		–		–		–		0.4	0	0.4	0	0.3	0	0.4	0
Communists	6.3	8	4.3	5	5.0	6	3.4	5	4.5	5	5.2	8	3.0	3	4.8	17	5.3	19	4.8	17	5.6	20
Social Democrats	46.1	112	46.1	110	44.6	106	46.2	111	47.8	114	47.3	113	50.1	125	45.3	163	43.6	156	42.7	152	43.2	154
Centre Party	12.4	30	10.7	26	9.4	19	12.7	32	13.6	34	13.2	33	15.7	37	19.9	71	25.1	90	24.1	86	18.1	64
People's Party (Liberals)	22.8	57	24.4	58	23.8	58	18.2	38	17.5	40	17.0	42	14.3	32	16.2	58	9.4	34	11.1	39	10.6	38
Joint Non-Socialist Lists (2 constituencies)	–		–		–		–		–		1.8	5	2.6	7	–		–		–		–	
Christian Democratic Party	–		–		–		–		–		1.8	0	1.5	0	1.8	0	1.8	0	1.4	0	1.4	0
Moderates (Conservatives)	12.3	23	14.4	31	17.1	42	19.5	45	16.5	39	13.7	32	12.9	29	11.5	41	14.3	51	15.6	55	20.3	73
Others	0.1	0	0.1	0	0.1	0	0.0	0	0.1	0	0.0	0	0.0	0	0.0	0	0.2	0	0.1	0	0.4	0
TOTAL	100%	230	100%	230	100%	231	100%	231	100%	232	100%	233	100%	233	100%	350	100%	350	100%	349	100%	349

Note: The 1982 election result was: Communists V 5.6%, S 20; Social Democrats V 45.6%, S 166; Centre Party V 15.5%, S 56; People's Party (Liberals) V 5.9%, S 21; Christian Democratic Party V 1.9%, S 0; Moderates (Conservatives) V 23.6%, S 86; others V 2.0% (of which 1.7% was for the New Environment Party; also including small Communist parties) S 0; total V 100%, total S 349.

NOTES

1 In Norway and Sweden, an MP can temporarily be replaced by a substitute member who will also have been nominated on the party list in the election. Most importantly, ministers are replaced in Parliament by substitute members while they hold office. Members of these Parliaments can be replaced by substitute members also for other reasons, such as serving as a delegate in an international assembly or being on 'sickness leave'.

2 For a full discussion of the thresholds of representation associated with different PR formulae, see Arend Lijphart and R. W. Gibberd, 'Thresholds and Payoffs in List Systems of Proportional Representation', *European Journal of Political Research*, 5, 3 (September, 1977), pp. 219–44. See also Markku Laakso, 'The Maximum Distortion and the Problem of the First Divisor of Different PR Systems', *Scandinavian Political Studies*, 1, new series (1979), pp. 161–9.

3 For a detailed description of the procedure, see Geoffrey Hand, Jacques Georgel and Christoph Sasse, eds., *European Electoral Systems Handbook*, (London, 1979); see also Ole Borre, 'The Social Bases of Danish Electoral Behaviour', in Richard Rose (ed.), *Electoral Participation: A Comparative Analysis*, (Beverly Hills, 1980).

4 The nomination procedure in Norway is described in Henry Valen, 'The Recruitment of Parliamentary Nominees in Norway', *Scandinavian Political Studies*, 1 (1966), pp. 121–66. For an account of the nomination procedure in Sweden, see Dan Brändström, 'Nomineringsförfarandet vid riksdagsval', *Statens offentliga utedningar*, 1972:17 (a study commissioned by an official committee of inquiry for constitutional reform).

5 In both Norway and Sweden, the voter can actually cross out names on the party list; in Sweden it is even possible to 'write in' additional names. But neither of these devices are of any practical significance.

6 See Morgens N. Pedersen, 'Preferential Voting in Denmark: The Voters' Influence of the Election of Folketing Candidates', *Scandinavian Political Studies*, 1 (1966), pp. 167–87. For an up-to-date description of the procedure see the chapter on Denmark in Hand, Georgel and Sasse, *European Electoral Systems Handbook*.

7 See Klaus Törnudd, *The Electoral System of Finland*, (London, 1968). Note however that the electoral law has been changed in one significant respect. Previously, it was possible for a candidate to be nominated in more than one constituency; a well-known politician could therefore help to attract votes in several constituencies, although he would of course have to settle for only one of these constituencies after the election. Under the new rules, a candidate can stand only in one constituency.

8 For a systematic comparative analysis of the effect of different proportional methods when applied to the Nordic countries, see M. Laakso and R. Taagepera, 'Proportional Representation in Scandinavia: Implications for Finland', *Scandinavian Political Studies*, 1, new series (1978), pp. 43–60. See also R. Taagepera and M. Laakso, 'Proportional Profiles of West European Electoral Systems', *European Journal of Political Research*, 8, 4 (December 1980), pp. 423–46; M. Laakso, 'Electoral Justice as a Criterion for Different Systems of Proportional Representation', *Scandinavian Political Studies*, 3, new series (1980), pp. 249–64; and Törnudd, *The Electoral System of Finland*, pp. 126–8.

9 See Richard S. Katz, *A Theory of Parties and Electoral Systems*, (Baltimore, 1980).

10 See Henry Valen, *Valg og politik – et samfunn i endring*, (Oslo, 1981), pp. 39ff.

SUGGESTIONS FOR FURTHER READING

Karl H. Cerny, *Scandinavia at the Polls* (Washington, DC, 1977)
N. C. M. Elder, 'The Scandinavian States', in S. E. Finer, ed., *Adversary Politics and
    Electoral Reform* (London, 1975)
John Fitzmaurice, *Politics in Denmark* (London, 1981), chap. 3
Kenneth E. Miller, 'The Danish Electoral System' *Parliamentary Affairs* (1964–5)
Björn Molin, 'Sweden: The First Year of the One-Chamber Riksdag', *Scandinavian
    Political Studies* (1972)
Mogens Pedersen, 'Preferential Voting in Denmark: The Voters' Influence on the
    Election of Folketing Candidates', *Scandinavian Political Studies*, 1 (1966)
Klaus Törnudd, *The Electoral System of Finland* (London, 1968)
Henry Valen, 'The Recruitment of Parliamentary Nominees in Norway', *Scandinavian
    Political Studies*, 1 (1966)
    and Daniel Katz, *Political Parties in Norway: A Community Study* (Oslo, 1964)

8

Benelux

DICK LEONARD

The three Benelux countries constitute an excellent laboratory for testing theories about the political consequences of electoral systems. They are small contiguous countries, with similar life-styles, a shared recent history and a comparable level of economic development. Each society, however, has sharply distinctive features, and though each elects its Parliament through a system of proportional representation, there is a considerable degree of difference in the systems used. Enough in common, then, for valid comparisons to be drawn, but enough diversity for more than marginal differences to be thrown up.

THE DATA

The elections under consideration are those held in the three countries between 1918 and 1982. The starting-point is chosen because the existing electoral systems in all three countries effectively date from the end of the First World War. At that period universal suffrage was adopted (though in Belgium women had to wait for the vote until 1948), and Holland and Luxembourg introduced proportional representation, which had already been in use in Belgium since 1899.

In the sixty-four years covered by this analysis there were twenty general elections in Belgium, eighteen in the Netherlands and sixteen in Luxembourg (of which seven were partial elections, usually covering only half the country – see below). In the case of Belgium and Holland only the results of elections to the Lower House are taken into account. Luxembourg has a unicameral Parliament.

Before attempting an analysis of the elections, a brief description is given of the electoral systems of the three countries, followed by a very broad outline of the party formations.

BELGIUM

The Chamber of Representatives is elected by universal adult suffrage under the d'Hondt system of proportional representation. The Chamber had 186 members until 1925, when it was increased to 187. In 1936 it went up to 202, and in 1949 to 212, which is its present size. In 1919 the vote was restricted to men over the age of twenty-one and to mothers and widows of soldiers killed in the war. Women were enfranchised in 1948, and the voting age was reduced to eighteen in 1969. Voting is compulsory.

The country is divided into thirty electoral districts, the smallest of which returns two members and the largest (Brussels) thirty-four. The districts are grouped into nine provinces to allow a second allocation of seats if, as is normally the case, all the electoral quotas have not been attained at district level. This has the effect of lowering the electoral threshold.

The elector has one vote, which he may cast either for a list of candidates, printed in the order decided by the party concerned, or, preferentially, for a single name on the list. This could have the effect, if a sufficient number of other voters behave in the same way, of promoting the chosen candidate to the top of the list.

Seats at the district level are allocated to parties on the basis of the number of *electoral divisors* (total number of votes cast divided by number of seats available) obtained by each party. Unfilled seats are transferred to a provincial pool, to which the residual votes of party lists after allocation of district seats are also transferred. The party votes are then divided by 1,2,3, etc. in the normal d'Hondt method until all the remaining seats have been allocated.

NETHERLANDS

The Second Chamber of the Dutch Parliament is also elected by universal adult suffrage under the d'Hondt system. The major difference from Belgium is that the whole country forms a single constituency – a feature shared only with Israel. The Chamber had 100 members before 1956, when its size was increased to 150.

Adult male suffrage dates from 1917, and women were accorded the vote on the same basis in 1919. The voting age was set at twenty-five, being reduced to twenty-three in 1946, twenty-one in 1956 and eighteen in 1972. Compulsory voting, introduced in 1917, was abolished in 1970.

As in Belgium, the elector has a single vote which he may cast either for a list, or, preferentially, for a candidate not heading a list. Seats are allocated to those parties which attain or exceed the *electoral quota*. This is calculated by dividing the total number of votes cast in the whole country by 150. In the 1977 election, for example, when 8,294,261 votes were cast the quota was 55,295.0. The number of votes cast for each party is divided by the electoral quota and seats are allotted accordingly. Normally, the number of quotients is less than 150, and remaining seats are allocated by the d'Hondt method of successive divisors.

There is one minor qualification to this 'extreme' form of proportional representation, in the existence of an electoral threshold. But this has been set at the extremely low level of 0.67% of the votes cast – only just above the natural threshold implied by the d'Hondt rules, and it has been rare for parties to be deprived of representation because of it.

The Chamber of Deputies has been elected by universal adult suffrage since 1918. The voting age was twenty-one until 1972, when it was reduced to eighteen. Voting is compulsory.

The electoral system used is the Hagenbach-Bischoff method of proportional representation. The country is divided into four multi-member constituencies, and each voter has as many votes as there are seats to be filled. He may distribute these votes between candidates on different lists, if he so chooses, and may even plump by giving two (but no more) of his votes to a single candidate. The constituencies are of uneven size, currently returning from six to twenty-four members.

The Chamber had fifty-two members until 1964, when it was increased to fifty-six. Since 1974 it has had fifty-nine members.

Before 1954 it was normal to have elections every three years, but only two of the four constituencies would vote each time, electing their members for a six-year term. Since 1954 the whole country has voted together, and members have normally been elected for a fixed five-year term.

PARTY STRUCTURES

Each of the three countries has produced a party structure whose principal axis has followed the classical West European pattern. Catholic, Socialist and Liberal parties have predominated, with, in each case, the Socialists replacing the Liberals as one of the two largest parties after the First World War. In Belgium and Holland the Liberal parties have since moved further Right, leaving the Catholic parties in the middle of the political spectrum. In Luxembourg the Catholic party (formerly Party of the Right, now Christian Social Party) has retained its right-wing berth, and the Liberals (Democratic Party) are in the Centre. Each of the three countries has also had a relatively small Communist Party.

A major difference has been that, whereas in Luxembourg these four parties have covered by far the largest part of the political spectrum (often monopolising representation in the Chamber), in both Holland and Belgium there has been an additional cleavage which has led to the formation of further significant parties.

In Holland this cleavage has been religion, with two medium-sized Protestant parties successfully competing for votes during most of the period

under discussion. These were the Calvinist Anti-Revolutionary Party (ARP)
and the orthodox Protestant Christian Historical Union (CHU). These two
parties usually obtained together, and occasionally singly, more support than
the Liberal party, and were effectively the third political force in the country. In
1977 both these parties combined with the Catholic People's Party to form the
Christian Democratic Appeal (CDA) which, like the CDU in West Germany, has
directed its appeal to both Catholics and Protestants. Other newer political
parties in the Netherlands, notably Democrats '66, are referred to below.

   In Belgium the additional significant cleavage has been linguistic. Although
Flemish groups enjoyed some success in the interwar period, it was only some
years after the formation of the Volksunie (Flemish People's Party) in 1953 that
linguistic issues began to have a major impact on the Belgian political scene.
The influence of the Volksunie in imposing bilingualism in the early 1960s led
to the creation of Francophone linguistic parties in Brussels (Front Démocratique des Francophones) and in Wallonia (Rassemblement Wallon). By
1978 the linguistic parties were polling some 15% of the votes, but – perhaps
equally significantly – by then each of the existing leading political groups –
Social Christians, Socialists and Liberals – had split up into separate French-
and Dutch-speaking parties. Of the traditional parties only the Communists
have maintained an organisation which straddles the linguistic divide.

THE RAE VARIABLES

It is clear that in each of the three countries peculiar factors independent of the
formal provisions of the electoral system have had a significant impact on the
development of electoral politics. It is also evident that the electoral system
itself has had a measurable effect, as will be revealed by assessing the election
results in each of the three countries over a sixty-three-year period against the
variables defined by Douglas W. Rae in his seminal work, *The Political
Consequences of Electoral Laws* (New Haven, 1967).

   The relevant characteristics of the three electoral systems are set out in
Table 1. Of the three countries, the Netherlands can be characterised as having
a medium-sized legislature (100, and later 150 members), a very high district
magnitude (100, and later 150) and a low legal threshold (0.67% of the
national vote). Belgium has a larger sized legislature (186 rising to 212
members), and a high average district magnitude (7.1 according to Rae, who,
however, appears not to have taken account of the secondary distribution of
seats. When this factor is included, as it should be, the average magnitude rises
to 23.5). There is no legal threshold in Belgium, but in the average province it is
effectively about 4%, though in Brabant (which includes Brussels) it falls to less
than 2%.

   Luxembourg has had a small Parliament (48 rising to 59 members), and a
fairly high district magnitude of 12–15. There is, again, no legal threshold, and

Table 1 *Electoral systems in the Benelux countries, as at 1981* [a]

Country	Ballot type	Number of MPs	District magnitude	Formula
Belgium	Categorical: simple party-list ballot	212	23.5	Proportional representation: d'Hondt highest average
Netherlands	Categorical: simple party-list ballot	150	150	Proportional representation: d'Hondt highest average
Luxembourg	Multiple: *panachage* with limited cumulation allowed	59	14.8	Proportional representation: Hagenbach-Bischoff largest remainder

[a] This table has been adapted from table 2.1 of Rae, *Political Consequences*. Two notable alterations have been made, as Rae appears to have been relying on incomplete information. First, the district magnitude listed here for Belgium is based on the provincial distribution of seats rather than those of the districts, which misleadingly gives the much smaller figure of 7.1. Secondly, the Luxembourg ballot type is clearly a multiple one rather than ordinal as defined by Rae.

because of multiple voting and the limited plumping permitted it is difficult to calculate what it might be in practice. But an examination of detailed election results over six successive elections[1] shows that the smallest vote obtained by a party winning representation in any of the four constituencies was 4.8%. In another constituency in a later year, however, 7.3% was insufficient to obtain a seat. In practice, the threshold is clearly substantially higher than in Belgium – mainly due to the smaller number of members to be elected.

Rae's variables, which provide the most scientific basis yet devised for comparing the political consequences of different electoral systems, can be briefly summarised. First is *fractionalisation*, defined as the probability that any two randomly selected electors vote in a different way. The more parties, and the more evenly distributed their support, the higher the level of fractionalisation. In a one-party system F_e (fractionalisation among electors) is zero. In an extreme multi-party system in which everybody voted for a different party it would be one. Rae also measures fractionalisation among legislators (F_p): this, he argues, is almost invariably lower as all electoral systems tend to have a defractionalising effect.

Rae's second concept is the *average deviation of vote and seat shares* (I) – which, he suggests, is high in plurality systems and lower in proportional ones: the more proportional the system the lower the value of I. Then comes the *number of parties* contesting elections (N_e) and the number obtaining seats in parliament (N_p), both of which he suggests are higher under PR systems. Next comes the *vote share of the leading party* (P_e) and its *seat share* (P_p). The latter is almost invariably higher than the former, though to a lesser degree under PR. The extent to which larger parties, in general, are favoured by electoral systems is measured by the vote (W_e) and seat (W_p) share of the *two largest parties.*

Finally, there is the concept of the *minimal parliamentary majority* (A) – the smallest number of parties which could form a coalition with a parliamentary majority. This is purely a mathematical measure, taking no account of ideological affinities – so that, in practice, A may not be a meaningful measure. Rae's general expectation is that the more proportional a system the higher the value of A.

Rae took the results of 121 elections in twenty different countries and tested them against each of the above concepts, as well as some others. He found substantial differences between plurality (first-past-the-post) and PR systems, virtually all of them in the expected direction. He then compared different PR systems and found a much smaller degree of variation. The most important source of variance was *district magnitude,* the number of members to be elected from each electoral district. Put in the crudest terms, the larger the magnitude the more proportional the results.[2]

Let us now test the results of the Benelux elections against the concepts set out by Rae. In the light of his discussion, we would expect a country with a very high district magnitude (the Netherlands) to be associated with:

1. Greater fractionalisation among voters (F_e).
2. Greater fractionalisation among parliamentarians (F_p).
3. A more proportional allocation of seats (I).
4. Larger numbers of parties contesting elections (N_e).
5. Larger numbers of parliamentary parties holding seats (N_p).
6. Slightly weaker first parties (elective) (P_e).
7. Slightly weaker first parties (legislative) (P_p).
8. Leading two parties which are together slightly weaker (elective) (W_e).
9. Leading two parties which are together slightly weaker (legislative) (W_p).
10. Slightly larger minimal parliamentary majorities (A).

On all the above propositions, the predicted rank order would be (1) Netherlands, (2) Belgium, (3) Luxembourg. The actual data for the three countries are set out in Table 2, which shows the position for three separate years – around 1918, 1954 and 1978 – with the average for each country in the final column. The extraordinary result appears that in each of the first nine cases the rank order is exactly as predicted. In the tenth category, Belgium leads Holland, but this is a purely theoretical category, and in its practical application the predicted order is maintained. That is to say that, whereas in theory only two parties were required to form a government in all three reference years in the Netherlands, and on one occasion three parties would

Table 2 *Relative scores on Rae variables*

Belgium	1919	1954	1978	Average
F_e	0.70	0.67	0.87	0.74
F_p	0.67	0.60	0.85	0.70
I	1.1	2.16	1.1	1.45
N_e[a]	7	7	13	9
N_p	7	6	13	8.6
P_e	36.6	41.1	26.1	34.6
P_p	39.2	44.8	26.9	37.0
W_e	73.2	78.4	39.1	63.6
W_p	76.8	85.4	42.0	68.1
A	2	2	3	2.3

Netherlands	1918	1952	1977	Average
F_e	0.82	0.95	0.75	0.84
F_p	0.83	0.78	0.73	0.78
I	0.47	0.57	0.44	0.49
N_e[a]	14	9	13	12
N_p	15	8	11	11.3
P_e	30.0	29.0	33.8	30.9
P_p	30.0	30.0	35.3	31.8
W_e	52.0	57.7	65.7	58.5
W_p	52.0	60.0	68.0	60.0
A	2	2	2	2

Luxembourg	1919	1954	1979	Average
F_e	0.68	0.68	0.76	0.71
F_p	0.61	0.62	0.71	0.65
I	1.68	3.48	2.29	2.48
N_e[a]	5	5	8	6
N_p	5	4	7	5.3
P_e	52.5	42.4	34.5	43.1
P_p	56.3	50.0	40.7	49.0
W_e	71.8	77.5	58.8	69.4
W_p	75.1	82.7	66.1	74.6
A	1	2	2	1.7

[a] See n. 8, which explains why the value of N_e is likely to be consistently understated, particularly for the Netherlands.

have been necessary in Belgium, in point of fact more parties have had to be included in Dutch governments because the two largest parties have often been incompatible. If reference is made to the classified election results on pp. 162–4, it will be seen that, on average, Dutch governments have been formed from 3.4 parties, Belgian from 2.5 and Luxembourg from 2.3.

CHANGE OVER TIME

The discussion so far has treated the three systems as if they were static
entities, whereas significant developments over time can be traced in both
Holland and Belgium and, to a lesser extent, in Luxembourg. The changes in
Holland and Belgium have been in opposing directions, leading in fact to a
certain degree of convergence.

In the Netherlands a significant degree of elective defractionalisation had
occurred by 1977 compared to 1952 (see Table 2). Legislative defractionalisation had also occurred, though to a smaller extent; this despite the emergence
of several new parties which successfully contended for seats in the Second
Chamber. The largest of these is Democrats '66, a left-wing liberal grouping
which by 1981, with 11.1% of the votes, had become the fourth largest political
party in the Netherlands, and provided ministers for two governments, those of
1973–7 and 1981–2. Other new parties which achieved parliamentary
representation were the Pacifist Socialist Party, the Farmers Party, Democratic
Socialists '70, the Netherlands Middle Class Party, the Radical Political Party,
the Reformed Political Union and the Roman Catholic Party.

Yet the emergence of these new groupings was much more than offset, in
overall terms of fractionalisation, by the amalgamation of the three largest
religious parties to form the Christian Democratic Appeal, prior to the 1977
general election. This amalgamation, which has had far-reaching consequences in Dutch politics, was certainly not imposed by intrinsic pressures of
the electoral system. This had shown itself extraordinarily hospitable to
political heterogeneity, permitting the existence for over eighty years of two
substantial right-of-centre Protestant parties (the Anti-Revolutionary Party
and the Christian Historical Union) without their suffering any apparent
electoral handicap. Even more striking has been the survival of the smaller
extreme Calvinist Political Reformed Party, founded in 1918 as a breakaway
from the ARP and still appealing to fundamentalist Protestants in 1981. The
stability of the vote for this party is remarkable: it has fluctuated only between
1.9% and 2.5% since 1925, and has invariably returned either two or three
Members of Parliament. Probably in no other democratic country has a party
with such a small, but rock solid, basis of support been able to maintain its
parliamentary representation over such a long period.

What brought the three bigger parties together was the weakening hold of
religious loyalties (apart from those of strict Calvinists) over voting behaviour,[3]
and the growing success of the secular parties – not only Labour, but also the
Liberals and D'66 – in winning the votes of church members. The attrition of
confessional voting had been a steady process in the postwar period, but the
1972 election result administered a particularly nasty shock to the three
largest religious parties. Their total vote in 1972 was less than that of the
Catholic People's Party alone some nine years earlier, while the Labour Party

seemed decisively to have replaced the CPP as the biggest party in the Netherlands. What particularly concerned the leaders of the religious parties was the quasi-presidential appeal of the popular Labour Party leader, Mr Joop Den Uyl.

It was the need to produce a convincing alternative focus of support to Mr Den Uyl which finally brought the three parties together before the 1977 election. The person who emerged was the then Justice Minister, Mr Andries Van Agt, 'a Catholic who nevertheless could inspire Calvinist voters'.[4] The crucial factor in breaking the long-established mould of Dutch politics has not been any change in the electoral system, which has undergone only relatively minor adaptations since 1918,[5] but the impact of the media, with its need to focus on a small cast of nationally known figures.

It is also arguable that this has been the major factor in the rise of D'66, whose leader, Mr Jan Terlouw, is a riveting performer on television. It can, however, be said of the electoral system in this context that, though it does not impose change on party alignments, it does not inhibit them either. If it is possible for a PRP to husband 2% of votes over a sixty-year period, it is equally feasible for a D'66 to come up from nothing to 11% in little over a decade.

In Belgium there has been a marked increase in fractionalisation since the early 1960s – almost all of which is attributable to the growing salience of the linguistic issue. A few statistics will illustrate the point. Before 1965 there had never been a significant vote for Francophone parties or candidates, as such. There had been fluctuating support for Flemish nationalist groups, which had peaked at 8.3% in 1939, but which had ranged between 0% and $3\frac{1}{2}$% in postwar elections.

In 1965 this rose to 6.4%, with Francophone parties polling 2.4%. By 1971 the Flemish parties were up to 11.1%, and the Francophones to 11.3%, together claiming the support of more than a fifth of Belgian voters. The two opposing groups reacted to each other and fed on each other's successes. The Flemish nationalists had had a long-standing and well-justified grievance in that Dutch-speakers had been discriminated against in many aspects of Belgian life. It was their success in persuading the Catholic–socialist coalition government in 1963 to pass a series of language laws which sparked off the Francophone reaction.[6]

A principal effect of the 1963 laws was to impose bilingualism in many parts of the public service, especially in Brussels. This has resulted in a virtual Flemish monopoly, as middle-class Dutch-speakers normally have an excellent command of French, while few French-speakers have taken the trouble to acquire more than a rudimentary knowledge of Dutch. The immediate consequence was the foundation of the Front Democratique des Francophones Bruxellois, in 1964, which within a few years became the largest political party in Brussels, outstripping Socialists, Social Christians and Liberals.

In 1967 the Rassemblement Wallon was formed in Wallonia (the French-speaking part of Belgium). Less successful than the FDF, with whom it collaborates at general elections, the RW has achieved a small representation in the Belgian Parliament, but more significantly has forced the Socialist Party – much the largest party in Wallonia – to adopt a stridently pro-Francophone line, for fear of being outflanked.

The full force of the language issue cannot be gauged only by the impact of the linguistic parties. Each of the three main Belgian parties – Social Christians, Socialists and Liberals – has split into two separate bodies, one comprised of Dutch-, the other of French-speakers. Formally, this has greatly increased the level of fractionalisation, both elective and parliamentary. In practice, this is hardly the case, as the parties are not competing with each other for votes. Only the Dutch-speaking parties nominate candidates in Flanders, and the French-speaking ones in Wallonia. In Brussels different lists are presented for the same ballot, but for the overwhelming majority of voters this does not present itself as a widening of choice. For example, a French-speaking Socialist would be unlikely to vote for the Socialistische Partij rather than for the Parti Socialiste.

In parliamentary terms, the increased fractionalisation is more real, as more parties have to be accommodated in order to form a government. In practice, four parties are now normally required, whereas previously two would suffice. Virtually all Belgian governments include the Social Christians, the question usually boils down to whether there is going to be a Centre–Left coalition, with the Socialists, or a Centre–Right one, with the Liberals. Occasionally there has been a grand coalition of all three major groupings, and both the Flemish nationalist Volksunie and the Francophone FDF have been included in some recent coalitions.

In theory, one linguistic wing of a major party grouping could be in government, while its counterpart remains in opposition, but this is made more difficult by the provision that exactly half the ministerial posts should go to each language group. So far at least, each of the political families has remained in harness, both parties going together into government or remaining in opposition.

The Belgian system appears reasonably welcoming to the challenge of new political formations. While, unlike in Holland, no small minority grouping besides the Communist Party has been able to maintain itself over a long period of years, it is relatively easy for new parties to force their way into the Chamber. An anti-tax party, the UDRT,[7] gained its first representative in 1978, when it polled only 0.9% of the votes, while the Ecologists, who just missed out in 1978 with 0.8%, elected four members three years later when their vote shot up to 4.8%. The small Vlaams Blok, a more extreme Flemish group than the much larger Volksunie, has been represented in the last two Parliaments on a vote hovering just over 1%.

The conclusion seems to be that the Belgian electoral system puts no more constraints on, and imposes no more penalties against, large- and medium-sized parties that split up, but that at the lower end it is rather more effective than the Dutch system at keeping small parties out, though the threshold is low by international standards. According to Mackie and Rose's data, there has been an average of three more parties contesting Dutch elections and an average of 2.7 more parties represented in the legislature.[8] The major reason for this is the lower threshold, both theoretical and actual, in Holland.

The Luxembourg system has produced the least change over time, and though the 1979 election showed an increased level of fractionalisation this may well prove to have been only a passing phase. The major element was the split in the Socialist Party, resulting in the formation of the more right-wing Social Democratic Party in 1971, and the presentation, in addition, of a list of dissident Socialists in the 1979 election. By 1982, however, most of the dissidents had returned to the Socialist Party fold, or left the political scene, and both new groups had virtually petered out. Luxembourg seemed set to return to the four-party system it has enjoyed since the Second World War.

Between the wars a number of independent groupings managed to obtain representation, but these were mostly based on local interest groups, and reflected the 'county council' type politics of a tiny country, then almost entirely rural except for the steel-making area in the South. As there is one Luxembourg MP for every 5,500 residents, it will always be open to an energetic independent campaigner to hope to build up sufficient support to obtain election. But Luxembourg seems too small and too cohesive a society to have much need for continuing political groupings outside the four traditional ones. So, although the electoral threshold in Luxembourg is undoubtedly substantially higher (in percentage terms) than in either Belgium or Holland, it is doubtful if this is the main reason why many fewer parties have been represented in the Luxembourg Parliament.

GOVERNMENTAL STABILITY

One important factor remains to be discussed – the effect of the different electoral systems on the stability of governments. If the electoral system were the only, or the principal variable, one would predict a rank order of (1) Luxembourg, (2) Belgium, (3) the Netherlands.

Three measures might be used to gauge government stability: the frequency of elections, the durability of governments following elections and the amount of time taken to form a government following on a general election.

The first measure is vitiated by the differing lengths of statutory parliamentary terms, and the different provisions for holding an election out of term. Luxembourg held partial elections every three years before 1954, and thereafter the term has been five years. Both Belgium and Holland have four-year terms. In fact, Luxembourg has had the fewest elections – sixteen, then the Netherlands eighteen, while Belgium has easily had the most, with twenty.

The average length of time that governments formed following a general election have remained in office has produced the same order – Luxembourg (3.5 years), Netherlands (2.7), Belgium (2.5). The fact that Belgium has shown up as more unstable than Holland on these two measures is perhaps an indication that the linguistic factors (and continuing economic difficulties) have had a more destabilising effect than factors arising directly from the electoral system.

On the other hand, there is no doubt that the initial formation of a government is more difficult in Holland, where more parties have typically to be accommodated. In Holland, the average length of time taken to form a government since 1965 has been 95 days, with a record of 207 days in 1977. In the postwar period as a whole, over three years have been spent forming governments. In Belgium and Luxembourg the period is much shorter.

This chapter has concentrated on seeking out differences between the three Benelux countries which can be traced to their distinctive electoral systems. Yet it would be misleading to exaggerate their importance. In many respects, the similarities between the three countries have been obvious, and are much more significant than the differences.

One glaring similarity has been the dominating governmental role which the leading Catholic political party has played in each country. In the Netherlands the Catholic People's Party (and its successor, the Christian Democratic Appeal) has been included in every government except one since 1918. In Luxembourg the Party of the Right (later the Christian Social Party) has missed only two governments during the same period. In Belgium the Christian Social Party has been only marginally less omnipresent, spending six years out of sixty-four in opposition. In all three countries it is the Catholics, also, who have provided most of the Prime Ministers.

In Belgium and the Netherlands the Catholics' predominance has rested not only on the fact that they have usually been the largest party, but even more on their central position in the political spectrum which has made them an essential component of either a Right–Centre or a Left–Centre coalition. In Luxembourg, where their position has been on the Right, their presence in government has rested more directly on the strength of numbers.

In all three countries the Catholic party has acted as the anchor of the system, ensuring a great deal more stability than would otherwise have been the case. Because it has almost invariably been in government, either as the largest or as the second largest party, it has moreover been able to ensure a high degree of policy continuity, even during periods with a high turnover of cabinets.

CONCLUSION

Most of the differences discerned between the political systems of the three countries have been in the direction which one would have predicted on the basis of a knowledge only of their electoral systems. Yet the actual divergence has been less than might have been expected, and this suggests that each of the countries has been operating well within the theoretical limits of its system. In the Netherlands, for example, the degree of fractionalisation could have been a great deal more than has in fact been the case. For nearly all the time under consideration five parties have dominated the system,[9] together polling well over 80% of the vote, whereas, arguably, there was room for ten.

From this one might well conclude that, while electoral systems set ultimate parameters, the actual contours of party formations are shaped far more by economic, social and psychological factors. If Belgium and Holland could somehow have contrived to swap electoral systems, it seems doubtful whether the broad outlines of their party divisions would have varied to any considerable extent. What changes there might have been would have been around the edges, and particularly affecting the fate of very small parties. The Luxembourg system seems more directly designed for its own situation, and the party alignments in both Belgium and Holland would have rubbed up much more sharply against its limits. In particular, it is questionable whether Holland could have managed the luxury of two medium-sized Protestant parties for so long under such a system.

Finally, the similarities between the three countries confirm that the big divide between electoral systems is between plurality and proportional systems rather than between systems producing more or less proportional results. Advocates of extreme PR will be heartened by the evidence that the Dutch system does indeed result in greater fractionalisation, a more proportional allocation of seats and a fairer deal for smaller parties. Yet those who hold that other factors besides pure proportionality should be taken into account will be reassured by the fact that the difference in results obtained under the 'extreme' PR system of Holland and the more 'mainstream' PR system utilised by Belgium is so small.

APPENDIX – ELECTION RESULTS IN THE BENELUX COUNTRIES

Belgium: twenty in sixty-two years

	Total seats	Social Christians (Catholics)		Socialists (Workers)		Liberals		Communists		Dissident Catholics		Flemish Nats.		Francophile Parties		Others a		Government		
		Seats	%Votes	Seats	%Votes	Seats	%Votes	Seats	%Votes	Seats	%Votes	Seats	%Votes	Seats	%Votes	Seats	%Votes	No. of parties	Type b	Duration c
1919	186	73	36.6	70	36.6	34	17.6	–	–	0	2.1	5	2.6	–	–	4	4.4	3	L–R–C	1
1921	186	76	37.0	68	34.8	33	17.8	0	0.0	4	4.3	4	3.0	–	–	1	3.0	2	R–C	4
1925	187	75	36.1	78	39.4	23	14.6	2	1.6	3	2.5	6	3.9	–	–	0	1.8	3	L–R–C	3
1929	187	71	35.4	70	36.0	28	16.6	1	1.9	6	3.1	11	6.3	–	–	0	0.8	2	R–C	2
1932	187	79	38.5	73	37.1	24	14.3	3	2.8	0	0.2	8	5.9	–	–	0	1.1	3	R–C	3
1936	202	61	27.7	70	32.1	23	12.4	9	6.1	2	1.1	16	7.1	–	–	21	13.5	3	L–R–C	2
1939	202	73	32.7	64	30.2	33	17.2	9	5.4	–	–	17	8.3	–	–	6	6.2	3	L–R–C	5
1946	202	92	42.5	69	31.6	17	8.9	23	12.7	0	0.0	–	–	–	–	1	4.3	3	L–R	1
1949	212	105	43.5	66	29.7	29	15.2	12	7.5	0	0.1	0	2.1	–	–	0	1.8	1	L–C	1
1950	212	108	47.7	77	34.5	20	11.3	7	4.7	0	0.0	–	–	–	–	0	1.8	1	C	1
1954	212	95	41.1	86	37.3	25	12.1	4	3.6	1	0.9	1	2.1	–	–	0	2.7	2	L–R	5
1958	212	104	46.5	84	35.8	21	11.1	2	1.9	–	–	1	2.0	–	–	0	2.8	1	C	1
1961	212	96	41.5	84	36.7	20	12.3	5	3.1	1	0.8	5	3.5	–	–	1	2.1	2	L–C	5
1965	212	77	34.4	64	28.2	48	21.6	6	4.6	0	0.3	12	6.4	5	2.4	0	2.1	2	L–C	3
1968	212	69	31.8	59	28.0	47	20.9	5	3.3	–	–	20	9.8	12	5.9	0	0.3	2	L–C	1
1971	212	67	30.1	61	27.2	34	16.4	5	3.1	–	–	21	11.1	24	11.3	0	0.9	2	L–C	1
1974	212	72	32.3	59	26.7	30	15.2	4	3.2	–	–	22	10.2	25	10.9	0	1.5	2	R–C	3
1977	212	80	36.0	61	26.5	33	15.5	2	2.1	–	–	20	10.0	16	7.7	0	2.2	4	L–C	2
1978	212	82d	36.1d	58d	25.4d	37d	16.4d	4	3.3	–	–	15	8.4	15	7.2	1	3.3	5 (3)e	L–C	1
1981	212	61d	26.4d	61d	25.1d	52d	21.5d	4	2.3	–	–	21	10.9	8	4.2	7	9.6	4 (2)e	R–C	–

a Other parties elected:
1919 Ex-Servicemen 2, Middle Class Party 1, Renovation Nationale 1
1921 Ex-Servicemen 1
1936 Rexists 21
1939 Rexists 4, Frenssen and Combattants 2
1946 Democratic Union 1
1961 German List 1
1978 Anti-tax (DDRT) 1
1981 Anti-tax (UDRT) 3, Ecologists 4.
b Political complexion of government: R =Right, C=Centre, L=Left.
c Number of years that elected government remained in office. 1=up to 1 year, 2=up to 2 years, etc.
d After 1977 the three largest parties each split into French- and Dutch-speaking components. The figures given for the 1978 and 1981 elections are in each case the combined totals of two separate, but aligned, parties.
e Indicates number of parties that would have been included if the major parties had not split along linguistic lines.

	Total seats	Catholics/Chr. Dems		Anti-Revolutionary P		Chr. Hist. Un.		Soc. Dems/ Lab.		Liberals and Radicals		Communists		Pol. Ref. P (PRP)		Democrats 66		Others[a]		Government		
		Seats	%Votes	Seats	%Votes	Seats	%Votes	Seats	%Votes	Seats	%Votes	Seats	%Votes	Seats	%Votes	Seats	%Votes	Seats	%Votes	No. of parties	Type[b]	Dura-tion[c]
1918	100	30	30.0	13	13.4	7	6.5	22	22.0	15	15.3	2	2.3	0	0.4	–	–	11	10.4	2	C–R	4
1922	100	32	29.9	16	13.7	11	10.9	20	19.4	16	13.9	2	1.8	1	0.9	–	–	3	9.5	2	C–R	3
1925	100	30	28.6	13	12.2	11	9.9	24	22.9	15	14.8	1	1.2	2	2.0	–	–	3	8.4	2	C–R	1
1929	100	30	29.6	12	11.6	11	10.5	24	23.8	15	13.6	2	2.0	3	2.3	–	–	3	6.6	2	C–R	4
1933	100	28	27.9	14	13.4	10	9.1	22	21.5	13	12.1	4	3.2	3	2.5	–	–	6	6.7	5	C–R	2
1937	100	31	28.8	17	16.4	8	7.5	23	21.9	10	9.8	3	3.4	2	1.9	–	–	6	11.1	3	C–R	2
1946	100	32	30.8	13	12.9	8	7.8	29	28.3	6	6.4	10	10.6	2	2.1	–	–	0	1.0	2	L–C	2
1948	100	32	31.0	13	13.2	9	9.2	27	25.6	8	7.9	8	7.7	2	2.4	–	–	1	2.3	4	L–R–C	2
1952	100	30	28.7	12	11.3	9	8.9	30	29.0	9	8.8	6	6.2	2	2.4	–	–	2	4.8	4	L–C	7
1956	150	49	31.7	15	9.9	13	8.4	50	32.7	13	8.8	7	4.7	3	2.3	–	–	0	1.4	4	L–C	4
1959	150	49	31.6	14	9.4	12	8.1	48	30.4	19	12.2	3	2.4	3	2.2	–	–	2	3.8	4	R–C	4
1963	150	50	31.9	13	8.7	13	8.6	43	28.0	16	10.3	4	2.8	3	2.3	–	–	8	7.4	4	R–C	4
1967	150	42	26.5	15	9.9	12	8.1	37	23.6	17	10.7	5	3.6	3	2.0	7	4.5	12	11.2	4	R–C	1
1971	150	35	21.8	13	8.6	10	6.3	39	24.6	16	10.3	6	3.9	3	2.3	11	6.8	17	15.2	5	R–L–C	1
1972	150	27	17.7	14	8.8	7	4.8	43	27.3	22	14.4	7	4.5	3	2.2	6	4.2	21	16.0	5	L–C	4
1977	150	49	31.9d	–d		–d		53	33.8	28	17.9	2	1.7	3	2.1	8	5.4	7	7.0	3	L–R	4
1981	150	48	30.8d	–d		–d		44	28.3	26	17.3	3	2.1	3	2.0	17	11.1	9	8.5	3	L–R	4
1982	150	45	29.3d	–d		–d		47	30.4	36	23.1	3	1.8	3	1.9	6	4.3	10	9.2	2	R–C	1

a Other parties elected:
1918 Christian Democrats 3, Socialist P 1, Economic League 3, Farmers P 1, Middle Class P 1, Others 2
1922 Farmers P 2
1925 New Reformed State P 1, Farmers P 1
1929 New Reformed State P 1, Farmers P 1, Middle P 1
1933 Roman Catholic Peoples P 1, Christian Democrats 1, New Reformed State P 1, Revolutionary Socialist P 1, Farmers P 1, League for Nat. Renewal 1
1937 Roman Catholic Peoples P 1. Christian Democrats 2. National Socialist Movement 4
1948 Catholic National P 1
1952 Catholic National P 2
1959 Pacifist Socialist P 2
1963 Reformed Political Union 1, Pacifist Socialist P 4. Farmers P 3
1967 Ref. Pol. Un. 1, Pacifist Socialist P 4. Farmers P 7
1971 Ref. Pol. Un. 2, Ref. Pol. Un. 2, Dem. Soc. '70 8, Farmers P 1, Middle Class P 2
1972 Rad. Pol. P 7, Rom. Cath. 1, Ref. Pol. Un. 2, Pac. Soc. P 2, Dem. Soc. '70 6, Farmers P 3
1977 Ref. Pol. Un. 1, Pac. Soc. P 1, Farmers P 1, Rad. Pol. P 3
1981 Rad. Pol. P 3, Ref. Pol. Fed. 2, Ref. Pol. Ass. 1, Pac. Soc. P 3.
1982 Pac. Soc. P 3, Rad. Pol. P 2, Ref. Pol. Fed. 2, Centre P. 1, Ref. Pol. Ass. 1, Evangelicals 1.

b Political complexion of government: R = Right, C = Centre, L = Left.
c Number of years that elected government remained in office. 1 = up to 1 year, 2 = up to 2 years, etc.
d In 1976 the Catholic Peoples Party, the Anti-Revolutionary Party and the Christian Historical Union came together to form the Christian Democratic Appeal. For 1977, 1981 and 1982 the CDA totals are shown in the first party column.

Sources: Mackie and Rose, International Almanac; Keesing's Contemporary Archives.

Luxembourg: sixteen in sixty years

	Total seats	Christian Social P (Right) Seats	% Votes	Socialists Seats	% Votes	Liberals (Democrats) Seats	% Votes	Communists Seats	% Votes	Others a Seats	% Votes	No. of parties	Government Type b	Duration c
1919	48	27	52.5	9	19.3	7	16.9	—	—	5	11.3	2	R–C	2
P 1922	25	13	n.a.	2	n.a.	6	n.a.	—	—	4	n.a.	1	R	4
1925	46	22	n.a.	8	n.a.	4	n.a.	—	—	12	n.a.	3	L–C	2
P 1928	27	12	39.8	10	41.3	2	7.9	—	—	3	10.9	2	R–L	6
P 1931	27	14	44.2	5	22.1	2	7.7	0	1.3	6	24.7	2	R–C	4
P 1934	29	12	37.0	10	36.7	3	12.9	1	6.4	3	7.0	2	R–C	2
P 1937	26	13	44.0	7	25.7	2	10.7	—	—	4	19.6	2	R–C	2
1945	51	25	41.4	11	26.0	9	16.7	5	13.5	1	2.4	4	R–C–L	3
P 1948	26	12	41.0	9	35.8	5	20.7	0	2.5	0	—	2	R–C	3
P 1951	26	9	33.3	10	41.4	3	8.4	4	16.9	0	2.8	2	R–L	4
1954	52	26	42.4	17	35.1	6	10.8	3	8.9	0	0.7	2	R–C	6
1959	52	21	36.9	17	34.9	11	18.5	5	9.1	2	6.0	2	R–L	5
1964	56	22	33.3	21	37.7	6	10.6	6	12.5	0	0.4	2	R–C	5
1968	56	21	35.3	18	32.3	11	16.6	6	15.5	0	10.3	2	R–C	5
1974	59	18	27.9	17	29.1	14	22.2	5	10.5	5	10.3	2	C–L	
1979	59	24	34.5	14	24.3	15	21.3	2	5.8	4	14.1	2	R–C	

P = partial election. Voting figures for the 1922 partial and the 1925 general election are not available.

a Other parties and independents elected:
1919 Ind. Nat. P 3. Ind. Pop. P 2
1922 Ind. Nat. P 4
1925 Ind. Nat. P 4. Ind. Right P 1. Left P 2. Rad. Socialists 5
1928 Independents 1. Left Independents 2
1931 Rad. Socialists 2. Independents 1. Farmers and Middle Class P 2. Prog. Democrats 1
1934 Independents 3
1937 Democratic List 2. Peasants. Middle Class. Workers P 1. Liberal P 1
1945 Independents 1
1964 Popular Independent Movement 2
1974 Social Democratic P 5
1979 Social Democratic P 2. Ind. Socialists 1. Enrôlés de Force 1.

b Political complexion of government: R = Right. C = Centre. L = Left.

c Number of years that elected government remained in office. 1 = up to 1 year. 2 = up to 2 years. etc.

Sources: Mackie and Rose. International Almanac; Keesing's Contemporary Archives.

NOTES

1 *Annuaire Statistique du Luxembourg*, published by Statec (Service Central de la Statistique et des Études Economiques) (Luxembourg, Annually), 1981–2, p. 366.
2 Rae also found that largest remainder systems tended to be more proportional than highest average ones, but that the differences were far less marked. This is borne out by the research of the present author. Luxembourg has a largest remainder system, while both Holland and Belgium utilise highest average. It is clear from the findings reported here that whatever additional proportionality Luxembourg has gained from using a largest remainder formula has been more than cancelled out by its lower district magnitude.
3 See Galen A. Irwin, 'The Netherlands', in Peter H. Merkl, ed., *Western European Party Systems* (NY, London, 1980), pp. 166–9, 174–6.
4 Irwin, ibid., p. 175
5 Arend Lijphart, 'Extreme Proportional Representation, Multipartism and Electoral Reform in the Netherlands', typescript. Paper prepared for 'Journées d'études sur les modes de scrutin européens', University of Paris II, 7–8 January 1977.
6 See Keith Hill, 'Belgium: Political Change in a Segmented Society', in Richard Rose, *Electoral Behavior: A Comparative Handbook* (New York, 1974).
7 Union Democratique pour le Respect du Travail.
8 The Mackie and Rose data (Thomas T. Mackie and Richard Rose, *The International Almanac of Electoral History*, 2nd edn (London, 1982)), which aggregates the votes obtained by very small parties, understates the number of parties presenting candidates – and this, in particular, understates the extent to which more parties have contested elections in the Netherlands than in the other two Benelux countries. For example, Mackie and Rose list the votes obtained by fifteen parties in the 1972 Dutch election, whereas, according to Lijphart, 'Extreme Proportional Representation', p. 9, twenty parties presented lists. This difference is not likely to have affected the calculations, on fractionalisation, etc., in Table 2, to any significant degree, as all the parties not taken into account polled a very small number of votes.
9 These five parties, the Catholic People's Party, the Anti-Revolutionary Party, the Christian Historical Union, the Labour Party and the Liberals, were also the only parties to be included in Dutch Cabinets until 1973, when Democrats '66 were included.

SUGGESTIONS FOR FURTHER READING

Annuaire Statistique du Luxembourg (published by Statec (Service Central de la Statistique et des Études Economiques) (Luxembourg, Annually)
H. Brény and J. Beaufays, *Le Rôle et la Place de l'Apparentement dans les Élections Législatives Belges à la Lumière du Calcul de la Dévolution des Sièges selon Différents Modes* in *Respublica* (1974)
Hans Daalder, 'Extreme Proportional Representation: The Dutch Experience', in S. E. Finer, ed., *Adversary Politics and Electoral Reform* (London, 1975)
'The Netherlands', in Stanley Henig, *Political Parties in the European Community* (London, 1979)

Keith Hill, 'Belgium: Political Change in a Segmented Society', in Richard Rose, *Electoral Behavior: A Comparative Handbook* (New York, 1974)

Mario Hirsch, 'Luxembourg' in Henig, ed., *Political Parties*

Arend Lijphart, 'The Netherlands: Continuity and Change in Voting Behaviour' in Rose, *Electoral Behavior*

'The Politics of Accommodation: Pluralism and Democracy in the Netherlands', 2nd edn (Berkeley, 1975)

'The Dutch Electoral System in Comparative Perspective', *Netherlands Journal of Sociology* (1978)

Xavier Mabille and Val R. Lorwin, 'Belgium', in Henig, *Political Parties*

9

The Republic of Ireland

PAUL McKEE

The original constitution, enacted in December 1922, of what was then called the Irish Free State directed that deputies to the Dail be elected 'upon the principles of Proportional Representation' (Article 26). There was no mention in the constitution of the way in which such principles were to be implemented – the details of the electoral system were to be specified by ordinary law and it was the Electoral Act (1923) which set out the detailed rules for operating the single transferable vote system.

The constitution was revised in 1937 primarily to replace those elements of the British Commonwealth model which had been incorporated in the original constitution, e.g., the replacement of a Governor General by an elected President. At the same time the opportunity was also taken to be more specific in the constitution regarding the type of electoral system. The current constitution, enacted in 1937, states in Article 16.2.5 that members of the Dail 'shall be elected on the system of proportional representation by means of the single transferable vote'. Somewhat paradoxically the system is still referred to in Ireland as 'the PR system' as though the system was a perfect proportional representation system and no other proportional representation system existed. It is rare that this system is ever described in Ireland as the single transferable vote system in multi-member constituencies, its correct technical description.

As often happens, some of the main reasons behind the adoption of the system turned out to be ephemeral. In particular the hope that it would ensure that Unionists (i.e., mainly Protestants) in the south of Ireland would achieve due representation in the Dail was not fulfilled. Such Unionists who were interested in politics quickly became absorbed in the main parties in the Dail, did not form a separate party and hence did not achieve separate representation. Additionally the use of the same electoral system in both the twenty-six southern counties of Ireland, i.e., the Republic of Ireland, and the six northern counties of Ireland, i.e., Northern Ireland, turned out to be temporary. In Northern Ireland the single transferable vote system was abolished for local elections in 1923 and for elections to the Northern Ireland House of Commons in 1929. But it was reintroduced in 1973 for both local government and Northern Ireland Assembly elections and has been used for all elections in

Northern Ireland (with the exception of UK parliamentary elections) since that time.

THE SINGLE TRANSFERABLE VOTE SYSTEM

The single transferable vote system requires the voter to select between the candidates listed on the ballot paper by ranking them in order of preference. The voter does this by marking the figure '1' beside the name of the candidate who is the first preference of the voter, the figure '2' beside the name of the second preference and so on for as many candidates as the voter chooses.

Whilst this system can be used within constituencies for which a single member is to be elected, when it is known as the alternative vote, the more normal approach is for several members to be elected for each constituency. In the Republic of Ireland, the traditional pattern is to have a mix of three-member, four-member and five-member constituencies.

The counting procedure used to determine which of the candidates are to be elected is relatively straightforward, although it does take longer than any of the other systems employed in Western Europe. The main reasons for this are first that the system does not allow for counting at individual polling stations but requires all the ballot papers for a particular constituency to be counted together at one count centre, and secondly that a large proportion of the ballot papers have to be processed more than once.

The first stage in the count is the determination of the total number of valid votes. Apart from technical factors which may invalidate a vote, e.g., lack of an official mark, the main reason for an invalid vote is the lack of an unambiguous first preference. Later preferences may be ambiguous, e.g., two second preferences would make the vote non-transferable if the second preference had to be considered but would not make the vote an invalid one. In the last five general elections in the Republic of Ireland the average number of spoilt votes has been 1.0% of the total votes cast. This can be compared with the average of around 0.15% in UK parliamentary elections. It should not be necessarily concluded that the electoral system itself has a tendency to increase the proportion of spoilt votes. It may be, and probably is, one of the options an Irish voter considers appropriate to exercise since the proportion of spoilt votes is very similar to that in UK parliamentary elections in Northern Ireland (average of 0.94% in the last three general elections).

Having determined the total number of valid votes the next stage in the counting process is the calculation of the quota, which is the number of votes a candidate has to achieve in order to be elected. This is calculated via the Droop[1] formula:

$$\text{Quota} = \frac{\text{Total Number of Valid Votes}}{\text{Number of seats} + 1} + 1 \text{ (ignoring any fractions)}$$

The quota amounts to the smallest number of votes which enables just enough candidates to be elected to fill all the seats whilst being just large enough to prevent any more candidates being elected. In other words the quota tends to maximise the number of votes being used to contribute to the election of winning candidates and minimises 'wasted votes' if these are defined as votes which fail to contribute to the election of a candidate. For instance in a four-seat constituency the quota would be one vote more than one-fifth of the valid poll, i.e., one vote more than 20% of the valid vote. Since each winning candidate has to achieve the quota this implies that just above 80% of the valid vote has been used to contribute to the election of the winning candidates and just under 20% has been 'wasted' in the sense outlined above. Obviously the larger the number of seats in any one constituency then the smaller the 'wasted' vote, but this aspect has to be balanced against the larger geographical area implied by a very large number of seats and the obvious inconvenience of extraordinarily long ballot papers.

Following the calculation of the quota the first preference votes for each candidate are counted and any candidate who achieves a number of first preference votes greater or equal to the quota is declared elected. The votes obtained by any such candidate in excess of the quota can be regarded as 'surplus' votes and these are distributed in accordance with second preferences. The problem of which votes to distribute is solved by sorting all the votes for an elected candidate by the next preferences. The same proportion of votes for each next preference is distributed as the total surplus divided by the total transferable vote for the elected candidate. If, for example, the surplus represents 10% of the total transferable vote of an elected candidate then 10% of the ballot papers of each next preference are physically transferred to the 'parcels' of votes already obtained by the next preference candidates.

The ballot papers which are transferred in this way are taken from the last ones added to each pile of ballot papers. Consequently in the later stages of the count the ballot papers involved are likely to be ones which themselves have already been transferred.[2]

If no candidate has obtained a number of votes equal to or greater than the quota, then the candidate with the lowest number of first preference votes is eliminated and the votes for that candidate are distributed in accordance with the second preferences indicated on the ballot papers.

The process of distributing surplus votes and eliminating candidates continues until the total number of seats has been filled. Precedence is given in this process to distributing the surplus votes rather than eliminating a candidate if the surplus is greater than the difference in votes between the bottom two candidates. (In this case the distribution of the surplus could conceivably alter the relative positions of the bottom two candidates.) Otherwise a candidate is eliminated before a surplus is distributed.

Table 1a *Galway West result, general election February 1982*

Galway West (5 seats)
Total valid poll 48,572   Quota 8,096
Turnout 67.5%

Candidate and party	Count 1[a]	Count 2[b]	Count 3[c]	Count 4[d]	Count 5[e]	Count 6[f]	Cou
*Molloy (FF)	9,545*	−1,449					
*Donnellan (FG)	6,105	+38	+51	+30	+2,181		
		6,143	6,194	6,224	8,405*		
*Higgins (Lab)	5,718	+129	+715	+214	+554	+2,970	
		5,847	6,562	6,776	7,330	10,300*	−2,2
Fahey (FF)	6,019	+352	+99	+294	+97	+379	+4
		6,371	6,470	6,764	6,861	7,240	7,6
*Geoghegan-Quinn (FF)	4,139	+475	+47	+1,716	+87	+221	+1
		4,614	4,661	6,377	6,464	6,685	6,8
*Killilea (FF)	5,624	+198	+35	+242	+29	+212	+1
		5,822	5,857	6,099	6,128	6,340	6,4
McCormack (FG)	3,952	+24	+38	+41	+1,014		
		3,976	4,014	4,055	5,069**		
Coogan (FG)	3,746	+47	+145	+105			
		3,793	3,938	4,043**			
O'Connor (FF)	2,513	+171	+33				
		2,684	2,717**				
Brick (SFWP)	1,211	+15					
		1,226**					
Spoilt/non.-trans.	391	0	63	75	81	1,287	1,4

Table 1b *First preference votes*

Party	N votes	% Votes	% Change from 1981
FF	27,840	57.3	+2.2
FG	13,803	28.4	−1.6
Lab	5,718	11.8	−0.5
SFWP	1,211	2.5	+0.4
Other	–	–	−0.5

General notes

i The quota $= \dfrac{48.572}{5+1} + 1 = 8.096$ (ignoring any fractions).

ii The party abbreviations following each candidate's name are:

FF   Fianna Fail. (Literally translated this party name is 'soldiers of destiny'. In party

THE SYSTEM IN OPERATION

The counting procedure can be illustrated in Table 1 which sets out the result of each count in Galway West in the February 1982 election. This example also serves to indicate many of the relevant implications of the system. The votes in the Count 1 column are the first preference votes for each candidate. Molloy (FF) obtained 9,545 votes which was 1,449 votes more than the quota and hence was elected and would subsequently be spoken of as 'topping the poll in Galway West'. This was not without significance since Bobby Molloy was, to phrase it diplomatically, not a strong supporter of the leader of Fianna Fail, Charles Haughey, whereas some of Molloy's running mates, in particular Mark Killilea, were strong supporters of Haughey. A

Notes to Table 1b (*cont.*)

	literature the sub-title The Republican Party is often added. Leader from December 1979 – Charles J. Haughey. Party founded by Eamon de Valera in 1926. Largest party in Ireland.)
FG	Fine Gael. (Literally translated the party name is 'family group of the Gaels'. Sometimes referred to as United Ireland Party. Successor party to Cumann na nGaedheal which accepted the Anglo-Irish Treaty of 1922. Leader from July 1977 – Garret FitzGerald. Second largest party in Ireland.)
Lab	Labour. (Oldest, but smallest of the three principal parties. Leader from October 1982 – Dick Spring.)
SFWP	Sinn Fein the Workers' Party. (The party was previously known as Sinn Fein, then Official Sinn Fein and only as Sinn Fein the Workers' Party from 1977. Renamed the Workers' Party from April 1982. Campaigns primarily for economic and social reform.)

iii An asterisk preceding a candidate's name, e.g., *Molloy, indicates a member of the previous Dail, i.e., a sitting member.

A single asterisk following a number of votes indicates that the votes of that candidate have exceeded the quota and hence the candidate has been elected on that count.

A double asterisk following a number of votes indicates that the candidate has been eliminated as a result of that particular count and the votes are to be transferred in the following count.

iv The candidates are listed in descending order of the final vote obtained by the candidate. This vote will be obtained in the count which results in the candidate being elected or eliminated. An alternative presentation[3] which could be used is to list the candidates in alphabetical order, as they are on the ballot paper.

a Count 1:   first preference votes counted, Molloy (FF) elected.
b Count 2:   distribution of surplus votes of Molloy (FF), Brick (SFWP) eliminated.
c Count 3:   transfer of votes of Brick (SFWP), O'Connor (FF) eliminated.
d Count 4:   transfer of votes of O'Connor (FF), Coogan (FG) eliminated.
e Count 5:   transfer of votes of Coogan (FG), Donnellan (FG) elected, McCormack (FG) eliminated.
f Count 6:   transfer of votes of McCormack (FG), Higgins (Lab.) elected.
g Count 7:   distribution of surplus votes of Higgins (Lab.) Fahey (FF) and Geoghegan-Quinn (FF) elected without reaching quota.

Table 2 *Distribution of surplus from Molloy (FF)*
– Count 2, Galway West, February 1982

To other Fianna Fail candidates	1,196	(82.6%)
To Labour candidate	129	(8.9%)
To Fine Gael candidates	109	(7.5%)
To SFWP candidate	15	(1.0%)

conclusion which could be drawn from the disparity in performance between Molloy and Killilea, who failed to be re-elected, and came fifth in order of first preference votes as compared with second in the June 1981 election, was that the anti-Haughey tendency within the Fianna Fail party had found increasing public support. In other words the pattern of first preference votes among Fianna Fail candidates could be interpreted 'as sending a message' regarding the leadership of Fianna Fail.

In Count 2, Molloy's surplus of 1,449 votes is distributed and not surprisingly the bulk of these votes go to other Fianna Fail candidates. In summary the 1,449 votes are distributed as shown in Table 2. There are no non-transferable votes since one of the rules of the system is that only transferable votes are normally distributed in a surplus, any non-transferable votes are considered as part of the 'quota' votes.

The distribution of Molloy's surplus (83% being obtained by other Fianna Fail candidates) is illustrative of the high degree of party discipline which can be applied to the transfer of votes from one candidate of a party to other candidates of the same party. The national analysis of transfer patterns in the general election of 1982 was similar to that in Galway West with Fianna Fail candidates nationally retaining 86% of the votes transferred from another Fianna Fail candidate either as a result of a surplus or from the elimination of a candidate.

As a result of the distribution of Molloy's surplus no candidate obtains a number of votes at least equal to the quota and consequently the candidate with the lowest number of votes is eliminated, i.e., Brick (SFWP), and his 1,226 votes are transferred in Count 3 in accordance with the next preferences. This total of 1,226 votes is made up of 1,211 first preference votes and fifteen second preferences from the distribution of Molloy's surplus. As will be seen from the votes in Count 3, sixty-three of the votes were non-transferable, i.e., did not have second preferences indicated in the case of Brick's original votes or third preferences if the votes came from the distribution of Molloy's surplus. In summary Brick's 1,226 votes are distributed as shown in Table 3.

The fact that a majority of these SFWP votes went to the Labour party candidate indicates quite clearly the nature of the support for the SFWP candidate, although it should be noted that the proportion of Labour votes

Table 3 *Transfer of votes of Brick (SFWP) –*
Count 3, Galway West, February 1982

To Labour candidate	715	(58.3%)
To Fine Gael candidates	234	(19.1%)
To Fianna Fail candidates	214	(17.5%)
Non-transferable	63	(5.1%)

Table 4 *Transfer of votes of O'Connor – Count 4,*
Galway West, February 1982

To other Fianna Fail candidates	2.252	(82.9%)
To Labour candidate	214	(7.9%)
To Fine Gael candidates	176	(6.5%)
Non-transferable	75	(2.7%)

obtained in this transfer was above the level in the three other constituencies with a similar pattern of candidature. Taking the four comparable SFWP transfers together, Labour candidates obtained, in 1982, 45% of SFWP transfers with Fianna Fail taking slightly more than Fine Gael at 21% and 19% respectively with 15% non-transferable. In some ways this pattern of transfers confirms SFWP support as being primarily drawn from those voters who considered themselves on the Left of the anti-Fianna Fail alliance.

The effect of the majority of votes going to Higgins, the Labour candidate, is to move him from third place behind Fahey (FF) and Donnellan (FG) at the end of Count 2 to ahead of both. No candidate achieved a quota as a result of this count and so O'Connor (FF) as the candidate with the lowest vote is eliminated and his 2,717 votes are transferred in Count 4 with the bulk of his votes going to other Fianna Fail candidates as in the parallel distribution of votes in Count 2. In summary the 2,717 votes are distributed as shown in Table 4.

The consistency of the pattern of transfers between Count 2 and 4 in terms of the proportion of votes retained by Fianna Fail candidates, 82.6% in Count 2 and 82.9% in Count 4, is a further illustration of the party discipline which can be utilised within the single transferable vote system.

Somewhat less obvious but equally important, at least to the candidates involved, is the distribution of votes between candidates of the same party. In Count 2, although Fianna Fail candidates retained 82.6% of the transferred votes, not all Fianna Fail candidates benefited equally and the variation between candidates as a result of the transfer of votes in Count 4 was even more marked as can be seen from Table 5.

Table 5 *Transferred votes received by Fianna Fail
candidates from other Fianna Fail candidates – Count 2
and 4, Galway West, February 1982*

	Count 2 Molloy's surplus	Count 4 O'Connor's transfers
Geoghegan-Quinn	475 (40%)	1,716 (76%)
Fahey	352 (29%)	294 (13%)
Killilea	198 (17%)	242 (11%)
O'Connor	171 (11%)	–
TOTAL	1,196	2,252

The effect of the considerable gain of votes by Maire Geoghegan-Quinn in
Count 4 is that she jumps ahead of her fellow party candidate Mark Killilea.
Previously she lagged Killilea by 1,196 votes, now she leads by 278 votes.
Clearly such a marked discrepancy in the transfer of votes must have an
obvious cause. The reason is likely to be that Nicholas O'Connor lives deep in
the Connemara end of the constituency, i.e., the western end which contains a
high proportion of people who use Irish as their first language. Maire
Geoghegan-Quinn was from 1979–81 the Minister for the Gaeltacht, i.e., the
department which deals with the particular problems of those areas where the
majority of the inhabitants speak Irish as their first language. Consequently,
since most of Nicholas O'Connor's votes are likely to come from the Gaeltacht
area, the natural next preference for such votes is likely to be a fellow party
candidate who was previously Minister for the Gaeltacht – especially since no
other candidate of any party in the contest had any direct association with the
Gaeltacht.

The discrepancy between the votes received by the other Fianna Fail
candidates as a result of the distribution of Molloy's surplus in Count 2 is less
marked than in Count 4 and is likely to arise from the fact that Geoghegan-
Quinn originates from the same part of Galway City as Molloy. Fahey also
benefited somewhat more than the other two candidates, possibly since he was
generally regarded as Molloy's running mate. These two particular examples
illustrate locational aspects of intra-party competition which can be extremely
important in determining in the Republic of Ireland which particular
candidate of a party is elected. It is also not without significance that Galway is
often referred to as the 'City of the Tribes' and it is likely that differentation
between candidates is somewhat accentuated.

With no candidate achieving a number of votes at least equal to the quota in
Count 4, the candidate with the lowest vote i.e. Coogan (FG) is eliminated and
his votes, totalling 4,043 are transferred in Count 5. In summary Coogan's
4,043 votes are distributed as shown in Table 6.

Table 6 *Transfer of votes of Coogan (FG) – Count
5, Galway West, February 1982*

To other Fine Gael candidates	3,195	(79.0%)
To Labour candidate	554	(13.7%)
To Fianna Fail candidates	213	(5.3%)
Non-transferable	81	(2.0%)

On a preliminary inspection this analysis would indicate that Fine Gael party discipline has been slightly less effective than in the case of Fianna Fail transfers since Fine Gael has retained only 79% of the transferred votes, whereas in Counts 2 and 4 Fianna Fail had retained 83% of the transferred votes. However it should be remembered that Fine Gael and Labour formed the Coalition government then in power and leaders of both parties had urged their supporters to include the candidates of the other party in their list of preferences. As a Fine Gael advertisement put it 'Vote Fine Gael and continue your preferences for Labour.' Consequently it can be argued that in terms of measuring party discipline, Fine Gael and Labour transfers should be considered together and on this basis 92.7% of the transferred votes remained within the Fine Gael plus Labour group – a considerably higher proportion than Fianna Fail retained.

Of the 3,195 votes retained by the remaining two Fine Gael candidates, more than two-thirds (68%) went to the sitting deputy, John Donnellan, who had been a deputy from Galway since 1964 when he won a by-election caused by the death of his father, who had been a deputy for the area from 1943 to 1964. The family relationship between successive generations of deputies in the Dail is a particularly notable aspect[4] of Irish politics and is perhaps well illustrated not only by John Donnellan but also by Maire Geoghegan-Quinn who also succeeded her father who was deputy for Galway West from 1954 until his death in 1975. In addition Mark Killilea is the son of the Dail deputy for Galway from 1923 to 1932 and 1933 to 1936, and the unsuccessful Fine Gael candidate, Fintan Coogan, is the son of the deputy for Galway West from 1954 to 1977.

John Donnellan also illustrates one other route of entry for successful candidates to the Dail, namely the sporting connection particularly in respect of prominence in the Gaelic Athletic Association. In John Donnellan's case he was the captain of the Galway team which won the All-Ireland Football Final in 1964 and a team member when the Galway side was similarly victorious in 1965 and 1966. (Tragically his father died while attending the 1964 final.)

These two characteristics of the candidates in Galway West, i.e., the family connection with previous deputies to the Dail and the sporting prominence are repeated in many other constituencies. Of the deputies elected in the General Election of 1981, 23% had direct family connections with previous or current deputies or members of the Senate and 30% were or had been prominent in sporting activities especially those involving Gaelic sports. Such characteristics being particularly marked in respect of Fianna Fail deputies.

This phenomenon is not a recent aspect of Irish politics. Of the deputies elected in 1961, 23% had direct family connections with previous or current members of the Dail or Senate with the proportion rising to 28% in 1965 and 1969. The prominence in sporting activities was, however, one which grew in importance during the 1960s since only 13% of the Dail deputies elected in 1961 came into this category, rising to 15% in 1965 and 30% in 1969.

One other marked characteristic of Dail deputies is the very high proportion with current or previous local government experience, with some 77% of those elected in 1981 being current or past members of local authorities; all the elected members for Galway West in 1982, with the exception of Maire Geoghegan-Quinn, being in this category.

Whatever the principal reasons behind the disparity between the votes received by the two Fine Gael candidates remaining in Count 5 the end result was that Donnellan obtained enough votes to exceed the quota and was elected on this count with a surplus of 309 votes. This surplus was smaller than the difference between the two bottom candidates remaining in the count, i.e., Killilea (FF) and McCormack (FG) who differed by 1,059 votes. Consequently distributing the surplus would make no difference to the relative order of the candidates. For this reason McCormack (FG) was eliminated since the votes involved (5,069) were considerably larger than the surplus and transferring these would hasten the overall progress of the count as compared with the distribution of a 309 vote surplus. The transfer of the 5,069 votes of McCormack (FG) in Count 6 enables a different measure of party discipline to be assessed since no Fine Gael candidate remained in the count.

This type of transfer is known as a terminal transfer, i.e., a transfer in which no candidate of the same party remains in the count but candidates of the other two major parties remain. In summary terms McCormack's 5,069 votes were distributed as shown in Table 7.

This pattern of transfers again indicates a high degree of party discipline with 59% of votes following the party guidance to 'continue your preferences for Labour' despite the fact that Michael D. Higgins, the Labour candidate in receipt of these preferences was a noted opponent of the Fine Gael and Labour Coalition. Perhaps as important is that only 16% of the transferred votes benefited the principal party opposed to Fine Gael, i.e., Fianna Fail, and 84% did not. The 2,970 votes received by the Labour candidate were more than sufficient to take him well over the quota and hence become the third candidate to be elected. This surplus of 2,204 votes is larger than the surplus remaining to be distributed from the previous count, i.e., 309 votes, and consequently it is the Labour surplus which is distributed in Count 7.

This count is distinguished by the large number of non-transferable votes. This is somewhat unusual in a count concerned with distributing a surplus.

Table 7 *Transfer of votes of McCormack (FG) –*
Count 6, Galway West, February 1982

To Labour candidate	2,970	(58.6%)
To Fianna Fail candidates	812	(16.0%)
Non-transferable	1,287	(25.4%)

for, as has been noted previously, non-transferable votes are normally excluded from the distribution of any surplus votes. Consequently in the distribution of a surplus one would expect to find zero votes in the non-transferable line. However, as can be seen from Table 1, 1,432 votes were found to be non-transferable in the distribution of Higgins' surplus in Count 7. What has happened is that there are insufficient transferable votes to make up a surplus so that a number of non-transferable votes have been included in order to ensure that a total number of votes equal to the surplus have been distributed.

Of Michael D. Higgins' total of 10,300 votes apparently only 722 (7.5%) had subsequent preferences marked and the remaining part of the surplus had to be made up of non-transferable ones. This represents a non-transferable per-centage of 92.5% of Higgins' vote in Count 6. This is another example of a very high degree of party discipline, indicating as it does that the overwhelming bulk of Labour and Fine Gael voters who supported Higgins had not gone on to include Fianna Fail candidates in their list of preferences.

After this count there are three candidates remaining and two seats yet to be filled, together with a surplus of 309 votes remaining to be distributed as a result of Count 5. The difference between the two lowest candidates remaining in the poll was 396 votes. Consequently the distribution of the surplus would not affect the order of these two bottom candidates and the returning officer then had the option of eliminating the third candidate, which would be to a large extent a meaningless exercise since only two candidates would remain in the count and hence both must be elected. The returning officer therefore terminated the process at Count 7 and declared the two highest candidates, i.e., Fahey (FF) and Geoghegan-Quinn (FF) elected 'without having reached the quota'.

Killilea was essentially defeated by 396 votes, this being the margin that he was behind Geoghegan-Quinn on Count 7. It is perhaps interesting to note that leaving aside the transfer in Count 4 of O'Connor's votes which did so much to ensure the election of Maire Geoghegan-Quinn she also succeeded in attracting more votes than Killilea on every other transfer of votes.

The counting process having started at 9 am on Friday 19 February 1982 concluded just after midnight with three Fianna Fail, one Fine Gael and one Labour deputies elected.

THE CONSTITUENCIES AND TOTAL MEMBERSHIP OF THE DAIL

The operation of the single transferable vote system is of course crucially dependent upon the definition of constituencies and the number of deputies in any individual constituency. Within the current constitution of the Republic of Ireland are set the following constraints on these factors:

> The number of members shall not be less than one member per thirty thousand of population and not more than one member for each twenty thousand of the population.

> The ratio between the number of members to be elected for each constituency and the population of each constituency, as ascertained at the last preceding census, shall, so far as it is practicable, be the same throughout the country.

> The constituencies shall be revised at least once in every twelve years.

> The number of members to be returned for any constituency shall not be less than three.

Table 8 sets out the population per member following each review of constituency boundaries. As can be seen the tendency has been to approach more closely the upper limit of the number of members of the Dail (i.e., calculated on the basis of one member per 20,000 population) than the lower limit (i.e., one member per 30,000 population). For instance in the 1980 revision of constituencies the membership of the Dail could have been fixed at any number between 113 and 168 inclusive and remained compatible with the provision of the constitution, but the terms of reference of the commission which specified the constituency boundaries limited the range they could consider to between 164 and 168 members.

The relatively low population per member is one characteristic which, as will be shown later, could explain some of the political consequences of the electoral system of the Republic of Ireland. It is worth noting that, within the European Community, the Republic of Ireland, with the exception of Luxembourg, has the lowest population per member of any legislature. The only country which approaches the Ireland ratio is Denmark with the 179 members of the unicameral Folketing representing a 1979 population of 5,111,534, i.e., 28,556 population/member. On a somewhat broader international comparison New Zealand has a population very close to that of the Republic of Ireland but the ninety-two members of the unicameral New Zealand House of Representatives represents a 1980 population of 3,148,500, i.e., 34,222 population/member for a land area nearly four times as large as that of the Republic of Ireland. Finally, if the population/member ratio in the Republic of Ireland was applied to the United Kingdom House of Commons then the number of members would rise from the present 635 to a total of the order of 2,750 members.

The second constitutional provision listed above, namely that the ratio of

Table 8 *Total membership of the Dail at each constituency boundary revision*

Year of revision	Total No. of members	Total population (and year of census)	Average population per member
1923	153	3,139,688 (1911)	20,521
1935	138	2,971,992 (1926)	21,536
1947	147	2,995,107 (1946)	20,103
1961	144	2,898,264 (1956)	20,127
1969	144	2,884,002 (1966)	20,028
1974	148	2,978,248 (1971)	20,123
1980	166	3,368,217 (1979)	20,290

Source: Dail Eireann Constituency Commission Report (April 1980).

members to the population of each constituency shall, as far as is practicable, be the same throughout the country has resulted in some considerable legal and political controversy. In an action commenced in 1960 in the High Court by Dr John O'Donovan (then a Fine Gael Senator) a revision of constituencies which had been rushed through in 1959 in order to meet the constitutional provision that constituencies should be revised every twelve years was ruled unconstitutional. Dr O'Donovan argued successfully that the variation in population/member between constituencies, which ranged from 16,575 population/member in South Galway to 23,128 in Dublin South West, i.e., variation of +14.9% to −17.6%, around an average population/member for the country as a whole of 20,127 violated the constitutional provision that as far as practicable the ratio of member to population of each constituency should be the same.

This judgement has been subsequently interpreted that a variation of up to 1,000 from the national average number of persons per member would probably be in accordance with the constitution. The variation is approximately equivalent to departing 5% from the national average of population per member in any one constituency. This appears to have been the guideline used in 1961 and subsequent revisions. However, in 1980, five constituencies slightly exceeded this guideline with the largest discrepancies being in Carlow–Kilkenny – the population per member of 21,565 being 6.3% above the national average of 20,290 – and Mayo East – the population per member of 18,988 being 6.4% below the national average. In all cases these divergences were justified on the basis of retaining compatibility between constituency and county boundaries.

This variation in population/member is considerably smaller than the variation in the number of electors/member. At the time of the last two elections in June 1981 and February 1982 the electorate per member ranged

Table 9 *Number of constituencies and members per constituency*

Electoral Act	Number of constituencies	Number of members per constituency							Total number of members	Average per constituency
		9	8	7	6	5	4	3		
1923	30	1	3	5	–	9	4	8	153	5.1
1935	34	–	–	3	–	8	8	15	138	4.1
1947	40	–	–	–	–	9	9	22	147	3.7
1961	38	–	–	–	–	9	12	17	144	3.8
1969	42	–	–	–	–	2	14	26	144	3.4
1974	42	–	–	–	–	6	10	26	148	3.5
1980	41	–	–	–	–	15	13	13	166	4.0

from 10,795 in Dublin North East (21.2% below the national average of 13,708) to 17,287 in Dublin South East (26.1% above the national average). Such wide discrepancies in electorate per member arise principally from demographic differences between constituencies and are only marginally due to the differences between population/member. The two constituencies mentioned are, however, exceptional cases, the remaining thirty-nine constituencies remaining within +10% and −13% of the national average number of electors per constituency, while twenty-three were within ±5.0% of the national average. However, the fact remains that despite the implication within the constitution that the aim shall be mathematical equality in terms of the distribution of members throughout the country, the constraint of settling constituency boundaries inherent within the single transferable vote system ensures that this aim is virtually impossible to achieve.

The final constraint set in the constitution is that there shall be at least three members per constituency and Table 9 sets out for each revision of constituency boundaries the number of constituencies and the breakdown in terms of number of members/constituency. Until 1980 the responsibility for determining constituency boundaries had been that of the government of the day, and this in part had led to the gradual decline in the average number of members per constituency in the period 1923–74.

The advantage which each government hoped to achieve by decreasing the average number of members per constituency arises from the fact that the quota is directly controlled by the number of seats in a constituency. If the quota can be set at an optimum level in each constituency in relation to a party's strength then the party involved could maximise its support in terms of seats. In order to calculate the optimum number of seats in any constituency, Table 10 needs to be consulted. This sets out the approximate size of the quota for varying sizes of constituencies together with the proportion of valid votes required to obtain a specific number of seats.

Table 10 *Variation in quota dependent upon number of seats in constituency*

No. of seats in constituency	Quota as % of valid vote	% Proportion of votes required to obtain set number of seats					
		1	2	3	4	5	6
1	50	50	–	–	–	–	–
2	$33\frac{1}{3}$	$33\frac{1}{3}$	$66\frac{2}{3}$	–	–	–	–
3	25	25	50	75	–	–	–
4	20	20	40	60	80	–	–
5	$16\frac{2}{3}$	$16\frac{2}{3}$	$33\frac{1}{3}$	50	$66\frac{2}{3}$	$83\frac{1}{3}$	–
6	$14\frac{2}{7}$	$14\frac{2}{7}$	$28\frac{4}{7}$	$42\frac{6}{7}$	$57\frac{1}{7}$	$71\frac{3}{7}$	$85\frac{5}{7}$

Consequently if a party is confident of achieving slightly over 50% of the vote in any particular area then the optimum strategy is to so organise the constituencies in that area in a pattern of three-seaters. This is likely to ensure that the party obtains two-thirds of the seats. The alternative of a pattern of four-seat constituencies and the same 50% share of the vote would result in only half the seats being obtained by a party and similarly for any even number of members per constituency. A further alternative of a pattern of five-seat constituencies and the same 50% share of the vote would result in a party obtaining three-fifths of the seats – nearly but not quite as advantageous as a three-seat arrangement.

In order to maximise the potential gain from any redistribution of boundaries a party should therefore organise three-seat constituencies where it is strong, four-seat constituencies where it is weak and reduce the number of five-seat constituencies to an absolute minimum. This approach was followed more and more strictly by Fianna Fail who were responsible for the boundary revisions in 1935, 1947, 1961 and 1969. For instance in 1969 Fianna Fail, who were weaker in Dublin City and County than in other parts of the country, allocated to the Dublin area eight four-seat constituencies and two three-seat constituencies whereas in the rest of the country three-seat constituencies predominated. This worked extremely well for Fianna Fail which at the subsequent election in 1969, won its fourth successive general election victory, increasing its number of seats from 72 to 75 despite dropping 2% in total first preference votes. The Minister responsible for the revision, Mr Kevin Boland, later wrote 'The only political reputation I have is as an expert constituency reviser.'

In 1974 it was the turn of the National Coalition government formed by Fine Gael and Labour to revise constituency boundaries. Mr James Tully, the Minister responsible for the revision, said in the Dail 'I cannot improve on it anyway. I think it is great. Fantastic.' In this revision the number of three-

Figure 1 Constituency map as established by the Constituency Commission April 198C

seaters in the Dublin City and County area increased from two to thirteen in
order to maximise the National Coalition strength and in the remainder of the
country the number of three-seaters was cut from twenty-four to thirteen
Despite what was considered to be an unfavourable boundary revision the
results of the subsequent election in 1977 gave Fianna Fail an overwhelming
victory, achieving its second highest share ever of first preference votes and a

record majority in the Dail. What had happened was that the Fianna Fail advance had been such as to turn strong areas of support for the National Coalition into marginal Fianna Fail areas and this party had been the beneficiary of the boundary review. So was born the word 'Tullymander', i.e., a failed gerrymander, after the Minister responsible for the boundary revision who himself only just managed to be elected on the 10th count in Meath.

Further political controversy was bound to arise if the Fianna Fail government in turn revised constituency boundaries and in his first speech to the Dail as Taoiseach (Prime Minister), Jack Lynch announced that the government intended to establish an independent electoral Commission to advise and report on the formation of constituencies. Such a Commission was duly established and reported in April 1980. Not surprisingly the Commission proposed a considerably altered pattern of constituencies, as can be seen from Table 9. The majority of constituencies were now to be five-seaters and the number of three-seaters was cut by half. These constituencies were used in the elections of June 1981 and February 1982, and the geographical arrangement of the constituencies is shown in Figure 1.

THE POLITICAL CONSEQUENCES

An important characteristic of the electoral system in use in the Republic of Ireland is that it appears to provide considerable elector satisfaction. This is a characteristic which, as applied to electoral systems, can be difficult to measure. However, in Ireland there have been two attempts to change the system, both of which have been initiated by Fianna Fail and approved by the Dail but rejected at referendums and this provides some indication of elector support.

The first referendum on this subject was in 1959 when on 17 June electors went to the polls to take part in a presidential election together with a referendum on a proposed change to single-member constituencies and a single non-transferable vote. In the presidential election Eamonn de Valera, the founder of Fianna Fail and a pre-eminent figure in Irish politics since the foundation of the state, was the party's candidate for the presidency. Despite the attempt to utilise support for de Valera, who initiated the proposed change in the electoral system, as a way of assisting his party in the referendum, the proposals were defeated by a majority of 33,667 votes in a poll of nearly 60% (see Table 11) and de Valera was elected President by a majority of 120,576 votes.

The second attempt to change the constitution followed the election of 1965 in which Fianna Fail obtained a majority of one seat over all other parties. The referendum held on 16 October 1968 included two proposed amendments to the constitution. The first one specified that the population per deputy should be not greater than nor less than the national average by more than one-sixth

Table 11 *Results of 1959 and 1968 referendums on change in the electoral system*

	June 1959 Single-member constituencies single non-transferable vote	October 1968 Straight vote
No	486,989 (51.8%)	657,989 (60.8%)
Yes	453,322 (48.2%)	423,496 (39.2%)
Turnout	58.4%	65.8%
Spoilt votes	4.0%	4.3%

Table 12 *Comparison of turnout at general elections Republic of Ireland and United Kingdom*

Republic of Ireland		United Kingdom	
General election	Turnout – average	General election	Turnout – average
1951/54/57	73.6%	1951/55/59	79.4%
1961/65/69	73.8%	1964/66	76.5%
1973/77/81/82	75.7%	1970/74/74/79	74.9%

and the second amendment proposed replacing the single transferable vote system by plurality voting in single-member constituencies. Both proposals were rejected by similar margins, and the majority (see Table 11) against the change in the electoral system was considerably larger than in 1959. Since that time there have been no serious proposals for changing the electoral system.

One other indirect measure of elector satisfaction is turnout. In the Republic of Ireland there have been ten general elections since 1951, whilst in the United Kingdom there have been nine general elections. In Ireland turnout has increased by 2.1% over the period from the three elections of the 1950s to 1973–82. In the United Kingdom turnout has dropped by 4.5% over the same period – see Table 12. Consequently, whilst turnout in general elections in the Republic of Ireland used to be significantly below that in the United Kingdom it is now the case that the General Elections in Ireland have turnout figures very similar to those in the United Kingdom.

Whilst these two features, i.e., the referendum results and turnout trends, are indicators of elector satisfaction, they do not explain the reasons for it.

There are those who would argue that it could arise from the fact that the system tends to ensure that a minimum number of votes are 'wasted', defined in the sense that such votes do not contribute to the election of a candidate. This allows a much larger proportion of the electorate to feel associated with an elected deputy from the constituency. Moreover, the system allows the elector to 'send messages' of political relevance without breaking any party allegiance ties. This can easily be done by suitable adjustment of the order of preference within a party framework, as was seen in the Galway West example. Other more subtle ways can also be utilised for the elector to indicate political messages via the operation of the counting process.

The first stage in the counting process is the opening of each ballot box and a count to ensure that the number of ballot papers in each box corresponds to the number issued. In this operation the ballot papers are straightened and counted face upwards in order to conceal the number on the back of the ballot paper and this exposes the front of the ballot paper, i.e., the opposite of the procedure in the UK. Each party is allowed to have a number of agents at a count to observe the count and a large number of these agents, known as 'tally-men', note the pattern of votes as the ballot papers are counted. Since the location of the polling station from which the ballot box originated is known this enables the parties to collect extremely detailed voting patterns for small localities. Of course tally-men cannot achieve 100% accuracy or completeness but surprisingly early indications of a final result can be achieved with this process.

This operation is an aspect of the process which is well known to electors, and one way in which some electors have used this to convey a political message is to use all the preferences available to the voter except one. If the candidate who is not included in the list of preferences belongs to one of the major parties then the tally-men for the party in question are bound to note the omission. Whilst this specific aspect of the electoral system could be considered particularly Irish it is one further illustration of the options open to an interested elector.

It is also possible that the variety of ways in which an elector can utilise the electoral system has a significant effect on the high level of party activity at a general election. This high level of party activity is perhaps best illustrated by the amount of personal canvassing which takes place. In an *Irish Times*/Irish Marketing Surveys poll taken five days before polling in February 1982, 54% of those interviewed said that they had been visited by Fianna Fail representatives during the campaign, 47% said they had been visited by Fine Gael representatives, and 21% by Labour Party representatives. These figures can be compared with the 15% of respondents who said, in a Market and Opinion Research International poll conducted at the time of the 1979 UK election, they had been visited by a party representative.

Overall the evidence points to the conclusion that the single transferable

Table 13 *Result of February 1982 general election*

	Seats	% Seats	% First preference	Seats in proportion to votes	Gains	Losses	Net change
Fianna Fail	81	49.1	47.3	78	6	3	+3
Fine Gael	63	38.2	37.3	61	3	5	−2
Labour	15	9.1	9.1	15	2	2	0
SFWP	3	1.8	2.3	4	2	0	+2
PSF	–	–	1.0	2			
IRSP	–	–	0.2	–			
Other	3	1.8	2.8	5	1	4	−3
Ceann Comhairle	1	–	–	1			
TOTAL	166	100	100	166	14	14	

Notes:
i The Ceann Comhairle (Speaker) is automatically returned and the percentages in the second column have been based upon 165 seats.
ii In addition to the 14 seats which changed hands between the parties there were 11 other seats which changed hands within a party, e.g., a Fianna Fail candidate displacing a sitting Fianna Fail TD.

vote system in the Republic of Ireland is strongly supported by electors and party activists. Some would say that it makes politics – at least for the spectators – more enjoyable and more satisfying and perhaps even more fun.

But more serious questions remain to be answered, in particular is it 'fair', does it produce 'an effective government' and does it result in an effective and competent Dail. The fairness critique is often equated to mathematical equality of each vote together with a close relationship between the proportion of votes obtained by a party and the proportion of seats. As has been pointed out previously the fact that the single transferable vote system operates within constituencies, the boundaries of which are strongly influenced by consider- ations other than mathematical equality, means that all votes are not of equal value in terms of electoral effect. The Irish system compounds this problem since the constitution requires constituencies to be compared in terms of population size rather than electorate size. However, it can be argued that set against the deviation in mathematical equality of votes is the tendency of the system to minimise 'wasted' votes.

As far as the relationship between votes and seats is concerned the system tends towards proportionality, especially now that the constituency boun- daries are being set irrespective of party considerations. This is illustrated in Table 13 which sets out a summary of the results of the February 1982 general election. The close relationship between votes and seats is clearly marked. Also Table 13 indicates one other aspect of the system in that although the net change in seats was extremely small, a total of fourteen seats changed hands, i.e., 8.4% of the seats in the Dail.

CONCLUSION

In summary, one can conclude that the electoral system in the Republic of Ireland does command considerable popular support and in a country where most subjects are the cause of argument and controversy this is in itself surprising. The evidence, such as, e.g., the large amount of canvassing, also indicates that local party organisations and workers are also strongly in favour of the system. The only group who appear not to be enthusiastic are many deputies and some party managers, particularly within Fianna Fail. It could be argued that this lack of enthusiasm among deputies and party managers is due to the fact that it makes their position more difficult and unpredictable.

One aspect of the Dail which is often referred to is the role of a deputy 'as a constituency messenger' and the emphasis that constituents place on the role of the deputy in serving the needs of the constituency. It is likely that this aspect is one which is primarily related to the nature of Irish political culture rather than the electoral system and is particularly influenced by the relatively low number of electors per deputy.

The effects of the electoral system on the stability of the political system, seem to be broadly neutral. There have been ten elections since 1951 in the Republic of Ireland, one more than in the United Kingdom. The average length of a government has been of the order of three years, which is by no means short by European standards.

The electoral system also seems to have a neutral effect on the number of parties, since it tends to encourage change and development within, rather than the fragmentation of, parties. Such changes are likely to be influenced by the ability of the electoral system to provide electors with the means of 'sending messages' without being constrained to break party ties.

APPENDIX

General elections 1923–1981 (party seats and % first preference votes)

Election	Total seats	Fianna Fail (Anti-Treaty to 1927) Seats	% Votes	Fine Gael (Cumann na nGaedheal to 1937) Seats	% Votes	Labour Seats	% Votes	Farmers Clann na Talmhan	Other parties[a]	Ind.	Govt	Taoiseach (President of Executive Council to 1937)
1923	153	44	27.6	63	38.9	14	12.4	15	–	17	C na nG	W. T. Cosgrave
1927 June	153	44	26.1	47[b]	27.5	22	13.8	11	13	16	C na nG	W. T. Cosgrave
1927 Sept.	153	57	35.2	62[b]	38.7	13	9.5	6	2	13	C na nG	W. T. Cosgrave
1932	153	72	44.5	57[b]	35.3	7	7.7	4	–	13	FF	E. de Valera
1933	153	77[b]	49.7	48	30.5	8	5.7	–	11	9	FF	E. de Valera
1937	138	69[b]	45.2	48	34.8	13	10.3	–	–	8	FF	E. de Valera
1938	138	77[b]	51.9	45	33.3	9	10.0	–	–	7	FF	E. de Valera
1943	138	67[b]	41.90	32	23.1	17	15.7	14	–	8	FF	E. de Valera
1944	138	76[b]	48.9	30	20.5	12[c]	11.5	11	–	9	FF	E. de Valera
1948	147	68[b]	41.9	31	19.8	19	11.3	7	10	12	Inter-party	J. A. Costello
1951	147	69[a]	46.3	40	25.7	16	11.4	6	2	14	FF	E. de Valera
1954	147	65	43.4	50	32.0	19[b]	12.0	5	3	5	Inter-party	J. A. Costello
1957	147	78	48.3	40	26.6	12[b]	9.1	3	5	9	FF	E. de Valera to S. Lemass
1961	144	70	43.8	47	32.0	16[b]	11.6	2	3	6	FF	S. Lemass
1965	144	72	47.8	47	33.9	22[b]	15.4	–	–	3	FF	S. Lemass to J. Lynch
1969	144	75[b]	45.66	50	34.10	18	17.02	–	–	1	FF	J. Lynch
1973	144	69[b]	46.24	54	35.09	19	13.67	–	–	2	Nat. coalition	L. Cosgrave
1977	148	84	50.63	43	30.49	17[b]	11.63	–	–	4	FF	J. Lynch to C. J. Haughey
1981	166	78[b]	45.26	65	36.46	15	9.89	–	2	6	Nat. coalition	G. FitzGerald
Feb. 1982	166	81	47.26	63	37.30	15	9.12	–	3	4[b]	FF	C. J. Haughey
Nov. 1982	166	75	45.20	70	39.20	16	9.60	–	2	3[b]	Nat. coalition	G. FitzGerald

a Other parties.
1927: (June) National League 8, Sinn Fein 5
1927: (Sept.) National League 2
1933: Centre Party 11, later merged with Fine Gael
1948: Clann na Poblachta 10
1951: Clann na Poblachta 2

1954: Clann na Poblachta 3
1957: Sinn Fein 4, Clann na Poblachta 1
1961: National Progressive Democrats 2, Clann na Poblachta 1
1981: SFWP 1, SLP 1
Feb. 1982: SFWP 3.

NOTES

1 So named after H. R. Droop who first suggested this approach in 1869.
2 The electoral rules used in Northern Ireland for this process are slightly different. Under the Northern Ireland electoral rules the distribution of 'surplus' votes is organised by distributing all votes for a winning candidate but with each vote counting not as a whole vote but as a fraction of a vote equal to dividing the surplus by the total number of votes of the candidate with the surplus.
3 This alternative presentation is used in the official compilation of the results. See *Election Results and Transfer of Votes – General Election, June 1981*, and similar title for the general election of 1982. Both published by the Stationery Office, Dublin.
4 See Brian Farrell, 'Dail Deputies: The 1969 Generation', *Economic and Social Review*, 2, 3 (1971).

SUGGESTIONS FOR FURTHER READING

M. Bax, *Harpstrings and Confessions: An Anthropological Study of Politics in Rural Ireland* (Assen, 1976)
V. Browne, ed., *The Magill Book of Irish Politics*, (Dublin, 1981)
R. K. Carty, *Party and Parish Pump: Electoral Politics in Ireland* (Waterloo, Ontario, 1981)
B. Chubb: 'Going About Persecuting Civil Servants: The Role of the Irish Parliamentary Representative', *Political Studies* (1963)
The Government and Politics of Ireland (London, 1970)
Election Results and Transfer of Votes (Dublin Stationery Office, 1981 and 1982)
M. Gallagher, 'Disproportionality in a Proportional Representation System: The Irish Experience', *Political Studies* (1975)
E. Nealon, *Nealon's Guide to the 21st Dail and Seanad* (Dublin, 1977)
Nealon's Guide to the 22nd Dail and Seanad, Election '81 (Dublin, 1981)
P. Mair and M. Lever, 'Proportionality, PR and STV in Ireland', *Political Studies* (1975)
C. O'Leary, *Irish Elections 1918–1977* (Dublin, 1979)
H. R. Penniman, ed., *Ireland at the Polls: The Dail Elections of 1977* (Washington, DC, 1978)
P. Sacks, *The Donegal Mafia* (New Haven, 1976)
J. H. Whyte, 'Ireland: Politics Without Social Bases', in R. Rose, *Electoral Behaviour: A Comparative Handbook* (New York, 1974)

10

Greece

RICHARD CLOGG

Greece's electoral system has changed with bewildering frequency since 1926, when the country effectively abandoned majority voting, conducted through a cumbersome but effective arrangement of dropping lead balls in a ballot box. In the postwar period manipulation of the electoral system has been one of the principal means by which the Right has sought to contain the Left and to perpetuate its hold on power. Parties of the Right, and sometimes of the Centre, have been systematically over-represented in Parliament (at times, as in 1952, grotesquely so), at the expense of the far Left, represented for most of the period by the United Democratic Left (EDA) and, after 1974, by the Communist Party(ies) (KKE and KKEes). Yet, while successive electoral systems (for the most part variants of proportional representation) have been undoubtedly discriminatory, and intentionally so, they have been less weighted against minority interests than, say, the British plurality system. Moreover, despite the manipulation of the electoral system, the postwar monopoly of power enjoyed by the Right has been successfully challenged on two occasions, by the Centre in 1963/4 and by the Centre–Left in 1981.

Clearly no analysis, however brief, of the political consequences of electoral systems employed in postwar Greek elections can be divorced from some consideration of the country's specific historical experience and the way in which this has shaped the country's political culture[1] and, in particular, of the turbulent postwar history of the country, which has been radically different from that of the other countries considered in the present volume. Greece acquired the forms of Western parliamentarianism in the early years of her independent existence, with effective universal manhood suffrage being conceded as early as 1844. Yet this grafting of the forms of Western constitutionalism onto a traditional society did little to undermine attitudes and values shaped by the long centuries of Ottoman rule. Endemic arbitrariness and corruption had contributed powerfully to the development of antagonistic attitudes towards the state and to the creation of defensive clientelist networks based on the extended family. Given the rudimentary level of economic development in the new kingdom, the state assumed a disproportionate importance as a source of secure employment and this enhanced the significance of parliamentary deputies as dispensers of patronage. Party loyalties were tenuous as politicians sought above all to retain and develop their clientage networks. *Rousfeti*, the distribution of favours, and *mesa*, influence, were the watchwords of the new polity.

The fact that so many Greeks were left outside the embryonic Greek state and that the 'redemption' of the 'unredeemed' Greeks depended on the active support, or at least the benevolent neutrality, of the Powers, led to attitudes of dependency towards outside interests. The disparity between the grandiose aspirations of the new state and the resources at its disposal, together with the chronic factionalism of the politicians, prompted the military to play an ever-increasing role in political life, particularly after the Goudi coup of 1909. Disagreements over foreign policy during the First World War engendered the National Schism, the division of the country into two sharply antagonistic and at times warring camps. The feud between supporters and opponents of the liberal statesman, Eleftherios Venizelos, was to be exacerbated by the consequences of Greece's disastrous entanglement in Asia Minor between 1919 and 1922 and was to colour the whole of interwar politics. The antagonism between Venizelists and anti-Venizelists, together with a 'hung' Parliament in 1936, elected under a system of simple proportional representation, was to enable the quasi-fascist dictator General Metaxas to seize power. His total proscription of political activity, coupled with the anomalous circumstances of the tripartite German, Italian and Bulgarian occupation between 1941 and 1944, were to project the hitherto insignificant Greek Communist Party (Kommounistiko Komma Elladas) to the forefront of the political stage. The domination by the Communists of anti-Axis resistance and the armed insurgency of December 1944, directed against George Papandreou's national government and its British allies, added a new dimension to the country's political strife, with a Right/Left, Nationalist/Communist cleavage now being superimposed upon the existing Venizelist/anti-Venizelist schism.

The first postwar election in Greece, that of 31 March 1946, the first since the fateful election of 1936, was held in highly anomalous circumstances. Just over a year earlier, the Varkiza agreement of February 1945 had concluded the bloody confrontation between the Communist-controlled forces of ELAS (National Popular Liberation Army) and the Government of National Unity, which was backed by British forces. The bitterness engendered by the fighting, and in particular the killing of hostages taken by the Left, provoked a savage right-wing backlash, which the weak, British-controlled post-Varkiza governments proved quite unable to control. The Varkiza agreement had provided for a plebiscite on the bitterly divisive issue of monarchy versus republic, to be followed by elections for a constituent assembly. This sequence was reversed when, under strong pressure from a Britain anxious to divest itself of its Greek commitment, the government headed by the elderly Liberal Themistocles Sophoulis reluctantly agreed to the holding of elections on 31 March 1946.[2]

The far Left abstained, as did a number of prominent non-Communis
republicans, arguing that the lawlessness, bordering on civil war, which
prevailed in many parts of the country, together with the impossibility o
compiling adequate electoral registers in the dislocation caused by foreigr
occupation and internecine strife, nullified the election as a true test of publi
opinion. The 1946 election has a particular significance in Greek electora
history in that it was observed by the Allied Mission to Observe the Gree
Election (AMFOGE), consisting of British, American and French, but no
Soviet, representatives.[3]

The result was an overwhelming victory for the right-wing monarchists
These were largely grouped in the United Camp of the Nationally Minde
(Inomeni Parataxis Ethnikophron*), the dominant constituent of which wa:
the pre-war People's Party (Laikon Komma). This alliance achieved a 55%
share of the vote and 58% of seats. The largest opposition grouping, the
National Political Union (Ethniki Politiki Enosis), achieved a 19% share of both
votes and seats, with the Liberal Party (Komma Phileleftheron) receiving 14%
of both (see Table 1). AMFOGE declared the election, held under ar
uncomplicated system of proportional representation, to have been a vali
expression of the people's will and estimated the number of politically
motivated abstentions at 9.4%. The Communists, on the other hand, urge
that since only 49% of those on the electoral registers had voted, the remaining
51% should be considered as having abstained. The true level of politically
motivated abstention must remain a matter of conjecture. It is incontestable
that no election in postwar Greece was held in such anomalous anc
unsatisfactory circumstances as that of 1946 and yet, paradoxically, in n
other election was there such a close correspondence between the percentage
of votes cast for a given party and its share of seats in Parliament. The election
was followed six months later by a plebiscite on the issue of the monarchy. This
resulted in a 68% vote for the return of King George II, with 32% voting for a
republic.

The conduct of the 1946 election and plebiscite clearly played some part in
the genesis of outright civil war which broke out in 1946 and ended with the
defeat of the Left in 1949, as a consequence of internal divisions within the Left,
a massive influx of American military aid and the East–West balance of power.
It is noteworthy that although the national government was at times very
hard pressed and the country for a long period under martial law, parliamentary government survived intact, although the Communist Party was
outlawed in 1947. Under American pressure a People's Party/Liberal coalition,
headed by the octagenarian Liberal Themistocles Sophoulis, was in power
through most of the period of the civil war.

---

* *Ethnikophron*, with its connotations of super-patriotism and virulent anti-Leftism, has no real
  equivalent in English.

The defeat of the Communist Democratic Army in the autumn of 1949 was followed by elections in March 1950. The most remarkable aspect of the result was the decline of the traditional right-wing vote and the strength of the Centre vote, albeit split among a number of groupings. The Centre (three groupings) secured 136 seats in a 250-seat Parliament and the Right 86 (four groupings), with the left-wing Democratic Camp (Dimokratiki Parataxis) securing 18 seats with a 9.7% share of the vote. It would seem that despite, or perhaps indeed because of, the experience of three years of a bitterly fought civil war, the Greek electorate had voted for moderation and to some degree for reconciliation. The Centre, however, was divided, mainly over the question of an amnesty for Leftists involved in the civil war, and over the next eighteen months there were five unstable Centre coalition governments. From an electoral point of view the 1950 election was noteworthy for a reduction in the number of parliamentary seats, from 354 to 250, for the large number of parties that participated and for the fact that, although the same electoral system was employed as in 1946, the correspondence between share of votes cast and share of seats received was not as close. Forty-four parties contested the election, twenty-five of which were grouped in nine alliances. Most of these parties were quite insignificant and only ten (five of them in alliance) were actually represented in Parliament. The large number of parties resulted in 46% of the seats being allocated in the second and third distributions, as opposed to 10% in 1946.[4]

In new elections, held in September 1951, the electoral system was changed from a fairly straightforward proportional system to a 'semi' or 'reinforced' proportional system. The principal feature of the new system was that participation in the second and third distributions was restricted to the three parties with the largest share of the votes, subject to a 17% minimum for parties and a 20% minimum for alliances. Nine parties contested the elections, as opposed to forty-four in the elections held in March of the previous year. Among these was the United Democratic Left (Eniaia Dimokratiki Aristera), which represented the forces of the far Left and to a large extent reflected the interests of the illegal Communist Party. A new grouping also appeared on the Right of the political spectrum in the form of the Greek Rally (Ellinikos Synagermos), founded in conscious imitation of de Gaulle's Rassemblement Français by Field-Marshal Papagos, the victor of the civil war who had resigned from the armed forces the previous May. This served as a focus for almost all Rightists (including the bulk of the People's Party) and, indeed, a number of Centrists.

Although the Right significantly improved its performance over the previous year, the two main Centre groupings the National Progressive Centre Union (Ethniki Proodeftiki Enosis Kentrou) and the Liberal Party (Komma Phileleftheron) still enjoyed a majority in the new Parliament, with 131 seats out of 258. The new system of 'reinforced' proportional representation did

prove of benefit to the three largest parties, but not to any very significan
degree. The Greek Rally, for instance, achieved a proportion of parliamentar
seats 7.6% higher than its share of the popular vote, whereas the number c
parliamentary seats received by the United Democratic Left was some 6.7%
lower than its share of the vote would have warranted in a system of pur
proportional representation. A Centre coalition government was formed
headed by General Nicholas Plastiras.

It was the prospect of the continuation of the pattern of unstable Centris
governments following the 1951 election that prompted perhaps the mos
blatant, and certainly the most overt, instance of American interference in
Greece's domestic affairs. American disapproval of the course of events in
Greece was signalled soon after the 1951 election by the announcement of a
significant reduction in economic aid, while in March 1952 the US Am
bassador in Athens, John Peurifoy, publicly warned that the failure of the
Greeks to adopt a plurality system in the elections scheduled for November o
that year would have 'destructive results upon the effective utilization o
American aid to Greece'. In August Peurifoy issued a further statement to the
press in which he stressed that the political situation would have to be clarified
a remark that was universally interpreted as constituting American endorse
ment of Field-Marshal Papagos.[5]

Despite protests in the press from Centre and Left politicians, and althougl
the Plastiras government had itself publicly declared that 'it belongs to the
Greek people and government to decide with what election system the country
will be administered',[6] the plurality system was adopted for the 1952 electio
and duly yielded the desired result. Only two groupings were represented in the
new Parliament, the Greek Rally and the Union of the Parties (Enosi
Kommaton), an alliance of three Centre parties. With 247 members out of 300
Papagos won 82.3% of the seats in Parliament as opposed to his 49.2% share c
the popular vote. This contrasted with the 17% share of the seats (fifty-one
achieved by the Union of the Parties on the basis of a 34.2% share of the vote. The
United Democratic Left, with 9.6% of the popular vote, was unrepresented in
the new Parliament. If the purpose of adopting the plurality system was to
secure greater governmental stability then the move was successful, for the
Papagos administration lasted until his death in October 1955, whereas there
had been no less than sixteen administrations between the elections of March
1946 and those of November 1952. The defection of Spyros Markezinis with
twenty-nine deputies to found the Progressive Party (Komma Proodeftikon
did little to dent Papagos' grip on Parliament. On the Marshal's death, King
Paul passed over Stephanos Stephanopoulos, who was generally considered to
be Papagos' heir and had acted as a Deputy Prime Minister during Papagos
illness, in favour of the then little-known Constantine Karamanlis. In
preparation for the elections scheduled for February 1956 Karamanlis
dissolved the Rally and replaced it by the National Radical Union (Ethnik

Rizospastiki Enosis), to which he was able to attract most of the deputies belonging to the Rally, many of whom had earlier also been active in the People's Party. Abandoning a law enacted by Papagos which would have perpetuated the majority system, Karamanlis utilised his still handsome parliamentary majority to pass an electoral law (Decree 3457/1955) of truly Byzantine complexity, the undoubted purpose of which was to ensure a victory for his National Radical Union.

In nine electoral districts with up to 3 seats (26 seats in all) a straightforward plurality system was adopted. In electoral districts of from 4 to 10 seats (183 seats in all) there was a mixed majority/semi-proportional system. In electoral districts of more than 10 seats (91 seats in all) a proportional system was in force, although only the two groupings receiving the largest share of the seats were eligible to participate in the distribution of seats. Moreover, it was no accident that the plurality system was applied in rural areas where the National Radical Union vote was strong and the proportional system in urban areas where the opposition parties gained their greatest degree of support. Karamanlis' massive majority enabled him to railroad the new electoral law through Parliament over the protests of the opposition parties, most of which combined together to form an electoral alliance, the Democratic Union (Dimokratiki Enosis), which ran the whole gamut from the rump of the People's Party on the Right to the far Left United Democratic Left. The new system produced the desired result, for the National Radical Union with 47.4% of the popular vote secured 55% (165) of the 300 seats in Parliament whereas the Democratic Union, whose overall share of the popular vote at 48.2% was actually higher than that of the National Radical Union, secured only 44% (132) of the seats in Parliament. Moreover the army and civil service vote,[7] which was counted separately, at 76.5%, was significantly and suspiciously at variance with the National Radical Union's overall share of the vote. Paradoxically, although the Right's primary purpose had been to isolate the far Left, the manifest bias of the electoral system had forced the United Democratic Left for the first time into a temporary alliance with the Centre parties. The 1956 election was also noteworthy in that, for the first time, women were entitled to vote in a parliamentary election with the result that the number of registered votes in 1956 was more than twice that of 1952.

Two years later, following an internal party crisis prompted in part at least by further proposals to tinker with the electoral system, Karamanlis called new elections. The 1958 election, as all subsequent elections, was held under the system of 'reinforced' proportional representation. The threshold for participation in the second distribution was raised, in the case of individual parties, from 17% to 25%, in the case of alliances involving two parties to 35% and in the case of a greater number to 40%. Although the new law came in for much criticism in Parliament, it was supported not only by those National Radical Union deputies who remained loyal to Karamanlis but also by the Liberal

Party, which had been reorganised the previous year under the joint leadership of George Papandreou and Sophocles Venizelos. They believed that the new system would both obviate the need for an alliance with the United Democratic Left and encourage the divided Centre to rally under their leadership, failing which they would be ineligible to participate in the second distribution.[8]

In the event the expectations of both conservative and liberal politicians were confounded, for, whereas the National Radical Union, as expected, gained a comfortable majority, it was the United Democratic Left that emerged as the largest opposition party, with 79 seats, benefiting from the continued divisions of the Centre and from an upsurge of anti-NATO feeling as a consequence of the campaign for the *enosis* of Cyprus with Greece. Although the United Democratic Left's share of the vote at 24.4% was less than the 25% prescribed for the second distribution, it did participate as the party securing the second largest share of the popular vote. The United Democratic Left's share of the seats in Parliament, at 26.3%, was marginally higher than its share of the popular vote, the only occasion when this occurred during the postwar period (see Figure 1).

Besides the continual tinkering with the electoral law, another form of electoral manipulation that characterised the 1956 and 1958 elections concerned the determination of the size of electoral districts. In both 1956 and 1958 (and in thirteen electoral districts in 1961) the boundaries were drawn up on the basis of the 1940 census rather than that of 1951. This meant that no account was taken of the wartime occupation, civil war and the consequent flight to the towns. Moreover the decade of the 1950s was itself to witness a very considerable rate of demographic change, which was not reflected in the drawing up of electoral boundaries. This failure to adjust electoral boundaries so that they reflected demographic realities more closely demonstrably benefited the Right. In 1958 in the Second (suburban) Athens Electoral District 23,246 votes were needed for the return of one deputy, whereas in the remote and backward province of Thesprotia on the Albanian border a mere 6,862 sufficed to return one deputy. In the same election the National Radical Union's share of the vote in the Second Athens Electoral District was 29.2%, against a 57.8% vote in its favour in Thesprotia.[9]

By the time of the 1961 elections George Papandreou, alarmed by the sudden surge in support for the far Left in 1958, had managed to unify the disparate elements of the Centre into the Centre Union (Enosis Kentrou). This was not a mere electoral alliance, of which there had been so many in the postwar period, but rather represented a serious effort to fuse together the various heirs to the Venizelist liberal tradition, together with one or two small groupings on the Centre–Left and even on the Right. Each of the constituent elements that made up the Centre Union was dissolved and recognised George Papandreou as the leader of the new party. But the appearance of unity was to prove illusory. Inevitably the electoral law was further modified in 1961. The basis of the electoral system was still 'reinforced' proportional representation, with the main difference over 1958 being that the threshold for participation in the second distribution was reduced from 25% to 15% for single parties, to 25% for a two-party alliance and to 30% for larger groupings. This produced results less weighted in favour of the winning party than in 1958 but the result of the 1961 election was greeted with uproar by the opposition parties, the Centre Union, which had fought in alliance with the Progressive Party (Komma Proodeftikon), and the United Democratic Left, which had joined with the National Agrarian Party (Ethniko Agrotiko Komma) to form the Pandemocratic Agrarian Front of Greece (Pandimokratiko Agrotiko Metopo Ellados). Although the electoral system had come under attack for bias in favour of the Right and for its failure to reflect the pace of demographic change in postwar Greece, the rhetoric of opposition politicians in the 1961 election was principally aimed at what they considered to be outright fraud on the part of the Right. Both the Centre Union and the United Democratic Left published 'Black Books' in which they detailed their charges of electoral skulduggery. Papandreou alleged that in Athens alone some 100,000 fraudulent votes had been cast. There were also allegations of fraud, undue pressure and violence in rural areas, particularly on the part of the National Security Battalions, an anti-Communist militia. The 83.5% vote cast for ERE in the separately recorded army and civil service vote was the target of particularly fierce criticism.

Claiming that his party had been the victim of an 'electoral coup d'état' Papandreou now launched his 'unrelenting struggle' for new elections. These were held in November 1963, amid indications that the traditional Right was losing its nerve, and in the wake of the precipitate departure of Prime Minister Karamanlis from the country after a quarrel with the Palace. The opposition parties threatened to boycott the elections unless the electoral law was modified and unless guarantees were given as to its proper conduct. In the event the electoral system in force was a marginally revised version of that employed in 1961. Electoral districts were defined on the basis of the 1961 census. The 'service' government, headed by the President of the Supreme Court, took a number of measures to ensure that the conduct of the elections was beyond reproach. These resulted in a narrow victory for the Centre Union over the National Radical Union but no overall majority in Parliament. With 42.1% of the votes the Centre Union secured 46% of the seats, as against 39.4% and 44% respectively for the National Radical Union. Both parties therefore were beneficiaries, even if somewhat marginally, of the electoral system. The United Democratic Left, on the other hand, with 14.3% of the votes and 9.3% of the seats was under-represented. The army and civil service vote (61.5% for the National Radical Union as opposed to 39.4% nationwide) was still disproportionately in favour of the Right.

Unwilling to be forced into dependence on the support of the United

Democratic Left in Parliament, Papandreou, a staunch anti-Communist, called a new election for February 1964. This was held in accordance with the 'reinforced' proportional system used in the election of the previous November and resulted in an outright majority of the popular vote and seats in Parliament for the Centre Union. Moreover the army/civil service vote for the National Radical Union at 48.3% was no longer so wildly out of congruence with the nationwide voting pattern. But although Papandreou had success-fully challenged the eleven-year hegemony of the Right, his triumph was to prove short lived. A major confrontation with young King Constantine in July 1965 resulted in Papandreou's resignation and the fragmentation of his party. The defection of some forty-five Centre Union deputies, who came to be known as the 'apostates', demonstrated the essential fragility of Papandreou's fusion of the forces of the Centre. It also enabled, with some difficulty, an 'apostate' Centre Union government, enjoying the support of the National Radical Union and the Progressive Party in Parliament, to cling to power, much to the outrage of Centre Union supporters who vociferously demanded the holding of fresh elections. After a considerable degree of political turmoil, agreement was finally reached for elections to be held in May 1967, under the same electoral law as had been in force for the 1963 and 1964 elections. These elections were, however, forestalled by the military coup of 21 April 1967, which signalled the beginning of the seven-year Colonels' dictatorship. The constitutional pro-posals, ratified in wholly spurious referenda in 1968 and 1973, put forward by the military fall outside the purview of this chapter. It is worth noticing in passing, however, that Article 57 of the 1968 constitution contained the reasonable provision that while the electoral system and size of electoral districts were to be enacted in Parliament as previously, they were to come into force only after the first election following its enactment.[10] A similar provision was contained in the draft constitution of 1948 but was omitted when the constitution was enacted in 1952. The 1975 constitution, which like that of 1952 authorises the legislature to determine the electoral system, also contains no such provision.

   The downfall of the Colonels' dictatorship in July 1974, in the wake of the Cyprus debacle, and the return of Constantine Karamanlis from his eleven-year self-imposed exile to oversee the return to democracy was followed remarkably quickly by elections in November 1974, the first to be held for ten years. This in turn was followed by a plebiscite on the issue of monarchy versus republic, which resulted in a 69% vote for the republic. Karamanlis' decision to seek to legitimise his position through early elections was much criticised by his political opponents on a number of grounds. Among these were that, because parties had been proscribed for the duration of the seven-year dictatorship, too little time had been allowed for the resuscitation of party organisations and for the organisation of a proper campaign; that the elections would be held on the basis of outdated electoral registers; that a truly free campaign could not be conducted, particularly in rural areas, until there had been a thorough-going purge of supporters of the dictatorship; and that the maintenance of a minimum voting age of twenty-one effectively disenfranchised a large section of a student population which had been a major focus of resistance to the military dictatorship. (The voting age was lowered to twenty in 1977). There was, however, little criticism of the unanimous decision of the provisional government to hold the elections under a form of the 'reinforced' proportional representation that had been employed in all elections held since 1958. Nor was there criticism of the manner in which the elections were conducted.

The electoral system used in all three general elections (1974, 1977 and 1981) held since the downfall of the military dictatorship was established by Presidential Decree 650/1974 and has been marginally modified by Decrees 526/1977 and 1180/1981. Constituencies correspond to the fifty-six *nomoi* or prefectures into which the country is divided. Because of the great concentration of the country's population in the two major cities of Athens and Thessaloniki, the *nomos* of Attica has been divided into five constituencies and that of Thessaloniki into two. The 1975 constitution set the minimum number of seats in Parliaments at 200 and the maximum at 300, which has been the size of all Greek Parliaments since 1975. The current system of 'reinforced' proportional representation is based on the Hagenbach-Bischoff system and provides for three distributions of seats. Voting is compulsory.

In determining the seats allocated in the first distribution the number of votes cast for a given party in a constituency are divided by the electoral quota. This quota is arrived at by dividing the number of votes cast in each constituency by the number of seats allocated to that constituency plus one.[11] For the second distribution, constituencies are grouped together into nine major electoral districts. Since 1974 participation in the second distribution has been dependent on parties securing 17% of the vote, two-party alliances 25% and alliances of more than two parties 30%. The electoral quota for the second distribution is established by dividing the total number of votes cast for eligible parties in each major electoral district by the total of seats not yet distributed. Seats are then allocated by dividing the vote of each eligible party by the electoral quota. The quota for the third distribution is determined by dividing the total vote cast for eligible parties in the country as a whole by the number of seats remaining for distribution. Seats are then allocated by dividing the national vote cast for each eligible party by the quota. Since 1974, 12 of the 300 deputies, known as state deputies, have been selected from lists nominated by the parties in proportion to the number of votes cast for parties eligible to participate in the second distribution. In fifty-three of the constituencies electors are entitled to express one preference. In the first and second Athens and first Thessaloniki electoral districts voters are entitled to express one or two preferences. Leaders of parties or alliances and former elected Prime Ministers are deemed to have secured as many preference votes as ballot papers cast for their party lists in the constituency concerned. In the November 1981 election seats were distributed as below.

	1st distribution	2nd distribution	3rd distribution	State deputies	
Panhellenic Socialist Movement	140	19	6	7	172
New Democracy	95	12	3	5	115
Communist Party of Greece	13	–	–	–	13

The way in which the system of 'reinforced' proportional representation has, in the words of one leading Greek authority, resulted in 'a systematic and organic over-representation of the larger parties and under-representation and non-representation of the smaller ones'[12] can be seen in the disproportion of seats in Parliament compared to votes in the country at large of the winning party in the last three elections (1974: New Democracy 54.3% of seats in the country, 73.3% in Parliament; 1977: New Democracy 41.9% in the country 57.8% in Parliament; 1981: Panhellenic Socialist Movement (Panellinic Sosialistiko Kinima) 48.1% in the country, 57.4% in Parliament (see Figure 1)

It is unquestionably the case that, in their anxiety to secure its own party advantage and to prevent the development of a popular front, uniting Centre and Left, which might constitute a serious challenge to its own virtual monopoly of power, the Right in Greece has during the postwar period manipulated the electoral system. But the system employed throughout most of the period has not been as heavily weighted against minority representation as straightforward plurality systems. Moreover, manipulation of the electoral system was only one means by which the Right sought to isolate and contain the far Left in the 1950s. A whole battery of repressive legislation was enacted whose purpose was to discriminate against the vanquished during the civil war, and the Communist Party, banned in 1947, was legalised only in 1974, by which time it had split into two wings, the Orthodox Communist Party of Greece (KKE) and the broadly 'Eurocommunist' Communist Party of Greece (Interior) (KKE-Esoterikou).

Furthermore, whatever its imperfections, the system has allowed for the peaceful and orderly transition of power. It is true that the first challenge to the entrenched power of the Right by the forces of the traditional Centre in 1963/4 ended within eighteen months in a major constitutional crisis, which in turn was to provide the pretext for the imposition of a military dictatorship between 1967 and 1974. But the legitimacy of Greece's newly re-established democratic institutions has been convincingly asserted with the accession to power of Andreas Papandreou's Panhellenic Socialist Movement (universally known by its initials PASOK) in 1981. The programme of the younger Papandreou's PASOK was a great deal more radical than that of George Papandreou's Centre Union in 1963/4 but there was no sign of any significant reaction to his accession to power by the armed forces. It has to be recognised, too, that the claim of its proponents that 'reinforced' proportional representation has contributed to political stability has some force. The system, with the exception of 1963, has produced governments with a comfortable working majority and it has tended to promote unity, if at times an artificial unity, among traditionally fissiparous political forces. The 1981 elections, indeed, produced a Parliament in which, for the first time for many years, only three parties, broadly representative of the three main *parataxeis*, or political 'camps', of the postwar period, were represented.

Discussion of the November 1981 election, which propelled the Panhellenic Socialist Movement to power, and of the nature of Andreas Papandreou's idiosyncratic brand of populist socialism is not possible within the confines of this paper. It is perhaps worth noting in passing that, despite the successful effort to give the party, founded as recently as 1974, both a proper organisational structure (hitherto found in Greece only on the far Left) and to develop a coherent ideological base, PASOK is very much in the tradition of Greek politics in the extent to which it relies on the appeal of a charismatic leader. What principally concerns us here are the proposals made by PASOK in the course of the election campaign for changes in the electoral system.

In its 'Contract with the People', issued by the PASOK Central Committee in July 1981 as the principal exposition of PASOK's electoral programme, a number of significant proposals for electoral reform were put forward. It was proposed to reduce the voting age from twenty to eighteen and to enable emigrants, seamen and students studying abroad to vote. Most importantly it committed a PASOK government to the implementation of a system of simple proportional representation 'so that the people's will can be registered without distortions'. At the same time the system of preference voting would be abolished 'so as to raise the level of the political struggle and of parliamentary life'.[13] Some indications as to how the introduction of a system of simple proportional representation might affect voting behaviour in a parliamentary election was afforded by the elections to the European Parliament that were held concurrently with the parliamentary election in November 1981. In part, at least, as a result of tactical voting in the parliamentary elections both main parties received a substantially lower share of the vote, with PASOK's share falling from 48.1% to 40.3%, and New Democracy's from 35.9% to 31.5%. The Communist Party increased its share from 10.9 to 12.7%. At the same time, a number of smaller parties, unrepresented in the national Parliament, significantly increased their share of the vote and gained a seat in the European Parliament. The Party of Democratic Socialism (Komma Dimokratikou

Sosialismou) in alliance with the Party of Peasants and Workers (Komma Agroton kai Ergazomenon) registered an almost six-fold increase in its share of the vote to 4.2%, while that of the Communist Party of the Interior increased almost four-fold to 5.2%. The ultra-right-wing Progressive Party increased its share of the vote only marginally, from 1.7% to 2.0%. But this was enough to win it a seat.

It is still too early to say whether PASOK, which is of course a beneficiary of the distortions inherent in the current electoral system, will in fact choose to implement a system of simple proportional representation.[14] Nor is it possible, in the present transitional and somewhat volatile stage of Greek politics, to predict the effect that such a system would have on parliamentary stability. The principal beneficiary would undoubtedly be the Communist Party, whose 10.9% share of the popular vote in 1981 resulted in only a 4.3% share of the parliamentary seats, and small groupings such as its arch-rival the Communist Party of the Interior, the social-democratic KODISO-KAE and the far Right Progressive Party. If PASOK were able to retain the level of support it enjoyed in 1982, then it would have a comfortable working majority in Parliament under simple proportional representation, as any kind of combination between the conservative New Democracy and the Communist Party would be out of the question. If, however, PASOK proves unable to fulfil the high, and perhaps unrealistic, expectations that it has raised of radical social transformation coupled with a bold attempt to assert an independent line in foreign policy, and if simple proportional representation is introduced, then we might see a return to the kind of unstable coalitions that characterised the very early 1950s. What can be said with some confidence is that political parties in Greece will, in the future as in the past, doubtless find it difficult when in power to resist the temptation to manipulate the country's electoral system to their advantage.

Election	Electoral system	Total seats	Seats % Votes %Seats	Seats % Votes %Seats	Seats % Votes %Seats	Seats % Votes %Seats	Seats % Votes %Seats	Seats % Votes %Seats
1946	Proportional	354	Inomeni Parataxis Ethnikophronon[a] 206 55.1 58.1	Ethniki Politiki Enosis[b] 68 19.3 19.2	Komma Phileleftheron[c] 48 14.4 13.6	Ethnikon Komma Ellados[d] 20 6.0 5.6	Enosis Ethnikophronon[e] 9 2.9 2.5	Others 3 2.3 1.0
1950	Proportional	250	Laikon Komma 62 18.8 24.8	Komma Phileleftheron 56 17.2 22.4	Ethniki Proodeftiki Enosis Kentrou[f] 45 16.4 18.0	Komma Georgiou Papandreou[g] 35 10.7 14.0	Dimokratiki Parataxis[h] 18 9.7 7.2	Politiki Anexartitos Parataxis[i] 16 8.2 6.4
			Metopon Ethnikis Anadimourgias[j] 7 5.3 2.8	Ethnikon Komma Ellados 7 3.7 2.8	Parataxis Agroton kai Ergazomenon[k] 3 3.6 1.2	Neon Komma[l] 1 2.5 0.4	Others[m] – 3.9 –	
1951	Reinforced Proportional	258	Ellinikos Synagermos[n] 114 36.5 44.2	Ethniki Proodeftiki Enosis Kentrou 74 23.5 28.7	Komma Phileleftheron 57 19.0 22.0	Eniaia Dimokratiki Aristera[o] 10 10.6 3.9	Laikon Komma 2 6.7 0.8	Komma Georgiou Papandreou – 2.1 –
			Synagermos Agroton kai Ergazomenon 1 1.2 0.4	Others – 0.4 –				
1952	Majority	300	Ellinikos Synagermos 247 49.2 82.0	Enosis Kommaton[p] 51 34.2 17.0	Eniaia Dimokratiki Aristera – 9.6 –	Laikon Komma – 1.0 –	Others 2 6.0 1.0	
1956	Combination of Majority and Proportional[q]	300	Ethniki Rizospastiki Enosis[r] 165 47.4 55.0	Dimokratiki Enosis[s] 132 48.2 44.0	Komma Proodeftikon[t] – 2.2 –	Others – 1.0 –		
1958	Reinforced Proportional	300	Ethniki Rizospastiki Enosis 171 41.2 57.0	Eniaia Dimokratiki Aristera 79 24.4 26.3	Komma Phileleftheron 36 20.7 12.0	Proodeftiki Agrotiki Dimokratiki Enosis[u] 10 10.6 3.3	Enosis Laikou Kommatos[v] 4 2.9 1.4	Others – 0.2 –
1961	Reinforced Proportional	300	Ethniki Rizospastiki Enosis 176 50.8 58.7	Enosis Kentrou[w] in alliance with Komma Proodeftikon 100 33.7 33.3	Pandimokratiko Agrotiko Metopo Ellados[x] 24 14.6 8.0	Others – 0.9 –		
1963	Reinforced Proportional	300	Enosis Kentrou 138 42.1 46.0	Ethniki Rizospastiki Enosis 132 39.4 44.0	Eniaia Dimokratiki Aristera 28 14.3 9.3	Komma Proodeftikon 2 3.7 0.7	Others – 0.5 –	

Table 1 (cont.)

Election	Electoral system	Total seats	Party	Seats	% Votes	% Seats
1964	Reinforced Proportional	300	Enosis Kentrou	171	52.7	57.0
			Ethniki Rizospastiki Enosis in alliance with Komma Proodeftikon	107	35.2	35.7
			Eniaia Dimokratiki Aristera	22	11.8	7.3
			Others	–	0.3	–
1974	Reinforced Proportional	300	Nea Dimokratia[y]	220	54.3	73.3
			Enosis Kentrou–Nees Dynameis[z]	60	20.4	20.0
			Panellinio Sosialistiko Kinima[aa]	12	13.6	4.0
			Eniaia Aristera[bb]	8	9.5	2.7
			Ethniki Dimokratiki Enosis[cc]	–	1.1	–
			Others	–	1.1	–
1977	Reinforced Proportional	300	Nea Dimokratia	173	41.9	57.8
			Komma Neophileleftheron[gg]	2	1.1	0.7
			Panellinio Sosialistiko Kinima	92	25.3	30.2
			Others	–	0.8	–
			Enosis Dimokratikou Kentrou[dd]	15	12.0	5.0
			Kommounistiko Komma Elladas	11	9.4	3.8
			Ethniki Parataxis[ee]	5	6.8	1.8
			Symmakhia Proodeftikon kai Aristeron Dynameon[ff]	2	2.7	0.7
1981	Reinforced Proportional	300	Panellinio Sosialistiko Kinima	172	48.1	57.4
			Nea Dimokratia	115	35.9	38.3
			Kommounistiko Komma Elladas	13	10.9	4.3
			Others	–	5.1	–

a United Camp of the Nationally Minded. Alliance of Laikon Komma (People's Party: 156 seats); Komma Ethnikon Phileleftheron (Party of the National Liberals: 34); Metarrythmistikon Komma (Reformist Party: 5); others in alliance: 11.

b National Political Union. Alliance of Komma Venizelikon Phileleftheron (Party of the Venizelist Liberals: 31); Dimokratikon Sosialistikon Komma (Democratic Socialist Party: 27); Ethnikon Enotikon Komma (National Unity Party: 7); others in alliance: 3.

c Liberal Party.

d National Party of Greece.

e Union of the Nationally Minded. Alliance of Komma Ethnikophronon (Party of the Nationally Minded) and Laikon Agrotikon Komma (People's Agrarian Party).

f National Progressive Centre Union. Alliance of Komma Proodeftikon Phileleftheron Kentrou (Party of Progressive Liberals of the Centre) and Dimokratikon Proodeftikon Komma (Democratic Progressive Party).

g George Papandreou Party.

h Democratic Camp. Alliance of Enosis Dimokratikon Aristeron (Union of Democratic Leftists); Sosialistikon Komma-Enosis Laikis Dimokratias (Socialist Party-Union of Popular Democracy); Komma Aristeron Phileleftheron (Party of Leftist Liberals).

i Politically Independent Camp. Alliance of Komma Ellinikis Anagenniseos (Party of Greek Rebirth) and Komma Ethnikophronon.

j National Reconstruction Front. Alliance of Ethnikon Enotikon Komma; Laikon Proodeftikon Komma (People's Progressive Party) and Panellinion Komma (Panhellenic Party).

k Camp of Farmers and Workers. Alliance of Synagermos Agroton kai Ergazomenon (Rally of Farmers and Workers) and Agrotikon Ethnikon Proodeftikon Komma (National Agrarian Progressive Party).

l New Party.

m These included four alliances (with one of seven parties) as well as eight miniscule parties running independently. Altogether forty-four parties contested the elections. most of them in alliance.

n Greek Rally.

o United Democratic Left.

p Union of the Parties. Alliance of Ethniki Proodeftiki Enosis Kentrou (26 seats); Komma Phileleftheron (25); and Sosialistikon Komma-Enosis Laikis Dimokratias.

q This was the first general election in which women had the right to vote. Registered votes numbered 4.507.907 compared to 2.123.150 in 1952.

r National Radical Union.

s Democratic Union. Alliance of Philelefthera Dimokratiki Enosis (Liberal Democratic Union: 43 seats); Komma Phileleftheron (26); Dimokratikon Komma Ergazomenou Laou (Democratic Party of Working People: 20); Eniaia Dimokratiki Aristera (18); Ethniki Proodeftiki Enosis Kentrou (15); Komma Agrotikon kai Ergatikon (Agrarian and Workers' Party: 7); Laikon Komma (3).

t Progressive Party.

u Progressive Agrarian Democratic Union. Alliance of Komma Proodeftikon; Ethniki Proodeftiki Enosis Kentrou; Komma Agroton kai Ergazomenon (Party of Farmers and Workers); Dimokratikon Komma Ergazomenou Laou (Democratic Party of Working People).

v Union of the People's Party. Alliance of Laikon Komma; Laikon Koinonikon Komma (People's Social Party); Komma Ethnikophronon; Metarrythmistikon Komma: Dimokratikon Metarrythmistikon Komma (Democratic Reformist Party).

w Centre Union.

x Pandemocratic Agrarian Front of Greece. Alliance of Eniaia Dimokratiki Aristera and Ethnikos Agrotiko Komma (National Agrarian Party).

y New Democracy.

z Centre Union-New Forces.

aa Panhellenic Socialist Movement.

bb Electoral alliance of Kommounistiko Komma Elladas (Communist Party of Greece: 5 seats); Kommounistiko Komma Elladas-Esoterikou (Communist Party of Greece-Interior: 2); Eniaia Dimokratiki Aristera (1).

cc National Democratic Union.

dd Union of the Democratic Centre: the result of the fusion of the Enosis Kentrou with Nees Dynameis.

ee National Camp.

ff Alliance of Progressive and Left-Wing Forces. Alliance of Kommounistiko Komma Elladas-Esoterikou (2 seats); Eniaia Dimokratiki Aristera: Socialistiki Poreia (Socialist Course) Sosialistiki Protovoulia (Socialist Initiative); and Khristianiki Dimokratia (Christian Democracy).

gg New Liberal Party.

Sources: Based on Meynaud. *Les Forces Politiques en Grèce;* Werner Voigt. 'Ergebnisse der Wahlen und Volksabstimmungen', in Klaus-Detlev Grothusen. ed... *Griechenland.* Südosteuropa Handbuch Band III (Göttingen, 1980). pp. 663–75 and *Odigos eklogon ap' to* 1961: *Elavon . . . Pliri eklogika apotelesmata kai vouleftes kata periphereia* (Athens. 1977).

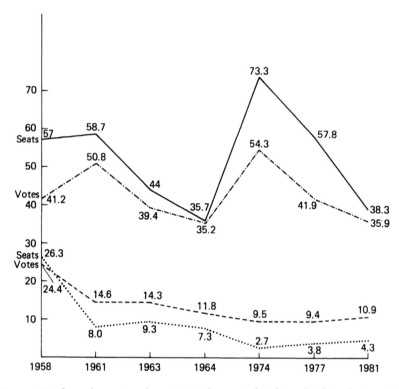

Figure 1 % of popular vote and seats in Parliament of Right and Left in elections held
under reinforced proportional representation 1958–81 (adapted from Contiades
'Griechenland', p. 595)

NOTES

1 On Greek political culture see P. Nikiforos Diamandouros, 'Greek Political Culture in Transition: Historical Origins, Evolution, Current Trends', in Richard Clogg, ed., *Greece in the 1980s* (London, 1983).
2 For a detailed analysis of this crucial period see George Alexander, *The Prelude to the Truman Doctrine: British Policy in Greece 1944–1947* (Oxford, 1982).
3 For an analysis of the 1946 election see George Th. Mavrogordatos, 'The 1946 Election and Plebiscite: Prelude to Civil War', in John O. Iatrides, ed., *Greece in the 1940s: A Nation in Crisis* (Hanover, NH, 1981), pp. 181–94.
4 Jean Meynaud, *Les Forces Politiques en Grèce* (Lausanne, 1965), p. 89.
5 Laurence Stern, *The Wrong Horse: The Politics of Intervention and the Failure of American Diplomacy* (New York, 1977), p. 16; John O. Iatrides, 'American Attitudes towards the Political System of Postwar Greece', in Theodore A. Couloumbis and John O. Iatrides, eds., *Greek–American Relations: A Critical Review* (New York, 1980), pp. 68–9.
6 Stern, *The Wrong Horse*, p. 17.
7 In respect of civil servants working away from the community in which they were registered.
8 Meynaud, *Les Forces Politiques en Grèce*, p. 105.
9 Ion Contiades, 'Griechenland', in Dolf Sternberger and Bernhard Vogel, eds., *Die Wahl der Parlamente und anderer Staatsorgane: Ein Handbuch*, vol. 1, *Europa* (Berlin, 1969), pp. 590–1.
10 D. George Kousoulas, *Greece: Uncertain Democracy* (Washington, 1973), p. 121.
11 The number of seats allotted to each constituency is determined by dividing the number of registered voters in the constituency by a quota arrived at in turn by dividing the total number of registered voters in the country by 288 (the number of deputies in Parliament minus the state deputies).
12 Phaedo Vegleris, 'Greek Electoral Law', in Howard R. Penniman, *Greece at the Polls: The National Elections of 1974 and 1977* (Washington, DC, 1981), p. 35.
13 *Diakiryrixi Kyvernitikis Politikis: Symvolaio me to Lao* (Athens, 1981), pp. 40–1.
14 PASOK, following its election victory, moved swiftly to carry out its commitment to lower the voting age to eighteen, a move which has increased the electorate by an estimated 300,000.

SUGGESTIONS FOR FURTHER READING

Two indispensable guides to the intricacies of the Greek electoral system are Ion Contiades, 'Griechenland', in Dolf Sternberger and Bernhard Vogel, eds., *Die Wahl der Parlamente und anderer Staatsorgane: Ein Handbuch*, vol. 1 *Europa* (Berlin, 1969), pp. 555–603; and Phaedo Vegleris, 'Greek Electoral Law', in Howard R. Penniman, *Greece at the Polls: The National Elections of 1974 and 1977* (Washington, DC, 1981), pp. 21–48.
  The literature in accessible languages on the Greek political system in general is sparse but Jean Meynaud (with P. Merlopoulos and G. Notaras), *Les Forces Politiques en Grèce* (Lausanne, 1965), and Keith R. Legg, *Politics in Modern Greece* (Standford, 1969),

are useful for postwar politics up until the establishment of the Colonels' dictatorship in 1967. On the inter-war period see George Mavrogordatos, *Stillborn Republic: Social Coalitions and Party Strategies in Greece, 1922–1936* (Berkeley, 1982), and on the nineteenth century Hariton Korisis, *Die politischen Parteien Griechenlands: Ein neuer Staat auf dem Weg zur Demokratie 1821–1910* (Nürnberg, 1966).

For a summary discussion of the 1981 elections see Richard Clogg, 'The Greek Elections of 1981', *Electoral Studies*, 1 (1982), pp. 95–9. For a more detailed analysis see George Mavrogordatos, *The Rise of the Green Sun: The Greek Election of 1981*, Centre of Contemporary Greek Studies, King's College, Occasional Papers, No.1 (London, 1983), obtainable from the Department of Byzantine and Modern Greek Studies, King's College, London WC2R 2LS.

11

Japan

J.A.A. STOCKWIN

Few countries in the world today have had longer or more extensive experience with elections than Japan. Elections for the House of Representatives have been held regularly, even during wartime, since 1890.[1] While it is true that until after the Second World War Parliament had a severely limited part to play in the political system as a whole, its role was not completely negligible, and the experience gained over a long period in both the holding of elections and the organising of political parties was of lasting value. Although in early elections under the Meiji constitution,[2] the size of the electorate was small as a result of imposition of a strict property franchise, the number of those males entitled to vote grew by several stages until in 1925 universal male franchise was introduced, with a lower age limit for voting of twenty-five years.[3] Under American auspices following the Japanese defeat of 1945, both men and women over the age of twenty obtained the vote, while a battery of other reforms were introduced, including a new constitution, enshrining the principle of popular sovereignty, and designed to ensure freedom of political organisation with a role for Parliament in the centre of the political stage.[4]

A principal concern of those who have investigated Japan's social, economic and political development since the American Occupation following the end of the Second World War has been the question of continuity and discontinuity. How far did the reforms of the Occupation open up a different path for Japan from that which she had been pursuing before? Or did indigenous norms and practices reassert themselves through the veneer of institutional reforms enacted under American auspices? The argument, indeed, is part of a broader concern about Japanese modernisation from the nineteenth century onwards. Japan was virtually a closed country for some two and a half centuries before the 1850s, and the socio-political culture of Japan, emerging as a member of the comity of nations in the late nineteenth century, was highly idiosyncratic from a Western point of view, or even by comparison with most of the rest of Asia. The opening of the country to the outside world involved much absorption of Western norms and ways of doing things, but indigenous values and modes of socio-economic organisations and behaviour proved persistent in many spheres.

The practice of voting in elections was, like many other institutions and practices at the time, imported from the West rather than handed down as part of the traditional culture. The behaviour of voters, however, as well as the behaviour of candidates competing for votes, tended to reflect norms and values of the pre-modern society which underlay the operation of an introduced institution. Burke's definition of 'party' as 'a body of men united, for promoting by their joint endeavours the national interest, upon some particular principle in which they are all agreed' was slow to develop in the Japanese political culture. Early parties were much closer in essence to a term which in English has generally had a pejorative connotation: 'faction'.[5] Behind-the-scenes politics conducted in and between cliques and cabals was fairly typical of the Japanese scene from the late nineteenth century to 1945 and beyond. The local community was the most important focus for electoral activity, with local solidarity (often enforced through a variety of social sanctions) being the most important factor determining the way people voted. Since the American Occupation, which introduced and reinforced a range of 'democratic' political practices and norms, much of the population has moved from close-knit rural communities, capable of ensuring that their members vote as a bloc in favour of the 'local son', to much more impersonal and mobile urban environments. Nevertheless, though there has been some change in electoral behaviour in the recent period, older patterns have proved re-markably persistent.

The main proposition to be argued in this chapter is that the electoral system constitutes an important independent variable tending to reinforce more traditional forms of electioneering and electoral behaviour, and to retard change. A logically subsequent proposition is that the failure of many proposals to revise the electoral system[6] has hitherto reflected the lack of interest in electoral revision on the part of the ruling Liberal Democratic Party, which continues to gain considerable advantage from the reinforce-ment of traditional modes of behaviour inherent in the present electoral system.

The Japanese Parliament is called the National Diet (Kokkai), and consists of two Houses, the House of Representatives (Shūgiin) and the House of Councillors (Sangiin). The House of Representatives, or Lower House (equi-valent in a very general sense to the House of Commons in the British Parliament) has 511 members – a number which has increased through several jumps from 466 in the immediate postwar period. The House of Councillors, on the other hand, has 252 members (250 before the reversion of Okinawa to Japan in 1972), and is also known as the Upper House. It has much more limited powers in relation to legislation than the Lower House.[7]

The electoral system for the House of Representatives is practically unique, though it has a long history in Japan. It may be described as a system based on the principle of a single non-transferable vote in a multi-member constituency. The voter, upon entering the voting booth, is handed a ballot paper which contains two instructions. The first is to write the name of one candidate, and one candidate only, in the appropriate place. The second is not to write the name of a person who is not a candidate. No indication is given on the ballot paper of who the candidates are, let alone their party affiliations, though the names of the candidates are posted within the voting area. A space is reserved for the voter to write the name of the candidate for whom he or she wishes to vote.[8] Voting is voluntary.

Constituencies are multi-member.[9] At present there are 130 constituencies throughout Japan, including forty-seven which elect three members, forty-one which elect four members, forty-one which elect five members and one which elects one member only. There is no mechanism for transferring votes from one candidate to another. Those declared elected are quite simply those three candidates in a three-member constituency (or four candidates in a four-member constituency, or five candidates in a five-member constituency) who respectively attract the largest number of votes. For example, in the Lower House general elections of 22 June 1980, there were 502,572 electors registered in the first constituency of Niigata Prefecture, which is located on the Japan Sea coast of Honshū. Five candidates (two Liberal Democrats, one Socialist, one Democratic Socialist and one Communist) stood for election in this three-member constituency. The results were as shown in Table 1.

It will be observed that votes cast for the LDP* heavily outweighed votes cast for any other party. Indeed the LDP had an absolute majority over all other parties of 202,540 votes to 173,447. Nevertheless, the Socialist was elected, with just 20% of the vote. Also it will be readily apparent that while LDP voters divided their votes about equally between Ozawa and Kondō, a large party such as the LDP could be severely disadvantaged by allowing its vote to be spread among too many candidates or by putting forward a candidate who was conspicuously more popular than its other candidates.

The term of the House of Representatives is four years at maximum, and in practice the government of the day has freedom to dissolve more or less when it likes.[10] In contrast the House of Councillors has a fixed term of three years. At each three-yearly election one half of the 252 seats come up for re-election for a six-year term. Constituencies for the House of Councillors are of two types: 152 members (seventy-six every election) are elected from prefectural constituencies, in which each of the nation's forty-seven prefectures are treated as one constituency. The remaining 100 members (fifty each election) are elected from a national constituency, in which the whole country is treated as one constituency. Unlike elections for the House of Representatives, where each

---

* The following abbreviations of party names are used in this chapter: LDP (Liberal Democratic Party); JSP (Japan Socialist Party); DSP (Democratic Socialist Party); JCP (Japan Communist Party); NLC (New Liberal Club); SDL (Social Democratic League); NLCDL (New Liberal Club Democratic League). Kōmeitō is left untranslated because of the difficulty of finding an adequate translation.

Table 1

Name	Party affiliation	Votes	
Ozawa	Liberal Democrat	102.416	
Kondō	Liberal Democrat	100,124	Elected
Yoneda	Socialist	75,318	
Yamamoto	Democratic Socialist	74,169	Not elected
Hayashi	Communist	23,960	

Source: Asahi Shimbun Senkyo Hombu (Asahi Newspaper Election Head-quarters), *Asahi Senkyo Taikan: Dai 36 Kai Shūgiin Sōsenkyo, Dai 12 Kai Sangiin Tsūjō Senkyo, Shōwa 55 nen 6 gatsu* (Asahi Election Survey: The 36th General Election for the House of Representatives and the 12th Regular Election for the House of Councillors, June 1980) (Tokyo, 1980), p. 71.

voter has one vote, in House of Councillors elections a voter has two votes, one for the constituency formed by the prefecture in which he is registered, and one for the national constituency. He thus votes for two candidates, but as in Lower House elections, there is no way that either of these two votes can be transferred from one candidate to another.

Because of the widely different population size of the various prefectures, the number of candidates in prefectural constituencies ranges from two in the case of the least populated to eight in the case of heavily populated. Since, however only half of the seats for the prefectural constituencies are renewed at each election, the number of seats in contention at any one election varies from one to four. Numbers are in fact weighted heavily at the lower end of the scale there are twenty-six one-member contests, fifteen contests for two members four for three members and only two (Hokkaidō and Tokyo) for four members This means that in twenty-six constituencies scattered around the country there are regular three-yearly elections in which the system of election is first past-the-post in a single-member constituency. This, as we shall see, provide us with the possibility of making an interesting check on the hypothesis that the predominant multi-member ('medium size') constituency system substan tially affects electoral behaviour. Unfortunately, however, since these Upper House single-member contests take place mostly in highly conservative rural areas, the sample is in no sense random. A fairly typical result of a contest of this kind was that fought in Nagasaki Prefecture in the Upper House genera elections of 22 June 1980, with 1,076,590 electors on the roll, as shown in Table 2.

The most unusual (and controversial) constituency in Japan is the nationa constituency of the House of Councillors. As we shall see, the decision has been taken to reform it. At each election fifty members are elected by an electorate which at the 1980 Upper House elections numbered 80,925,034. Quite simply the first fifty place-getters are declared elected. At the 1980 elections the

Table 2

Name	Party affiliation	Votes	
Hatsumura	Liberal Democrat	452,561	Elected
Tatsuta	Socialist	267,786	Not elected
Furuki	Communist	55,376	

Source: Asahi Shimbun Senkyo Hombu (Asahi Newspaper Election Head-quarters), *Asahi Senkyo Taikan: Dai 36 Kai Shūgiin Sōsenkyo, Dai 12 Kai Sangiin Tsūjō Senkyo, Shōwa 55 nen 6 gatsu* (Asahi Election Survey: The 36th General Election for the House of Representatives and the 12th Regular Election for the House of Councillors, June 1980) (Tokyo, 1980), p. 80.

octogenarian Miss Ichikawa, standing as an Independent, came first with 2,784,998 votes, while the candidate placed fiftieth, a Socialist called Wada, attracted a mere 642,554 votes. Apart from the fifty elected, there were a further forty-three unsuccessful candidates.

Besides the two Houses of the National Diet, regular elections are held for an enormous number of chief executive and local assembly positions at the local level. As of December 1972 there were elections for 47 prefectural governor-ships, 643 mayors of cities, 2,641 heads of towns and villages, 2,788 members of prefectural assemblies, 20,325 members of city assemblies, 49,777 members of town and village assemblies and 1,091 members of special ward assemblies in Tokyo. Chief executive elections were all single-member first-past-the-post affairs, whereas the number of members per constituency in local assembly elections varied widely. When one considers the number of elective positions in both national and local politics, it becomes clear that the act of voting and the routine of elections is a regular and familiar experience for much of the Japanese population.

Turning from a description of the electoral system to an analysis of electoral results and trends, a number of most interesting factors become apparent. Before the Second World War, when political parties were much less important in the political system as a whole than they subsequently became, there was much fluidity in electoral behaviour. Two major parties – both essentially conservative – dominated the scene, and more or less alternated in possession of parliamentary majorities, though this did not necessarily mean alternation in power, since power did not securely lie with the parties.

Following the 1945 defeat a further decade of fluidity ensued, though with the difference that parties professing various forms of socialism had come to constitute a major minority force in the electorate and in Parliament. Briefly, in 1947 and 1948, the JSP entered a coalition government together with two parties from outside the socialist side of politics. The year 1955 marks a turning point. In that year for the first time the Socialists mustered enough parliamentary seats to block revision of the constitution,[11] and both the Socialists and the Conservatives successively amalgamated into single parties.

Subsequently the Conservatives, with their far greater access to power and patronage, were able to control strong internal fissiparous tendencies to the extent that, apart from the defection of a small splinter group in 1976, they maintained themselves as a single party. The Socialists, on the other hand, were much more prone to destructive internal squabbling, and found it difficult either to avoid the defection of splinter groups or to stem the tide of electoral decline which in turn permitted the formation of alternative parties of opposition.

The pattern of electoral trends from the late 1950s to the middle 1970s is extremely interesting. On the conservative side of politics the proportion of the total vote which went to the LDP declined slowly but steadily, and there was no Lower House general election between those of May 1958 and December 1976 at which the LDP did not do worse in terms of proportion of the total votes cast than it had at the previous election. In 1958 the percentage was 57.8, but by 1976 it had fallen to 41.8 – a fall of 16.0% over eighteen years. Not surprisingly, during the middle 1970s many commentators were basing their predictions on the assumption that this trend would inexorably continue, and that the LDP therefore could not long hope to maintain its majority of Lower House seats.[12] There was some surprise, therefore, when towards the end of the 1970s the trend began rising again, to 44.6% in the 1979 elections and to 47.9% in the elections of 1980.

If we examine this trend in more detail, we see that the downward tendency was most pronounced in the middle 1960s, which was precisely the period when economic growth was at its most rapid, urbanisation was proceeding fastest and the problems facing those living in the big cities were becoming most evident and acute.[13] Towards the beginning and towards the end of the eighteen-year period the rate of decline was much slower[14] (see Figure 1). The connection between urbanisation and a decline in the LDP voting percentage is strongly supported by an examination of the urban–rural breakdown of the vote. Whereas over the whole period the LDP vote held up well in the countryside, it suffered a sharp decline in the big cities, particularly during the high economic growth period of the 1960s and early 1970s.[15]

When we turn to the opposition parties, we see, on the part of the JSP, a rather similar but much more marked pattern of secular decline, with the decline most acute in the cities. In the Socialist case, however, there is no recent evidence of recovery. The principal difference between LDP and JSP performance relates to the much poorer record of cohesion and perceived competence of the latter when compared with the former. Whereas, apart from a single small occurrence of defection in 1976 (the formation of the New Liberal Club) the LDP has managed almost to monopolise conservative votes at the national level, the Socialists have more and more had to share the non-LDP

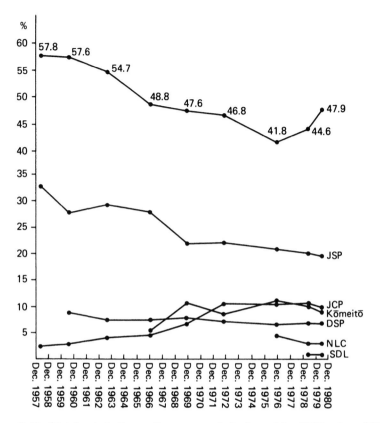

Figure 1 % of total vote in Lower House general elections, May 1958 – June 1980

vote with smaller and more dynamic parties, directing their appeal largely to urban voters. Since the late 1950s the JSP has suffered two defections, one major and one minor. In 1959–60 much of the right wing of the JSP defected and formed the Democratic Socialist Party (DSP), which has generally won 6% or 7% of the national vote and about 30 seats in Lower House elections. In 1977–8 there was a much smaller and less serious defection from the party's right wing, leading to the formation of the Social Democratic League (SDL),[16] which in 1981 merged at parliamentary level with the New Liberal Club (NLC) to form the New Liberal Club Democratic League (NLCDL). The best result so far of the SDL is three Lower House seats.

The earlier JSP monopoly of opposition seats was also challenged from the outside, by two dynamic and well-organised parties which began to do well in the 1960s. Despite their radically different origins and ideologies, these two parties have much in common organisationally and in terms of the base of their support. The first is the Kōmeitō (also sometimes known, rather inaccurately, in English as the Clean Government Party), the political offshoot of an energetically proselytising neo-Buddhist religion called the Sōka Gakka ('Value-Creation Association') having an appeal in particular to relatively under-educated sections of the population which in an earlier age might well have been called 'petit bourgeois'.

The second such party could in fact boast the longest history of any party in Japan, though between its original foundation in 1922 and its re-emergence as a legal party for the first time in 1945 that history was discontinuous to say the least: the Japan Communist Party (JCP), after a brief flowering during the Occupation, was reduced to marginal status in the 1950s, but under astute leadership in the 1960s came to attract about 10% of the national vote.[17] The JCP received support from among relatively alienated sections of the population, and although factory workers constituted its core backing, its support extended across the range of socio-economic groups, though it was very weak in the countryside.

What the Kōmeitō and the JCP had in common was a seriousness about grass-roots organisation that was largely lacking in the other parties. Strenuous and up to a point successful attempts were made to build up a body of devoted and dedicated members whose lives would revolve around their party, and whose commitment went far beyond that of personal convenience or gain. In both cases, also, organisation was, by comparison with other parties, centralised, hierarchical and carefully structured. They were both strong in the big cities and weak almost everywhere else. Unlike the JSP and DSP they were not dependent upon a kind of substitute organisation in the labour unions. Both experienced their most spectacular flowering in the late 1960s and early 1970s (the JCP a little later than the Kōmeitō) which was precisely the time when the social dislocations created by rapid urbanisation were most apparent, and when both the LDP and especially the JSP were losing urban support. Since the middle 1970s the electoral performance of these two parties has ceased to improve, and in the case of both has recently somewhat declined.

Finally, the New Liberal Club (NLC) is the only party of opposition to have originated as a splinter group from the LDP. Although it confounded observers with its capacity to attract votes in the 1976 Lower House elections, held in the aftermath of the Lockheed revelations, it found its initial success difficult to sustain, and was plagued by defections from members wishing to return to the LDP fold. It is a very minor party indeed, its support being virtually confined to the big cities (especially the Tokyo area), and despite its parliamentary union with the even smaller Social Democratic League, its future appears to be in doubt. The voting trends for the various opposition parties are shown in Figure 1.

Results of the House of Representatives election from 1958 to 1980 are given in Table 3. Results of the House of Councillors elections from 1971 to 1980 are given in Table 4.

Election	LDP	JSP	DSP	KP	JCP	NLC	SDL	Others	Indep.	Total
22 May 1958	287 (61.5) 22,977 (57.8)	166 (35.5) 13,094 (32.9)			1 (0.2) 1,012 (2.6)			1 (0.2) 288 (0.7)	12 (2.6) 2,381 (6.0)	467 39,752
20 Nov. 1960	296 (63.4) 22,740 (57.6)	145 (31.0) 10,887 (27.6)	17 (3.7) 3,464 (8.8)		3 (0.6) 1,157 (2.9)			1 (0.2) 142 (0.3)	5 (1.9) 1,119 (2.8)	467 39,509
21 Nov. 1963	283 (60.7) 22,424 (54.7)	144 (30.8) 11,907 (29.0)	23 (4.9) 3,023 (7.4)		5 (1.1) 1,646 (4.0)			0 (0) 0 (0)	12 (2.6) 1,956 (4.8)	467 41,017
29 Jan. 1967	277 (57.0) 22,448 (48.8)	140 (28.8) 12,826 (27.9)	30 (6.2) 3,404 (7.4)	25 (5.1) 2,472 (5.4)	5 (1.0) 2,191 (4.8)			0 (0) 60 (0.1)	9 (1.9) 2,554 (5.5)	486 45,997
27 Dec. 1969	288 (59.2) 22,382 (47.6)	90 (18.5) 10,074 (21.4)	31 (6.4) 3,637 (7.7)	47 (9.7) 5,125 (10.9)	14 (2.9) 3,199 (6.8)			0 (0) 81 (0.2)	16 (3.3) 2,493 (5.3)	486 46,990
10 Dec. 1972	271 (55.2) 24,563 (46.8)	118 (24.0) 11,479 (21.9)	19 (3.9) 3,661 (7.0)	29 (5.9) 4,437 (8.5)	38 (7.7) 5,497 (10.5)			2 (0.4) 143 (0.3)	14 (2.9) 2,646 (5.0)	491 52,425
5 Dec. 1976	249 (48.7) 23,654 (41.8)	123 (24.1) 11,713 (20.7)	29 (5.7) 3,554 (6.3)	55 (10.8) 6,177 (10.9)	17 (3.3) 5,878 (10.4)	17 (3.3) 2,364 (4.2)		0 (0) 45 (0.1)	21 (4.1) 3,227 (5.7)	511 56,613
7 Oct. 1979	248 (48.6) 24,084 (44.6)	107 (20.9) 10,643 (19.7)	35 (6.3) 3,664 (6.8)	57 (11.2) 5,283 (9.8)	39 (7.6) 5,626 (10.4)	4 (0.7) 1,632 (3.0)	2 (0.4) 368 (0.7)	0 (0) 69 (0.1)	19 (3.7) 2,641 (4.9)	511 54,522
22 June 1980	284 (55.6) 28,262 (47.9)	107 (20.9) 11,401 (19.3)	32 (6.3) 3,897 (6.6)	33 (6.5) 5,330 (9.0)	29 (5.7) 5,804 (9.8)	12 (2.3) 1,766 (3.0)	3 (0.5) 402 (0.7)	0 (0) 109 (0.2)	11 (2.1) 2,057 (3.5)	511 59,029

Notes: *i* For each entry: number of seats (% of total seats)

number of votes, in thousands (% of total votes).

ii Party name abbreviations

DSP: Democratic Socialist Party (Minshatō)

JCP: Japan Communist Party (Nihon Kyōsantō)

JSP: Japan Socialist Party (Nihon Shakaitō)

KP: Kōmei Party (Kōmeitō)

LDP: Liberal Democratic Party (Jiyūminshutō, Jimintō)

NLC: New Liberal Club (Shin Jiyū Club)

SDL: Social Democratic League (Shakaiminshurengō, Shaminren).

Sources: *Asahi Nenkan* (Asahi Yearbook), 1977 (Tokyo, 1977), p. 323; *Asahi Shinbun* (9 Oct. 1979); *Asahi Nenkan*, 1981, pp. 232–3.

Table 4 *House of Councillors election results 1971–1980*

	Prefectural constituencies			National constituencies			
	Seats		Votes	Seats		Votes	Total seats
	No.	%	%	No.	%	%	%
LDP							
1971	41	54.6	43.9	21	42.0	44.4	62
1974	43	56.6	39.5	19	35.2	44.3	62
1977	45	59.2	39.5	18	36.0	35.8	63
1980	48	63.2	43.3	21	42.0	42.5	69
JSP							
1971	28	37.3	31.2	11	22.0	21.3	39
1974	18	23.7	26.0	10	18.5	15.2	28
1977	17	22.4	25.9	10	20.0	17.4	27
1980	13	17.1	22.4	9	18.0	13.1	22
Kōmeitō							
1971	2	2.7	3.5	8	16.0	14.1	10
1974	5	6.6	12.6	9	16.7	12.1	14
1977	5	6.6	6.2	9	18.0	14.2	14
1980	3	3.9	5.0	9	18.0	11.9	12
DSP							
1971	2	2.7	4.8	4	8.0	8.0	6
1974	1	1.3	4.4	4	7.4	5.9	5
1977	2	2.6	4.5	4	8.0	6.7	6
1980	2	2.6	5.2	4	8.0	6.0	6
JCP							
1971	1	1.3	12.1	5	10.0	8.1	6
1974	5	6.6	12.0	8	14.8	9.4	13
1977	2	2.6	9.9	3	6.0	8.4	5
1980	4	5.3	11.7	3	6.0	7.3	7
NLC							
1971	–	–	–	–	–	–	–
1974	–	–	–	–	–	–	–
1977	2	2.6	5.7	1	2.0	3.9	3
1978	0	0	0.6	0	0	0.6	0
Minor parties (incl. SDL) and Inds.							
1971	1	1.3	4.4	1	2.0	6.0	2
1974	4	5.2	5.5	4	7.4	13.1	8
1977	3	3.9	8.3	5	10.0	13.6	8
1980	6	7.9	11.8	4	8.0	18.6	10

Table 4 (*cont*)

	Prefectural constituencies			National constituencies			
	Seats		Votes		Seats		Votes	Total seats
	No.	%	%	No.	%	%	%
Total							
1971	75	100.0	100.0	50	100.0	100.0	125
1974	76	100.0	100.0	54[a]	100.0	100.0	130
1977	76	100.0	100.0	50	100.0	100.0	126
1980	76	100.0	100.0	50	100.0	100.0	126

[a] In 1974 four candidates were elected to the national constituency for three-year terms to fill vacancies in seats filled in 1971.

Sources: Asahi Nenkan (Asahi Yearbook), 1972 (Tokyo, 1972); ibid., 1975; ibid; 1978; ibid., 1981.

To what extent has the electoral system affected the outcome of the electoral process and more broadly the nature of party politics in Japan? Several aspects of the system have clearly exerted a significant influence on both electoral results and political style.

One quite important aspect is the failure, in both House of Representatives elections and in elections for the prefectural constituencies of the House of Councillors, to redraw electoral boundaries to take into account changes in the distribution of population. In the case of the House of Representatives the failure is not absolute, since thirty-nine seats in densely populated urban areas have been added since the early 1960s.[18] Nevertheless, at the time of the Lower House general election of October 1979, the discrepancy in the value of a vote at the extremes – that is between the most and the least densely populated constituency – was 3.9 times.[19] This in part at least explains the consistently higher proportion of total seats won by the LDP in comparison with the proportion of votes, since that party enjoys more support in the countryside than in the towns. Without this advantage, the LDP could not have sustained an independent majority in several recent elections. It is not so clear that the JSP is disadvantaged by this factor (and indeed it may now marginally profit from it), but the smaller urban-based parties appear to suffer some disadvantage.

The second point is that the system has in practice fostered the fragmentation of the opposition. There have been instances in five-member constituencies of the Lower House where a candidate has been elected with as little as 10% of the vote. This means that parties with minority appeal, which in a British-type system would be eliminated altogether (unless their support were heavily concentrated in a particular region), are able to elect one candidate in each of a number of constituencies where their organisation is sufficiently strong to muster, say 15 or 20% of the total vote. It is worth noting that with

one exception the Kōmeitō, DSP, JCP, NLC and SDL have never elected more
than one candidate in a House of Representatives election in any single
constituency. The exception is in the Communist stronghold of Kyōto, in
whose first constituency the JCP elected two candidates in the 1972 and 1979
elections. It is possible to check this point by reference to those constituencies of
the Upper House where a single member is elected, as mentioned above. The
normal pattern in those constituencies is for the LDP, the JSP and the JCP to put
up candidates, though Independents also sometimes stand. The JCP has a
policy of contesting every constituency, in order to develop its local organisation, but its percentage of the vote in Upper House single-member constituencies is usually very small. In the 1974 House of Councillors elections the
Kōmeitō put up candidates in sixteen single-member constituencies, but all of
them did badly, and the experiment was not repeated. The DSP (and in 1977
the NLC) have on occasion put forward one or two candidates, but never to any
effect. For all intents and purposes, then, the Upper House single-member
constituencies involve contests between the LDP and JSP, or sometimes
between the LDP and a conservative Independent. They do not reward
opposition fragmentation.

It should be noted, however, that multi-member constituencies are merely
permissive towards the emergence of small parties; their existence does not
explain why the fragmentation has taken place in the ranks of the opposition,
but not in the LDP (except for the minor defection of the NLC in 1976). Several
factors may be advanced to explain this difference, though which is the most
important is not entirely clear. Up to the time of the formation of the LDP in
1955 the conservative camp was at least as prone to fragmentation as the
socialist camp, but since 1955 the conservative side of politics has been far
better at staying together in one party than have its opponents.[20] Probably the
key explanation is simply that the LDP has been in power, and no doubt the
prospect of losing power as a result of forming splinter groups is more of a
stimulus to stay together than the prospect of perhaps gaining power in a more
or less remote future is a stimulus to remain united when power has never, or
almost never, been tasted. In addition, the LDP is under pressure from business
to keep its house in order, and ideological disputation is more of a habit on the
Left than on the Right. But even in recent circumstances, where the ideological
temperature has been substantially reduced, the opposition has found it almost
impossible to merge into a smaller number of parties, let alone a single party.

This leads us to a third effect of the electoral system, which is that it appears
to encourage both factionalism and candidate-centred, rather than party-
centred, mobilisation of the vote. This effect is confined to those parties which
put up more than one candidate in a substantial number of constituencies.
This is overwhelmingly true for the LDP, and true now to a rather minor extent
for the JSP,[21] but not true for any of the other parties. What this means in effect
is that whereas candidates of the smaller parties are competing only with

candidates of other parties, candidates of the LDP (and to a much lesser extent the JSP) are not only competing with candidates of other parties but are also in the bulk of cases competing with each other. Since there is no possibility of transferring a vote from a candidate of one party to another candidate of the same party (or for that matter, to a candidate of another party), intra-party competition is an absolutely crucial problem for a big party.

The LDP copes with this problem by combining strict central control of candidate endorsement with decentralisation of candidate campaigns. In the Lower House electoral system it is crucial not to split the vote between too many candidates, and in recent elections the LDP has been extraordinarily successful in keeping down the number of candidates to a bare minimum that are capable of being elected. Indeed, in the 1980 Lower House elections, votes for successful candidates as a percentage of total votes cast for all LDP candidates amounted to 94.9%.[22] Since, however, in the bulk of cases there are two or more LDP candidates competing against each other in the same constituency, they rely not only on the party for backing, but also on intra-party factions. It is unusual for two LDP candidates for the same constituency to belong to the same faction, because of this competitive element. The faction, which is not in the LDP primarily a policy-oriented body, performs certain functions for its members, such as backing them for cabinet office and other positions, and in relation to their election campaigns it provides them with funds. The funds are used to 'service' a personal support organisation run by the candidate himself in his constituency. Many of the activities of this organisation are in fact of a rather innocuous social nature, but the candidate's *kōenkai* (as it is called) is an invaluable means of establishing and maintaining connections and thus creating a network of support.[23] Curtis refers to the 'hard vote' of those who will vote for the candidate through thick and thin, essentially because of involvement in such a network of connections.[24] Although this pattern is more typical of rural and small town Japan than of the big cities, the *kōenkai* may be met with in one form or another in most parts of the nation, where electioneering is in progress or in prospect. It should be noted that the 'hard vote' is directed towards a candidate rather than a party.

The difference between urban and rural patterns of electoral behaviour is well indicated by the at first sight surprising fact that voting turnout is substantially higher in rural areas than in the cities. This is a reflection of community solidarity, in that a village or rural community normally backs a particular candidate and failure to vote on the part of an individual would be regarded as letting the local community down. Whereas turnout rates in big cities are often in the 50% or 60% range, those in the remoter parts of the countryside are sometimes over 80%.

It is clear from this description that social patterns, as well as the electoral system as such, are responsible for the high level of personality, rather than party, voting. Nevertheless, the electoral system serves to reinforce rather than to counteract indigenous social patterns, and to retard change rather than promote it.

A fourth effect of the electoral system relates to the regulation of electioneering practices. In Japan these regulations are unusually severe, and include a total ban on door-to-door canvassing, restrictions on expenditure, numbers of posters, numbers of campaign vehicles, numbers of speech meetings, use of the media, the period of permitted campaigning, the giving of presents to supporters and so on.[25] Although many of these restrictions are unrealistic and are not widely observed (especially the regulations regarding campaign expenditure), they have the general effect of deterring a programmatic campaign effort, and giving substantial advantage to the sitting member whose political machine is well oiled through long use. It is much harder to break in from the outside.[26]

It remains to discuss the national constituency of the House of Councillors. It will be recalled that of the 126 Upper House seats renewed at each three-yearly election, 50 are elected in a constituency which encompasses the whole nation from Hokkaidō to Okinawa. Whereas elections for two-, or three- and four-member constituencies in the House of Councillors follow much the same logic as the three-, four- and five-member Lower House constituencies, the national constituency of the Upper House operates in a different fashion. Obviously with an electorate of some eighty million, the network approach adopted by many candidates for the House of Representatives would be utterly impracticable. In recent elections the minimum vote required to be elected for the national constituency is over 600,000 votes. To reach such a total, a candidate requires either broad-based organisation or nationwide fame. The latter approach has led to the election in most Upper House elections of a number of 'talent candidates', who are mainly television stars, sportsmen or the like. Ironically, many of them after six years in the House of Councillors have been forgotten by the electorate, and are defeated the second time round.

Organisation may be that of a political party or of some nationwide interest group, such as the Japan Dental Association, the Bereaved Families Association, the Japan Teachers Union, or various religions. Usually both party and interest groups are involved.[27] In the 1974 elections, for instance, Tanaka Tadao, a right-wing conservative backed by the nationalist religion, *Seichō no ie* (House of Light) stood for the national constituency on the LDP ticket, and narrowly failed to be elected (he won 550,689 votes).

The House of Councillors national constituency is the only constituency of either House to be unaffected by the gross imbalance in the value of the vote between rural and urban areas, mentioned above. It is also the most unpredictable of all constituencies, in which incumbency conveys less of an advantage than elsewhere. Tight organisation, such as that centrally exercised over its members and supporters by the Kōmeitō, is, on the other hand, an advantage. The Kōmeitō is able to estimate accurately the level of its support, and carves the nation up into regions, instructing its supporters to vote for one of its candidates in region A, for another candidate in region B, and so on. The success of this method of avoiding wasted votes is attested to by the results of the 1980 Upper House elections in the national constituency, where nine Kōmeitō candidates stood for election, and all were elected, their placings ranging between numbers twenty-seven and forty-six.[28] By contrast, the twenty-three LDP candidates were placed between number three and number fifty-eight. In 1980 only two candidates out of the LDP field of twenty-three were placed lower than fifty and so failed to be elected, but this was an election where the LDP in general did rather better than expected. In 1974, when the LDP fared slightly worse than had presumably been anticipated by the party's electoral strategists, it suffered the humiliation of finding that the seven candidates whose voting performance placed them immediately below the line dividing victory from defeat were from its own ranks.

The cost of campaigning in the national constituency is the most frequent reason advanced in criticism of the system used. The LDP has long been unhappy with it, and arguably it does less well in proportion to its percentage of the vote in the national constituency than in either the House of Representatives or the prefectural constituencies of the House of Councillors. The Suzuki government, 1980–2, introduced legislation to change the national constituency system to a system of proportional representation by list, with votes being distributed among candidates on different party lists according to the d'Hondt formula. A voter, therefore, will still have two votes when voting for the House of Councillors, but will vote for a candidate in his prefectual constituency and for a party list in the national constituency.

The reform is controversial, and is opposed particularly strongly by the smaller parties. This is no doubt partly because they appear to have done rather better out of the previous system than the LDP. There is, however, a more complicated reason why they oppose it. Hitherto much of the energy of the smaller parties in Upper House elections was taken up with the national constituency, and, as we have seen, they do not (except for the Communists) normally contest the numerous single-member prefectural constituencies. Under proportional representation for the national constituency, presumably there will be no real need for individuals to campaign since it will be a contest between parties. This – so it is argued – will mean that the parties will concentrate much more than previously on the prefectural constituencies. The failure, however, to present a candidate in a prefectural constituency will be likely to have an adverse 'spillover' effect on that party's vote in that prefecture for the national constituency. If this argument is correct, it is because of the extent to which a candidate's campaign is a crucial factor in generating enthusiasm for his party.[29]

A number of other arguments are used against the proposal. These include

the view that the Upper House ought to be readily distinguishable from the
Lower House, and that parties ought not to dominate it as they do the Lower.[30]
The 'listing' of Independents, a few of whom at present win large vote totals, is
seen as another problem, as is the question of how far factionalism will
intrude into the choice and order of candidates by the LDP. More seriously
perhaps, the change is vulnerable to the accusation that it fails to institute
reform of those Lower and Upper House constituencies which suffer from acute
inequality of vote values, favouring the LDP, while seeking to tamper with the
one constituency where the LDP appears somewhat disadvantaged. It should
be noted, however, that the LDP almost proved capable of turning even the
previous national constituency voting system to its advantage. Whereas in
1974 the LDP was severely disadvantaged under the existing system, in 1980 it
secured 42% of the seats with 42.5% of the vote.

In evaluating the political effects of the Japanese electoral system it is of
course important not to overstate the case that the electoral system as such has
shaped important aspects of postwar Japanese politics. Obviously much more
importance attaches to the broader political institutions that emerged, first
from the institution-building experiences of the late nineteenth and early
twentieth centuries, second from the period of mobilisation for war from the
early 1930s until 1945,[31] and third out of the American Occupation. We have
argued elsewhere[32] that in essence the Japanese political system today is closer
to the Westminster model than to any other, particularly since a government
commanding a secure parliamentary majority is in a position to exercise firm
authority, though the political arena is notably pluralistic.

The second set of variables apart from the electoral system which any
consideration of Japanese politics as a whole needs to take into account is that
stemming from the norms and practices of Japanese society. Habits of
deference to authority, a tendency towards voting for individuals rather than
parties, political factionalism and a general weakness of grass-roots party
organisation all plainly reflect aspects of Japanese social behaviour, even
though the features we have just listed should not be regarded as static or
unchanging.

The electoral system, nevertheless, can be seen as a not insignificant
independent variable which in recent years has tended to consolidate and
reinforce some of the more 'conservative' features of the system. The failure to
rectify gross electoral imbalance of population is the most obvious example.
More subtly, however, the system of multi-member constituencies without
provision for vote transfer has facilitated the fragmenting of the opposition as
well as factionalism within the ruling party. Perhaps most significantly of all in
terms of its long-term effects, the fact that the system is readily compatible with
personal political machines at the constituency level serves to reinforce the
conservatism of the political atmosphere in three principal ways. First, it gives
a big advantage to sitting members who merely have to service an existing

machine rather than build one from scratch, which is both inordinately expensive and also time-consuming. Second, it tends to give the edge to those candidates able to command, either through factional connections with monied interest groups or by means of actual membership of an organisation with substantial resources, the very large sums of money needed to be elected. And third, in a more general sense it has the effect of continuously importing into the political arena the values of a rather traditional rural and small town environment. The more freewheeling liberal values of the big cities, where parties, together with their policies and images, appear to count more now than the voter's personal feeling for the candidate, are correspondingly not allowed to exert the kind of influence that one might expect given the ultra-modernity of many aspects of contemporary Japanese life.

Given, therefore, the conservative bias of the electoral system reflected in the ways just outlined, it is hardly surprising that the LDP should be reluctant to embark upon wholesale reform. Indeed, its promotion of reform of the national constituency of the House of Councillors is consistent with its general anti-reform position, since the national constituency is the one part of the system which has failed to conform to the norms of the system as a whole.

NOTES

1 See R. H. P. Mason, *Japan's First General Election 1890* (Cambridge, 1968); and Ben-Ami Shillony, *Politics and Culture in Wartime Japan* (Oxford, 1981).
2 The Meiji Constitution of 1889 provided for a bicameral Parliament (the 'Imperial Diet') consisting of two Houses of approximately equal powers, the House of Peers and the House of Representatives. Only the latter was elective, and the constitution in general gave a very limited role to elected representatives while enshrining the principle of an executive with little responsibility to the electorate.
3 In order to take care of fears that universal male suffrage would open the floodgates of radicalism, a Peace Preservation Law, giving enhanced powers to the police, was brought down in the same year.
4 For further details, see J. A. A. Stockwin, *Japan: Divided Politics in a Growth Economy*, 2nd edn (London, 1982). It should be noted that nobody can be a candidate for the House of Representatives before the age of twenty-five and for the House of Councillors before the age of thirty.
5 Factions in Japanese parties and other organisations tend to involve strong bonds between the leader and at least his core followers. They also tend to be semi-permanent, rather than ephemeral.
6 A radical revision of the electoral system, substituting single-member for multi-member constituencies and including also a number of seats (in the Lower House) to be filled by proportional representation, was proposed by the then Prime Minister, Tanaka Kakuei, in 1973. It failed to be adopted. A recent decision to revise the electoral procedures for the national constituency of the House of Councillors, will be discussed later in the chapter.

7 For details, see Stockwin, *Japan*, pp. 88–97.
8 Because of the complexities of the Japanese writing system, it is often possible to write a particular name in several different ways, even though each person will have only one way of writing his name. The possibilities of writing a name incorrectly are, therefore, considerable, but it is the understanding of the writer that the election authorities are lenient towards incorrect writing of names, provided that there is no ambiguity between different candidates. Informal voting rates are low.
9 The present Lower House constituency system is known in Japan as a 'medium' constituency system, to distinguish it from a 'small' (i.e., single-member) system and from a 'large' (i.e., more than five-member) system. All postwar elections for the Lower House have involved 'medium' constituencies, except for the elections of 1946, in which they were 'large'. 'Small', 'medium' and 'large' constituency arrangements were all used at various times in elections before 1945.
10 D. C. S. Sissons, 'Dissolution of the Japanese Lower House', in D. C. S. Sissons, ed., *Papers on Modern Japan 1968*, (Australian National University, Canberra, 1968), pp. 91–137.
11 The postwar constitution has been a major issue in Japanese politics, in part because of the 'no-war' clause (Article 9), which the Socialists in particular have championed. See Stockwin, *Japan*, pp. 196–218.
12 The trend of voting for elections for the Upper was roughly similar.
13 Margaret A. McKean, *Environment Protest and Citizen Politics in Japan* (Berkeley, Los Angeles and London, 1981).
14 Most of the decline in LDP support in the 1976 Lower House elections is probably to be explained by the recent defection of several LDP members who then formed the New Liberal Club.
15 See Stockwin, *Japan*, tables 12 and 19–24, (pp. 118 and 193–5), and first edition (1975) of the same book, tables 11 and 17–21 (pp. 100 and 167–71).
16 This is also sometimes known in English as the United Social Democratic Party (USDP).
17 The Kōmeitō and the JCP pursue quite different strategies on the number of candidates they put forward. The Kōmeitō only puts up candidates in winnable seats, whereas the JCP has a candidate in nearly every constituency in order to build up its local organisation throughout the country.
18 In addition five Lower House and two Upper House seats were added with the reversion to Japan of Okinawa in 1972.
19 For the basis of this calculation, see Stockwin, *Japan*, pp. 108–11.
20 There was, however, a serious crisis within the LDP in May–June 1980. For details, see J. A. A. Stockwin, 'Japan's Political Crisis of 1980', *Australian Outlook*, 35, 1 (April 1981), pp. 19–32.
21 At the 1980 House of Representatives elections the JSP put up three candidates for only one constituency, and two candidates for a further seventeen constituencies. The total number of constituencies is 129. By contrast the LDP failed to endorse more than one candidate in only twenty-four constituencies.
22 See Stockwin, *Japan*, table 9 (p. 108).
23 See Gerald L. Curtis, *Election Campaigning Japanese Style* (New York and London, 1971), passim.
24 Ibid., pp. 38ff.
25 For details, see Stockwin, *Japan*, pp. 103–5.
26 Ibid., table 7 (p. 106).

27 Michael K. Blaker, ed., *Japan at the Polls: The House of Councillors Election of 1974* (Washington, DC, 1976), pp. 32–3.
28 Their placings were nos. 27, 30, 33, 37, 39, 40, 41, 42, 46, and their vote totals ranged between 689,042 and 814,953. Vote totals for all the fifty candidates elected in the national constituency ranged from 642,554 to 2,784,998.
29 The argument is put by Kiyoaki Murata in *Japan Times* (13 March 1982).
30 The number of Independents in the House of Councillors has in any case greatly declined since the 1950s.
31 One of the key legacies of this period was the network of close connections between government and large firms.
32 J. A. A. Stockwin, 'Understanding Japanese Politics', *Social Analysis* (Adelaide), no. 5/6 (December 1980), pp. 144–53.

SUGGESTIONS FOR FURTHER READING

For an overview of the Japanese political system, see J. A. A. Stockwin, *Japan: Divided Politics in a Growth Economy*, 2nd edn (London, 1982).

For scholarly writing in English on Japanese elections, see Gerald L. Curtis, *Election Campaigning Japanese Style* (New York and London, 1971); Bradley M. Richardson, *The Political Culture of Japan*, (Berkeley, Los Angeles and London, 1974); Michael K. Blaker, ed., *Japan at the Polls: The House of Councillors Election of 1974* (Washington, DC, 1976); Herbert Passin, ed., *A Season of Voting: The Japanese Elections of 1976 and 1977* (Washington, DC, 1979); John C. Campbell, ed., *Parties, Candidates and Voters in Japan: Six Quantitative Studies* (University of Michigan, Center for Japanese Studies, 1981); Ronald J. Hrebenar, 'The Politics of Electoral Reform in Japan', *Asian Survey*, 17, 10 (October 1977), pp. 978–96

12

The European Parliament

MICHAEL STEED

The case of the European Parliament is unique among those covered in this book. Only one popular election of the Parliament has yet taken place, so it provides no opportunity for the study of the cumulative effect of its electoral system on such matters as the development of its party system or the recruitment of its members. Yet that electoral system is of peculiar interest since the European Parliament – alone among democratically elected bodies – consists of members elected by a variety of electoral systems (currently thirteen of them).[1] The 1979 result was rich in examples of the interplay between electoral systems and party systems but without lessons on some of the more important political consequences considered in this book; it is best viewed as a special transitional case.

Under article 138 (3) of the Treaty of Rome, confirmed by the September 1976 Act of the Council of Ministers providing for the first election to take place by diverse national systems, the Parliament is required to draw up a uniform procedure upon which the Council of Ministers, acting unanimously, decides. Parliament did recently adopt (on 10 March 1982) a largely common electoral system, which would, if enacted, limit the effect of the diversity of the 1979 election. The Council of Ministers referred this proposal to a working party of experts representing national governments, which set aside many of the proposed common provisions – a proceeding of doubtful legality in the light of the treaty text. At the time of writing it seems unlikely that any further common provisions will come into effect for the 1984 elections, and it may be that the Council of Ministers will successfully substitute looser provisions, more closely resembling the 1979 diversity, for the European Parliament's common system.

Yet the proposed system remains a useful benchmark, as a test of the significance of the diversity of 1979, as a possible future system and as a standard set by the European Parliament. This chapter will first look at how the two systems, that of 1979 and the proposed common system, came into being. It will next look briefly at an effect common to both, the national allocation of seats. Then it will focus on a comparison of the two systems, using the 1979 voting figures (or 1981 in Greece) as a basis. This is both an exercise in measuring the precise political consequences of electoral systems and of potential practical application since in doing this we will also be offering a tentative prediction of the practical effects of adopting the common system.

THE 1979 SYSTEM

The arrangements for the 1979 elections contained two notably controversial features. The 410 seats in the European Parliament were allocated amongst the nine member states in an arbitrary fashion (an additional 24 were later given to Greece, bringing the total to 434); and each member state chose its own electoral system. Both involved departures from Article 138(3) of the Treaty of Rome, departures which, because they were made by an act of the Council of Ministers rather than by an explicit amendment to the Treaty, could be considered of doubtful legality.[2]

After direct elections had taken place, it was clear that the diversity of national electoral systems had significantly affected the political composition of the first directly elected European Parliament; and the debate about the electoral arrangements came to focus on a common system for the second elections. Yet in the period leading up to the act of the Council of Ministers of 20 September 1976 allocating the 410 seats in the newly enlarged Parliament, it had been the division of the seats between the member states that had proved most problematical.

The treaty requirement for a 'uniform procedure' seems clear enough, and the opinion of the legal affairs committee of the directly elected Parliament in October 1981 on the acceptance of national systems rather than a uniform procedure was robust: 'This decision was totally contrary to the letter of the Treaty, had no legal justification and was motivated solely by reasons of political expediency.'[3] But in fact, the acceptance of national diversity goes back to the first efforts of the Parliament to secure direct election. The draft Convention adopted on 17 May 1960 provided that during a transitional period 'the electoral system shall . . . fall within the competence of each member State'.[4] Thus, though the problem of securing a common electoral system has come to revolve more around the British tradition of first-past-the-post than any other national practice, the proposal to use national rather than common (or uniform) procedures pre-dates even the first British application for membership of the Community.

In the event, six countries (joined in 1981 by a seventh, Greece) adopted proportional representation at the national level; two (Belgium and Ireland) applied the principle of proportionality only at regional level while Great Britain adopted the single-member constituency system traditionally used for

national elections.[5] France, the other Community country using a single
member system for its national elections, switched to national proportionality
for the European Parliament. Several other countries made adaptations from
their national systems, most notably Germany and Greece. In general, these
were away from the particular type of proportional representation in use for
national elections towards a system incorporating national proportionality
according to the d'Hondt rule, with national lists. So, whilst the 1979 system
abounded in diversity in detail, some voluntary movement towards common
principles was already evident, a movement from which the United Kingdom
stood out starkly through the decision of the House of Commons by 321 to 225
votes to allow domestic political considerations to over-ride European ones.
Domestic politics in fact played a substantial part in the way that most
countries decided on their arrangements for direct elections but elsewhere they
happened to work in the general direction of common principles.[6]

THE COMMON SYSTEM

The newly elected Parliament took up its appointed task to 'draw up a proposal
for a uniform electoral procedure'[7] with more procedural prudence than
speed. The Political Affairs Committee (PAC) set up a sub-committee to work
on the subject; this had made little progress by the end of the first year when its
chairman, Jean Rey, resigned from the Parliament. Its main achievement was
to rule out the approach which Rey had been pressing – that of only laying
down broad principles (specifically that of proportional representation rather
than a particular system). British Conservative MEPs argued very effectively
that a uniform procedure had to mean more than this and that if the United
Kingdom was to be required to adapt its national procedures, so too should
other countries.[8] A first report, by Jean Seitlinger, the sub-committee's
rapporteur, was produced for PAC in autumn 1980 but found little favour and
was in due course passed to the political groups for comment. The groups
responded slowly and the next steps were not taken until October 1981, when
PAC took a series of votes on what principles a common system should embody
and then set up an ad hoc working party of political group representatives.
This working party proposed a compromise common system which was agreed
by PAC in December 1981. That agreement was put into the form of a draft act
at a PAC meeting on 28 January 1982 by 24 votes to 8, and was to survive all
attempts to change it when the European Parliament debated and adopted it
on 10 March 1982.[9]

   The agreed electoral system contains three uniform elements that will
require almost every member state to make some adaptation – proportionality

at national level, regional constituencies and the d'Hondt rule. Alterations in the 1979 system in each member state will be required as shown below.

	National Proportionality	Regional Constituencies[a]	d'Hondt Rule
Belgium	Yes	No	No
Denmark	No	Maybe	No
France	No	Yes	No
Germany	No	Partly	No
Greece	No	Yes	Yes
Ireland	Yes	No	Yes
Italy	No	Partly	Yes
Luxembourg	No	No	No
Netherlands	No	Yes	No
United Kingdom	Yes	Yes	[b]

[a]   Denmark and Luxembourg did not have regional constituencies in 1979; Luxembourg is too small to be required to subdivide itself and if Greenland remains a member of the Community, mainland Denmark could remain a single national fifteen-member constituency; Germany had regional constituencies in 1979 but they were only optional; Italy had five in 1979 and will have to have more.

[b]   Adaptation required in Northern Ireland where the single transferable vote with quota was used in 1979.

Thus although the United Kingdom is clearly called on to make the greatest change – as was inevitable given its decision on the 1979 system – the common system is a compromise containing a core of uniform requirements to which each country will have to adapt. It moves away from one general characteristic which emerged in 1979 by requiring regional constituencies of no more than fifteen members apiece, which only Belgium and Ireland had then. This constituency element was presented by Seitlinger as a move to incorporate some element of the British electoral tradition: 'an element, not of majority voting but of personalisation, so as to meet this criterion of forging a link between the electors and their representatives'.[10]

But whilst the common system can thus be presented as a careful, sensible compromise, which has gone a reasonable way towards meeting the habit of personal constituency representation in the United Kingdom and some other member states, it was – as the narrative above of its evolution implied – essentially a product of political compromise. The critical stage in reaching agreement came in the ad hoc working party of political group representatives. This was chaired by Niels Haagerup, one of the vice-chairmen of PAC, who took on the task on behalf of the chairman of PAC, Mario Rumor. But Haagerup is also a Danish Liberal, and therefore from the group most interested in securing a common system. In the working group a new compromise system agreed between the representatives of the two largest groups, both South German MEPs, Reinhold Bocklet (CSU) and Rudolf Schieler (SPD),[11] replaced both the earlier compromises of the original sub-committee and the apparent outcome of the votes of principle at the October 1981 PAC meeting. After PAC had accepted the deal made in the working group, the rapporteur brought his earlier report into line with the decisions taken.

With PAC's ratification of this inter-group agreement, paradoxically at a meeting in London, the natural majority inside the European Parliament in favour of the principle of proportionality asserted itself, sweeping aside the achievements of certain British MEPs over the two previous years. Two British Conservative MEPs, Adam Fergusson and the Marquess of Douro, had played a particularly active role in the original sub-committee during a period when the other groups had displayed less interest. Their influence is evident in the first report, which proposed two alternative compromises between proportionality and majority voting, both of which would have enforced on most countries a distinctly less proportional system in return for Britain coming a little way towards proportional representation.[12] British Labour MEPs were able to obtain an even more negative opinion of what was to be the common system from their group in the summer of 1981; in a letter to the chairman of PAC dated 16 June 1981 (PE 73.743/ANN) the Socialist group leader expressed the view that it would be unwise to try to adopt a uniform electoral system for 1984 and proposed that attempts to do so should be abandoned.

But in the six months before the adoption of the common system, the two British parties represented in the European Parliament failed to maintain these victories. A number of Conservative MEPs fought unsuccessfully to obtain a common system based on the German domestic system, mixing single-member constituencies with overall proportionality. The failure of the British MEPs to block or significantly affect the system adopted had something to do with the technical problems of applying the German system to European parliamentary elections,[13] but more to do with presidential rivalries in the European Parliament, the standing of the British Conservative and Labour Parties among their European partners and the personal position of the Conservative leader (an unsuccessful presidential candidate, who then lost his leadership) – in other words, politics.

When the proposed system came to the floor of the European Parliament, it was carried by the overwhelming support of the two largest groups, Christian Democrat and Socialist, with the Conservatives broadly against and the Communist, EPD and Liberal groups divided or abstaining. However, the division was as much national as political as the following analysis of the ninety-seven MEPs who voted against in one or both of the two divisions shows.

	Voted Against		
	Act only	Resolution only	Both
Danish	–	2	2
French Gaullist	1	1	1
French Liberal	1	5	5
Greek	1	3	1
Irish Labour	1	–	–
Italian Communist	8	2	6
UK: Conservative	8	5	30
Labour	–	2	10
Unionist	–	–	2
TOTAL	20	20	57

The opposition was an unholy alliance. Many of the British, Danish and Ulster votes were cast in opposition to the concept of a common electoral system, or to the proportional principle. The French, Greek and Italian votes were in favour of purer proportionality or stricter uniformity (e.g., opposition of principle to the clause allowing for thresholds or insistence on national list systems).

NATIONAL ALLOCATION

The European Parliament had proposed that 355 seats be divided between the member states by a weighted formula taking account of population, after considering an alternative but similar formula for 550 seats; the French government proposed a formula more favourable to the populous countries (with 284 MEPs) and the Irish government one more favourable to the smaller countries (with 384 MEPs). In the end, the European Council seized on a simple allocation of around 400 seats – 80 to each of the four larger countries and 80 shared (25:25:15:15) between the next four, with Luxembourg keeping its six places. In the final discussion the four large countries obtained one more seat each to facilitate a third seat for Northern Ireland, and a Belgian seat was surrendered to Denmark to assist the provision of a special seat for Greenland.[14] When Greece came in, it was allocated the same number as Belgium.[15]

The effect of this allocation can be compared with any of the more sophisticated formulas considered earlier, or with a simple proportional allocation according to national electorates or populations.[16] Table 1, which uses electorates and assumes a minimum of only one seat (i.e., an unrealistically extreme degree of proportionality between states) shows relatively little difference compared with the actual allocation. The biggest difference (the increase in the size of the Conservative group) is one that would be reversed by

Table 1 *The effect of national weighting*

	Change	Comm.	Soc.	Lib.	CD	EPD	Cons.	Others
Germany	+16	–	+6	+1	+9	–	–	–
Italy	+15	+4	+2	+1	+6	–	–	+2
United Kingdom	+14	–	(+3)	–	–	–	(+11)	–
Belgium	– 9	–	(–3)	(–2)	(–4)	–	–	–
Denmark	– 8	–1	–1	–1	–	–1	– 2	–2
France	– 1	–	–1	–	–	–	–	–
Greece	– 9	–2	–3	–	–2	–	–	–2
Ireland	–10	–	(–3)	(–1)	(–2)	(–3)	–	(–1)
Luxembourg	– 5	–	–1	–2	–2	–	–	–
Netherlands	– 3	–	–2	–	–1	–	–	–
Net effect	–	+1	–3	–4	+4	–4	+ 9	–3
Composition	434	49	120	35	120	18	72	20

Note: For this table, the 434 seats in the European Parliament were distributed between the member states on the basis of their registered electorates at the time of direct elections (except that Luxembourg was guaranteed one seat). The first column (change) shows how this would affect the total representation of each country. The votes cast in 1979 (or 1981 in Greece) were then used to determine the division of that number of seats, using the electoral system in force in each state. In the three countries whose figures are shown in brackets this involved necessarily arbitrary assumptions about constituency boundaries; in the other seven there is no problem in making the simulation. The results are shown in the form of the change in the composition of each political group compared with the actual result.

a common electoral system. The political effects of the particular formula used for national weighting were not very great, and any of the other formulae would have produced a broadly similar European Parliament.

THE 1979 SYSTEM AND THE COMMON SYSTEM

Table 2 shows a simulated 1979 result (1981 for Greece) making certain necessary assumptions about party lists and voting (see appendix). The most important assumption is the absence of thresholds, which the common system leaves to national discretion, but which operated in France and Germany in 1979 (see p. 238). We make the comparison this way so as to examine fully the effect of different methods of allocation on the smaller parties.

The most significant change compared with the actual 1979 result is the effect of proportional representation in Great Britain. This not merely alters the political balance among the British MEPs by nearly twenty seats; it contributes to several further effects on the political balance within the European Parliament.

First the Liberal group would be restored to its pre-direct election place as the third group of the Parliament while the European Democrats (the name the Conservatives adopted after direct election) drop from the third place to fifth

Table 2 *The European Parliament on a common system*

	E–L	Comm.	Soc.	C–L	Lib.	CD	Cons.	EPD	E–R	Eco.	Reg.	Misc.
Belgium	–	–	6 (–1)	–	4	10	–	–	–	1 (+1)	3	–
Denmark	– (–1)	–	4 (+1)	–	3	–	3	1	–	–	1	4
France	2 (+2)	17 (–2)	20 (–2)	1 (+1)	–	23 (–2)[a]	–	13 (–2)	1 (+1)	3 (+3)	–	1 (+1)
Germany	–	–	34 (–1)	4	4	41 (–1)	–	–	–	2 (+2)	–	–
Greece	–	4	11 (+1)	1	–	8	–	–	(–1)	–	–	1
Ireland	–	–	3 (–1)	–	–	5 (+1)	–	5	–	–	1	1
Italy	1 (–1)	25 (+1)	12 (–1)	3	5	30 (+1)	–	–	4	–	1	–
Luxembourg	–	–	1	–	2	3	–	–	–	–	–	–
Netherlands	–	–	9	2	4	10	–	–	–	–	–	–
United Kingdom	–	–	26 (+9)	–	10 (+10)	–	41 (–19)	–	–	–	4	–
TOTAL	3	46 (–1)	126 (+5)	7 (+1)	48 (+9)	114	44 (–19)	19 (–2)	5	6 (+6)	10	6 (+1)

Note: The Classification in this and subsequent tables is explained in the appendix. This table shows the result with a d'Hondt allocation on a national basis without a threshold or (in the Danish case) list alliances upon the assumptions set out in the appendix. The figures in brackets compare this result with the actual 1979 result.

[a] Elected on a list covering parties in both the Liberal and Christian groups: seventeen chose to sit with the former and eight with the latter – it is assumed that the two lost seats would come one from each group.

Next the political balance within the Liberal group would alter. The British Liberals place themselves, broadly, on the Left within the diverse family of Liberal parties represented in the group, so the presence of ten British Liberal MEPs within it would not simply have reduced the dominance of the French parties, but tilted the group towards the Centre. The French Liberal MEPs tend to be among the most Right-wing within the group (as well as being distinctly less integrationist), so this change could have been substantial.

Within the Socialist group, there would have been a different tilt. The internal Left–Right balance would probably not have been much different, but the group's coherence on European integration would have been lessened. In the simulated Socialist group of Table 2, eighty-two Socialist MEPs come from the original six countries, in which commitment to European unity both among their populations and in the Socialist parties remains strong, whilst forty-one come from Britain, Denmark and Greece, where the party is either hostile to Community membership or divided. In the actual group, this ratio is rather different: 87:30.

The other political difference in Table 2 lies in the hypothetical entry into the European Parliament of half-a-dozen Ecologists (mainly due to the assumed absence of thresholds). Since several of the Centre–Left parties also have a green view (notably D'66 and Partito Radicale) this opens up the possibility that a Green/Left of Centre political grouping of some ideological coherence · in which some of the regionalists could also have found a natural home · might have emerged. This, rather than the very miscellaneous 'technical co ordination group', could have been the seventh grouping.

The effect of the common system actually proposed can be compared with the alternatives proposed to see its potential effects more fully. Elaborate simulations of the first semi-proportional proposals of the sub-committee were made both by the Parliament's staff on behalf of the sub-committee and by the political groups. However, as a key characteristic of these proposals was the large discretion they left to national governments as to how proportional the system was to be in each country there is no simple way of summarising this comparison.[17] In any event, by the time the common system came to the Parliament, no one supported either of the original proposed alternatives.

Table 3 illustrates in a very limited manner what one of them, allocation purely within regional constituencies, might have produced. It is limited to those member states which actually used, or considered using, regional constituencies; a more precise simulation of this effect would require necessarily very arbitrary decisions as to what regional constituencies should be used.[18] The main effect of regional rather than national allocation is to favour the larger parties; Table 4 illustrates an opposite effect, that of applying the natural (Hare) quota plus largest remainder system. This was employed by Italy in 1979 with Greece using a minor variant of the same principle in 1981 and an amendment (No. 7) to put it into the common system was proposed by one of the small Italian parties.

Table 3 *The effect of regional allocation*

	E–L	Comm.	Soc.	C–L	Lib.	CD	Cons.	EPD	E–R	Eco.	Reg.	Misc.
Belgium			+1							−1		
Germany			+1		−2	+3				−2		
Ireland			+1			−1						
Italy	−1	+3			−2	−4	+4					
United Kingdom			+2			−3		+1				
Net effect	−1	+3	+5	−2		−9	+6	+1	−	−	−3	−	−

Note: This table compares a regional allocation in certain countries with the outcome in Table 2. In Belgium and Ireland it shows the outcome in the two and four constituencies actually used; in Italy the effect of making the allocation at the level of the five constituencies used; in the UK the effect of an allocation within the twelve regional constituencies proposed by the government in 1979; and in Germany the effect of an allocation within the ten *Länder*.

Table 4 *The effect of quota plus remainder*

	E–L	Comm.	Soc.	C–L	Lib.	CD	Cons.	EPD	E–R	Eco.	Reg.	Misc.
Belgium			+1			−1						
Denmark	+2		−1		−1							a
France			−1	+1	−1[b]					+1		
Germany			−1		+1	−1				+1		
Greece			−1						+1			
Ireland	+1		−1									
Italy	+1	−1	+1			−1						
Luxembourg					+1	−1						
Netherlands	+1	−1				−1				+1		
United Kingdom							−2				+2	
Net effect	+4	+1	−5	+2	−1	−5	−2	−	+2	+2	+2	−

Note: This table compares the effect of a national allocation by simple (Hare) quota plus largest remainder with the outcome of Table 2.
[a] One seat lost by anti-EEC list; one gained by Retsforbundet (Georgist).
[b] One seat lost by joint Lib.–CD (UFE) list.

Putting these effects together in Table 5 shows how the major impact of variations in the system of proportional representation to be used for the European Parliament elections lies in the representation of the smaller parties outside the six established political groups. A common system would have been a little more favourable to the Left in 1979, essentially because of the over-representation of the British Conservative vote. But it could, in principle, as easily have worked in the opposite direction.[19] Variations in a common proportional system do not significantly alter the Left:Right balance. But the

Table 5 *Summary of effects*

	1979/81 outcome	Table 2 (uniform)	Table 3 (regional)	Table 4 (quota)
2 large groups	235	240	251	230
4 middle groups	170	157	152	155
Others	29	37	31	49
Left	171	175	182	175
Right	242	230	228	224

Definitions: 2 large groups: Soc. and CD; 4 middle groups: Comm., Lib., Cons. and EPD. Left: E–L, Comm. and Soc.; Right: Lib., CD, Cons., EPD and E–R.

representation of the smaller parties can vary greatly, even without considering the effect of any thresholds.

To add the effect of thresholds to the simulations in Tables 2–5, one can simply adjust the French and German base result in Table 2 back to what it was in 1979 when both employed a 5% threshold. In most other member states, the limited number of seats at stake already provides a significant threshold so the discretionary power within the proposed common system to impose a threshold is a largely academic issue outside the four large countries. In Italy small parties are too important in government formation for a threshold to be likely, and in any event the adoption of the d'Hondt rule already involves a change there which is unfavourable to small parties. The United Kingdom is more likely to look with favour at the principle of thresholds, but since its small parties tend to be regionally based and it might feel obliged to adopt only a regionally operative threshold, it could well be of no effect there either.

DYNAMIC EFFECTS

We can thus make some precise statements about the more mechanical effects of using different electoral systems for the European Parliament. But perhaps the less predictable dynamic effects are the more important.

The political arrangements within the Parliament contain two notable features. In the first place, the MEPs have, from the start, sat by political groups rather than nationality. In the internal ordering of the Parliament's business, these groups have established a considerable dominance. Yet those who see this development as signifying trans-national politics often fail to note the second feature – the six political groups do not reflect issue-differences within the Parliament but have grown directly out of historic national cleavages.

Thus three of the six are dependent on particular national histories – those of French Gaullism and British Conservatism – or the long-standing strength of

Communism peculiar to France and Italy. But the lines distinguishing the three more trans-national ideologically defined groups, Christian Democrat, Liberal and Socialist, are often arbitrary. If one were to take, say, British Labour and Italian Communist MEPs and compare them with French Communist and Socialist MEPs, one would very likely find that on both basic ideological orientation and attitudes towards European integration a more logical line-up than the existing alignment in political groups would be British Labour/French Communist versus French Socialist/Italian Communist. The only clear logic in the present groups on the Left is the attitude towards Lenin's Third International over sixty years ago. It is similar on the Centre and Right. Between the Christian Democrat and Liberal groups there is a clear difference on the historic battle over church versus state education and a significant difference of emphasis today on issues such as human rights. But on European integration the two groups are essentially alike, and on most economic and social issues they are similarly diverse. In Germany the Liberal FDP plays a Centrist role, as a hinge party between the CDU/CSU on the Right and the SPD on the Left. Just across the border, the Netherlands has a superficially very similar party system – a Christian CDA, Liberal VVD and Socialist PvdA. In Dutch politics, however, it has been the CDA which spans the Centre, with the VVD and PvdA as alternative partners to the Right and Left respectively. In national role, and position in the political spectrum, the FDP and CDA are similar, as are the VVD and CDU/CSU. But in the European Parliament the Christian CDA and CDU/CSU sit together, as do the Liberal FDP and VVD.

So long as national parties dominate European parliamentary elections, and national political allegiances and issues dominate the behaviour of those who vote in them, those paradoxical alignments will persist without difficulty. But if the European Parliament is to become a force in Community politics, it will need to develop political alliances and alignments which have more of a European logic. Whether and how it can do so depends on many factors, amongst which the electoral system is unlikely to be of major importance. But it may have a role to play, nonetheless.

If fresh alliances and alternative formations are to emerge out of the existing political groups then the internal balance of these groups and the existence of certain MEPs outside them could be crucial. That is why potentially the most important effect of Britain's failure to adopt proportionality in 1979 was not on the size of the three groups affected or on the Left:Right balance, but its impact on the internal character of the Socialist and Liberal groups. The evidence, demonstrated in this chapter, that comparatively small changes in the precise form of proportional representation can have large effects on which, and how many, small parties win seats is similarly critical. A tiny three or four person trans-national group might turn out to be the catalyst that sets off a chemical reaction undoing the bonds holding together one of the larger groups. The electoral formula which allows that small group to form, or strangles it by refusing it representation, might have a major effect on how trans-national politics develops: the loss of a nail for which the kingdom was lost.

But of course one cannot predict at what point the internal strains in an existing group or an external catalyst may produce a chain reaction. In general, however, one might conclude that versions of proportional representation conducive to the entry into the European Parliament of more small and diverse political bodies (especially if not necessarily already organised as parties) could be more likely to be an agent of disturbance; provisions, such as the d'Hondt rule or thresholds, which tend to keep them out, are more likely to help to preserve the status quo. However, the uncertainties of the future development of politics at the European Community level are such that even this reasonably plausible prediction could turn out to be wrong.

Whenever the provisions for the first direct elections were discussed in the two decades that led to them, one prediction that must have been made many times was that a common date would be conducive to a common, Community-wide event: coincidence of European with national parliamentary elections would lead to the domestic obscuring the Community considerations. Yet in the two synchro- or near synchro-elections of 1979 (Italy and Luxembourg) together with the 1981 synchro-election in Greece, there was more clear evidence of differential voting between European and national elections than in the rest of the Community.[20] Some such differential behaviour is probably an essential accompaniment to the changes we have been discussing, and its presence in the first direct elections – albeit on such a limited scale – evidence that there is some chance of their happening. But that it would prove easier for a few people to vote against their national political preference when faced with simultaneous European and national elections rather than the purely European event to which Europeanists had looked forward is paradoxical.

APPENDIX 1

Classification of Small Parties

Extreme-Left (E–L) Socialistik Folkeparti and Venstresocialisterne in Denmark; Extrême-Gauche trotskiste in France; Sinn Fein – The Worker's Party in Ireland; Partito Democratico di Unita Proletaria and Democrazia Proletaria in Italy.

Centre-Left (C–L) Emploi-Egalité-Europe (J. J. Servan – Schreiber's list) in France; KODISO (Social Democrats) in Greece; Partito Radicale in Italy; Parti social-démocrate in Luxembourg; Democraten '66 in Netherlands.

Extreme-Right (E–R) Eurodroite in France; KP (Progressives) in Greece; Movimento Sociale Italiano in Italy; Staatkundig Gereformeerde Partij in Netherlands.

Ecologist (Eco.) Ecologistes in Belgium; Die Grünen in Germany; Ecologistes in France; *Regional/Nationalist* (Reg.) FDF/RW and Volksunie in Belgium; Siumit (Greenland Representative) in Denmark; Independent (Blaney) in Ireland; Südtiroler Volkspartei in Italy; Plaid Cymru, SNP and all Northern Irish representatives in United Kingdom.

Miscellaneous (Misc.) Anti-EEC list and Retsforbundet (Georgist) in Denmark; Défense interprofessionelle in France; Independent (Maher) in Ireland.

Assumptions made in Simulations for Tables 2–4

Belgium: the Christelijke Volkspartij and Parti Social Chrétien would have presented separate Flemish and Francophone lists, but the Ecologists would have presented a single national list or linked regional lists.

Denmark: the facility of alliances between competing lists (which in 1979 led to the Anti-EEC list with 21.0% taking four seats to the Social Democrats three seats for 21.9% because two smaller parties were linked to the Anti-EEC list) would have been absent, since no provision for such alliances exist in the proposed common system, although it is not explicitly prohibited.

Great Britain: The votes cast for individual candidates would all have been cast for the parties of those candidates, so (a wholly unrealistic but necessary assumption) a party list would gain no votes where in 1979 that party had no candidates. Both the Ecologists and an anti-EEC list could have won enough support nationally to secure representation, to judge by the few constituencies in which their candidates stood – but there is no reasonable way of measuring such a possibility.

Ireland: the votes used for party list support are the effective preferences between the parties' candidates as expressed during the count. These differ significantly from the first preferences, which are widely but misleadingly used to measure party support in the single transferable vote system, in June 1979, as shown below.

	% First preferences	% Party preferences
Fianna Fail	34.7	33.1
Fine Gael	33.1	31.1
Labour	14.5	17.0
Independents	14.2	15.0
Sinn Fein	3.3	3.5
Others	0.3	0.3

This question is further explored in Michael Steed. *Twelve into One: The Effect of Using Diverse Procedures for the First European Parliamentary Elections*, in *Das Europa der zweiten Generation: Gedächtnisschrift für Christoph Sasse* (Baden-Baden, 1981), vol.1. pp. 297–302.

Special exceptions; since Article 4(2) of the common system allows special exceptions to be made on constitutional, ethnic and geographical grounds, it is assumed that the Berlin, Greenland and Northern Ireland MEPs would have been elected as in 1979 and that the Südtiroler Volkspartei would have similarly been enabled to win a seat

Results of the first direct elections to the European Parliament (7–10 June 1979, except in Greece, 18 Oct. 1981)

	Total seats	E-L		Comm.		Soc.		C-L		Lib.		CD		Cons.		EPD		E-R		Eco.		Reg.		Misc.	
		S	%V	S	%V	S	%V	S	%V	S	%V	S	%V	S	%V	S	%V	S	%V	S	%V	S	%V	S	%V
Belgium	24	—	0.9[a]	—	2.7	7	23.4	—	—	4	16.3	10	37.7	3[a]	20.2[a]	1	5.8	—	—	—	3.4	3	13.6	—	2.0
Denmark[b]	15	1	8.2[a]	—	—	3	21.9	—	3.3	3	14.5	—	1.8											4	24.4
France	81	—	3.1	19	20.5	22	23.5	—	1.8	25	27.6					15	16.3			—	4.4			—	1.4
Germany[b]	78			—	0.4	34	40.8			4	6.0	40	49.2							—	3.2			—	0.4
Great Britain[b]	78					17	33.0			—	13.1			60	50.6					—	0.2	1	2.7	—	0.4
Greece	24	—	3.5	4[a]	17.9[a]	10	40.3	1	4.2	—	2.1[a]	8	31.5					1	2.0					—	2.0
Ireland	15					4	17.0			—	0.3	4	31.1			5	33.1					2	15.0		
Italy	81	2[a]	1.8[a]	24	29.6	13[a]	15.3[a]	3	3.7	5[a]	6.2[a]	29	36.5					4	5.8[a]			1	1.1		
Luxembourg	6			—	5.0	1	21.7			2	28.1	3	36.1												
Netherlands[b]	25	—	3.3[a]	—	1.7	9	30.4	2	9.0	4	16.4	10	35.6					—	3.3[a]					—	1.6
Special[b]	7					1						2										4		—	0.4
TOTAL	434	3		47		121		6		39		114		63		21		5		—		11		4	

[a] A figure combining two parties with competing lists.

Belgium: Most figures combine the results of an ideological pair of distinct Flemish and Francophone parties.

Denmark: The miscellaneous figure includes 21.0% (4 seats) for the anti-EEC list.

France: The Union pour la France en Europe list combined nominees of two Liberal parties, and one Christian Democratic one together with independent personalities. Of the twenty-five top names initially elected seventeen sat in the Liberal group and eight in the Christian Democratic one; but this ratio can alter as vacancies occur and replacements enter.

Ireland: Three independents polled 15.0%; T. J. Maher (6.8%, elected) was a Farmers' organisation leader; N. Blaney (6.4%, elected) a hard-line Nationalist and the third (1.8%) Ecologist in outlook.

Italy: There were special provisions for ethnic minority lists; whilst the Südtiroler Volkspartei did win 0.6% of the vote for its own list, the seat it obtained was on the Christian Democratic list.

[b] Elections were held under separate provisions in Greenland (1 seat) and Northern Ireland (3 seats). All the votes cast in Greenland and 99.8% of those in Northern Ireland were cast for local parties, classified here as regionalist. No direct election was held for the 3 German MEPs assigned to Berlin who were appointed (2 CDU, 1 SPD) by the Berlin Senate. The British, Danish and German figures exclude those special areas.

This table shows an election result rather than a parliamentary outcome. The Danish Socialistik Folkeparti MEP sits in the Communist group and Maher in the Liberal group. Of the regionalists, two (Greenland and Northern Irish SDLP) sit in the Socialist group, and one each in the Christian Democrat (Südtirol), Conservative (Official Ulster Unionist) and EPD (Scottish National Party) groups.

Sources: *European Journal of Political Research*, 8, 1 (1980), pp. 150–7, adjusted for (a) the trotskyite and worker-control lists in Belgium (b) British instead of United Kingdom figures (c) party preferences instead of first preferences in Ireland (see p. 241); plus *Electoral Studies*, 1, 1, 241 p. 98 for Greece.

NOTES

1 In addition to the electoral system adopted for each of the ten member states, special provisions were applied to Berlin, Greenland and Northern Ireland.

2 The view that the '434 individuals, styled (and paid) as "Members of the European Parliament" are not the Assembly set up by the Treaties' is set out in Philip Goldenberg, 'When is Parliament Not Parliament?', *New Law Journal* (24 September 1981).

3 *Working Documents of the European Parliament 1981–8*, No. 1–988/81/B, p. 36.

4 Article 9 of the draft Convention, published in the *Official Gazette of the European Communities*, 37 (2 June 1960).

5 See n. 1.

6 The systems in use in June 1979 are fully examined in Christopher Sasse, et al., ' *The European Parliament: Towards a Uniform Procedure for Direct Elections'*, European University Institute, 11, (Florence, 1981); the processes by which they were determined in Valentine Herman and Mark Hagger, eds., *The Legislation of Direct Elections to the European Parliament* (Farnborough, 1980). Greece, which for national elections was using a version of proportional representation 'reinforced' to deter smaller parties (see chapter 10), switched to a system of national list proportional representation without thresholds in which the formula for distribution (quota plus largest remainder as in Italy) was more generous to small parties than the d'Hondt rule.

7 Article 7(2) of the Act of the Council of Ministers of 20 September 1976; the wording differs subtly from that of the Treaty of Rome, notably in that Article 138(3) of the latter refers to 'proposals' whereas the Council of Ministers defines 'a proposal'. At a later stage this difference could become a matter of substantial importance.

8 In pursuing this approach, Rey, a Belgian Liberal, was following the policy adopted by the Congress of the European Liberals and Democrats in February 1980. Thus, insofar as Rey's approach delayed matters, ELD, which had most to gain from getting a common system speedily through the Parliament, did not assist its own cause.

9 Ninety-five amendments were proposed, many of them substantial. Only ten were successful, of which eight were minor or redrafting and not opposed by Seitlinger. The two controversial amendments passed did not affect the electoral system, being about the right of EEC residents living outside their country of citizenship to vote and to stand for election.

10 Debates of the European Parliament, 10 March 1982 (282/74).

11 In addition, the German leader of the Liberal group, Martin Bangemann, had been pressing for such a political compromise throughout 1981, and had initially tried to secure one by personal agreement with the German leader of the Christian Democratic group, Egon Klepsch. This marked German influence on the final agreement was used to prevent the adoption of the domestic West German system for the European Parliament (see n. 13), giving the technical objections against doing so the weight of national experience.

12 The draft report of the sub-committee proposed that PAC choose between two systems. In alternative A representatives would be elected partly by proportional representation with national lists and partly by 'absolute majority of the votes cast in a single ballot in single-member constituencies' (sic), but (unlike the West German domestic system) the proportional allocation would not correct the

outcome in the single-member seats to produce overall proportionality. In alternative B proportional representation would have operated only at the level of regional constituencies which were to have between three and nine members apiece. At this stage the sub-committee defined its objective (and both alternatives) as incorporating 'both the principle of proportional representation of the political forces and features of the majority system' (PE 64. 569/rev IV, p. 9).

13 In the German system, the number of seats in the various *Länder* is allowed to vary according to the regional distribution of the parties' votes, and sometimes additional seats (*Überhangsmandaten*) have to be created (see p. 97). Several minds in the European Parliament were exercised in the summer of 1981 over how such questions could be coped with in the European Parliament, with its fixed national allocations of seats. One British Conservative MEP (Ben Patterson) eventually put forward personal amendments (Nos. 41, 42 and 43) which solved the problem by reducing the number allocated to each member state by one-third, and electing 145 members 'by the Community as a whole'. But for those who did not wish to disturb the national allocation of seats, the technical problems of applying the German system were substantial, though not, as Bocklet claimed in the final debate, insuperable.

14 Chris Cook and Mary Francis, *The First European Election: A Handbook and Guide* (London, 1979), pp. 106–11, gives full details of all the allocations discussed in the 1974–6 period.

15 The twenty-four Greek MEPs who joined the European Parliament in January 1981 were nominated by the national Parliament; their successors were directly elected at the same time as the next national election. on 18 October 1981.

16 M. L. Balinski and H. P. Young, in 'Fair Representation in the European Parliament', *Journal of Common Market Studies*, 20 (1982), pp. 361–73, explore different formulae for the future allocation of seats in the European Parliament according to national populations.

17 Under one alternative the seats filled non-proportionally in single-member constituencies could have ranged from a quarter to three-quarters; under the other alternative, the regional constituencies could have ranged in size from nine-member to three-member. The effect of this range can be seen in the simulations of the 1979 British results as shown below.

		Seats		
	Con.	Lab.	Lib.	SNP
$\frac{3}{4}$ single-member; $\frac{1}{4}$ PR	56	20	2	–
$\frac{1}{4}$ single-member; $\frac{3}{4}$ PR	46	24	7	1
Three-member PR	45	29	3	1
Nine-member PR	42	25	10	1
Exact PR	39.4	25.8	10.2	1.5
Actual Result	60	17	–	1

18 Simulations by David Brew involving twenty-two regions in France and eight or nine in Italy (rather than the five adopted) are included in Sasse, et al., *The European Parliament*.

19 Were the 1979 system to continue, and were the two leading British parties to become more integrated into Left and Right blocks in the European Parliament, the exaggerative quality of the single-member plurality election of Britain's seventy-

eight MEPs could mean that a swing of political opinion in Britain would determine the overall political majority in the European Parliament.

20 In Italy the PSI and PLI were able to claim that Socialism and Liberalism were more substantial forces in Europe than in Italy; they polled, together, 14.6% in the European election compared with 11.7% a week earlier in the national election. In Luxembourg, the Parti Démocratique led by the European personality and President of the Federation of Liberal parties Gaston Thorn polled very much better in the European election. In Greece the European bonus went principally to the Eurocommunist KKE-interior and to the Social Democratic KODISO, led by a notably pro-European figure (Ioannis Pezmazoglou). Together they polled 9.4% in the European elections but only 2.1% in the national election on the same day. The different electoral systems in use could also have produced tactical voting.

SUGGESTIONS FOR FURTHER READING

Geneviève Bibes, et al., *Europe Elects Its Parliament*, Policy Studies Institute (London 1980)

Jay G. Blumler and Anthony D. Fox, *The European Voter: Popular Response to the First Community Election*, Policy Studies Institute (London, 1982)

David Butler and David Marquand, *European Elections and British Politics* (London and New York, 1981)

European Journal of Political Research, 8, 1 (1980), Special Issue on the First European Elections

Valentine Herman and Mark Hagger, eds., *The Legislation of Direct Elections to the European Parliament* (Farnborough, 1980)

Geoffrey Pridham and Pippa Pridham, *Transnational Party Co-operation and European Integration: The Process Towards Direct Elections* (London, 1981)

Christoph Sasse, et al., *The European Parliament: Towards a Uniform Procedure for Direct Elections*, European University Institute, 11 (Florence, 1981)

Michael Steed, 'Twelve into One: The Effect of Using Diverse Procedures for the First European Parliamentary Elections', in *Das Europa der zweiten Generation: Gedächtnisschrift für Christoph Sasse* (Baden-Baden, 1981), vol 1, pp. 287–310

P.R. for Europe: A Guide to the European Parliament Proposals, Parliamentary Democracy Trust (London, 1982)

13

Conclusion: electoral systems and party systems

VERNON BOGDANOR

I

Traditionally, analysis of the consequences of electoral systems has concentrated upon two central topics – the influence of the electoral system upon
the number of parties, and its effects upon the political stability of a country.
Yet political scientists have been unable to establish clear connections of cause
and effect between these factors. At the same time, they have tended to neglect
other ways in which electoral systems might influence a country's political life
where perhaps well-founded conclusions can more easily be reached. The
chapters in *Democracy and Elections* show that the electoral system can also
affect the party system through its effect upon the internal cohesion and
discipline of parties. There is considerable scope for comparative analysis in
looking at the effects of an electoral system allowing voters to choose between
candidates as well as between parties. Ireland, Italy and Japan offer excellent
case studies in the effects of different electoral systems whose only shared
characteristic is that of offering choice of candidate. In all three countries, the
electoral system permits the politics of brokerage and clientelism to operate
alongside the more normal divisions of party competition. In Ireland and
Japan, this combination operates within conservative societies dominated by
traditional norms which the electoral system tends to reinforce. In such
societies the effects of personality politics are likely to prove profoundly
conservative in nature.

The electoral system can also play an important role in encouraging or
militating against alliances or other forms of co-operation between political
parties. The history of France since 1945 shows that the two-ballot system has
cemented stable electoral alliances more than party list PR (even with
apparentement) was able to do. For the success of a party under the second-
ballot system depends not only upon the number of votes it receives and their
geographical distribution, but also upon the party's ability to maintain
effective alliances.

Other proportional systems have enabled voters to signal coalitions more
effectively than in Fourth Republic France. In West Germany, electors were
able to display their support for the SPD/FDP coalition by casting their

247

constituency vote for the SPD and list vote for the FDP; while in Ireland the
single transferable vote has enabled voters to endorse or reject the Fine
Gael–Labour coalition. The plurality system, by contrast, militates against
political alliances, and the only way in which two like-minded parties can co
operate is through recriprocal withdrawal of candidates at constituency level
One need only consider how differently the relationships between the Liberal
and the Labour Party in Britain might have been in the 1920s, or relationship
between the Liberals and SDP today under a PR system encouraging electoral
alliances, to appreciate the importance of electoral systems in shaping the
political life of a country.

Electoral systems may exert considerable influence also upon campaign
strategy; they provide incentives and disincentives for the operation of different
strategies. Where the electoral system allows intra-party competition and
candidates find themselves fighting others of the same party as well as their
political opponents, the role of centralised campaign strategy will be correspondingly diminished. Rigid list systems, on the other hand, are more likely
to encourage centralised control. They may also, as in Weimar Germany or
Fourth Republic France, make it more profitable for parties to ensure the
loyalty of the ideologically committed rather than seek converts. The
plurality system, by contrast, can encourage parties to woo the voter in the
Downsian Centre. Yet this will occur only where the basic cleavages are socio-
economic rather than territorial. In Canada, for example, where Liberals have
little chance of winning in the West, and Conservatives little chance of gaining
representation in Quebec, the parties may not think it worthwhile to attend to
the grievances of electors in regions dominated by their opponents. The
consequence, according to Pierre Trudeau, has been to encourage Liberals in
Quebec to use 'their voting bloc as an instrument of racial defence, or of
personal gain'[1]; while in South Africa since 1945 and Britain since 1964
convergence towards the middle ground has hardly been a prominent feature
of political life.

Electoral systems can also profoundly affect the relationships between
elected members and their constituents. These relationships are, of course
likely to be weakest under party list systems where there is no choice of
candidate. In such systems, as Duverger pointed out, 'the parliamentary
representatives are chosen by the inner circle; the party in this case is a closed
circuit'.[2] Yet one must beware of attributing to the electoral system
phenomena which result from constitutional arrangements. In Sweden, for
example, members of the Riksdag are not expected to deal with constituency
problems, but this is not a result of the electoral system but rather of the nature
of the Swedish administrative process and the role of the Ombudsman; while in
West Germany, constituency matters tend to be resolved at local or Land rather
than federal level.

Finally, the effects of the electoral system upon political recruitment need to

	% Women
Plurality system	
Canada (1980)	5.0
New Zealand (1980)	4.3
USA (1978)	3.7
United Kingdom (1981)	3.0
Majority systems	
France (1977)	1.7
Australia (1979)	0.0
Semi-proportional systems	
Japan (1980)	1.8
Single transferable vote	
Ireland (1981)	6.6
Malta (1981)	4.6
Party list systems	
Finland (1979)	26.0
Denmark (1979)	23.4
Sweden (1981)	22.6
Norway (1977)	22.5
Netherlands (1977)	15.3
Switzerland (1981)	10.5
Austria (1981)	10.0
West Germany (1980)	8.5
Italy (1977)	8.4
Portugal (1981)	7.5
Belgium (1978)	7.5
Israel (1981)	6.6

Sources: Vernon Bogdanor, *The People and the Party System* (Cambridge, 1981), p. 243; and Francis G. Castles, 'Female Legislative Representation and the Electoral System', *Politics* (November 1981), p. 22.

be considered. Here, it is possible to present one conclusion with a striking degree of confidence. For, 'It is the unanimous finding of all those studies which have been explicitly concerned with the linkage between women's legislative representation and the nature of the electoral system that systems of proportional representation appear to favour higher levels of female representation.'[3] Under party list systems of proportional representation, the proportion of women in the legislature is likely to be considerably higher than under plurality systems; while under the single transferable vote, it is likely to be marginally higher. The above table gives the comparative percentages of women elected to the Lower Houses of different legislatures. The figure for France, in fact, rose in the 1981 election which led to a victory for the Left; but, as Castles remarks, 'Comparison with other cases suggests that in non-list systems, where women tend to be selected for a party's "hopeless seats", their representation may rise dramatically following a "landslide" result.' In West Germany, in 1976, the representation of women in constituencies was under 3%; on the *Land* lists nearly 12%, 'an illustration of the same electorate voting to quite different effect under different electoral systems'.[4]

The single transferable vote and party list systems both give an advantage to a female candidate, since, with multi-member constituencies and party lists, a balance of types of candidate is necessary. Otherwise, votes will be lost to an opposition party with a balanced ticket. The same argument, of course, applies to candidates representing ethnic, racial or regional minorities. By contrast, in the single-member constituency characteristic of the plurality and majority systems, the requirement of balance is not present and parties will seek to avoid hurting the prejudices – or what they imagine to be the prejudices – of the majority of the electorate. It is for this reason that women, and members of minority groups, fare so much worse under such systems.

Yet, as the table shows, party list systems seem to favour women more than the single transferable vote. In a refinement of the above argument presented in Vernon Bogdanor, *The People and the Party System*, Castles has shown why this should be so. The single transferable vote allows the local elector to choose the candidate. Therefore, if the elector is prejudiced, he will not vote for women. In party list systems, on the other hand, it is the party which plays the dominant role in deciding which candidates are to be elected to the legislature. Provided that women secure a sufficiently high place on the list, they will be returned. The single transferable vote is a more transparent electoral system whereby the attitudes of the electorate are more directly reflected in politics. For this reason, 'Under list systems, the percentage of women representatives will be a reflection of the elite political culture, whereas in other systems it is more likely to reflect the mass political culture.'[5] And elite opinion is more likely than mass opinion to favour women candidates. Thus in countries such as Italy, Portugal and Switzerland, where cultural norms are markedly hostile to the participation of women in public life, these norms can be circumvented through the operation of the party list; while in countries such as Ireland and Malta, where traditionalist attitudes also reign, this cannot happen: nevertheless the single transferable vote will still give a marginal benefit to women candidates as compared with plurality and majority systems, while if attitudes towards the participation of women in politics were to change, this change would be rapidly reflected in the legislature.

II

Any analysis of the political consequences of electoral systems must, therefore, if it is to be complete, consider the effects upon:
1. The stability of the political system
2. The number of parties

3. The nature of the parties:
   (a) the degree of internal cohesion and discipline
   (b) party alliances and other possibilities of co-operation
4. The relationships between members of the legislature and constituents
5. Campaign strategy
6. Political recruitment

Most of the literature on the political consequences of electoral systems has concentrated on topics 1 and 2, which clearly involve issues of considerable complexity; and the rest of this chapter will discuss what conclusions can be drawn about them from the essays in *Democracy and Elections*.

III

If there is one central conclusion which clearly emerges, it is the extent to which the working of the electoral system is influenced by the political traditions of the countries in which they operate. The same electoral system can have quite dissimilar effects in different countries; or even in the same country at different periods of its history. The plurality system was generally held to have produced moderate government in Britain in the inter-war period and for twenty years after 1945. Since then, however, it has been seen by many as a de-stabilising factor and blamed for Britain's economic decline. In Canada, by contrast, the plurality system makes the country appear more geographically polarised than in fact it is by denying representation to the Conservative minority in Quebec and the Liberal minority west of Winnipeg. Indeed, the paradox is that the country the results of whose electoral system display the most similarity to that of Britain and New Zealand is not one operating the plurality system, but Australia where the alternative vote sustains what is in effect a two-party battle.

The two-ballot system, however, whose mechanics seem on the surface so similar to that of the alternative vote, has yielded very different political consequences in France, not only between Republics but even within them. In the early part of the century, the two-ballot system sustained moderate government by reinforcing the Radicals as a hinge party of the Centre; since 1974, on the other hand, the electoral system has allowed polarisation into Left and Right blocs while weakening the extreme forces in each bloc and giving tremendous power to the Centre voter despite the absence of a Centre party. In this respect at least it operated like the alternative vote in Australia, yet the dynamics of a two-bloc system are bound to be very different from those of a two-party system (even though one of the 'parties' – the Liberal/Country Party coalition – is a tight electoral alliance).

What is clear is that plurality and majority systems will work less successfully in ideologically or ethnically divided societies where each side fears the consequences of giving supreme power to its opponents. It is noticeable, indeed, that the earliest moves towards proportional representation were in ethnically heterogeneous societies – Denmark, which introduced PR into the indirectly elected Upper House in 1855 in an unavailing attempt to meet the problems posed by the German minority in Schleswig; the Swiss cantons which began to adopt PR in 1889; and Finland, with its Swedish minority, which adopted PR in 1906. It seems, then, that a national culture unified both ideologically and ethnically is an essential precondition for the success of territorial representation of the type offered by the plurality or majority systems.[6]

Yet whereas on the Continent the response to such tensions was generally to introduce a proportional electoral system, in the United States and Commonwealth countries the plurality system was retained and minorities given protection (except in Britain and New Zealand) through federal institutions and a Bill of Rights. The effects of plurality and majority systems will be very different in a society in which federalism creates alternative centres of political power from one in which the traditional doctrine of the supremacy of Parliament is retained. From the perspective of the protection of minorities, therefore, federal institutions may be seen as a surrogate for PR. In France, by contrast, a majority electoral system proved compatible with the absence of institutional measures for minority protection because the executive was subservient to a legislature which saw its role not as sustaining a disciplined party government, but as protector of local interests. It is perhaps no coincidence that the Fifth Republic which has seen the growth of coherent majorities has also seen the development of a form of judicial review by the Constitutional Council, an important modification of traditional French doctrines of the sovereignty of Parliament.[7]

German history offers a good illustration of the dangers of generalising about 'proportional representation', two very different examples of which have operated in dissimilar ways in the Weimar and Federal Republics. Proportional representation has been held to have contributed to the rise of Hitler, yet a similar system to that operating in Weimar Germany worked in Czechoslovakia throughout the inter-war period serving to enhance democracy rather than undermine it, since 'The leading parties of democratic Czechoslovakia – unlike those of its neighbouring states – were agreed as to the bases of political, economic and social life of the country and also with regard to tactics.'[8]

In Pulzer's view, the central difference between Imperial Germany and the Weimar Germany was not the change from the second ballot to proportional representation, but the constitutional transformation from Wilhelmine oligarchy to responsible government. This required the parties to assume a new role, since they were now expected actively to assist in the process of governing, rather than remaining mere vehicles for ideological assertion. The central question to ask of proportional representation in the Weimar Republic therefore, is whether it prevented the parties from making the necessary adjustment in their behaviour so as to bring about responsible party government. It seems doubtful, however, whether a change in the electoral system could of itself have been sufficient to achieve a radical transformation in long-established habits of behaviour; nor that changes in institutional rules could have saved the representative system in a country humiliated by defeat in war, ravaged by the slump and faced with an anti-democratic movement of the sweep and force of Hitler's Nazis.

In Italy, by contrast, proportional representation has sustained, in the postwar years, a polarised and unstable, yet still functioning, democracy. Here too, it would be a mistake to attribute too much blame to the electoral system. In a deeply divided polity, proportional representation provides an element of flexibility which the plurality system, by polarising politics into a battle between the Christian Democrats and Communists, could destroy, leaving the Christian Democrats perpetually in power. The two-ballot system has been advocated by a number of prominent Italian political scientists; yet whether it could improve the efficacy of Italian democracy in the absence of other institutional changes – or an Italian de Gaulle! – remains highly problematical.

Scandinavian experience is sufficient to explode the notion that proportional electoral systems lead to political weakness and instability. For, while the impact of the slump in Germany was to strengthen rival extremisms, in Scandinavia it was a prime factor in social democratic dominance and a style of government which owed more to the theories of Eduard Bernstein than Karl Marx. Except in Finland, extremist groups were characterised only by their failure to make any impact upon the electorate. Indeed, even under German occupation, the Danish Nazis in the only free election ever permitted under Nazi rule secured only 2.2% of the total vote in 1943.

The Low Countries and Greece also display the contrasting effects of proportional systems. In Greece, a system of reinforced proportional representation produced unstable coalitions in the 1950s, while fear of the Left resulted in a military take-over in 1967; yet since 1974 a similar system has allowed for stable government, a peaceful alternation of power and a reduction in the number of parties. In the Low Countries, proportional systems gave stable coalition government until the 1960s when social changes in Holland and the impact of the linguistic question in Belgium led to the growth of new parties. Yet, although the Dutch electoral system with its low threshold ought to have proved more hospitable to new parties, the Belgian system has proved the less stable, with more frequent elections, and governments lasting for shorter periods of time. Linguistic conflict and economic decline have proved more destabilising than the electoral system.

Ireland and Japan offer examples of electoral systems assisting the growth of factions so that the political systems of these countries are as much candidate-based as party-based. In each country, a balance is secured between the requirements of centralised party discipline and decentralised constituency campaigning. In Ireland and Japan, the electoral systems fit happily into a conservative political culture, reinforcing and consolidating it. In a different political culture, the political effects of the same electoral systems would, no doubt, be very different. In Australia, for example, where the single transferable vote is used for elections to the Senate, the parties issue 'How-to vote' cards indicating to electors the order in which they should cast their preferences. There is, so far, no case in Senate elections of electors ignoring these instructions so as to allow a candidate to secure election in place of one more strongly preferred by his party. In this way, the parties have succeeded in converting the single transferable vote into a party list system. In Tasmania, by contrast, where the single transferable vote is used for elections to the local Lower House as well as the Federal Senate, there have been frequent occasions when electors have ignored the requests of their party leaders; while in Ireland such exhortations would prove counter-productive because of the profoundly localist nature of the Irish polity. Generalisations about how the single transferable vote might work in different political cultures are as dangerous as generalisations about 'proportional representation' which ignore the context of society and the constraints of history.

IV

It should be clear, then, that any theory making the electoral system a fundamental causative factor in the development of party systems cannot be sustained. Yet when political scientists first came to consider the influence of electoral systems, they saw them as the key variable. Hermens claimed that proportional representation invariably led to unstable government and political extremism; while only the plurality system could be guaranteed to sustain democratic values. Duverger proffered scientific laws in an attempt to prove that the plurality system would yield a two-party system and political stability, while proportional representation would fragment the parties and cause unstable government.[9]

Such theories failed to give sufficient weight to the complexity and diversity of democratic systems. It is in any case far too simplistic to divide party systems into 'two-party' and 'multi-party'. Britain and New Zealand, where two parties with contrasting socio-economic bases and ideologies compete for power in a unitary political structure are very different from the two-party system in the United States where decentralised 'catch-all' parties compete in a political system fragmented by federalism and the separation of powers. To assimilate functioning multi-party systems such as those of Scandinavia to those of less stable systems such as the French Fourth Republic or postwar Italy is to reveal a colossal failure of political perception.

In reality, both Hermens and Duverger were illegitimately generalising from the experience of their own countries. Hermens translated the concerns of German anti-Nazis of the Weimar period into a universal theory; while Duverger sought a remedy for the chronic instability of French politics, with its ill-disciplined parties and feeble executive, in the British electoral system, which, he hoped, would produce a two-party system and responsible government.

The reaction to such theories was not slow in coming, although when it did, it took too extreme a form. For, by contrast to theories which made electoral systems fundamental, there arose theories claiming that electoral systems were wholly consequences and not causes. They resulted from party configurations which were themselves the product of social and historical factors. Such theories, put forward by political scientists such as Grumm and Lipson,[10] were based upon a much more accurate understanding of a diverse range of countries than the theories of Hermens and Duverger; and they reached their apogee in the work of the great Norwegian, Stein Rokkan, whose theory of electoral systems, elaborated with the aid of S. M. Lipset, was but a part, and a comparatively small part, of a massive geopolitical construction whose purpose was nothing less than to explain the whole course of political development in the West.[11]

The essence of these new theories was that the development of party systems depended not upon the electoral system, nor indeed any institutional factor, but upon the number and type of cleavages in society. If there were a large number of social cleavages, there would be a multi-party system even under an electoral system of the plurality or majority type. A multi-party system would then be as 'natural' as Duverger had held a two-party system to be. For it might be just as natural for a society to sustain a diversity of interests and therefore a multi-party system, as to sustain only a duality of tendencies.

These theories emphasised, through the consideration of actual historical examples, that the introduction of proportional representation into the countries of Continental Europe had occurred after rather than before the coming into existence of a multi-party system. In Belgium, for example, a three-party system was already a reality by 1894 with the rise of the socialist Belgian Workers Party as a challenger to the Catholics and Liberals. Proportional representation was to come in 1899. Similarly, in Denmark, four parties were competing for office before the introduction of PR in 1920, while in Norway there were three major parties and a number of minor ones; and in Imperial Germany between six and twelve.

The correlation between PR and multi-party systems, therefore, could not be explained by the electoral system, but by explicitly political factors. In Belgium, the development of a three-party system could have made election results highly unpredictable. Socialists feared that the bourgeois parties might gang up against them, Catholics faced the possibility of an anti-clerical alliance, while the Liberals feared that they would be submerged in a battle between progressive socialists and clerical reactionaries. Similar motives were present in other Continental countries. In Italy and Norway, Liberal parties attempted to rescue themselves from the threat of under-representation under universal suffrage by pressing for PR. In the Netherlands, the Catholic party sought PR as a way of minimising the dangers of an anti-clerical alliance; while in Denmark and Sweden, Conservative parties insisted on PR as an insurance against the tyranny of the majority.

PR was the Conservative price for accepting universal suffrage, but an insurance for Socialists against under-representation under second-ballot systems where the bourgeois parties combined against them, as in Imperial Germany and pre-1914 Italy. Before 1914, every Continental socialist party with the exception of those in Belgium and Sweden, favoured proportional representation. In Britain, by contrast, Labour in alliance with the Liberals did not fear a bourgeois combination against it, the Conservatives were confident enough to believe that they could survive under conditions of universal suffrage, while the Liberals, through a colossal misjudgement, failed to secure PR in 1917–18 although it had been unanimously recommended by an all-party Speakers Conference.[12]

In each case, therefore, it seems as if the electoral system changed because it suited the interests of the political parties. In Särlvik's words which can be generalised beyond the Scandinavian experience, 'changes in the electoral order have always come about as the result of a change in the balance of forces or in the structure of party systems. Electoral systems are devised by political parties in response to political circumstances.' Electoral systems are consequences, therefore, even more than causes; and if, for example, PR were to come about in Britain, this would be because the challenge of a three-party system (counting the Liberal–SDP Alliance as a single party) offered too great a threat to the predictable relationship between votes and seats. For the nearer the system approaches to that of three equal parties, the more unpredictable and volatile this relationship will be; and neither the parties nor the electorate would be willing to accept the wild disparities which could result. In such circumstances, PR would constitute a recognition that multi-party politics had become a reality; it would not have caused it.

Duverger attempts to reply to this line of argument by claiming that many of the Continental countries which changed to PR in the first two decades of the twentieth century did so not from the plurality system but from a two-ballot system, and so cannot be used as a test of his hypothesis. But this is a feeble reply, firstly because the mechanics of the two-ballot system (and the alternative vote) can easily operate in a similar manner to the plurality system. More important the two-ballot system was adopted in countries such as Belgium and Germany in the nineteenth century precisely for reasons which invalidate Duverger's argument. They adopted it because there were *already* more than two parties which could not be accommodated within the plurality system without producing unpredictable and intolerably unfair results.

There is, then, no reason to believe that the plurality system will necessarily reduce the number of political parties any more than that proportional systems will necessarily have a multiplicative effect. Indeed, under first-past-the-post systems, regionally concentrated parties may fare better than they would under PR. It has been said, for example, of the Irish Nationalists that 'It took more than the electoral system to get rid of the Irish', for in 1886, they succeeded in securing 86% of the Irish seats in the Commons for 67% of the Irish vote, leaving Conservative and Liberal opinion in the south of Ireland totally unrepresented. It is not surprising, therefore, that some politicians concerned to preserve the Union with Ireland came to regard PR as an essential element in a Unionist strategy. Similarly, the British electoral system today gives excessive parliamentary weight to the Ulster parties and, between 1974 and 1979, the SNP, as compared to the Liberals whose electoral strength is more evenly distributed across the country as a whole.

Generalisations about the multiplicative effects of PR are equally suspect. Because Duverger treated 'proportional representation' as the name of a single electoral system, he did not notice that any supposed multiplicative effects can be mitigated by a threshold. In West Germany, for example, ten parties (counting the CDU/CSU as one party) competed in the first elections in the Federal Republic in 1949; whereas at the time of writing only three are represented in the Bundestag. No party which has been excluded by the threshold has succeeded in surmounting it at later elections.

Nor is there any evidence that the single transferable vote exerts a multiplicative effect. In Malta, only two parties are represented in the legislature, while Tasmania is the only Australian state in which the two-party system has never been effectively challenged by splinters. Ireland between 1969 and 1981 had only three parties in the Dail, while the introduction of STV in local elections in Northern Ireland in 1972 did not prevent a reduction in the number of parties in the mid-1970s.

Recent electoral evidence shows fairly conclusively that PR is *not* a brake preventing a reduction in the number of parties even where there is a very low threshold. In Israel, for example, Mapai together with two small splinter parties merged in 1968 to form the Labour Party; while four bourgeois parties merged to form Likud in 1977. Thus, although ten parties were represented in the Knesset in 1977, four of them shared 93 out of 120 seats; while, after the 1981 elections, the two main parties held 95 out of the 120 seats. Similarly in Holland, the three religious parties came together in 1977 to form the Christian Democratic Appeal, and in 1977 the three main Dutch parties gained nearly 84% of the vote; while in 1981, the four main parties secured 87% of the vote.

The party system, therefore, seems to be a reflection of basic social cleavages; and these cleavages will prevent new parties establishing themselves if such new parties do not reflect real social factors. Habit, it has been said, is also a threshold.

Proportional representation may appear to have a de-stabilising effect in

unstable multi-party systems such as those of Weimar Germany, Fourth
Republic France or Italy, which Sartori calls 'polarised pluralism',[13] characterised by the existence of powerful anti-system parties, centrifugal
competition, a tendency to irresponsible opposition and a high ideological
temperature; yet precisely because ideological conflict has been heightened
plurality voting will be unacceptable, and it may be that PR actually plays a
positive role in maintaining a precarious kind of equilibrium between opposites

Where, on the other hand, such pathological conditions are absent, anti-
system parties, if they exist at all, will be weak, and the parties will have well-
established social roots reflecting developed partisan alignments; and in
countries such as West Germany, Holland, Ireland, Sweden, Denmark
Norway and Switzerland, proportional representation will not encourage
instability. Indeed, it may perform a positive function as a precondition of
stability by balancing the claims of different religious or linguistic groups, as in
Holland or Switzerland; or, as in Ireland and Sweden, by ensuring that there is
alternation of power rather than perpetual one-party rule.

The great strength of what one may call the sociological approach to the
analysis of electoral systems is that it offers an explanation of the stability of
political alignments in Western Europe since the advent of universal suffrage; a
stability which seems to have lasted from the 1920s to the 1960s, and was
hardly undermined by the ravages of the Second World War. When the first
elections in the German Federal Republic were held in 1949, it was discovered
that patterns of support for Christian, Conservative and Socialist parties
mirrored almost exactly the voting patterns of pre-1930 free elections, before
Hitler. In Italy, despite political instability and an electoral system encouraging
the formation of new parties, 92% of the seats in the Chamber of Deputies in
1979 were occupied by deputies belonging to parties present in the 1946-8
Constituent Assembly; and these in turn all had their roots in the political
traditions of the pre-fascist era. Parties without such deep roots had a record of
almost unredeemed electoral failure.

Lipset and Rokkan explained these phenomena by means of the so-called
'freezing hypothesis'. The main cleavages in industrial society – socio-
economic, linguistic, religious and territorial – had all developed before the
advent of universal suffrage, and there was a 'freezing of the major party
alternatives in the wake of the extension of the suffrage and the mobilisation of
major sections of the new reservoirs of political supporters'. There was an
element of historicity in voting behaviour, since 'The voter does not just react
to immediate issues but is caught in an historically given constellation of
diffuse options for the system as a whole.' Party choice was based less upon
appraisal of immediate policy issues, than upon the voter's ties with his class
region, subculture or *famille spirituelle*. Party identification provided the key to
the stability of political alignments, and for this reason Lipset and Rokkan were
able to say that 'the party systems of the 1960s reflect with few significant
exceptions the cleavage structures of the 1920s'.[14]

V

Yet, for all its subtlety and historical insight, the sociological approach cannot be accepted as a final analysis of the relationship between party systems and electoral systems. It is too deterministic, underplaying the potentialities for change inherent even in the most stable political structures, and ignoring the existence of political divisions which are not the product of social cleavages. It is difficult, for example, to offer a complete explanation of the success of parties where one element in this success is allegiance to a charismatic leader – whether de Gaulle, de Valera or Hitler – without bringing in non-sociological factors. The changing fortunes of Irish nationalism in the nineteenth century cannot be understood without paying attention to the rise and fall of Parnell, just as the failure of Scottish nationalism in the twentieth century must be in part ascribed to a failure of leadership. In nineteenth-century Britain, political divisions were fundamentally affected by the widespread hostility to Disraeli which, in the 1840s and 1850s prevented a reunion between Peelites and Tories; while Gladstone's espousal of Home Rule in 1886 transformed the political alignment by causing the defection of the Radical Joseph Chamberlain who might otherwise have revitalised the British Left. Similarly, party configurations in modern France cannot be explained without considering the careers of de Gaulle and Chirac; nor West Germany without evaluating the roles of Adenauer and Brandt, nor Ireland without noticing that Fianna Fail and Fine Gael began life as the parties of de Valera and Cosgrave.

Sociological theories of parties are better at explaining persistence than explaining change. They have found it difficult to explain why electoral change and volatility have affected different political systems in different degrees; for the melting of traditional alignments in many Western European countries since the 1960s has occurred at different rates. Here, too, part of the explanation of change lies in the skills – or lack of them – displayed by individual politicians. The formation of the SDP in Britain surely owes as much to the failure of Gaitskell's attempt to modernise the Labour Party and to his early death as it does to socio-economic developments. The electoral success of the French Socialists owes as much to Mitterrand's subtle strategy as it does to social factors. If they are to survive, political parties cannot be purely passive mechanisms content to reflect long-established social cleavages. They must act positively, adapting to social change if they are not to become rapidly outmoded. Party systems, then, are not merely reflections of social cleavages. Although rooted in cleavages, they also 'record past victories in the struggle to define the terms on which politicians will compete'.[15]

It is, perhaps, not too speculative to suggest that just as the work of Hermens and Duverger has been so greatly influenced by the circumstances of their countries of origin, so also the theories of Rokkan owe something to their author's Scandinavian background, where political leaders are expected to play a rather more passive role than in many other Western democracies, and it is therefore easier to understand political leadership as a reflection of socia forces, rather than as a causal influence in its own right.

Of course, it would be wrong to press this argument too far. For politician cannot operate in a social vacuum. The keys to history, in Koestler's words may be 'shaped by subjective individual factors', but the locks are determine 'by objective constellations in the structure of society'.[16] The scope for th individual politician is not likely to be so great when there is social stability a when old alignments are melting, or when there is a change of regime. It is a such periods that the choice of electoral system may well prove, contrary t sociological theories, of fundamental importance. Goldey and Williams argu that the two-ballot system in France was a necessary but not sufficien precondition of political recovery between 1958 and 1962; the same can be sai of the adoption of the West German electoral system in 1949.

It is when a party system is in the process of formation or when it is ossifyin; that the influence of the electoral system is likely to be greatest. For it ca critically affect the *speed* with which social changes are reflected in the part system. A 'pure' party list system of the type used in Israel or the Netherland; and the single transferable vote, are likely to be the most transparent system and to reflect more accurately than other systems the process of social change That, of course, will be welcomed only if the direction of social change i regarded as beneficent. If social changes are creating support for extremist an anti-democratic parties, then it might well be thought desirable to select a electoral system which dampens down or refracts change – although n electoral system will be able to dampen change permanently. Of all electora systems, the plurality system is probably the least transparent, and the leas likely to reflect social change.

This argument can be illustrated from the experience of the Unite Kingdom. A change in the electoral system would clearly have had a majo effect if it had come about – as it might easily have done – in 1917–18 when th modern party system was being formed. It would certainly have transforme British politics if PR had been in existence in February 1974 when the Liberal secured 19% of the vote, but gained only 2.2% of the seats. It would also, c course, transform the prospects of the Liberal/SDP Alliance at a time when, i the view of many, the two-party system with its emphasis on a class alignmen of politics, has become ossified. In the 1950s, however, when a stable part configuration reflected widespread public satisfaction with the performance c parties and their leaders, the introduction of PR would probably not hav changed British politics very much. When society is fundamentally stable, a electoral system which reflects what is happening in society will, *ex hypothesi* not lead to much change in the political system. When society is changing, proportional system will reflect that change. One crucial consequenc therefore, of electoral systems is the extent to which they are likely to reflect c refract the process of social change, a factor peculiarly relevant to cor temporary Western Europe where there are clear signs of the melting of frozen alignments; and perhaps particularly to Britain which may be on the threshold of a period of major political and electoral change.

VI

The relationships between electoral systems, party systems and the process of social change are, therefore, reciprocal and highly complex. They are not such as can be summed up in scientific laws, whether these laws are arithmetical, institutional or sociological. Electoral systems must be understood against the background of a society's historical development, which is in turn profoundly affected by political choices. The interactions between these factors can best be understood by using the methods of the historian, rather than by an attempt to assimilate the study of politics to the natural sciences. The comparative study of electoral systems and party systems is likely to be of more use in shedding light on what is unique and particular than in yielding generalisations which do justice to the historical experience of different countries. That, at least, is the spirit in which the chapters in *Democracy and Elections* have been written.

NOTES

1 Pierre Trudeau, 'Some Obstacles to Democracy in Quebec', *Canadian Journal of Economics and Political Science* (1958).
2 Maurice Duverger, *Political Parties*, 2nd edn (London, 1959), pp. 151–2.
3 Francis G. Castles, 'Female Legislative Representation and the Electoral System', *Politics* (November 1981), p. 22.
4 Ibid., pp. 22, 26.
5 Ibid., pp. 25–6.
6 Stein Rokkan, *Citizens, Elections, Parties* (Oslo, 1970), p. 166.
7 See Barry Nicholas, 'Fundamental Rights and Judicial Review in France', pts. I and II, in *Public Law* (Spring and Summer 1978).
8 Václav L. Beneš, 'Czechoslovak Democracy and its Problems, 1918–1920', in Victor Mamatey and Radomír Luža, *A History of the Czechoslovak Republic* (Princeton, 1973), p. 67.
9 F. A. Hermens, *Democracy or Anarchy? A Study of Proportional Representation* (Notre Dame, 1941); and Maurice Duverger, *Political Parties* (London, 1954).
10 John H. Grumm, 'Theories of Electoral Systems', *Mid-West Journal of Political Science* (1958); Leslie Lipson, 'Party Systems in the United Kingdom and the Older Commonwealth: Causes, Resemblances and Variations', *Political Studies* (1959); Leslie Lipson, *The Democratic Civilization* (New York, 1964).
11 Rokkan, *Citizens*; and Seymour M. Lipset and Stein Rokkan, 'Cleavage Structures, Party Systems and Voter Alignments: An Introduction', in Seymour M. Lipset and Stein Rokkan, eds., *Party Systems and Voter Alignments: Cross-National Perspectives* (New York, 1967).

12 See Vernon Bogdanor, *The People and the Party System* (Cambridge, 1981), pp. 126–35.
13 Giovanni Sartori, 'European Political Parties: The Case of Polarized Pluralism', in J. La Palombara and M. Weiner, eds., *Political Parties and Political Development* (Princeton, 1966); and Giovanni Sartori, *Parties and Party Systems: A Framework for Analysis*, vol. 1 (Cambridge, 1976), chap. 6.
14 Lipset and Rokkan, *Party Systems*, pp. 50, 53.
15 R. K. Carty, *Party and Parish Pump: Electoral Politics in Ireland* (Waterloo, Ontario, 1981), p. 151. This book is a brilliant case study of the thesis argued for in this chapter.
16 Arthur Koestler, *The Yogi and the Commissar* (London, 1945), p. 44.

SUGGESTIONS FOR FURTHER READING

F. A. Hermens, *Democracy or Anarchy? A Study of Proportional Representation* (Notre Dame, 1941)
Maurice Duverger, *Political Parties*, 1st edn (London, 1954), 2nd edn (London, 1959)
John G. Grumm. 'Theories of Electoral Systems', *Mid-West Journal of Political Science* (1958)
Leslie Lipson, 'Party Systems in the United Kingdom and the Older Commonwealth. Causes, Resemblances and Variations', *Political Studies* (1959)
   The Democratic Civilization (New York, 1964)
Seymour M. Lipset and Stein Rokkan, 'Cleavage Structures, Party Systems and Voter Alignments: An Introduction', in Lipset and Rokkan, eds., *Party Systems and Voter Alignments: Cross-National Perspectives* (New York, 1967)
Stein Rokkan, *Citizens, Elections, Parties* (Oslo, 1970)
Douglas Rae: *The Political Consequences of Electoral Laws*, revised edn (New Haven, 1971)
Giovanni Sartori, *Parties and Party Systems: A Framework for Analysis* (Cambridge, 1976)
Vernon Bogdanor, *The People and the Party System* (Cambridge, 1981)

Index

263

Lightning Source UK Ltd.
Milton Keynes UK
UKOW03f0622270814

237647UK00001B/50/P